FRONTIER CAVALRY TROOPER

Frontier Cavalry Trooper

The Letters

of Private Eddie Matthews

★ 1869–1874 ★

Edited by

Douglas C. McChristian

University of New Mexico Press
Albuquerque

© 2013 by the University of New Mexico Press
All rights reserved. Published 2013

Library of Congress Cataloging-in-Publication Data

First paperback edition, 2020
Paperback ISBN: 978-0-8263-5227-9

Matthews, Eddie (William Edward) 1851–1932.
  Frontier cavalry trooper : the letters of Private Eddie Matthews, 1869–1874 / edited by Douglas C. McChristian.
    p. cm.
  Includes bibliographical references and index.
  ISBN 978-0-8263-5226-2 (cloth) — ISBN 978-0-8263-5228-6 (electronic)
  1. Matthews, Eddie (William Edward) 1851–1932—Correspondence 2. Fort Union (N.M.)—History—19th century. 3. Indians of North America—Wars—1815–1875—Biography. 4. United States. Army. Cavalry Regiment, 8th—Biography. 5. Soldiers—United States—Correspondence. 6. United States. Army.—Military life. 7. Frontier and pioneer life—New Mexico. 8. New Mexico—History, Military—19th century. I. McChristian, Douglas C. II. Title.
  F804.F67M37 2013
  978.9'56—dc23
                    2012037665

DESIGN AND COMPOSITION: Catherine Leonardo
Composed in 10.5/14 Adobe Garamond Pro
Display type is Ashwood Condensed WF, Arcana GMM Std Manuscript, Helvetica Neue LT Std

For Jerome A. Greene

in appreciation for his friendship, guidance,

and encouragement through the years.

CONTENTS

Illustrations   viii
Acknowledgments   ix
Introduction   xi

CHAPTER ONE   "Away from Home and Friends"
SEPTEMBER–DECEMBER 1869   1

CHAPTER TWO   "His Throat Was Cut from Ear to Ear"
JANUARY–APRIL 1870   35

CHAPTER THREE   "Wind, Wind, and Sand All the Time"
MAY–DECEMBER 1870   72

CHAPTER FOUR   "We Only Shot to Scare Them"
JANUARY–DECEMBER 1871   125

CHAPTER FIVE   "Have Had All the Indian Fighting I Wish"
JANUARY–DECEMBER 1872   147

CHAPTER SIX   "Soldiers Are Not Given to Shedding Tears"
JANUARY–JUNE 1873   193

CHAPTER SEVEN   "I Shall Never Soldier Again"
JULY–DECEMBER 1873   242

CHAPTER EIGHT   "Every Day Is One Less for Me to Serve"
JANUARY–MARCH 1874   298

CHAPTER NINE   "When Eddie Comes Marching Home"
APRIL–AUGUST 1874   337

Epilogue   393
Abbreviations Used in This Volume   400
Bibliography   401
Index   409

ILLUSTRATIONS

FIGURE 1: William E. Matthews   184
FIGURE 2: Recruits drilling at Carlisle Barracks   184
FIGURE 3: Triple-tier army bunk   185
FIGURE 4: Fort Whipple, Arizona Territory   185
FIGURE 5: Fort Union, New Mexico Territory   185
FIGURE 6: Plan of Fort Union, 1877   186
FIGURE 7: Company Quarters, Fort Union   187
FIGURE 8: Sutler's Store, Fort Union   187
FIGURE 9: Las Vegas, New Mexico Territory, 1867   188
FIGURE 10: Interior of Barracks Squad Room, ca. 1873   188
FIGURE 11: Cavalrymen in the field, New Mexico Territory, 1867   188
FIGURE 12: Eighth Cavalryman in the regulation full dress uniform   189
FIGURE 13: District of New Mexico Headquarters Building, Santa Fe   189
FIGURE 14: Gordon Granger as a Major General   189
FIGURE 15: Plat of Fort Bascom, New Mexico Territory   190
FIGURE 16: Colonel John I. Gregg, Eighth Cavalry   190
FIGURE 17: First Lieutenant Edmund Luff   191
FIGURE 18: Captain William McCleave, Eighth Cavalry   191
FIGURE 19: Cavalry trooper wearing the full dress uniform introduced in 1872   192
FIGURE 20: Hospital at Fort Union, New Mexico Territory   192

Maps

MAP 1: Arizona Territory, 1870   34
MAP 2: Southwestern Frontier, 1865–1875   71
MAP 3: Fort Union Military Reservation   241

ACKNOWLEDGMENTS

Authors customarily give a nod of appreciation to their spouses at the end of their acknowledgments, but in this instance I want to express my heartfelt thanks to my wife, Frances, who contributed so much to this project. It was she, in fact, who discovered the old issue of *American History* in which John Koster first published a portion of the Matthews letters. She recognized that the article would be of interest to me for another project in which I was already involved and brought it to my attention. Neither of us could have imagined at that time that her discovery would eventually lead to this volume. As work progressed a few years later, Frances devoted many hours to scanning and formatting the original typescript and proof-reading my manuscript to ensure the two agreed. Additionally, her abilities as a native Spanish speaker proved extremely useful in translating place names and terms found throughout the letters.

I am especially indebted to Dr. Robert L. Spude, a former National Park Service colleague and my boss during the last few years of my career. Bob both encouraged me to pursue this project and enthusiastically assisted by locating Matthews family descendants, researching ownership and copyright issues, coordinating my work with Superintendent Marie Sauter at Fort Union National Monument, and initiating contact with the University of New Mexico Press for publication of the letters.

Bob also located and put me in touch with John Koster, who originally discovered and recognized the historical importance of the Matthews letters. I am grateful to John for graciously relinquishing the copyright he held for that portion of the letters he had previously published, and for readily supporting my effort to bring all of the Matthews letters before the public.

Retired NPS Historian Susan Kopczyski, formerly on the staff at Delaware Water Gap National Recreation Area, kindly took time from her schedule to locate Eddie Matthews' death certificate in the New Jersey state records.

As with every historical work, librarians and archivists were essential in facilitating and assisting with my research for this book. First and foremost among those were Librarian Tibor K. Remenyik and Park Interpreter Claudette Norman who hosted me at Fort Union National Monument, Watrous, N. Mex. Sara Good and Donna Humphrey at the Bucks County (Pa.) Historical Society went beyond the call to ferret out tidbits from their collections concerning Eddie Matthews' later life. Additionally, I appreciate the assistance offered by the Old Military Records staff at the National Archives, Main, Washington, D.C.; the staff at the Center for Southwest Research, Zimmerman Library, University of New Mexico, Albuquerque; the Donnally Library staff at Highlands University, Las Vegas, N. Mex.; Archivist Jill Ludlum with the Maryland State Archives; and the staff of the Carroll County (Md.) Historical Society, Westminster, Md.

Daniel Kosharek, photo archivist, was most helpful and efficient in assisting with my work at the New Mexico History Museum in Santa Fe. Jane Winton, Print Department, Boston Public Library, and George Moore and Russ Ronspies, at the Frontier Army Museum, Fort Leavenworth, Kans. expediently processed my requests for photographs in their respective collections.

My longtime friend and colleague, R. Eli Paul, with the Kansas City Public Library, gave the manuscript a careful critique and offered many thoughtful suggestions for improving it. I greatly appreciate the time he devoted to that effort.

—Douglas C. McChristian
Tucson, Arizona

INTRODUCTION

The post-Civil War era witnessed the resumption of the U.S. Army's role as the vanguard of the nation's westward expansion. Acting in this role was a daunting challenge for a force whose numbers were always inadequate for the task, a reflection of the Founding Fathers' predisposition against a large standing army controlled by the central government. The volunteer force raised in response to the Southern rebellion swelled to more than a million men, but by the end of 1865, nearly all of the units assembled had been disbanded and mustered out, leaving the regular army at a strength of only about forty-three thousand men. Congress increased the size of the army to some fifty-four thousand men the following year in an attempt to provide enough troops to both police the Reconstruction of the South and contend with the Indian situation in the West. But in 1869, a parsimonious Congress burdened with wartime debt dealt the army a serious blow by directing it to consolidate its forty-five infantry regiments to twenty-five, while retaining ten cavalry and five artillery regiments. The army's woes were further exacerbated by casualties, discharges, and sluggish recruiting, all of which translated to a force that was consistently 10 percent smaller than its new official strength of 37,313.

This pitifully small army was tasked with manning fortifications along both seacoasts from Maine to Texas and from Alaska to California, besides maintaining a couple hundred posts, arsenals, and camps scattered throughout the interior. Frontier garrisons, geographically isolated and composed of only one or two understrength companies, were common. Much of the trans-Mississippi West, particularly west of the hundredth meridian, was only partially settled, with enormous tracts of land still entirely devoid of non-Indian inhabitants. The regulars, therefore, were tasked with protecting routes of travel and communication and dealing with recalcitrant tribesmen residing in the territories.

Many of the men who joined the regular army in the latter 1860s were Civil War veterans who had found that military life agreed with them. A high percentage of new recruits were recent foreign immigrants, while men unable to find employment in the postwar economy constituted another large segment. Throughout the rank and file was a smattering of young, adventure-seeking Americans who had not reached military age during the war, but were motivated to enlist after hearing of thrilling experiences told by their veteran relatives. Still others had encountered problems at home or with the law and sought refuge in the army.

Typical of the last group, nineteen-year-old William Edward Matthews, known to family and friends as Eddie, quickly regretted his decision to enlist in September 1869. The regular army, noted for unquestioning obedience and strict discipline enforced by harsh punishment, was not the army his father had known as a member of the volunteer force during the war. However, unlike many of his contemporaries who contributed to a notoriously high desertion rate, Matthews resigned himself to abide by his oath and make the best of the experience.

His parents, John and Judith Matthews, exemplified the foreign-born immigrants who came to America during the mid-nineteenth century. Both were natives of Cornwall County, England, a tin- and copper-mining region on the island's southwestern peninsula. By the age of twenty, John, like most of the men in the area, was employed in the backbreaking, dangerous work of a miner. Not long after his marriage to Judith Newton early in 1847, he concluded that eking out an existence on a miner's wages was an economic dead end, with hardly better prospects for his offspring. Electing to cast their fortunes in America, the Matthewses boarded a ship bound for the United

States in March 1848, shortly after the birth of their first child, Elizabeth ("Lizzie").[1]

Within two years of their arrival, the couple migrated to western Maryland's Allegany County, where John again found familiar work in the mines. By that time, the Matthews family included a second child, Eddie, born in Frostburg on April 26, 1850. John improved his status sometime during the following decade when he became postmaster at nearby Oakland, Maryland.[2]

The Civil War directly impacted Allegany County in the fall of 1861, when the Third Regiment Potomac Home Brigade, Maryland Volunteers began recruiting five companies from among area residents. Despite his age—he was then forty-one—and being a father of eight, John offered his services to his adopted nation. He was readily mustered in on March 13, 1862, as the regiment's quartermaster with the rank of first lieutenant.

As soon as the regiment's first battalion was complete, it was assigned to General Frederick W. Lander's division of the Army of the Potomac and detailed to defend Harpers Ferry. Although the once-vital U.S. armory there had been burned by Union forces and subsequently plundered of its machinery by the Confederates, the location itself continued to be strategically important. The town occupied a rugged point of land at the confluence of the Potomac and Shenandoah Rivers on the Maryland-Pennsylvania border and served as a bridge crossing for the Baltimore & Ohio Railroad. When General Robert E. Lee's Army of Northern Virginia invaded Maryland in 1863, General Thomas J. "Stonewall" Jackson's troops handily defeated and captured the poorly led Union garrison at Harpers Ferry. The entire Third Regiment Potomac Home Brigade was made prisoners of war until exchanged soon thereafter. Lieutenant Matthews's unit later confronted General Jubal Early's Confederates during his invasion of the North the following year, and was subsequently engaged in the Shenandoah Valley Campaign as a component of General Philip H. Sheridan's army. John returned home to his family upon his muster out of the service in January 1865.[3]

---

1 *1841 England Census*, last modified 2010, Ancestry.com; *England and Wales, Free BMD Marriage Index: 1837–1915*, last modified 2006, Ancestry.com; *New York Passenger Lists, 1820–1957*, last modified 2010, Ancestry.com.

2 *1860 U.S. Federal Census*, last modified 2009, Ancestry.com; *1850 U.S. Federal Census*, last modified 2009, Ancestry.com; Death Certificate, William Edward Matthews, Vital Statistics, New Jersey Department of Health.

3 Allison, Jarrett, and Vernon, *Roster of Maryland Volunteers, War of 1861–5*, 569–71; and McPherson, *Battle Cry of Freedom*, 534–36, 756. Eddie suggests that he accompanied his father for some period of time during the war and that experience gave him an early exposure to military life.

In addition to Lizzie and Eddie, the Matthews household by that time included Susan M. ("Susie," or "Sue," b. 1852), Margaret ("Maggie," b. 1854), Frances (b. 1856), John J. ("Johnnie," b. 1858), Arthur W. (b. 1860), and George B. McClellan ("Clellee," b. 1862), namesake of the dynamic and wildly popular first commander of the Army of the Potomac. Frances, whose death Eddie alludes to in a letter, was gone by 1870, apparently a victim of one of the childhood diseases so prevalent during the nineteenth century.

Once back in civilian life, John concluded that a large family required more income than he could earn as a postmaster in the mining regions. He therefore decided to relocate to Westminster, a thriving town along the Western Maryland Railway in the rolling countryside northwest of Baltimore. John apparently discovered that his experience as an army quartermaster suited his natural talents and it provided a foundation for his new venture as a retail grocer. He maintained a store for a number of years, though by 1874, business declined to the point that he had to take supplemental employment as a shoe salesman and as a property assessor for the City of Westminster to make ends meet.[4]

Eddie, not unlike other boys his age who resided in rural American towns, spent his formative years working in the family store, attending classes, riding horseback, ice skating, flirting with girls, and chumming with schoolmates. Like many teenagers then and now, he was not a saint. We know that he indulged in liquor, sometimes to excess; he also chewed tobacco and smoked a pipe. Just what prompted Matthews to leave home is not clear, but his letters suggest that he fell in with bad company and that those associations led to behavior that was unacceptable, if not embarrassing, to his parents. He also admits to having been jilted by a local girl with whom he apparently had had a romantic relationship, though he remains close-mouthed about the details.[5]

Restless by the summer of 1869, Matthews and two companions, Bill Baumgartner and another identified only as Shorb, left home seeking

---

4 *U.S. IRS Tax Assessment Lists, 1862–1918*, last modified 2008, Ancestry.com.
5 A public notice in the Westminster newspaper warned the adolescents who had been smoking, talking loudly, and running up and down stairs in the vestibule of the Lutheran Church that if they persisted with such activities, they would be arrested. Shortly thereafter, another public notice admonished "boys and young men" for swimming, presumably in the nude, in ponds near the railroad in full view of passengers. We do not know if Matthews was involved in these incidents, but the articles reflect the sort of behavior that may have placed him at odds with his parents (*Democratic Advocate*, June 17 and July 1, 1869).

adventure.⁶ Shorb may have initiated the trip for the purpose of visiting friends or relatives in far-off Ohio, while Baumgartner and Matthews probably tagged along to experience something of the world beyond Carroll County. Shorb, apparently, had always intended to return to Westminster, but Matthews and Baumgartner decided to stay "out West" and find employment.

By late August, the trio found themselves in Cincinnati, where they discovered that work was more difficult to come by than they had anticipated. As their prospects and funds diminished with each passing day, the relationship between Baumgartner and Eddie soured. Despite their pact to stick together through thick or thin, Baumgartner unexpectedly changed his mind, announcing that he would return to Maryland with Shorb. Eddie, feeling double-crossed by his friend and chagrinned by the strained relationship with his father, was too embarrassed to go back home, just then at least. Faced with being alone and destitute, a despondent Eddie sought out an army recruiting office, which happened to be the cavalry rendezvous in Cincinnati. He was soon a regular soldier clad in army blue.

For a time, Eddie performed the normal duties of a soldier in the ranks, but his superiors took note that he obviously possessed more formal education than an average private, many of whom were illiterate. Company commanders, always mindful of men who could perform the myriad clerical duties necessary to maintain accountability for men, horses, equipment, and supplies, detailed him for various periods throughout his enlistment as either company or adjutant's clerk. For a time, he held the rank of company quartermaster sergeant. Those roles, although demanding in their own right, allowed him to remain in garrison much of the time, rather than participating in patrols and escorts with the rest of his company. His assignment of such roles was fortuitous for history because it placed Matthews in a situation in which he had the time and means to write home with some regularity.

The Matthews letters comprise an unparalleled firsthand narrative of one regular soldier's service during the Indian campaigns in the West. Personal accounts of army life in any form left by soldiers of that period are

---

6 William N. Baumgartner was the twenty-one-year-old son of Westminster attorney John J. Baumgartner. William later became a dentist and took up practice in his hometown (*1850 U.S. Federal Census*, last modified 2009, Ancestry.com; *1880 U.S. Federal Census*, Ancestry.com). Eddie's other companion was probably Joshua Shorb, age eighteen, whose father was an architect and builder in Westminster and a partner in the furniture-manufacturing firm of Shorb, Leister, and Shaeffer (*1870 U.S. Federal Census*, last modified 2009, Ancestry.com). See also business advertisements in the 1869 issues of the *Democratic Advocate*.

comparatively rare for several reasons. Chief among those, as has been discussed, was the small size of the army at that time. The Union Army of the Civil War, by contrast, averaged approximately a million men, most of them volunteers, over a four-year period. For most of those men, the war was the highlight of their lives, a factor that resulted in thousands of diaries, letters, and published reminiscences. By contrast, nearly half of the men who joined the army in the postwar era hailed from foreign countries, and many of them had little or no command of the English language. Those who did, even native-born Americans, were often from the lowest rungs of society, where they had not been afforded an education. With few exceptions, those who bothered to leave any sort of record kept only simple field diaries, blandly recording the day-by-day marches of troops on campaign with little useful detail or perspective.

In this respect, Eddie Matthews was exceptional. His was not a later reminiscence clouded by time and dimming memory. Eddie's letters record a vivid chronicle of daily life in the frontier regulars as he was experiencing it. Included are operational details of his company, candid observations of people and places, intimate views of frontier society, and personal opinions that probably would have been forgotten or moderated had he recorded his experiences later in life. Subtler are his valuable references to the state of transportation and communication in the Southwest during the early 1870s. The keen-eyed reader will note, for example, how he marks the progress of the Kansas Pacific and the Atchison, Topeka & Santa Fe Railroads into the territories of Colorado and New Mexico, thus heralding the doom of major wagon roads like the Santa Fe Trail. Matthews probably did not realize until later years that he was not only a witness to the nation's rapid westward expansion, but was himself a tiny cog in the machinery that made it possible.

His letters, never intended to be read by anyone outside his immediate family, reflect a rather cocky, vain young man out on his own for the first time. Suffering pangs of guilt for the problems he had caused at home, he went out of his way to impress his parents with a newfound sense of maturity and a desire to improve himself. His cheeky sense of humor is evident throughout, though at times he could turn sarcastic, particularly when family members failed to write him as frequently as he expected. Today's reader may fault Matthews for his racist and sexist views. While his prejudices may violate today's sensibilities, we must consider his opinions within the context of societal norms of the mid-nineteenth century. That Eddie openly expressed these unvarnished biases to his family adds significantly to the historical value of the letters.

I am deeply indebted to John Koster, a former New Jersey newspaper reporter, for initially bringing the Matthews letters to public attention. During a serendipitous encounter with Ora Bublitz, Eddie Matthews's granddaughter, Mr. Koster was shown a three-foot-high stack of manuscript letters dating to the late nineteenth century and bearing addresses from various military posts in the American Southwest. Recognizing their importance as a chronicle of one soldier's experience on the Western Frontier, Koster selected a journal Matthews kept during a six-week period in the field and published it as an article in *American Heritage* (1980). Although Koster intended to publish the full collection in cooperation with Mrs. Bublitz, the project never came to fruition. However, Bublitz, a stenographer by profession, did prepare a typescript of the letters and each party retained copies. One of those eventually found its way to the archives at Fort Union National Monument.

Regrettably, the original letters disappeared after Ora Bublitz's passing and could not be located for this project. I was unable to determine through contacts with other surviving descendants whether they had simply been lost, or had been destroyed. Thanks to John Koster, however, the typescript survived to enable all of Eddie Matthews's letters to finally be shared with the historical community and the public at large.

It is appropriate at this juncture to offer some explanation about the methodology used in editing the letters for this book. As the editor, I have considered it important to preserve as fully as possible Matthews's writing style to convey to the reader a sense of his personality, attitudes, and views of events as he witnessed them. His salutation invariably read, "To the Loved Ones at Home," and he usually closed with, "With much love and kisses to you all," or something similar. I have deleted those redundant elements in the interest of maintaining a narrative flow. Matthews's address and date headings, now uniformly formatted, have been retained to aid the reader in tracking the chronology of events and his whereabouts at any given time.

Matthews's original spelling, capitalization, punctuation, and usage have been preserved throughout, except in those instances where clarity would be enhanced by providing the corrected word in brackets. One of his writing habits involved the frequent omission of the word *I* at the beginning of sentences. Accordingly, [I] in brackets has been added where necessary for readability. Throughout his letters, Matthews substituted the letter *e* for the letter *y* in adverbs such as *possibly* and *comfortably*, and thus they appear as *possible* and *comfortable*, respectively. He also frequently used *y* in place of *i*, as, for example, in *satisfyed*. Not surprisingly for someone who found himself in a foreign environment, he often used phonetic spellings of place names, particularly those of Spanish origin.

In those instances in which it appears that the original typist has erred in deciphering Matthews's handwriting, or has not correctly interpreted a particular word (for instance, army slang, proper names, and military terms), I have either corrected the word or inserted [*illegible*] when it could not be deciphered. Words were sometimes missing from the original typescript. We have no way to know whether the omissions were on the part of Matthews or Mrs. Bublitz. I have either entered [*missing*], or, in those instances when the missing word could be conjectured, it has been added in brackets with a question mark. Matthews had a habit of underlining some words for emphasis and those have been retained. He frequently omitted periods, and never used question marks. He also had a habit of running his sentences together, which at times resulted in long, rambling paragraphs. In those instances, I have made sentence breaks at appropriate locations to improve readability without altering the text's meaning. Punctuation has been added or modified only where necessary for clarity, and paragraph breaks have been made as necessary to improve cohesiveness.

As might be expected of letters written to home folks, Eddie often digresses into family chitchat and commentary relative to acquaintances and events in Westminster. Most of those passages have been deleted so as not to distract from the central narrative, except where they related in some way to his army life. With few exceptions, no attempt has been made to identify the friends he mentions in his hometown, though where possible the correct spellings of most proper names have been verified.

Finally, I have added commentary in italics to introduce the chapters and to provide some historical context for Eddie's activities and those of the Eighth Cavalry. In one instance, it was necessary to bridge a thirteen-month gap in the original correspondence. Military personnel have been identified wherever possible, and biographical sketches have been provided in footnotes. However, I was unable to accomplish this in a few instances in which information concerning individuals, usually enlisted men, could not be found in available sources. I was placed at a disadvantage because the muster rolls for the Eighth Cavalry, which would have provided those names, are no longer available for public use at the National Archives, and microform copies have not been produced.

Now we join Eddie Matthews as he embarks on a five-year adventure that will take him across the continent to California, to the wilds of Arizona and New Mexico, to Colorado, and back again.

CHAPTER ONE

"Away from Home and Friends"

SEPTEMBER—DECEMBER 1869

*T*hinking he might be able to endure the army for three years, which would be enough time for his domestic troubles to subside, Eddie Matthews introduced himself to the recruiting officer, Captain James S. Tomkins. Eddie's spirits plummeted, however, when he learned that Congress had recently increased the term of enlistment to five years, an eternity to a nineteen-year-old.[1]

The option of joining the army now seemed less appealing, and, having arrived at the office too late in the day to undergo a physical examination, Matthews told Captain Tomkins that he would reconsider and return with his decision the next day, after seeing his companions off at the train station. Uncertain just what to do after that, Eddie procrastinated for most of another week, hoping some other alternative might present itself. At length, literally down to his last penny, and having no other prospect for supporting himself, he enlisted in the U.S. Cavalry

---

1 He could not have known that the Army Reorganization Act of March 3, 1869, had just changed the term of enlistment for all branches of the army from three to five years. See Ganoe, *History of the Army*, 324.

on September 8.[2] *Following a short stay at the Cincinnati rendezvous, Eddie traveled with a party of other recruits to the Cavalry School at Carlisle Barracks, Pennsylvania. Ironically, Carlisle was only about fifty miles from his hometown, Westminster, Maryland. Nevertheless, going home was no longer an option; Eddie Matthews was in the regular army whether he liked it or not. After undergoing several weeks of recruit training, he was sent to join the Eighth Cavalry, then headquartered at San Francisco, California.*

Cincinnati, Ohio
SEPTEMBER 2, 1869

Shorb leaves here this morning for home and kindly consented to take this to you. He only came out here on a visit—but Bill Baumgartner who also is going home came out to stay, and declared to me before leaving Westminster that he would never, to use a common expression, go back on me, but I certainly ought to know by this time, how much dependence to place in a person like he.

We have all been unsuccessful in getting anything to do. I have tried most everything but in every instance was unsuccessful, and as last resort went down to the Recruiting Office for the purpose of enlisting in the regular Cavalry for 3 years, but found out that they were only taking men for 5 years. It was too late to be examined so promised to go down this morning "but don't like to," don't know whether I will or not, but if I possibly could get anything let it be what it may I would take it, but there is not much chance for anything else here. Baumgartner has acted very mean with me, and should I ever get back to Westminster or any place where he is, I will know how to reciprocate his kindness, just same as to Shorb he has been a friend in more than one instance.

How are all at home[?] Oh how I would love to see you all, but how

---

2 When Matthews enlisted, he stood five feet six and a half inches tall and had black hair, brown eyes, and a fair complexion. Eddie claimed to be twenty-one years old, the minimum legal age for military service. However, his true age was only nineteen. Suspecting that Eddie was underage, Captain Tomkins protected himself by inserting into the oath the handwritten phrase, "& that I am twenty-one years of age," in addition to the witnessed "Declaration of Recruit" on the enlistment form. See entry 214, p. 202, roll 36, ROE, AGO, RG 94, NA; and William E. Matthews, Enlistment Papers, AGO, RG 94, NA. Eddie mentioned in a subsequent letter that he treasured that last penny as a souvenir and reminder of his former destitute condition.

long en [until?] I have that pleasure would be hard to say. The time will come I hope when I will return a wiser and better boy. I cannot help but feel sad this morning to see Shorb & B leave me. Out here a stranger to every person and then to think of <u>you all at home</u>, with out knowing how long it will be before I can visit you, if not to stay all together, perhaps for a short time my feeling cannot be the best.

I cannot ask you to answer this yet, for I have not the remotest idea where I will be by the time you receive this. But soon as I get permanently settled then how much good it will do me to hear from you all.³ I am writing this at the Little Miami R.R. Depot, while Shorb & B are waiting for the train to start. Good bye to you all till you hear from me again.

A Troop, Carlisle Barracks⁴
SEPTEMBER 19, 1869

Father's long looked for letter was received this morning although mailed on the 14th inst. Oh you know not how I felt while pursuing its contents. It completely surprised me, I would [do?] anything in this world could I only be with you just now, but why do I write this way knowing I cannot be. I have just returned from dress parade and although it is getting quite dark I want to write this and send in tomorrows mail. We came to this place last tuesday morning and was assigned to this Troop. I went to the letter carrier for the barracks and told him to inquire for me, suppose he forgot to do so.

We had a game of Ball yesterday between Citizens & Soldiers. I was pitcher on S[oldiers]. Charlie Cassell from Wakefield came up to see the game, he goes to Dickinson's College. When he saw me he took one step backward and asked if he was dreaming. I said no you are awake, he was very much surprised. After I explained why I was here he said I was a

---

3 Recruits usually remained at the so-called rendezvous, or recruiting office, for a period of a few days after enlistment. When a sufficient number of men had congregated, a non-commissioned officer (noncom) at the station would escort them via public transportation to the appropriate recruit depot, where they would undergo basic training. See Rickey, *Forty Miles*, 32.

4 Carlisle Barracks was situated in the Cumberland Valley of Pennsylvania. First occupied as a U.S. military station in 1777, it later became the Cavalry School of Practice during the mid-1830s. It ceased being a recruit depot effective June 20, 1871. See Rodenbough, *From Everglade to Canyon*, 245–46 and Billings, *Hygiene of the Army*, 12–13.

fool, and I suppose he is right. I told him that I was positive that there was a letter in the P.O. for me. Said he would go and see soon as he went down to town and would bring it up to me this evening. I was looking anxiously till about three o'clock, then he came with the letter but no papers. Said he did not ask for papers. Will get them tomorrow, I sat down in the room and read awhile and cried awhile. I could not help it although there were about half dozen soldiers in the room. Of course some laughed and said I was home sick which is true. But I have to remain till my time expires. I am very anxious to hear how Mother is. Oh I hope and pray she is better.

When I think dear Parents how much trouble I have given you, it makes me feel wretched and it seemed that I never could mind my ways. Father I have done enough a thousand times to make you loose all faith in me, but you [always?] say, "I cannot be persuaded to loose faith in the integrity of our first born son." Oh dear Father how happy I feel to know that you still have some faith in me who has been so undeserving, Yet I have a heart and a tender one and if it has [been?] false it never shall again. Oh that I may live like Joseph to bless the last days of my parents is my prayer now and ever shall be. I cannot but think we will all gather around one fireside at home again after my time has expired. As you say life is very uncertain yet I hope to be with you all at home forever.

I am trying to do right in my new duty. How different this is from the Volunteer Service.[5] Officers are very strict, but you can get along very well if you only pay attention. We don't expect to remain very long in this place. Troops go away every week for some points, California, New Mexico & Kentucky are the points they are sent to, also out on the plains. I find that offices here are very well supplied with master men. I, [like?] lots of young men, are enlisting. I had no idea that there was so many. I guess I will have to do a soldiers duty.

We are kept pretty busy all day. First thing in the morning at day break a cannon is fired to arouse all up to roll call. Then we eat our breakfast composed of a little colored water with out any sugar called coffee and a slice of bread. Sometimes we have a little fat meat at other [times?]. Then we go to the stables where we have to groom the horses

---

5 This is a reference to what his father had undoubtedly related to him about his Civil War service with the Maryland Volunteers.

one hour, and should one of the horses kick you or bite you must not hit him for it. They are allowed to kick you but you are not allowed to hit them back. Soon as that is over we go and wash our faces. Like cats eat first and then wash. Then we have drill for 1 1/2 hours, have a little rest, then go to stables and water horses, then get our dinner. We get a slice of bread, some beef and vegetable soup for desert.

At twelve o'clock we drill another hour, get supper soon as [we?] get off of drill then are marched to the stables again where we groom the horses one hour again, then get ready for Dress Parade. If we don't have any, we have [inspection?] which is most the same and if you aint got your cloths clean, boots blacked and white gloves on, you are sent to the guard house or else do some fatigue duty. At 8 o'clock we have roll call, at nine lights must all be put out.

The roll is called for everything and if you don't answer to your name away to the guard house you go. I have never missed one roll call or had a cross word spoken to me yet. Every little thing you do the Officers curse you for it, and call you all kind of names. I have made up my mind to do what is right and should I do anything wrong it will be done in [innocence?].

You have to go on fatigue duty once a week. When I was on I had to mix mortar while another carried the Hod. We had a good laugh over it, did not have to work scarcely any, did not do one hours work all day.

Each man had to draw 3.00 dollars worth of Settler [sutler] checks to buy the little necessaries to keep clean and eat. You have to get a quart cup, tin plate, knife and fork, and spoon, blacking & brush, p[air of white gloves, towel and soap, plate, powder to clean your plate and buttons, a little thread.[6] For that you pay 2.30. I forgot a button brush but I did not take any, I use my tooth brush. Then you have 70 cents for anything you want. I bought ten sheets of paper and that many envelopes, a little looking glass for ten cents, a comb, some tobacco and mailed one letter.

---

6 The army provided no white cotton dress gloves or personal mess gear to soldiers prior to 1872. The men were required to purchase gloves, tin cups, plates, and utensils from their meager pay. See McChristian, *U.S. Army in the West*, 72, 98. Recruits also had to buy the cleaning material necessary to maintain their uniforms and personal equipment. It was not unusual for sutlers, who had a licensed monopoly to operate general stores at military posts, to charge exorbitant prices for these items. See Rickey, *Forty Miles*, 35, 38.

You must get payed off here unless you get in the permanent party.[7] You have to wait till you join your regiment, and whenever I am payed off I will send home just as much money as I possibly can. I will try to save something. It is very near roll call, I will add a line tomorrow. I want Johnnie, Arthur & Clellee, Susie & Maggie all to write something to me, for every word from home will be gladly received. Father don't let the little boys play around the store, if they do they will very likely bad Johnnie away as they did me. I do not want him or either of my little brothers to follow my path, and nothing will make them so bad as bad boys. I know from experience, and bitter experience to me it has proven.

A Troop, Carlisle Barracks
SEPTEMBER 27, 1869

Your letter and two papers was received yesterday also one from Lizzie the day before. You can imagine how delighted I was. It does me so much good to hear from you. I have become reconciled to my fate and will brave it out manfully. I received a splendid letter from Geo. Parke in answer to one I wrote while here, I would send it to you but want to write a long letter as this is Sunday and I have more time to spare than any other day. This is the substance of it. "Ed, Your letter was received yesterday, was very glad to hear from you, but sorry that you had no other choice but to join the Army. I think I can imagine your situation and I can't blame you for what you did. I have been there myself and I know what it is to be away from home and friends without money. Words can't express the contemp[t] I feel for B[aumgartner]. I never did or could desert a friend in need. I have divided the last crust with a friend, and others have done the same with me. I wish you could have held out longer, you might have succeeded to some Employment. If I had been with you, we would have gone down to first principals, <u>hard work</u>. B is living here as before; he is not much account any where. If I were you, I would go to California. You will like the Country. Now

---

7 The permanent party consisted of one or two companies of soldiers specially selected for duty at the recruit depots. Organizationally, these units belonged to the General Mounted Service, not line regiments. The noncoms acted as drill instructors and the privates as both assistants and examples for the recruits. Recruiting parties also were drawn from these units. Between recruit drafts, the permanent party performed the normal garrison duties.

that you are in for it, do all you can to raise yourself in the estimation of the officers. You would make a good clerk. And in time might better yourself—even in the Army. You are young yet and five years will soon pass away—Come out a good man. Don't throw yourself away, and never despair. All may yet come right. Your family are all well as far as I know."

He sent me the <u>Democrat</u> and said he would send me one when ever I would be interested in it. Don't you think that was a good letter[?] I always did like the <u>Parke family</u> the <u>daughter especially</u>.

Well I can't say how long we will remain here, but one thing certain we will not remain here very long. The barracks are full of [bunks?] no place to put any men unless in Huts. The Colored Troops are in tents now. Recruits are coming in most every day. So many rumors are flying around that you can't believe anything. The report now is that three hundred men are to leave here next Friday, some for the First Regiment in California. The rest for the Eighth in New Mexico. I can't say what they are a going to do.

You can't get in the permanent Troop here without you have been in the Army before. I would not go in it if I could. It would almost take your wages to keep clean and dress like some of them do. They are having nice times now, but soon as the recruits leave here they will have hard work. Will have to clean all the horses and stables as well as make all the garden in the Summer time. They have two large gardens here for the Soldiers. The recruits have to do all the work now. The permanent party does nothing.

I have been promoted from D Troop to A. I don't have any fatigue duty to do. Do guard duty instead. Have to go to the stables three times a day same as [I] did in D Troop, but have only groomed one horse. Other troops get there, then there is nothing for us to do. We don't have as many horses as men. Sometimes the Sergeant cuts about twenty of the Men off at Stable Call. He always cuts them off from the right of the company. I always manage to fall in on the right. Yesterday evening I was eleventh man in the front rank for stable, we fall in two ranks, and of course of the Sergeant cut off only twenty. I would have to go to the stables. He put his arm in between the man on my right, but took it out again and put it below me and told us to fall out of ranks. I did not feel like going to the stables so of course felt good on being excused.

The Sergeant has found me several times. I was detailed for guard

Friday but was fortunate again and got excused. There is always one man excused every morning from the detail for being the cleanest man.[8] When you are excused you don't have to do anything all that day or the next, till half past four in the evening. Of course every man tries to be the cleanest and have his arms and the [word missing] cleanest. I have been keeping myself clean as I possibly could under the circumstances. When the bugle blew for guard mount we fell in to ranks all looking clean as possible, boots blacked, white gloves on and buttons shining. After the Sergt. inspects your carbine he examines your cloth[e]s. After he had gone all around he came up and said to me you are excused Sir. Tell you what I felt good as it was my first time on guard mount, he gave me a pass all day Saturday to go where I pleased.

We played another match game of baseball in the morning with the Town Club and as luck would have it beat them 13 runs, score standing 25 to 38. Last Saturday they beat us more than that. I made 7 runs and 3 outs, best score on the nine, pitched also.

In the afternoon went in town first time since have been here. Went to Dickinson's College to see Charlie Cassell. I can't say that I fancy the place much. I must say it looked a great deal more dreamy than these Barracks. Guess it would have been more beneficial to me had I gone there instead of here. Saw Charlie and after spending an hour or so with him came back to camp, he accompanying me. I like Charlie very much.

Sue asked very particular about my pay. We get sixteen dollars a month and board, and are allowed four hundred dollars for cloths during the five years. If we have any clothing money left, we can draw, but if you over draw your monthly allowance they take it out of your pay.[9] The

---

8 Guard mounting at the depot prepared the recruits for a venerable army tradition they would experience when they reached their stations. Performing the ceremony flawlessly was the mark of a well-drilled command. One member of each day's guard detail was selected as orderly for the post commander. This was a position of honor, but had practical benefits too. The orderly was exempt from walking post and had an easy day standing by at the commander's quarters or office to convey any messages he might send to others on the post. Best of all, the orderly was relieved by evening and was allowed to sleep in his own bunk, rather than stay at the guard house. He often received a pass to go off post the next day. See Rickey, *Forty Miles*, 91–92.

9 Clothing was issued twice yearly, barring any emergencies. The money value of each item of clothing was published annually in a general order. A table in army regulations listed the items normally required by the average soldier during each year of his enlistment, the total of which formed the annual allowance. If he overdrew the established allowance in a given year, the extra items were deducted from his pay. Soldiers were encouraged to conserve their clothing because if they drew less than authorized, their accounts would be credited and the savings paid to them in cash upon discharge. See *Revised Regulations*, 169–71.

permanent troop get payed off every two months, but we would not be payed off if we stayed two years. We will not get our pay till we get with the Regiment, and there is no telling when that will be. Rest assured that I will send as much of my money home as I possibly can spare and let you use it as you see propper.

I was going to have a picture taken yesterday and send it home to you, but changed my mind because I had nothing but a blouse and you don't look well in them. I don't suppose we will get our jackets till we join the regiment.[10] We'll wait till then, or if you say so will have one taken the way I am next time I go down town. Don't know when that will be.

You must excuse the writing, my pen is miserable and I am perched up in the second story of a bunk that shakes worse than an old man with the [palsy?]. The bunk would not shake so much but the boys are running around the room jumping and romping. I will not write to Lizzie this time. She will get to read this and I can't afford to be so extravigant although I have plenty of stamps, thanks to you all at home for them. I bought a [word missing] of paper and package of envelopes yesterday. I am alright for letter writing for some time to come, but could soon dispense of all of them if [I] would give to all that asks for them. I don't give to any. I am not reading any continued stories in the <u>Ledger</u> so it does not make any difference how old they are when I get them. All of you read them at home then send to me, I mean after Lizzie has had them, anything so it is something to read.

Sue says I must not run myself down like I did in one of my letters. Says there is no black sheep in our family. Well perhaps there is not a black sheep, but there certainly has been a very bad boy, and one that has been very disobedient even to his own sorrow. See what disobedience has led me to, but I have no right to complain, it was brought on by myself, with no one to blame but me. I would be perfectly resigned to my fate were I only certain that you would all be alive and well when my time expires.

My wages are very good and certain, but the eating I can't enjoy or

---

10 Matthews refers to the 1858 fatigue blouse, sometimes termed a sack coat, a loosely fitting dark blue, single-breasted woolen garment that was the soldier's daily uniform. The blouse was made in lined and unlined versions, both having four brass buttons down the front. The jacket he mentions was the tight, waist-length cavalry jacket, piped with yellow braid, adopted in 1855. Although it was intended to be the mounted man's only uniform, the jacket was commonly reserved as the dress uniform by the postwar regulars. See McChristian, *U.S. Army in the West*, 12–13.

can I get use to it. It don't seem to satisfy my hunger. Some days I buy a slice of ginger bread from a boy that brings it in camp. I have never yet eaten all they gave me, but then it does me no good. I am just as hungrey when I get up from breakfast and supper as [I] was when sit down. The dinner I feel a little better on, but not very much.

Remember me kindly to all those that ask after me, but don't say a word to those that don't. I have been in the service just two weeks and a half.

Have just returned from Stables and dinner and will try to finish this epistle. A little circumstance occurred here yesterday which I think is worth relating. My bunk or bed fellow is a man about 37 years old.[11] He enlisted in Cincinnati and from his appearance I judged he had seen better days. He seemed to be a gentleman, more so than any of the rest. So I proposed that he and I bunk together, which he readily consented to do. We have been sleeping together ever since and I have found him to be just what I took him to be, a perfect gentleman. He is very ambitious and like myself wanted to do anything [to improve?] himself in the estimation of the officers. So when I was detailed for guard he done every thing to make me present a clean and neat appearance, so that I win the [inspection?] and be excused for being the cleanest man. How well we succeeded you already know.

Yesterday morning he was detailed for the same duty. So at it we went to trim and clean him up and did. So he was the cleanest man from our detail, but in inspection he made one or two mistakes and the Sergt. excused someone else. He was I think sure of being excused [and] no doubt was somewhat disappointed.

When you are on guard you are on duty two hours and off four. So last night when he had done his duty he layed down to sleep with the rest of the guards at the guard house. About twelve o'clock last night the officer at the day came around and all the guards had to be in ranks with their guns and belts. In the hurry to get out he forgot his belt and cartridge box. The Officer saw he had none on and ordered him in the guard house, where he is yet. Suppose he will get out tomorrow. I can imagine

---

11 Prior to the early 1870s, when single iron-frame bunks were adopted, the army furnished barracks with double bunks that were two or even three tiers high. A man's "bunky," therefore, was the one who shared the bed and blankets. This practice of sleeping two men in a tier was uncomfortable and unhealthy, and became an almost universal complaint of army doctors. See Brown, *Army Called It Home*, 71–75.

how bad he feels, but he can hardly be blamed. When our squad left Cincinnati & all [wagered he?] would get in the guard house first. So I had to bunk by myself last night. I am very sorry for him, but sympathy does little good under these circumstances. I guess I have written about enough, for one time. Direct to A Troop instead of D.

A Troop, Carlisle Barracks
SUNDAY, OCTOBER 3, 1869

Well we have not left Carlisle yet, but don't know how long we will remain here. About one hundred colored troops left here Friday. It is supposed that two or three hundred whites will leave here tomorrow, if so I expect to be one of the number. Will be sent to the first and eighth regiments [in] California. If I dont get off with this detachment, will be sent to New Mexico in about eight or ten days. Would sooner go off with the first detachment and go to California.

Friday I was detailed for guard again and got excused again. The first time I got excused, I had a white shirt and collar on. Some of the boys said that was the reason I got excused. Last Friday I had no white shirt, so had to put a government one on.[12] Cleaned myself up, but did not have much cleaning to do as we all generally keep ourselves clean. We are compelled to do so. I had no idea of being excused but was agreeable. Disappointed after the Sergeant examined us all, he came to me and said you are excused. You can hardly imagine how good I felt. It is no little honor to be excused for two days twice in succession, and the only times that [I] was detailed for guard.

The Capt of our troop asked the Sergt. yesterday to detail one out of the troop that understand driving horses for him. Said he wanted a man to drive his carriage and take his wife out a riding when he could not go. The Sergt. came over where I was standing and asked me how I

---

12 Although soldiers were not supposed to have civilian clothing in their possession, the rule was generally ignored when it came to underclothing. The men commonly wore cotton or muslin shirts under their woolen uniforms during the warm seasons of the year, rather than the regulation white or gray flannel article. Many men purchased white cotton shirts with separate linen collars for dress occasions. In this instance, surprisingly, the inspecting officer seems to have given preference to the smart appearance Matthews presented in a non-issue shirt. Another officer might have disqualified him under the same circumstances. See McChristian, *U.S. Army in the West*, 67–68.

would like to go with the Capt., said I would not have much to do. I thanked him very kindly and said I did not enlist for a waiter, I enlisted for a Soldier. I don't know who got the Situation, it would be a good place for any one that liked that kind of business. But we are too much of a slave for them now, without going in their houses. I don't want any such situations. If I can't get a clerkship in any of the departments, will do a Soldiers duty for my time of enlistment.

Don't think I will want to enlist again, although am getting along very well. The only thing that goes hard with me is the eating. I can't enjoy that, the cooks here swindel the men out of most everything. After we get away from here will get better eatings.

We were going to play another match game of Baseball yesterday, but a rain storm broke it up. It has been raining constantly since yesterday noon, and not much prospects of it clearing up for some time.

My bunk companion got out of the guard house last week.

I will not close this letter till tomorrow morning then perhaps I can give you some definite answer about leaving here. The Sergeant gave me a pass for all day this morning. I would go into Town and go to Church, but it is raining too hard.

Sunday evening 3 o'clock, great excitement in the barracks about the boys going away. Just signed my name on the clothing roll for a Overcoat. Am consigned to the Eighth regiment in California, will leave here tomorrow.

At 11 A.M. [a] great many of the men are disappointed. Some have to remain here. Hope I will get a letter from home tomorrow. It will make me feel good till I am in California. But if I have to wait till after I get there will not feel so well. Will add a few lines tomorrow. I would not like to remain here after the boys left. There will be no one to do the work. So am glad I am going. I wanted to go to California. One thing I care about will be so far away from home.

Monday morning:

Have not received the looked for letter. Will have to mail this if [I] want it to go this morning. Everything is excitement here, all in the room are packing up ready to start. Will leave here some time this morning. I will write to you soon as [I] arrive in California. Tell those that ask after me where I am going. Bid all good bye. It will be some time before I see any of you again. Don't grieve after me. I will try to be a good Soldier. I guess it is all for the best. Rest assured you are all foremost in my mind all the time. Soon as [we] get payed off I will send all home that I can possibly spare, for you to use in any way you see proper.

The Sergt. just said we would leave here at 11 A.M. Have about two hours yet. We are going via of Omaha. I don't know what else to write. Have written this in a great hurry so could mail it this morning. God bless and Keep you all well, till I come home.

The Eighth U.S. Cavalry was one of four new cavalry regiments authorized in 1866 for service on the Western Frontier. Unlike the other regular units, the Eighth was specially recruited in the far West. Headquarters and ten of the twelve companies were organized at the Presidio of California, north of San Francisco, while the other two were quartered at Angel Island, situated in the adjacent bay. Most of the men initially came from the immediate region, where they had worked as miners or lumbermen or at other laboring occupations. These hardened outdoorsmen, described as "typical specimens of the roving order of citizens," probably would have done well in the California Volunteers of the late war, but many of them proved unable to adapt to the discipline and spit-and-polish for which the regulars were legendary. By the end of 1867, with most of the companies still posted in California, nearly 42 percent of the men had deserted. Thus, the regiment desperately needed to be brought up to strength again if it were to effectively carry out its mission of protecting travel routes, mining regions, and settlements.[13]

By 1869, the Eighth Cavalry was fast losing its original complement of three-year men. Eddie Matthews, of course, had no way to see the larger picture when he entered the recruiting office that summer, but as fate would have it, he presented himself at just the critical moment to help fill the quota of needed cavalrymen.

Omaha, Nebraska
OCTOBER 7, 1869

Who would have supposed that when I left home not two weeks ago I would be in this God forsaken country. "Excuse the expression." I can think of no other word sufficiently strong to express myself. Also excuse this letter as I have to write on my Knapsack, which is not as convenient as a desk. When we left Carlisle I did not expect to write home till had

---

13 See Rodenbough, *Army of the United States,* 268.

arrived in California. Had to stop here for a day so concluded to write a line to you.

Monday morning about nine o'clock we were drawn up in line to hear what Regiment we were assigned to. It took about one and a half hours to call three hundred and forty names. Had to stand in line all that time with Knapsacks and accouterments on. I was assigned to the 8th Regt [in] California, just where I wanted to go. About 11 o'clock we left Carlisle under an escort of 20 men who were stationed at every door with orders to let no man pass out of the cars.[14] Not even from one car to the other.

I was unfortunate enough to be put in a car where there was most too much Binzine on board and the result was heavy skirmishing amongst the occupants of the car.[15] Several knock downs and considerable hair pulling, also a few black eyes was the result. I was not a participant. I perched myself up on the back of my seat and was a silent spectator, all quieted down at last. The rest of the ride was past in a more peacible manner.

Arrived in Pittsburg Tuesday morning at 4 o'clock. Changed cars for Chicago. Arrived in that place the following night about 12 o'clock. Took another change for this place, and arrived in town 11 o'clock last night, or at least arrived on the east side of the Missouri River which runs by the town. We were put on board of a Ferry Boat, crossed over to the west side, with marching orders for Omaha Barracks which are situated about six or eight miles west of Omaha on the Prairie. I tell you we got pretty tired before we got to the barracks. We were all cramped up and about half starved had only about half rations from Chicago here. Were on the cars three days and two nights.

Arrived at the Barracks at 2 A.M. this day. Got to bed at last and got the first sleep I had since Sunday Night. Could not sleep on the car, they were too crowded. Slept till 8 o'clock. Then got up took wash and looked for something to eat. Could get nothing till about 10 when we got a big peace of half raw beef and a loaf of bread. We looked like so many dogs gnawing at the beef which was as old as the hills. At 12 we got [a] cup of coffee.

---

14 Reliable soldiers from the depot's permanent party accompanied the recruits to discourage desertions while traveling to their assigned regiments.
15 Benzene, a common solvent of the day, was slang for liquor.

It was all a mistake that we stopped here. Major Foreman our officer in charge got left behind at some turn, so we had to stop here till he came up.[16] Will leave here tomorrow morning.

Just had two fights in the room, causes as before—too much Omaha this morning. We were called on by the citizens of this country, "Paunee Indians." About a doz of them came in camp with their [word missing] on begging for anything they could get. They created no little sensation among the boys. Did not like their looks much, an[d] dirty enough to have Buggy hair. No doubt they have them in abundance.

It is getting so dark I can scarcely see. This is an awful country to live in. I had lots of Omaha in me before I ever saw the place. But assure you it is all taken out now. Would not live here as a citizen under any c[ondition?]. Sometimes we were for hours without seeing a house or even a town. You could look all over the country, have no hills here as large as the Time Killer hill at home. Will have to close, but soon as get to C[alifornia] will write you a long letter. I did not get the expected letter in Carlisle. If any come for me it will be forwarded to California.

Angel Island, California

OCT. 15, 1869

Arrived on this Island yesterday. It is situated about four miles from San Francisco and is surrounded by the Pacific. It is the Head Qtrs of the 8[th] Cavalry.

We left Omaha last Friday morning, had to march from the Barracks a distance of Six Miles through mud shoe top deep and a cold rain. By the time we arrived at the cars we were pretty well drenched and had on our cloth[e]s about as much mud as we could carry. Was put aboard of the Great Union Pacific [Railroad?] Cars. Saw any amount of game along the Road, such as Prairie Chicken, Deer, Antelopes, Wolves & Foxes. Capt. [Samuel P.] Smith and Lieut [Thomas M.] Fisher the Officers in charge of the Detachment were shooting at them all along

---

16 Foreman has not been identified.

the Road, but did not hit any. At Cheyene, Nebraska or Wyoming Territory I don't know which.

Capt. Smith had me [assigned?] Orderly for him. I still hold the hon[ored?] position. One thing I know it is a good deal easier than doing Soldiers duty.

Well I am now about four thousand miles from home. Without any prospects of getting nearer. And more to go farther in a short time. We will be sent to Arizona to join our Companys. This is only the Head Qtrs. of the Regt.

We arrive[d after] ten days on the Cars traveling over the great Union Pacific R.R. Saw parts of Salt Lake, crossed the Rocky Mountains. Sometimes would be thousands of feet above the level, then you would be crossing works about twice as high as those at Rowlesberg W. Va. In a town called [illegible] on the Rocky Mountains they have built a Shed just like the cover over a bridge for "forty miles" to protect the track from the snow. You can't see anything all that distance but pine boards.[17] It is night along the [word missing] of the Mountain where the prettiest scenery is. I don't think I would care about passing over the road again. It is too dangerous for pleasure.

All along the road you can see any amount of Indians and Chinamen working on repairs. Don't have any white men except for Overseers.

Saturday Morning 16th. I had to stop writing yesterday to go down to Head Qtrs. with the Capt. This Island is just like the Maryland Heights, and we are [pos?]ted right on the top. Is one mile down to Head Qtrs.

About twenty five men deserted on the road. At Omaha we were put in companys with Sergeants and Corporals appointed to take charge till we arrived at this place. Lieut. [Michael J.] Fitzgerald Commanding at Omaha was assisting our Officers in forming us into Companys. When my name was called Lt. Fitzgerald came up and asked me if I ever was in the Army before. Told him was with my Father who was QM of the 3rd Md. He asked if it was not the P[otomac] H[ome] B[rigade]. I said it was. He said why young man I know you and your Father very well. Said he was in command of some

---

17 Matthews was describing one of the many snow sheds constructed in the Sierra Nevada range along the Central Pacific route. See Wheeler, *Railroaders*, 106, 112.

forces at Frederick during the War. Shook hands with me and said when I got to the Reg[iment] to go to the Col[onel] and give him his compliments, and ask him to assign me to G Company. He left me then to assist the Officers, but returned soon as [he] got through and said I need not go to the Col., said he would write to him and tell him to take care of me. I suppose G Co. is a good one, the reason he told me to get assigned to it.

After he left me, the men gathered around me to find out what he said, asked me lots of questions. It is strange, yet true, I meet friends and acquaintances where ever I go, but what does it amount to? None of them ever done me any good. But it is very pleasant to have a kind word spoken to you once in a while. I have been fortunate in that respect since have been in the Army. I have got kind words from the officers all the time, while some others get harsh ones. I have made up my mind now that I am in the Army to do my duty and obey every command cheerfully, till my time of enlistment has expired. One thing is certain I will never enter the Army again. This has taught me a lesson, and one I will never forget. It is a dear one to me. It is true I will get to see a good deal of this world, more than I ever would had I remained at Home, but what does that amount to, when you are separated from those that love you and are so dear to you.

At one of the towns on the route a nice looking Lady called to me from the Porch and handed me a very nice large apple. It brought tears to my eyes even to receive that little kindness from a stranger. It was just as much as I could do to raise my cap and thank her for it. She seemed inclined to talk to me, but I did not want to expose myself to her. Knew if I said two more words to her would have to cry. Kind words go a great way with me. I have been in the Army one month and nine days and it seems like that many years since have been away from home. When I get home again I don't think anything in this world will induce me to leave it again. I will spend the balance of my life trying to do all I can to help you all along at home and try to make some amends for the trouble I have caused you.

Don't think we will get payed off till [I] get to the Company. Don't use any thing but Gold and Silver out here. The Government pays us off with greenbacks which are considerable below par, thirty per cent discount on the dollar. I don't think that is right. If they discount paper money, the Gov't. ought to pay the Men off with money that is at par. I know one thing, there will be very little I will have discounted. I shall not keep one cent more than can do with.[18]

This separation from all that is dear to me is very hard to bear, but five years will pass away then, like the prodigal "that I am," I will return to my fathers house, never under any circumstances to leave it again. I know you will miss me equally as much as I shall you. Not because I am so all important, but still I am a member of the family, and one darling little sister has left us for a better land and only those that have suffered the same bereavement can sympathize with us. I have by no means bettered my situation, yet I am doing something that will feed and cloth myself and be able to send you some money to get along with.

Don't trouble for me, one thing I will promise you which I know will make your hearts glad, and that is I promise you dear ones never to drink a drop of intoxicating liquor while I am in the Army. I will never break this pledge, although I have broken one before. As I hope to meet you all again, so I hope to keep my word. I have some postage stamps left yet, but as we are going to Arizona and don't know whether will be able to get any or not. Wish you would send me a few.

Write immediately and give me all the news. Tell George Parke to write to me, he writes a splendid letter. Direct to me 8th Cavalry, Angel Island, California. If we should leave here before your letter arrives, it will be forwarded to me. Don't know whether I will be assigned to G. Co. or not, that will make no difference about the Company. Tell Parke where to direct.

I am not doing anything at present, so concluded had better fill this scrap of paper up with a description of this and surrounding Islands. We are in sight of San Francisco, and can see the Vessels coming in and leaving any hour of the day. Have lots of Cannons on the Island in case of an invasion. San Francisco I think is about as safe from any attack or invasion as any place I ever saw.

There is a little Island a short distance from us inhabited by Citizens. Boats stop here every day. You can get a pass and go to the City for a

---

18 Soldiers were paid bimonthly, or as soon thereafter as a paymaster could make his rounds. A private in his first enlistment received $13.00 per month, less $2.00 compulsory retained savings paid to him at the end of his term. Additionally, he forfeited twelve and a half cents monthly to support the old soldiers' home in Washington, D.C., even though he would probably never avail himself of it. By the time he also paid the company tailor, laundress, and barber for their services, and suffered a local discount for paper money, as Matthews describes, he had little discretionary money left. See *Revised Regulations*, 546.

change. A Government boat comes and leaves here once a day. If I had any money I think I would go to the City and look around, perhaps will do so [while?] am here. Want to see as much of this Country now I am out here as I possibly can for after I leave will never visit it again, unless do on my return home. Saw some of the great Gold and Silver Mines. People generally look rough out here. Sometimes you see a respectable looking Lady or Gentleman, but you will see more men with two revolvers and a large knife strapped around them than anything else. Every person looks out for it out here.

Fort Yuma, Lower California
SUNDAY, NOVEMBER 14, 1869

When I wrote to you from Angel Island Oct. 15th, I did not know whether we would remain there till I could hear from my dear home or not, but I know how anxious you all are to hear from me that it is a pleasure for me to write to you, and I certainly avail myself of every opportunity to do so, as this is the fifth letter that I have written to you without receiving one word in reply from you, but it is not your fault. Undoubtedly you have written to me long ere this, but have been continually on the move, not remaining long enough in one place to receive an answer from you and even now we have only stopped till Tuesday 16th when we will go on the move again. I am now Seven thousand miles from home and not done going yet. I intend to give you an account of all my doings since I wrote to you.

Oct. 20th we were assigned to our Companys and very much to my surprise I was assigned to L Co. instead of G, the Co. I made application for. And when I saw the men that was to go to my Company it made me feel bad. All looked [word missing] and ungentlemanly. Not one that I would have any association what ever with. None that I could call a friend, you of course can imagine my feelings then, something like they were in Cincinnati where the only two boys or persons that I knew in the west deserted me and left me no other resort but to join the Army.

Soon as the Roll was called and all the men assigned, I went up to Capt. Smith our Commander and asked him how I came to be assigned to L Co., when I made application for G. Capt said he did not know. Said he handed my application in to Lieut. [Pendleton]

Hunter, the officer that assigned us. Said he supposed it was over looked some way, and that I had better remain in the Company, that it was one of the best in the Regiment. I said that may be, but the men that are going with me are very rough. Capt said so much the better for you Orderly, the harder [word missing] you go with your chance for promotion is very good and that makes it so much the better. An other Capt. that was standing by said that is so young man. So I had to content my self and remain where I was put. From what I have seen and heard since have been in the Army, I am satisfied that I will not be a Private for five years.

21st. Heard of the death of Ex President Pierce. Were firing cannons at intervals all day. We could not imagine what all the firing was for till we were drawn up in line and the news read to us. On the night of the 22nd received orders to be ready to move by five o'clock next morning. It was good tidings of great joy to us as we were nearly starved, did not have enough to eat any one time while on the miserable place, I mean Angel Island.

So next morning bright and early all went to work striking Tents. Left the Island about 8 A.M. and was taken over to San Francisco on a Tug Boat and was at once put aboard of the Steamer "Continental" bound for "Arizona."[19] Left San Francisco about 10 P.M. on the 24th. I had lots of fun looking at the men vomiting although the water was quite calm, yet a number were sea sick.

Companies B, I, K, and L, Eighth Cavalry, had been transferred to stations in Arizona Territory in 1867 to contend with mounting Apache resistance to the influx of miners and ranchers into the region bounded by the Colorado and Verde Rivers. "[T]he few settlers and scattered miners of Arizona were the sheep upon which these wolves habitually preyed . . . ," wrote Brigadier General Edward O. C. Ord in his annual report, "therefore I encouraged the troops to capture and root out the Apache by every means, and to hunt them as they would wild animals." As a result, this battalion was in the field almost continuously during the next two years, patrolling and engaging the Apaches in numerous

---

19 The steamer was taking a course south along the coast of California, circumventing the Baja California peninsula, and then going up the Gulf of California to Fort Yuma at the mouth of the Colorado River.

skirmishes. Company L was posted at Fort Whipple, immediately northeast of Prescott, the territorial capital.[20]

The nature of western service necessitated the distribution of companies among posts and temporary cantonments throughout their assigned geographical divisions. Typically, regiments were rarely, if ever, together as a whole for years at a time; the Eighth Cavalry, for example, was never concentrated at one place for over two decades after its organization.

[continued] 25th was clear and fine. I was sitting up on deck thinking of my dear home and friends when one of the Sailors took me down in the hold and gave me a splendid meal. I enjoyed it very much as was quite hungrey. Thanked him very kindly for it and went up on deck again to meditate, have plenty of time for that, and I assure you that most of it is of home, that blessed place. I will be deprived of the pleasure of being with you for five years. But sure as that time is up, I will never leave you again. But this is only a repetition of what I have written to you [a] half dozen times.

In the evening I was on the hurricane deck again, and seeing the evening star I made three wishes. I have often heard that if you make three wishes while looking at the first star you see of an evening, they will come true. I thought I would try what virtue there was in it. First wished that you were all well at home. Second that you would all live and prosper till I return. Third that I would get a letter from you soon as [I] got to my Company.

The mail does not come by water but over land and probably a letter would arrive at the Company for me by the time I got there, for sure as your letter would come to Angel Island for me, it would be forwarded to me as they know to which Company we go to.

26th. I have often heard you say that it was very beautiful to see the Sun rise and set at Sea. It certainly is a very grand sight. Often when I would listen to you talking about the wonderful Sea, I would wonder if

---

20 Ord's quotation is found in *ARSW*, 1869, 121. The army established the post, initially called Camp Whipple, on December 21, 1863, in Arizona's Chino Valley, near the Verde River. Six months later, a new location was chosen near Prescott. It was named for Major General Amiel W. Whipple, killed at the Battle of Chancellorsville in 1863. Fort Whipple, as it was later known, was combined with Prescott Barracks in 1879 to become Whipple Barracks. The garrison was withdrawn in 1913. See Frazer, *Forts of the West*, 14–15.

I would ever see those wonder sights. And I always had a great mania for traveling, but I have been perfectly satisfied in that respect and have traveled to my hearts content and still am not to my journeys end, or do I know when [I] will be.

27th. Can see land this morning, it is Lower California. The weather is very warm, much warmer here than in Maryland anytime during the summer.

28th. Weather fine as usual, water smooth. I am detailed for Guard tomorrow. Very little guard duty I have done since have been in the Army, but I certainly have been shifted about from one thing to another a great deal since have been in the service of Uncle Sam. First Orderly for the Capt, then Clerking for him, then doing Guard duty.

Fort Yuma, Lower California
SUNDAY, NOVEMBER 14, 1869

29th. Running along side of the Mexican Shore, grass looks green, reminds me of spring. Came into Cape St. Lucas about 8 A.M., did not remain but short time. There is only two or three horses in sight. Suppose there is a Town inland some place near the Cape.

30th. All had a good wash about 4 A.M. Something on the order of a shower bath. All undressed and then had two men to turn the hose on us. Cleaned us up pretty well. Just one week aboard of the Boat, and have had quite enough of the Sea.

31st. Came in the harbor of San Blas this morning.[21] This is a very beautiful Town, the prettiest town [I] have seen in all my travels. We were boarded by an English man of war which was lying in the harbor. I said boarded by a man of war, I mean her Officers. Name of the Ship was the "Staletta." The Sailors looked quite nice in their clean uniforms. Much cleaner than us by a good deal.

Mustered for Pay this morning. This is the Sabbath and our services consist of a number of forms, some spending it reading, others sleeping, some playing cards and a number of other ways. For my part I am sitting on Deck watching the little boats come and go. Don't see but a few Americans. I have had the "Diarriah" suppose that is something too

---

21 San Blas is a port on the west coast of mainland Mexico.

and spelling it. It is the only way I know for some time and also was Sea Sick but got over that much easier than expected. It is not a very pleasant feeling which I suppose you are aware of.

Nov. 1st. Arrived at Mazathan [Mazatlán] and remained all day discharging cargo.[22] All hands took a good swim in the harbor. One man came very near drowning. Just rescued him in time. It like San Blas is a very pretty Town, situated along the Sea Coast. Saw plenty of oranges, lemons, bananas & cocoanuts growing, looked very nice.

2nd. Still at M. Had to unload a great many goods. It must be quite a business place. Dreamt last night that was shot in the back by an Indian. Was quite pleased when woke up and found it was only a dream.[23] Three of our men deserted last night. We have lost a great many men by desertion since left Carlisle.[24]

Left M. about 3 P.M. Had not gone very far before we got in some very rough water. Wind was blowing at a tremendious rate. Ship pitched about considerable, continued so all night.

3rd. Was very sick again today. The water still continues very rough. Water sometimes would fly all over the hurricane deck.

4th. Run in sight of a vessel that was driven ashore about a year ago in a storm. Cannot get her off till high water comes, don't know when that will be. La Paz is only nine miles from this point.

5th. Came to Harbor Island there saw a Lake of Salt. When the water is lower men working there cut blocks of Salt out. Took a big load aboard of our ship. It belongs to Lower California. Am on Guard again today.

Nov. 6th. Am two weeks aboard of the Continental today. Came to Guaymas in Lower California. Very strange looking place, looks like some of the towns in Virginia during the war. The Indians made a raid on it some time ago and came very near demolishing it. The young man that was bunking with me stole two Government Shirts of mine last night. I did not say anything to him but took my raps and moved them to another Bunk. He never asked me why I moved them. Could not look me in the face. I will have nothing to do with those kind of people.

---

22 Also on the coast of mainland Mexico, Mazatlán was a major port supplying the northern section of the country, and it was an outlet for fruit grown in the region.
23 This comment suggests that the realities of Indian fighting may have occupied more of Matthews's thoughts than he had previously revealed.
24 Landing at a Mexican port provided an unparalleled opportunity for soldiers inclined to desert. Once they were away from the ship, there was little chance of their being apprehended.

Lost nine men by desertion at "Guaymas." Can't imagine why men desert in such a Country as this.

8th. Just two months in the Army today. What a long long time it does seem since I left my dear home and all that is dear to me in the world to associate myself with the scrapings of the world, for I do think that the Army is composed of the scrapings of Penitentaries, Jails and everything else combined to make an Army suitable for this Government, both Officers and men. The Officers steal from the men and the men steal from each other. Everything is steal, steal, steal. Well I have only 58 months to serve yet. Arrived at the mouth of the Colorado River about five o'clock. We will be transferred to a River Boat tomorrow.

9th. Went aboard of the "Cocopah," the river boat that is to take us up the "Colorado." The river is very low, so low that a man has to stand on the Bow of the boat with a long pole and continually cry out the depth of the water, and then we would run a ground about every half hour, but could push off again in a few minutes. Could only run during the day, had to lay up at night. While on the "Continental" I saw any amount of Wales, Sharks, Porposes and all kind of fish, the Pacific seemed to be full of them.

10th. The banks of the River are lined with Civilized Indians. They look anything but civilized. Why do people call them noble, "the noble Red Man"[?] What can there be noble in a miserable, dirty, lousy, thieving piece of humanity, which all the Indians I have seen certainly are, and I have seen a goodly number since [I] have been in the Army. I would not trust my hair in reach of any of them, although they are very cowardly. Nevertheless if they got a chance they would [raise?] your hair in less than no time.

11th. We lost one man this morning while getting aboard. We all spent the night on stove cooking and sleeping. About 4 A.M. the whistle blew for us to get aboard and in the rush one man lost his balance and fell overboard and before anything could be done for him, he was carried off by the swift current. He had his Great Coat and Knapsack on at the time, and even had he been a good swimmer, there would have been very little chance for his life. Soldiers show very little respect for a comrade. I cannot tell how many times I thought of the circumstance since, although I did not know the young man.

12th. Came to this place Fort Yuma, where we will be divided and put to our different Companys. Some will go by land and others will go up the River by Boat. I go the latter way. I have heard since [I] have been here that L Co., the one I go to, is the best Company in the Regiment. Will find out when get to it. Soon as got here I was made Clerk for B, D, & L Companys. Those three Co. go together up the river. I will continue in that capacity till [we] get to our destination. Don't know when that will be.

The country I have travelled over since left Angel Island generally has been nothing but sand hills and as barron as it could possibly be. Can't imagine what the Gov't wants with such a country. Fort Yuma is in Lower California but right across the river is a little town called Arizona City, composed chiefly of Government buildings and Indian Huts. Those are the kind of citizens we have out here.

Well I have given you a little account of my travels since [I] wrote to you from Angel Island. It is not much of a description, but the best I can do just now. Perhaps some other time I will give you a better description of our trip and the country, "I mean verbally." Wish could do that now. Now will write about something which is of more importance to me than Arizona, Mexico or California, and that is my beloved home.

How are you all getting along[?] All well and prospering I hope. Did you receive my letter from Angel Island and did you answer it yet[?] If you did it will be forwarded to me by mail over land. Will be sent to my Company at Fort Whipple Arizona. Then it may arrive soon as I do. Oh how anxious I am to hear from you dear ones.

When you receive this I may be settled down with my Company. I don't know how long it will take us to get to our Company's yet, but the mails will not come the way we have.

Does Johnnie help Father in the store[?] I hope he does and is a good boy which no doubt he is. Who does he associate with, none but good boys I hope. Tell me their names, then I can tell what kind of company he keeps for I know all the boys both good and bad, large and small and my experience is that there is very few good boys in Westminster large or small and I would sooner my dear little brothers would not associate themselves with any boys at all unless they are real good boys in every respect. I have had a bitter experience and have been a miserable bad boy in every respect, and I should be an example for you my dear little Brothers, take warning and lead a different life from the one your elder brother has lived.

I have been in the Army now two months and one week. I count every day and think at night, well I have one more day less to serve Uncle Sam. I don't suppose I will get any pay for at least two months more, then I will be able to send you right smart. Oh how good I will feel when I send you my wages home. Then I will commence to repay you partly for the trouble I have given you, and it will make my heart glad to know that I am helping my dear Parents along. I know how hard times are. Do you think you will remain in Westminster[?] I hope you will, I like the town about as well as any place I have seen, and as for business I think yow can do equally as well as any place else. I will send you enough to pay the store rent and I suppose more but even that will be some help to you.

Answer this soon as possible and direct to me Co L 8th U.S. Cavalry, Fort Whipple Arizona.

Camp Whipple, Arizona Territory
DECEMBER 15, 1869

I arrived at this my destination last night, after a long and tedious march over land a distance of one hundred and seventy five miles. Almost the first thing after [we] entered camp was the joyful news that several letters and papers were at the Company's Head Qts. for me. I hastened to the Quarters and was handed three letters and two papers, they had been here for some time. One of the men standing by remarked that he had been in the service very near five years and had not received that many letters during that time. And now that I know you are all well and satisfyed at the step I have taken, I can content myself and feel like a new man. My anxi[e]ty for your welfare was troubling me a great deal. I have read and reread them a number of times, not only to myself but to some of my comrades, all said they were splendid and only wished they could get some like them. Oh you don't know how proud I am of you all, you dear ones.

It affords me great pleasure to show the few photographs which I have. All the men praise them very highly. One remarked that Lizzie looked like an Authoress, I thought to myself that she was good enough if not quite smart enough to be one. All admire little Annie's picture and someone always says "what a dear little thing," and when I show my little Brothers they say aint they nice little fellows.²⁵ I always say yes, they are just as good as they are nice. Sues and Maggies were not forgotten, but were praised equally as much as the rest. One of the Company said Matthews you [are] all splendid lookin, yourself included, that was stale news to me for I was awair of that fact long ere he told me. But still it made me feel good to know that others was of the same opinion as myself, "but how could they be otherwise in that respect." Another one of the Company said if those pictures belonged to him he would not take five years pay for them. If I only had my dear Mothers and Fathers now would have all the familys. You must have them taken for me soon. Will have mine taken and send to you soon as get payed off, which will not be very long. I am just one week and three months in the service today. Will I suppose draw four months pay or perhaps more. That will be a sorry little sum wont it[?] Will send the most of it home.

Will give you a little account of my trip [since I] last wrote to you from Fort Yuma, which I hope you have received ere this. We were separated at the above place, those that went to the First Cavy and one or two companys for the Eighth. We were put aboard the same Boat the "Cocopah" an Indian name, everything is "Indian" out here. Left Yuma on the 16th inst. and arrived at Fort Mojave in about two weeks.²⁶ Remained there two days. M is a small town situated along the banks of the Colorado River. The town consists of several Gambling & drinking saloons, and two or three stores. Each store having a bar and Gambling saloon attached to it. Whiskey sells at two bits equal to twenty five cents in coin a drink. One drink set some of our men almost crazy. Oh it must be miserable stuff to drink. I have been offered a number of drinks, but replyed very emphatically no, I don't indulge. I have no desire to partake of the poisonous stuff.

But I must say that some of the stores are much finer than any in Westminster and have more goods in them. It requires capital to do

---

25 "Annie" has not been positively identified, but may be a nickname for Matthews's deceased sister, Frances.
26 Established on the left bank of the Colorado River at Beal's Crossing in 1859, Fort Mojave protected the immigrant route across northern Arizona into California and controlled the neighboring Paiute and Mojave Indians. The rise of Confederate sentiment in southern California in 1861 caused the garrison at Fort Mojave to be transferred there, and the post to be temporarily abandoned. It was reoccupied in 1863 and remained active until 1890. The property was later transferred to the Interior Department for use as an Indian school, which operated until 1935. See Frazer, Forts of the West, 11–12.

business out here. All buy large stocks at a time, and charge very high for everything. The farther you go from the river the dearer everything is.

Well to return to my subject. We left Mojave with a wagon train for this point and Prescott City, which is about one mile from this post. First day we marched only nine miles, but it was enough for the most of us, me especially. It blistered my feet very badly, so much so that I had to remain behind with the wagon's next day and continued to follow them till within two days march of this place.[27] Found it much easier with the wagons than to keep up with the column, could ride sometimes. We were just twelve days marching the hundred and seventy five miles. We came in a north [*sic*, south] east direction from Fort Mojave and found the Country much finer than the southern part of the Territory. Water is very scarce in some parts, but what there is splendid good as any water I ever drank, cold and healthy. And the Country here is very healthy and very little danger of Indians.

This is the Head Quarters of the Territory and is the finest post. D and my Company of the Eighth Cavalry and one Company of the 12th Infantry. When we arrived yesterday evening we were welcomed heartily by our Company. Men came and shook hands and welcomed us the same as though they had known us for a number of years. It made me feel splendid. And when I saw the men that composed my Company I felt much better. All are young men, and seem to be Gentlemen in every respect. Officers as well as men, don't think I ever saw finer looking men in my life. All look like they were from good homes, and I flatter myself that I am an addition to them by no means discreditable, and will be one more addition to a good looking company. "Lizzie will say this is vanity I know." Mother will agree with me, which will over balance the other party, we having a majority, like the Democrats of Carroll County.

Now I am settled down at least till spring when the 8th cavalry is to be sent to New Mexico. What an extent of Country I have travelled over and what sights I have seen at Uncle Sams expense. It seems that I am always at some persons expense. Get payed for travelling over the Continent when hundreds have to travill at their own expense and see no more than I.

---

27 Even though these recruits were in the cavalry, they would not receive horses until they joined their companies. Therefore, they were essentially infantrymen, carrying their overcoats and other meager belongings in knapsacks and their rations in haversacks.

Lizzie spoke of curiosity. I have a few small shells that I gathered on the Mexican Coast. Could have gotten some very fine ones but had no way of carrying them. While we were aboard of the Steamer Continental we anchored off the Coast, and a party of us went fishing in a row Boat. That is the way I come by them. I will take care of them and perhaps will get a chance to send them home, if not will keep them till I return, which will be in the Short period of five years. I am in better spirits now that I have arrived at my Co. and find how nicely we are situated. I can jest on subjects now that would have troubled me a great deal while we were on the road.

I had a great laugh yesterday [a] short time after [we] came in. A Clerk from Head Qts. came in the building I was in and said where is Eddie Matthews[?] I want to see him. I supposed by the way he was talking that, he was an old acquaintance, I could not see his face as it was too dark. I spoke up and said that I was the individual he was in search of, he took me by the hand and said my dear fellow there is several letters and papers down at the Office for you, and I suppose they must be from some little sweet heart. Soon as he said letters my heart went straight up in my throat and choked me almost, for well I knew they were from home. My speach soon returned and I said no they were from home. He said allow me to welcome you to as good a home as any "home," still holding me by the hand. I interrupted him by asking him to excuse me till I had read my letters, then I would have no objections to talk to him all night if he was satisfyed. He said very well, and I knew by the way he was talking that he could almost talk a man blind.

He said come along and I will get the letters for you, which I did and after I had read those dear letters over very carefully I looked around for my man for I knew I could talk to him then for I felt so good. But he was not to be found any place. He was on the order of Theo Fritchey, only he seemed to talk a little faster. The men here are as different from the recruits that came with me as day light is to darkness. All try to make us feel comfortable as possible. We all had to draw new clothing, as the cloth[e]s we had on were pretty near played out.

Some of the lazy and dirty men of our detachment were carrying with them some of those little insects called "lice." As for myself in that respect can say had none, as I kept myself clean all the time, never letting one day pass without a good wash. Sometimes would only have a chance of washing once, but always had that, while a great many others went for three and five days without touching water to their faces. I have drawn less clothing than most of the men that came with me and certainly the cleanest with a few exceptions. "More Vanity."

Well boys I have got a very pretty little white horse, whos name is "Petrolium U Nasby." He was christened before I came to the company, otherwise I would have left him to all of you three little fellows to name for me. I guess he is pretty well aquainted with his name by this time and would not learn a new one very soon. But I think I will risk it and leave you to agree upon some pretty name for him. Be shure to name him, and let me know in your next letter to me. If you can not agree on a name each one send me his choice and I will be the judge. But I fear this latter plan will not work well as I might gain your displeasure by deciding my self. But mind if you do not agree upon a name and leave it to me which ever name I make, choice of the others must not think me partial, for I am not. I love you all equally. You are all very dear to me and I am very proud to have such handsome little Brothers.

Nearly all the Horses here are what is called Broncoes. When a man gets on them they Buck. I mean by that they jump off the ground with all four of their feet and Kick and rair up till they throw the rider. If they can not do so after a good many trials they walk off same as any other horse. It is the same thing every time you mount them. It is seldom that a man gets thrown off. My horse is the same as the rest, but he is so small that I can master him very easily. He is full of play, and is very proud. Wish you could see him.

If you want to know anything concerning this country or anything else which I am able to answer you must ask me in your letters, for when I am not writing I can think of plenty of news to write to you, but when I sit down I can think of scarcely anything. It takes about one month for a letter to come from home, the Mail comes and goes once a week.

Camp Whipple, Arizona Territory
DECEMBER 29, 1869

Your welcome letter of the Seventh inst. came safely to hand yesterday. It is useless for me to repeat my feelings always when I receive a letter from home, for you can imagine how one feels. It certainly made good time. It usually takes one month for a letter to come from the

States, but my letter from Yuma and your answer made the round trip in forty-four days.

You spoke of sending me some pictures and at least six letters. I have only received three since [I] left Carlisle Barracks, but suppose they will come all right after [a] while, at least [I] hope so. I wrote home to you last week, hope it will arrive safely. You speak of me being seven thousand miles from home. It is very near nine thousand to New York.

The only winter we have here is a little frost at night, but can look up on the mountains which are only a short distance from camp and see plenty of snow, but we have none here. I have only had one opportunity to tast[e] snow this winter and that was once while we were in the mountains. It is warm enough for me here, but it is nothing to compair with the southern part of this territory.

I am getting along fairly and am liked by all the boys. I am quite different from what [I] was at home, am becoming quite modest. It comes natural to me, don't know what has caused it. Suppose I am the most quiet of any of our Company. I have been offered a Clerkship in the Ad[j]utants office the first of the year, don't know whether we go or not, have been Company Clerk for 3 days, have been making out muster rolls, but assure you [I] do better writing than do when [I] write home. It is because I take more time, the Quarter Master Sergt. complimented me for my writing, and also the first Sergt. I get along finely but would prefer to do a little Escorting and Scouting for awhile.[28]

I am working for a commission even if it is only a non com [non-commissioned officer]. If I succeed, which [I] have not much doubts, [I] will be doing very well, for it is not every one that gets to become a Corporal. I have been told by a number of the men that I will get promoted after while. I am not [word missing] but know that I posess qualites enough to get along. The Non Commissioned officers are all young men. None of them more than twenty five years old.

Suppose will get payed off by the fifteenth of next month. Will muster for pay on the first of the month. Tell you what everything is

---

[28] The first sergeant, always on the lookout for capable men to perform various tasks in the company, noted that Eddie had been a clerk in civilian life. In addition to having a basic education, he had undoubtedly gained considerable experience in bookkeeping and maintaining inventory records under his father's tutelage. In an age when illiteracy was still widely prevalent, Private Matthews was a prize catch. Eddie remembered his father's advice to do whatever was asked of him and thereby gain advancement as quickly as possible. Consequently, he served as a clerk and quartermaster sergeant throughout most of his army career, thus avoiding much of the tedium of routine troop duty.

high out here. Merchandise of every kind is awful. Country produce such as Eggs and Butter are the same. Eggs one dollar and twenty five cents per doz. Butter one fifty per lb and very scarce at that. They have some very fine stores out here, but know how to charge. I went down to the sutlers a few days ago to get some writing paper and a few other articles that [I] had to have. Bought a quire of paper for one dollar, package of Envelopes 50 cents, bottle of ink 75 cents with about a gill in, pen holder and four pens 25 cents and a pipe for $1.50, in all four dollars. I got out of there very soon and will stay out, but I had to have them. I could have done without a pipe but it is a great pleasure to me. So concluded [I] would buy one. I will have to have a suit of cloth[e]s altered for inspection, but will stint myself much as possible.

You speak of trying to aid me in procuring a commission through Mr. Hamill. I don't think he can aid me any, at least I know of nothing at present, but after while may find out. If I do will certainly let you know, but I have given quite enough trouble during my life without giving you more now, have no fear. I will win a name yet. I seem to be confident don't I[?] Well I am, and if [I] should not succead would be greatly disappointed. I remember Gus Valoise and would like to come across him, he might aid me some. What branch of the service did he enlist in[?] Not the Cavalry I know, for he was not much of a horse man.[29]

Soon as [we] get payed off am going to have my Photo taken in full uniform and send home to you. I am going to write to J. W. Perkins and if he has not destroyed my negative will ask him to strike off a few pictures and give them to you. I want to see what five years will make in my appearance.

Dec. 30th. Will add a few more lines this morning before [I] go to the Sergt. room. Last night we sit up eating Venison and Bread, had wochestershire sauce to put on it, and assure you it was not bad eating. Most every night we have a lunch before going to bed. After we got

---

29 Apparently, Valois (real name, Gustavus Haenel) was an old army friend of John Matthews. A native of Prussia, Valois had served as a noncom and an officer in the Third Maryland Infantry from 1862 to 1865. As the regimental quartermaster sergeant, he and the senior Matthews would have worked closely. Eddie, however, was wrong in his assumption that Valois was not a horseman because he afterward enlisted in the regular army and rose to sergeant in the Fifth Cavalry. He was one of those rare individuals who managed to cross the void to the officer corps by being commissioned as a second lieutenant in the Ninth Cavalry in 1868. He rose to captain in 1884 and retired three years later. See Heitman, *Historical Register*, vol. 2, 980.

through I read Father's letter to them. The one that was written to Angel Island. All said it was splendid. After which I entertained the house with some of my travels. And was the hero till near twelve o'clock when we all retired to our couch to dream of loved ones at home.

This morning an escort goes out to Camp Date Creek which is some sixty miles from the post.[30] Suppose I would have been on it had I not been engaged making out muster rolls. Will get plenty of it to do before my five years has expired. It is almost a certainty that we are to be moved to New Mexico in the spring. Am very glad of it, don't want to stay out here five years.

Prescot City is just one mile from here, and every day some of the men go down, but I never go. I will wait till pay day, then go down and have a few pictures taken and get some little necessaries that I need.

How did you spend your Christmas[?] Don't suppose there was much going on. We had a very good dinner bought with some of the Company funds. Had roast beef in abundance, mashed potatoes, fried onions, cold slaw, bread and butter. Tea by the quart, condensed milk and current jellie. Not so bad was it. Tell you what, I made things fly, for a while. Was very few of the men drunk.

When I read your letter to the boys last night they said you only made one mistake and that was about the officers being true men. There is very few of them that I have had anything to do with but are the greatest thieves outside of Penitentiaries. Most of them would take the last penny from a poor soldier. Suppose there is some exceptions, but very few.

Tomorrow we muster for pay and have monthly inspection. The boys are having great times cleaning up. I will have to go at it. I will just be three months and twenty three days in the service. It seems a long time since I enlisted. Much longer than I have served.

The money I send home [I] want you to use to help make your selves comfortable and not save it for me, for I am young yet and able to work. What I say I mean, the boys are having a laugh at my expense.

---

30 Camp Date Creek was located southwest of Prescott at the strategic junction of the roads leading west to Ehrenberg, on the Colorado River, and south to connect with the main southern artery leading from Texas to California. Originally named for General James B. McPherson, killed in action during the Civil War, the camp was redesignated in 1868 to reflect its geographical location on Date Creek. It was active from 1867 to 1874. See Alexander, Arizona Frontier, 46–47; and Walker and Bufkin, Historical Atlas, 41.

One of the sergeants whose time will be out in a year, he says soon as he gets discharged he is going to Westminster and call on you. He said he is going to tell you I am very good soldier and praise me up very highly, so you will invite him to stay with him a week or so. And then when he is going away will say that I was the meanest boy in the regiment.

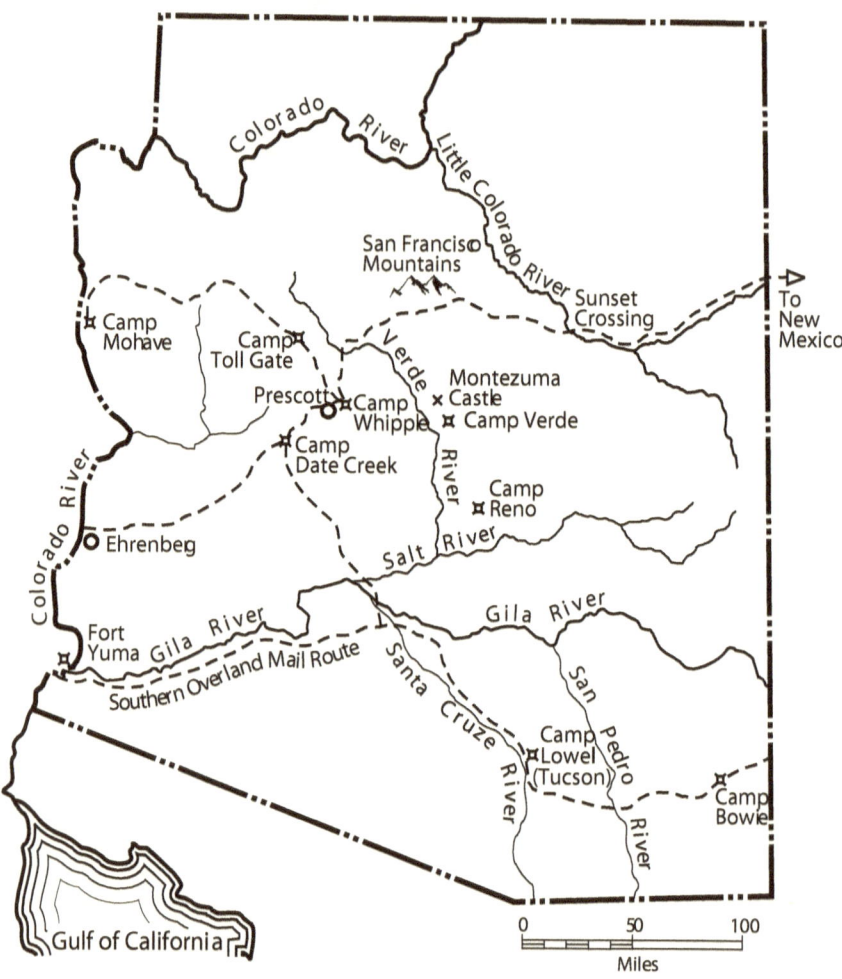

Map 1. Arizona Territory, 1870

CHAPTER TWO

"His Throat Was Cut from Ear to Ear"

JANUARY–APRIL 1870

By this time, Matthews had made a fairly comfortable adjustment to army life, even though he was already counting the days he had served. He liked most of the men in his company, which was somewhat unusual considering some of the hard cases who found their way into the ranks in those days, yet he had little respect for most of the officers. He was nevertheless making the best of his situation and was applying himself to being a good soldier. His superiors, however, were already aware of his abilities to read and write, and had detailed him as company clerk. Even the post adjutant had taken note of this and was vying for Matthews's services at headquarters. While Eddie appreciated the attention he was receiving, he knew that clerking would tie him to the fort. He considered himself to be a full-fledged soldier by this time and felt responsible for pulling his share of company duty. He especially yearned to experience some field service, and he was about to get it.

Camp Whipple, Arizona Territory
JANUARY 5, 1870

Your welcome letter of the 15th inst. came to hand this morning. I am very sorry that you have not received my letters yet. I have written two since [I] came to this post, but perhaps you have got them in this [by now]. Well I just got in Camp this evening from an escort of forty five miles and asure you [I] feel quite sore and tired, as this was my first trial, but will not go to bed till [I] have written to you.

Monday morning the first Sergeant came in my quarters and told me to get ready to go to Toll Gate, which is 45 miles from here, to escort Majors Price and Perkins.[1] We left here about half past eleven A.M. and rode in a gallop the whole way, did not walk one mile on the trip. We arrived at Toll Gate about 7 P.M. We cooked our suppers and then retired.

Next morning we were ordered to return, but our Corporal went to General [Andrew J.] Alexander commanding the post and told him that our horses were not able to go all the way back and asked him to allow us to go half the distance that day and then report here the next, "today."[2] The General consented so we left Toll Gate about 1 P.M. and rode to Williamson Vally and Camped for the night. Started from there about 11 o'clock this morning and arrived here about 4 P.M. I was good and sore when [I] got in here. It was a very pretty sight to see six Cavalry

---

1 Camp Toll Gate was established by Major William R. Price on Walnut Creek, northwest of Prescott, on May 9, 1869. The name derived from its location on a toll road leading to Hardyville in the region inhabited by the Hualpai Indians. The place was renamed Camp Hualpai on August 1, 1870, and was abandoned as being of no further military use in 1873. See Frazer, *Forts of the West*, 10. William R. Price, a native of Ohio, served with the Third Pennsylvania Volunteer Cavalry during the Civil War. He earned three brevets for his actions during the war and was appointed major in the Eighth Cavalry upon its organization in 1866. He was awarded an additional brevet to colonel in the regulars for gallant and meritorious service in an engagement with Indians at Walker's Springs, Arizona Territory on December 10, 1868. See Heitman, *Historical Register*, vol. 1, 807. Benjamin R. Perkins was commissioned as a lieutenant in the Twelfth U.S. Infantry in 1861 and served with that regiment until his death in 1871. He was brevetted twice for gallantry, the first time at Cedar Mountain and the second at Gettysburg. See ibid., 783. A brevet was an honorary rank awarded to an officer for gallantry or other exemplary service. Many officers were given brevets according to the highest rank they had achieved while serving with the volunteer forces during the Civil War. A regular officer could wear only the insignia of his permanent rank, but was entitled to be addressed according to his brevet rank. See McDermott, *Guide to the Indian Wars*, 23–25.

2 Alexander's permanent rank in 1869 was major, Eighth Cavalry. Matthews refers here to his brevet rank of brigadier general, conferred in 1865. See Heitman, *Historical Register*, vol. 1, 156.

men riding just as hard as there horses could run across the plains. To me it was a splendid sight. I imagined we were riding in Westminster and thought we created a Great deal of excitement. I know we would make a stir in the Town if a few of us blue coats were to dash in town, but no such good luck will happen to me I am shure.

We halted for a few minutes when we were going down while the Officers eat a lunch and disposed of some bad Whiskey. They handed the bottle around to us, all drank except me. When the Major offered it to me, I said "no I thank you I never drink." He was much surprised and said he would not insist. Major Perkins said you stick to that young man, and you will be shure to come out all right. It made me feel very good to refuse to drink with an officer. It is so seldom that they offer a soldier a drink and then for a man to refuse to drink surprised them. I have been offered whiskey I suppose a hundred times since [I] enlisted but in all cases refused and will continue to do so while I am in the Army.

I am going to make a scrap book for myself, and will take notes of all my doings, when on scouts, Escorts and in Camp. Guess [I] will have plenty of the two former duties to now have started. Nothing new in Camp. Some little talk about an outbreak in the Morman settlement. Have not heard much lately about going to New Mexico in the spring.

There is scarcely any danger of Indians around here now, they have been driven away off in the Mountains. It is too cold for them to show their selves now. Soon as spring breaks a big scouting party will be sent out and will perhaps remain out two or three months. It is a funny sight to see how everything mostly is carried over this Country. It is packed by mulls [mules]. Sometimes you see fifty or a hundred in a drove joging along the road or over the Mountains when there is only a small Indian trail. An Indian trail is a path, where one Indian walks after another. They always walk in single file.

I was in the first Sergeants Room a few days helping them to make out the Muster Rolls and doing some other writing. Guess [I] could get to be Company Clerk if wanted it. But I don't want it. I am working for something else, and will get it before I am in the Army two years, and that is promotion. I do not want to be a Private five years, and if I would get to be Company Clerk I would have to write all day and never get anything else. That is not my idea. The day will come when I will get two stripes on my coat sleeves, if not three. There is very few get a Commission that raise from the ranks.[3]

It is about ten o'clock or perhaps later. I think I will put this away till tomorrow and then perhaps can think of some thing else to write to you. Good night and happy dreams.

Thursday 6th. Will try to finish this letter today. Although [I] do not know what to write that would interest you. In my last letter I said eggs were worth $1.25 doz. & butter $1.50 lb. I made a slight mistake as the former brings $3.25 per doz. and butter $3.50 per lb. and very scarce at that. Flour from $25.00 to $30.00 per lb., Potatoes 15 cents lb., onions 15 cents lb., corn 15 cents lb. Most everything is sold by the lb. Every thing is very high. In the southern part of this State Lumber is worth 25 cts. per foot. It is not so high here as there is plenty of pine trees. Mechanics get from $3.00 to $10.00 per day in Gold. If I was to be discharged here tomorrow I would not remain in this Country longer than was actually necessary for anything. The Citizens here look like regular desparados and could not live in Civilization. Would much sooner be in the Army if had to remain out here than anything else.

I am ashamed almost to send this, but as there is nothing new, I can find nothing to write about, but I don't like to see the mail go away from here without a line to you dear ones at home. It only goes once a week and I would like to send you a letter in every one. This is the third letter I have written to you since [I] came to this post.

Remember me especially to Charlie Horner. I think more of him than most any other in town, outside of our own dear Family. Any papers you could send me would be thankfully received. Don't get to see much out here. Write often.

Camp Whipple, Arizona Territory
JANUARY 13, 1870

I was some what surprised upon the arrival of the mail this week to find that there was no letter from you, although there was one from Carroll

---

3 His reference to two and three stripes relates to the chevrons for corporal and sergeant, respectively. Some men aspired to noncommissioned rank while others preferred not to have the responsibility. Although it was rare for enlisted men to be commissioned as officers, it was not unheard of in the post-Civil War army. After the passage of an act of Congress in 1878, qualified noncoms were increasingly elevated to second lieutenants. See Foner, *Soldier Between Two Wars*, 70–71.

County. And a splendid letter it was, one of the best it has ever been my lot to receive. It was from "Capt. Rogers," and a nice long one, three sheets of letter paper filled close up. Was so glad to hear from him. He gave me the news in general. Gave me any amount of good advice. Simular to what you give me from home. I will tell you how much good it gave me, and not only me for I read it to a number of the boy's last night about 11 P.M.

I was sitting in the "Cook House" writing a reply to him when the door opened and in walked three of my company all slightually under the influence of Liquor. All three of them are fine young men, and old Soldiers. Hardly had they got up to the fire, when one of them produced a bottle about two thirds full of Whiskey and asked me to drink. I of course said no, for I drink nothing stronger than good strong coffee. They insisted upon me drinking, while I persisted in not drinking. When they found that I was determined not to drink they concluded to drink by themselves.

After they had all drank, I told them if they would listen I would read them a letter from an Ex Soldier, and one that would do them no harm to hear if it done them no good. All seemed anxious to hear it and seated themselves around me, and I read the Capt.['s] letter to them, from beginning to the end. While I was reading I noticed one of the three was either crying to himself or very near doing so, but all listened patiently and with interest till I had finished. Soon as [I] closed one of the three rose up and with a horse [hoarse] voice said, "Boy's, I have drunk the last glass of liquor that I ever will with you while I am in the Army." Says he, "that letter has touched my heart and reminds me of letters I use to get from home." It was as much as he could do to speak he was so near crying. One of the three said, "for you don't mean that do you[?]" He replyed that he did and was determined to keep his word, and said you, to Jim, had better say the same thing. Swear off with me before Ed, meaning me, and we will soon see how much [better?] off we will be when our time is out. Jim said he would do so, and never drink another drop while he was in the Army. Then to see those two men standing up holding each other by the hand and both feeling so good they could scarcely keep from crying. Oh it was a beautiful sight and one I will not soon forget. It would have made a grand picture. And me what was I doing, why I could do nothing but look at them and laugh. I felt so good. Oh my heart was full of gladness. I cannot describe my feelings, both I know are sincere, and I do hope they will be faithful to their promises.

I had finished my letter to the Capt. but had to add a postscript to tell him of the circumstance. I know it will make his heart glad to know the good his letter done.

I am now assistant Cook and have been for three days. Each man has to take his turn in the Cook House for ten days. It is not a very pleasant situation, but still each one must do his share, two men are in at a time.

Nothing new going on here. Some strong talk of us going to New Mexico soon. For my part I don't care how soon we have to go. I don't admire this part of the Country very much.

I gave you a little list of prices in my letter to you last week, but only of a few articles. Flour is $21.00 per hundred instead of a lb., Barley from $20.00 to $25.00 per hundred, Corn from $8.00 to $12.00 hundred, Potatoes from 10 to 15 cts. per lb., onions 25 cts lb., coffee 60 to 75 cts, sugar 40 cts, cigars common article 25 cts. <u>Whiskey</u> 25 cts. per drink, warranted <u>poison</u>. Syrup from $1.50 to $2.00, beef I don't know what, pork 40 cts, butter when it is plentiful $1.50, but when scarce $3.50 per lb., eggs same as butter when plenty $1.25, scarce $3.25.

These prices I have gained from Citizens. Mechanics wages from $3.00 to $10.00 per day, a pair of boots is worth from $14.00 to $25.00. Common suit of cloth[e]s $100.00, those are prices for you.

Well I have killed my little horse, not exactly killed him either, but have [exhausted?] him, so that he is no account now, or ever will be. Done it on the Escort to Camp Toll Gate. We rode in a full run all the way 45 miles. Five horses out of the six had to go on the sick report. That is the way business is done here, was no necessity for us riding so fast. It was the miserable officers fault, they in their drunkenness didn't care how many horses were killed.

I have a contract for writing letters, for about six of our company, those that came with me. I write them a <u>little</u> better than what this is written. Poor fellows are whorse off than me. I can manage to write a little, while they can't write any.

Well indeed I am at a loss for something to write to you that would be interesting. While I was travelling could always find something new, but here it is the same old routine. Except sometimes you go out scouting or on Escort. I will not be able to write such long letters now as [I] did on the march, as have not the news to write. I am going to collect a lot of c[actuses] out here and will label them with the place taken from, and what they are, and if sometime have an opportunity will send them home. If not will keep them till I return.

Have heard nothing of the Pay Master lately, would like to see him muchly.

Well it is about twelve o'clock P.M. and as I was up till half past two last night and have to get [up] about six it is high time I was in bed. I don't like to send this without filling this one sheet, but indeed I have not the news to write.

Camp Whipple, Arizona Territory
JANUARY 18, 1870

Lizzies letter was received this evening. I knew there would be one for me, so watched for the mail all evening, and when it did come shure enough there was the expected letter. I must say I felt slightually home sick after reading it, but that is always the case. Not only when I am reading your letters, but when ever I am not engaged I get to thinking of you dear ones at home and I get the blues most awfully.

A few mornings ago, I was sitting in Cook House studying over the last five months when our first Sergeant came in and said, "Whats the matter Matthews, are you home sick[?]" I said I was not exactly home sick but that I was just thinking of Home. He asked me if I was ever away from Home much, told him no. He said never mind five years will pass away. That is what every person says, but they will be a long time passing. Some of our Company only have a little over a year to serve, and they think that is an awful long time to serve. If that was all I had, I would be the happiest boy in the Country. I tell you what, five years is a long time, and I guess I will be home sick more than once before they have passed.

How I would have liked to have been at Home during the Fair. Know it must have been grand from the description you gave of it. How much did you make, or in other words more plainer, how much did they realize from it[?] We don't have either the Churches or the Fairs out here. All that is here is a few drinking Saloons, plenty of Indians and still more plenty of the boys in Blue to make both Citizen and Indian behave themselves. "<u>We</u> are the boys that fear no nois[e] although we are far from Home." How is that, ain't far, only about nine thousand miles. Well we will be nearer home in the course of a few months. It is now a certain thing that the 8th Cavalry is to be moved in to New Mexico in the spring.

I think I will like it better there than in this territory. I am sorry to hear that the Youths of Westminster are conducting themselves so badly. They had better look out for fear they might find themselves in a similar predicament to the one I am now in, or perhaps in a whorse capacity. This is the fruits of my folly and no telling what theirs will be.

Well it is quite late and as I have to get up in the morning about five o'clock to help get breakfast, for I am not out of the Cook House yet, but will be day after tomorrow. So good night and pleasant dreams. Will finish some time before the mail goes out.

Wednesday morning 19th. Have just finished washing my breakfast dishes and swept up. As it is not quite time to set the dinner table, will try to add a line or so.

I am getting awfull fat. I have gained "Eight" pounds since enlisted. I weigh now one hundred and forty four pounds. I have enjoyed excellent health all along, except while on the Steamer "Continental," when between sea sickness and starvation liked to have died. Most every man on board went on the sick report, but I never. I have not been on the sick list since [I] enlisted, or will I go on unless I am very sick. I don't want to take their miserable "<u>quinine</u>."[4] A great many soldiers go on the sick report just to get excused from duty, half of them are not sick.

Before I came in the Cook House the Capt. sent over first Sergeant to ask me, if I would not <u>Cook</u> for him. I told the Sergt. that I did not want any such situation as I knew nothing about Cooking. He said the Capt. would like to have me and that his, "the Capt.['s]," Wife would teach me. I then told him I had no desire to learn but was willing always to take my turn in the Companys Cook house, but any more cooking than that I did not want. No doubt it would have been a very

---

4 Extracted from cinchona bark, quinine was widely used to combat fevers, particularly malaria, as well as digestive disorders, and was employed as a poultice for snakebite. It was of crystalline consistency with a bitter taste. See Steele, *Bleed, Blister, and Purge*, 326.

"His Throat Was Cut from Ear to Ear" 43

good thing as far as eating is concerned and besides the Capt. always pays something.⁵

A number of the Company would have been glad to get the situation. For me I am after something else that [I] could not get in the Cook House. I get along nicely with both Officers and men now. I always do my duty with a will, and sometimes it is very disagreeable, but I never complain. Go at it as though it was a pleasure to do it. I will not loose anything by always doing my duty cheerfully.

I am a great advocater now of the temperance cause and have done some good I think. I have the promise of four of the Company that they will abstain from drinking while they are in the Army, and I have seen every one of them refuse to drink when some of their comrades have asked them. The boys don't think of asking me to drink any more. Sometimes when they have a bottle some one will say, "I guess it is no to ask you, <u>Ed</u>."

I want you to send me a paper once in a while. Reading matter is very scarce out here. We are expecting the pay master every day. Soon as [I] get some money will go in town and have my Photo taken for you. Photographs <u>only cost</u> $12.00 per doz. and not very good at that. Will only have one taken. Some of the boys tell me not to have my picture taken in Soldier cloth[e]s, say they don't like to see them. I tell them I am not ashamed of the <u>blues</u>.

I done four days writing in the Sergeants room, then was taken down to the company where I was kept at work three days more taking an Inventory of the whole stock, at least I was assisting, not doing it by myself. The Quarter Master is going to quit this place and is going inside. I mean in to the States. Colonel [Charles W.] Foster will now take charge of the Q.M. Stores, releaving Col. [Capt. Edward D.]

---

5 Many officers, considering themselves above doing menial household work, hired soldiers as servants to perform such tasks as chopping wood, hauling water, caring for personal horses, and sometimes cooking when women were not available for hire. Termed "strikers" or "dog robbers," these men were not looked upon with much favor by their comrades, who viewed them as shirkers because the officers usually saw to it that their soldier-servants were excused from most military duties. See Knight, *Life and Manners*, 128. Captain Charles Hobart commanded Company L during Matthews's enlistment. Hobart had migrated to the Pacific Northwest prior to the Civil War and served as an officer in the First Oregon Cavalry throughout the conflict. Mustered out of the volunteers in July 1866, Hobart was immediately appointed as a first lieutenant in the Eighth U.S. Cavalry. He was promoted to captain two years later. Hobart transferred to the infantry in 1873, and served with various regiments until he retired as a lieutenant colonel at the close of the Spanish-American War. See Heitman, *Historical Register*, vol. 1, 533.

Baker.⁶ Baker is about six thousand dollars behind that he cannot account for. Baker and Foster came very near having a little fight about it. I don't know how Baker is going to fix the affair. Suppose though he will account for the deficiency some way.

So Joe and Annie Shnois are married at last, and Al Cook and the fair Hellen. May love and happiness be their lot through life, that is all the harm I wish them. I have been unfortunate in this world in some respects, but that is no reason I should wish others to be. I don't mean in love affairs, although I was jilted in my childish attempt at love making, but assure you suffered no great harm from its effects. Did not shed many tears or break my heart over it, and still more had no notion of committing Suicide. The latter seems to be the popular mode of avenge after being duped by some of the fair daughters of En [Eden?]. For my part I don't think that piece of flesh has been modelled that would cause me to take that which I could never get back, my precious life, because she jilted me. Mother I know will say that is sound doctrine.

How does "Wip Joe" prosper now a days[?] Is she proud as ever. Well if she did think she had what Soldiers say is a soft thing when she had me, she was badly mistaken. Perhaps when I come home after five years on the frontier there will be some little fair Angel waiting for me. I went so far, when wrote to Lec, to ask her if she would not wait five years. "Guess she will."⁷

Thursday 19th. Have a few spare moments so will write a few more lines. In about two hours I will be out of the Cook House until my time comes around again. Oh if it was only out of the Army how much happier I would be. Father always said I lacked stability, and I guess he was right. But after I put this time in he will come to the conclusion "that I stick to a situation a long time." It is not every person that can retain a situation five years, without becoming dissatisfied. Or would I retain this one if it was not for compulsion. I am here

---

6 Charles W. Foster served for ten years as an enlisted man in the Corps of Engineers during and after the Mexican-American War. He was commissioned as a captain of volunteers at the outbreak of the Civil War and concluded the war as a major with two brevets, thus Matthews's addressing him as "Colonel." Foster spent the remainder of his career in the Quartermaster Department, retiring in 1891. See Heitman, *Historical Register*, vol. 1, 431. Edward D. Baker was an officer in the regular cavalry during the first two years of the Civil War, and then was promoted to captain and assistant quartermaster, a position he still held in 1869. Baker retired in 1879 at the rank of major and died four years later. See ibid., 183–84.

7 "Lec" presumably refers to a female friend in Westminster.

and here I will have to remain. When I return home I can say I stuck to one situation five years.

Some of our Company started for Alcatras Island California this morning with prisoners.[8] Some of them are sentenced for five years to wear a twelve lb. Ball with a chain six feet long and to be confined at hard labor, with all pay and allowances stopped. Most of them were deserters. I tell you they have commenced to give deserters severe punishment. A great many men have deserted out here. Most of them though get captured. Alcatras Island is about three miles from San Francisco and is just across the Harbor from where we were camped on Angel Island. It will take the men about one month to go in. Soon as the men turn the prisoners over they will get a furlough for 30 days. Wouldn't it be nice if I was one of the party and could come home for a few days[?] Could talk to you all night about my travels. These men that are going in have not been home for three jars [years]. Some have been away for a longer period. Never mind my time will come.

I bought a box from a Corporal of our Company to put my cloth[e]s in for one dollar, and in the bottom of [it] a pair of chevrons, "Corpl. Stripes." I took them out and offered them to him, but he would not take them.[9] He said you put them in the bottom of your box, it will not be long till you will need them. Several of the boys have told me I would get promoted soon, that I commence to think there must be something in it. Let it come I am ready for it.

It is time I was bringing this to a close as it is dinner time again. After dinner I get out of here. You must excuse this dirty paper as I had to write at intervals. Sometimes with dirty hands. Direct your letters to Camp Whipple, not Whimpple.

Friday Morning. It seems as though I will never finish this scrappy letter. I was sent to the Adjutants Office yesterday evening and was kept there writing till 11 o'clock last night. Had to write eight sheets of' Fools Cap. Making out reports of a Board of Survey which convened at this post a few days ago, to inspect and report upon the Quarter Master's

---

8 Alcatraz Island, sometimes called Fort Alcatraz, was situated in San Francisco Bay. The army acquired the island in 1850 and began constructing defensive works on it three years later. As one of several coastal fortifications in the Bay Area, Alcatraz was garrisoned during and after the Civil War. Its natural isolation perfectly suited it for use as a prison. Military convicts from all over the Division of the Pacific were interned there to serve their sentences. See Frazer, *Forts of the West*, 19.

9 Matthews refers to a foot locker.

Stores. In 1868 and 1869 these was furnished to E. D. Baker, Quarter Master. Seven hundred thousand pounds of Grain, (700,000) and the Board of Survey allowed him (2%) two per cent, fourteen thousand (14,000) pounds, for Shrinkage, those (14,000) thousand pounds would amount to nearly twelve hundred dollars. The Board recommended that he be allowed to drop that amount from his papers. That is the way he will get square with the Government.

The Adjutant wants me to Clerk in the Office, but under the present circumstances I will not do it. There is no extra pay attached to it and besides the officer that is acting Post Adjutant is <u>only</u> a second Lieut. and is very overbearing. When he asked me if I would not like to Clerk for him, I replied that I did not think I was capable. He said yes I was, that I wrote a very nice plain hand. Then I told him I would sooner rough it for awhile in the ranks, that I wanted to see as much of this country as I could while I am here, that I would never return again after once [I] got out. He said then that he would have me detailed for a few days till he got the papers fixed up. I of course consented to do so. One of the Clerks left on account of sickness, had to go to the Hospital.

I assure you I feel somewhat proud of the many Clerkships that have been offered me since [I] enlisted. I write a better hand when [I] take my time, and especially when I have a good Gold pen. Guess I have written "three cents" worth, or as much as three cents will carry.

Went out on Target Practice a little while this morning and missed the Target at twenty five yards, shot once at it, that distance and missed it. Threw down my Carbine, picked up a stone and hit it the first time. Was the whorse shot in the crowd, had to carry the Target home to the Quarters for shooting so badly.[10]

Camp Whipple, Arizona Territory
JANUARY 25, 1870

Am somewhat disappointed this evening because [I] did not get a letter

---

10 At this time, the Eighth Cavalry was armed with the seven-shot .56–50 Spencer repeating carbine. Although the Spencer was not reputed to be a particularly accurate weapon, especially beyond about three hundred yards, it seems remarkable that Matthews could have missed the target at a distance of only twenty-five yards. The army budget allowed each man only ten rounds of ammunition per month for practice, which was conducted haphazardly, as evidenced by his firing only one shot that day. This is also the first time Matthews mentions attending target practice. Marksmanship was not emphasized service-wide until about 1880. See McChristian, *Army of Marksmen*, 21–24.

from home. Perhaps though I should not be as this is the first week that I have been a new recipient of a mission. But nevertheless I cannot help but feel disappointed. Would not write to you to night only I had [have] to go away tomorrow morning and will not be back in Camp until Saturday.

Last week after I finished that scrappy letter I went down to the Adjutants Office and commenced to write. Had not been at work very long till a messinger came with orders for me to get ready at once to go on an Escort to Williamson Valley.[11] I was very glad to get released from the office so [I] hastened to finish what writing I had commenced and then went and got my Horse and acruitraments [accouterments] and in less than ten minutes was mounted and ready for the Escort. We were six altogether and had to Escort Quarter Master Baker & Lady, Mr. Beam & Lady, General Alexander and one or two other officials of less caliber. We rode in a gallop all day, and arrived at Waboreh [at] four o'clock P.M. where another Escort was waiting to take them on through.[12] Mr. Beam has a Ranch at W. and told us to remain at his House till Sunday when he would be back and we could Escort him in to Whipple. Told us we could get our meals in his Ranch which suited us exactly. I tell you we lived well while we were there.

Saturday morning two of the men that works on the place went out hunting and returned in a short time with a very fine Deer. During the morning one of our party went down a little stream that flows through the Valley and shot a very nice Duck. So we had plenty of meat, also potatoes, onions and several other kinds of vegatables, with abundance of rich Bread, and always a quart of Tea for each man to drink three times a day. How was that for high living[?]

Friday night we made our bed down on the floor, but the boards were much too hard for us, and we were continually rolling around till morning came. So [we] concluded [we] would not be so important next night, would go to the Hay Stack and make a soft bed of Hay. When night arrived we all spread our blankets around the Hay Stack and layed ourselves down for a good nights sleep. About 12 o'clock we were all aroused by a great noise all around and most on top of us. It was but a moment till six men could be seen standing up half dressed with Carbine in one hand and a Revolver in the other ready for any emergency. It was very dark and

---

11 Williamson Valley lies approximately twenty miles northwest of Fort Whipple.
12 "Waboreh" has not been identified.

we could hear plenty of moving around and could distinguish dark objects a little distance from us. One of the party took a step forward and run against something which give one loud howl and away went about fifty head of Cattle. We all looked at each other for a moment then all laughed and layed down to sleep again. The Cattle had broke out of the <u>Corall</u> and had come around to the Hay Stack to eat.

During Saturday two of our party went out in the hills for a hunt and finally came across some deer. One of the men shot three times and wounded one, but the deer continued to run and he started to follow it. The other party a Corporal who had charge of us, seeing some fresh Indian tracks as he supposed, followed them down the mountain and when he had almost got to the bottom he saw a Horse without a rider running at full speed and an <u>Indian</u> as he supposed running after it. He at once commenced firing at him, but failed to do any damage as the Indian was too far off. Looking up the Valley a little farther he saw two more objects, which he also took for Indians trying to head the Horse off. He at once made tracks for the Ranch where we were.

On his way in he came across the Government Herd which is Kept in the Valley, told the two herders about the Indians and came on in. The herders drove the Herd in on a double quick. The Corporal got in ahead of them and related his adventure to us. We were a little uneasy about the man that went out with the Corpl. as he was a Recruit that came with me and as he had not returned we thought perhaps he might get lost, and as it was getting near dark were afraid the Indians might jump him. We were thinking about moving our Horses and going after him, when I spied him away off coming down the mountain. We felt all right then as all the party was safe.

One of the Citizens in the Ranch said the horse that was running loose belonged to one of the settlers who had gone out hunting, and he supposed the Indians had jumped and killed him. The horse had come in to the Ranch while we were standing around waiting for our man to come up. We saw at a distance another man walking very fast towards us. After [a] while he came up and I must say he was a miserable specimen of humanity; any person would almost take him for an Indian at a distance. He was the owner of the horse and said while he was getting a drink of water his horse got frightened at something and ran off. He started after him and the first thing he knew he heard a shot fired and looking around saw our Corporal up the mountain side firing away at him. Said he tryed to make him understand that he was not an Indian but failed so went on his way after the horse, knowing the Corpl. could do him no harm as he was too far away. We all had a good laugh at the Corporals expense.

It seemed to be hard to be shooting at a white man instead of an Indian, and then coming in and telling us such a yarn about it. But as no harm was done it did not make much difference. The man that went out with the Corpl was a real old Irish man. Of the first mater, when he got in we asked him if he killed a deer, he said no but he came very near it. Said he shot over the Deer once and under him once. Said he saw a lot of buffalo tracks. At that we all burst out laughing again for we all knew that there was not a buffalo in the Territory or on this side of the Rocky Mountains. He had seen some large tracks made by Cattle and supposed they were Buffalo. So everything turned out all right with plenty of fun for us boys.

Sunday morning arrived and as Mr. Beam had not made his appearance we concluded [we] would start for Camp. Saddled up and left about 12 noon. We came to Lee's Ranch which is ten miles from this Camp, when we saw some of our company lying down sleeping, with their horses unsaddled. We woke them up and found out they were in search of a lot of Government Cattle. They told us that the Herd had got frightened the evening before and had stampeded, and that every man of the company was out after them. We took our time getting in Camp about 4 P.M. The Cattle in this country as a general thing are very wild and soon as [they] get frightened they stampede and when they start they sweep everything before them. They seem to get <u>mad</u>, roar like so many wild beasts. The first Sergeant with a squad of men came across some of them and while trying to bring them in one of them got after him, and ran him horse and all, till his horse was showing signs of fatigue, when he wheeled his horse around and shot the steer. The first shot knocked him down, but he jumped up again and made for the Sergt. again. The Sergt. fired and down goes Mr. Bull again, but not till four carbine balls had entered his head did Mr. B— give up the ghost.

They have succeeded in getting all but twenty-eight of them. I with nine others will start out tomorrow morning with three days rations to search the hills for the missing <u>bulls</u>.

Am getting along finely. Have become perfectly satisfied now, I like my Officers and men, and know they all like me, for any thing any of them can do for me is always done, and done cheerfully.

Last night the Sergeant came in our quarters and called for me. I answered and followed him out when he gave me a message to take down to Mr. Beam's house, down town. The Sergeant gave me the message and was going to leave, when I stopped him and asked where Mr. B. lived. He said, "Haven't you been to town yet[?]" I said no Sir. He said I must be an exception to the general class of men. Told him [I] did not suppose that I was. I came back in the quarters to get my Revolver on, for you have to have a Revolver strapped around you if you only want to go to the rear to obey nature. "As Mr. Bond the Lawyer use to say." When I took my Revolver the boys all asked me where I was going, told them downtown. Then they wanted to know on what business as I had never been in the town before. Of course I would not satisfy them. They could not imagine what was taking me downtown that time of night.

Arrived in the town which is only one mile from Camp, found Mr. Beams house which by the way is a very nice house outside and in. Knocked at the door, heard a female voice say, come in, entered where [I] found myself before a very pretty Lady. I asked if Mr. B lived there. She said yes Sir, asked if he was in. Said no he had gone down town. So [I] delivered the message to her. I was slightually confused as it is an unusual thing to talk to a Lady in this Country, and she being very pretty and not more than twenty one or two, I almost fell in love at first sight. But what is the use to talk this way, she is married I am shure. I did not make a very bad appearance as I had on what the boys call biled [boiled] Shirts, White ones, collar and nectie, also a very nice [vest?].

Fort Whipple, Arizona Territory
FEBRUARY 18, 1870

I have just returned to Camp after a hard days ride of forty five miles. I of course feel somewhat fatigued but will spend most of the night in writing and reading. Soon as came in and put my horse away, went to the 1st Sergeants to see if there was any mail for me. Imagine how I felt when [I] was handed four letters and a paper. The first one I opened was from Sue, a real nice letter. Then came a splendid letter from Aunt Kate, one from John Reese, and to wind up with a real splendid letter from

Jennie Zepp. How some of the poor boy's envied me when they saw me so deeply engaged perusing all those letters. I feel tired, but oh how good I feel after reading those letters, and I intend to answer every one before I go to bed. But by the time you receive this, I will be either in New Mexico, or on the road.

I wrote to you last week and in fact every week since [I] came here. How often do you receive my letters[?] I had a tolerable good rest last week, was in Camp most all week, something unusual for me. I have been constantly on the road since [I] came to this post. Monday night I retired after Tattoo, which is 8 o'clock. Had just got in a nice snoose when the 1st Sergt. came to my bunk, "Bed," and told me to Saddle up soon as possible, with one days rations to go to <u>Toll Gate</u> with some dispatches. Did not take long to dress and go down to the <u>Corall</u> after my Horse. When [I] got to the Corall, [I] found the Sergt. there with one of the fastest horses for me. Told me to ride him as we had to go through that night. I found two men there that was to accompany me.

Soon as [we] Saddled up reported to General [Frank] Wheaton at Head Quarters, found the Gen'l walking up and down the Porch waiting for us.[13] He gave me a lot of letters, and equally as many orders. Said he wanted us to go through as fast as the horses could carry us, and soon as we got to the Toll Gate to go to the Commanding Officer and deliver those letters and get a receipt for them, stating what time they were received. Said they were very important. Said not to spare the Horses any. If it killed them it was all right. We left here about 11 o'clock P.M. and arrived at Toll Gate precisely at 4 o'clock A.M., distance [by] the road we went fifty miles.

The night was bitter cold. A strong wind blowing all night. I came very near freezing my hands and feet. You can imagine how cold I must to have been when I fell asleep a half dozen times while my horse was running as fast as he could go. I could not help it, it was impossible to keep my eyes open. I certainly must have been very near frozen. Soon as [we] came in sight of the Camp I commenced to feel warmer. Suppose

---

13 Frank Wheaton's service dated back to 1855, when he was appointed as a first lieutenant in the First Cavalry. He attained the rank of captain just prior to the beginning of the Civil War. Transferring to the volunteer service, he was promoted to colonel and later to brigadier general. He accepted a commission as lieutenant colonel of the Thirty-Ninth Infantry in 1866 and was transferred to the Twenty-First Infantry during the army reorganization of 1869. Rising to colonel of the Second Infantry five years later, a position he held for the next eighteen years, Wheaton was promoted to brigadier general in the regulars in 1892 and retired in 1897. See Heitman, *Historical Register*, vol. 2, 1022.

thinking of what I had to do and say started my blood to circulate, and by the time [I] got in the Camp [I] felt warm as could be.

Found the officer of the day, told him [I] had some very important letters for the Commander of the Post, and that [I] would like to see and deliver the letters to him. He took me to his house and knocked at the door, Col. [Samuel Baldwin Marks] Young the Commander came to the door in his disabille [dishabille]. Gave the letters to him. He told me to come to his Tent during the day some time and he would give me a receipt for them and some letters to take back. Capt. Coffman the Officer of the day took me down to his Tent and said I must be very cold. Said he would give me something that would warm me, poured out a glass full of Whiskey and offered it to me. Thanked him for it, but refused saying I never drank anything of the kind. He said it would not hurt me after riding all night. Told him I felt very well and did not think it would help me any. He said I was a strange young man. Said if I did not drink any liquor while I was in the Army I would come out all right.

Told me to take the other two men and go down to his company's cook house, where we would find a good fire and plenty to eat. Done so and got a cup of warm coffee and a tolerable good breakfast. Felt much better after the meal. We then went back of the Stables where we built a fire spred our blankets and layed down and went to sleep. Sleep till dinner, then went back to bed again and sleep till supper. After supper the Sergt. gave us a tent to sleep in for the night.

Stayed at Toll Gate till the following evening, when [we] started for Williamson Valley which is half way between the two posts. We had four Horses to bring back to our company. We being short that many servicible horses. Among the four was a very beautiful little horse, and he could run very fast. I set my eye on him and soon as [I] came in this Post I asked the Captain for him. Our Captain is a very nice man but when he speaks he draws his words out long as possible. When I asked him for the horse, he looked at me a little bit and said "Y—e—s Matthews, you can have him." He is the smallest horse in the company. The boys say I ought to call him Baby. Guess I will call him Frank as that seems to be your choice.

We will soon be on the march to New Mexico. I understand that as soon as we get wagons we will move. The wind is blowing very hard, I guess the March wind has set in this month and March are said to be the most disagreeable months during the year. Will answer Sue's questions and close as I have nothing new to tell you. It keeps me pretty busy to find something new every week to tell you. Although there seems to be something new every day.

We are quartered in log Houses. Our company have three large Houses, besides a large building for the cook house. Each building has only one large room. The room is about the size of our Parler, dinning and sitting room all together. Each room contains six double Bunks, similar to those aboard Boats, one above the other, four men to each Bunk. We have straw ticks, for a pillow we roll up our Pants and blouses, which makes a very nice pillow. I sometimes spread my hand kerchief over my blouse, so as to make it have the appearance of a white pillow. We have four blankets and two Great Coats over us, sleep very warm.

When we are on the road and camp for the night at some of the Ranches, we go to a Hay Stack, spread some hay down lay our blankets on it and then pile about half a ton of hay on top of the blankets. Take our saddles for pillows.

Last night at Williamson Valley a lot of Hogs came around after we had gone to bed and rooted away in the hay stack under our heads. Kept up a continual grunt all night. It was very cold. So sooner than one of us to get out of bed to drive them out, we would content ourselves with hearing them grunt all night. Nice music to go asleep with. If some of the good people of Westminster should get such a sernade as that was some night, what would they think[?] They did not sing "I won't go home till morning," or "meet me by moonlight alone," but their song was, "Grunt, Grunt, Grunt."

Our camp is just one mile from Prescott City, situated on a hill very much like where the Lutheran Church is in W[estminster]. This is the best Post in the Territory. There is two company's of Cavalry here, D Co. of the 8th Cav. and our own, and one company of infantry. This is the Head Quarters of the Territory, General Frank Wheaton commands the Post. He use[d] to belong to the Sixth Corps, during the late war. The Infantry performs all the Guard duty at the Post. D Company have no horses, all theres being condemned. They cut the wood and do the extray duty. While our company has the hardest of the lot, we are on the road all the time, carrying dispatches from one Post to another, escorting etc.

Every Sunday we have inspection, where every man has to be as clean as a new pin, with Arms Shining, brasses so bright that you could almost see yourself in. Sometimes we have Mounted inspection. The

Officer will rub his white glove over your horse, and if a little dust should come off on his glove, away you go to the Guard House, where they will put a fifty or seventy five pound log on your shoulder and make you walk up and down with a guard all day. You are only allowed to stop to eat your meals. I have the praise of being a very clean soldier. You remember I was excused from Guard duty twice at Carlisle for being the cleanest man. I have never done a guard duty since [I] came here, in fact have only been on guard two or three times since [I] enlisted, now going on Six months. The time is passing. My five years will be up before we are aware of it.

You want to know what we have to eat. Well we have Beef seven days out of ten, when we are in Camp. When on the road [we] have Pork, sometimes Bacon. The three days you have Pork, for Breakfast we have Coffee, Bread and boiled beef, dinner Roast beef, sometimes Bean Soup, or Boiled Potatoes with their jackets on, as some of the boys say, supper Bread and Coffee. You get very near two quarts of Coffee a day. I never drink more than half of mine. I get as much of the kind as [I] can eat. We have soft bread all the time, have a post Bakery here. Get fresh Bread every morning.

We have a Sergt. in our Company from Baltimore, his time will be out in about one year and a half. Says he is coming up to Westminster to see you and tell you how I am getting along.

Am much obliged for the Stamps that were enclosed. Still have some on hand. I did intend to answer those other letters, but it is now getting late, and as I am tired, will read all the letters over again and retire for the night and write them tomorrow.

Camp Whipple, Arizona Territory
FEBRUARY 23, 1870

Another mail has come in with out bringing me a letter, but don't think I aught to complain, as last weeks mail brought me four.

In my letter of last week I spoke of leaving here for New Mexico, soon as we could get ready. This weeks mail brought an order countermanding to the movement till the first of April. Some of our Regt. are on their way now, but half of the Regiment will remain here till April. We were all ready for the move and had the order not come in the mail we would now be enroute to New Mexico. We had turned everything in to the Quarter Master that we did not actually need. Had even gone so far as to empty the hay out of our bed sacks. So as to turn them in, and did intend sleeping on the hard boards, but as soon as [we] received the order, [we] refilled the sacks again.

I have had a splendid rest of a week now, something unusual for me as I have been continually on the road ever since [I] came here. Am afraid though [I] will have to go out tomorrow. An escort is going to Camp Date Creek in the morning with some wagons to move Company B of our Regt. to New Mexico. Is sixty five miles from here and a very rough road for Indians. Although I was one of the last men that came in off an escort.

I have traded my little horse off, that I spoke of in last weeks letter. The Bugler of our Company took a great fancy to him and wanted me to trade with him. His was a very pretty little Horse, almost our Frank all over. My little horse now is the pet of the Company. He has saved two men's lives, and perhaps might be the means of saving mine. Our Q. M. Sergeant was on him once when several Indians fired at him from the road side, but fortunately did not strike him or the horse. Soon as they fired on him they jumped out into the road. He put spurs to the little horse and ran him three miles. [They] chased him so closely that he had to cut his Over Coat and everything loose from the little horse so that he could run fast. The other time was very much like the above. I was very glad to get him and would not trade now with any man in the Company. He is in splendid condition now and ready for the road any time. He is just like a pet dog, when you groom him he puts his mouth to the side of your head or else [he] will take your cap off. In fact he is the general pet of the Company, and is not slow on the run. There is only one or two faster horses in the Company than he is.

Yesterday the 22nd the Anniversary of the Nations Father was celebrated here with a Horse race, for five hundred dollars a side.[14] The race track is only a couple of hundred yards from Camp, and of course we all went to see it. It was a queer sight to see the Stile [style] displayed there. People came in very many of vehicles you could think of. In old carriages, broken down wagons drawn by mules, etc. I had no idea there was so

---

14 George Washington's birthday was universally celebrated in the army by the suspension of all but essential duties. See Rickey, *Forty Miles*, 207.

many females in the Territory as I saw on the grounds yesterday. There was at least one dozen females which is an unusual sight to see together out here. All seemed to be delighted. After waiting at least three hours the Horses run started where considerable speed was shown for a few seconds. The distance to be run was three hundred & seventy five yds., so you can imagine how long a time it takes a horse to run that distance. After the race was over, all started for home, feeling very good I suppose except those who had invested on the loosing horse.

At night I attended a kind of Minstrel performance in Prescott City, given by some of the Soldiers of this Post. One of my Co. invited me and as anything of this kind is very unusual out here, I accepted but must say was not very well payed for my trouble in walking one mile to see any thing of that kind. Don't think [I] will attend any thing of the kind again as long as [I] remain in this part of the country.

I am lost for something to write about. Everything seems to be quiet along the lines at present. Think [I] will not close this today and perhaps something will turn up to write about. Good bye till tomorrow.

9 o'clock PM. Have just got orders to go on the road tomorrow morning with three days rations. So I will only wind this up. Perhaps next letter will be a little better. I certainly ought to write a good letter, and write a good hand for I certainly have practice enough. I am secretary for at least a half dozen of my company, and all like to send lots of letters, and because I write long letters home to you, they want the same kind, and are not satisfied unless you write five or six sheets of note paper or two or three of letter paper. I just finished writing a long letter for my Bunkey and as I promised another of the company to write one for him this week will have to do so tonight, as I will not be in again till Sunday or Monday, and perhaps not then. It is hard to tell when you will get back when you go out on the road.[15]

Camp Whipple, Arizona Territory
MARCH 3, 1870

Yours of the second inst. came to hand yesterday. It was real nice and long just the Kind for me. Also some writing paper, please accept my

---

15 "Bunky" was army slang for one's best friend. It derived from the custom, as Matthews described earlier, of two men sleeping side by side in each of the two tiers of the regulation wooden-frame bunk in use at that time. See ibid., 57.

thanks for it. Will come in very handy. I use considerable, and if I had to buy it all at one dollar per [quire?] would soon run into my months pay. I told you in one of my former letters that I was corresponding secretary for several of my company. And of course they furnish there own writing materials. As I have a box to put those things in they make me keep the stock and allow me to use as much as I want, by that means I am always supplied.

Please allow me to extend to you my heart's felt thanks for your high "Corn the left" appreciation of my writing so very accurately on unruled paper. I think in the future I will only use ruled, as I am not so very particular about keeping straight and especially when writing home, for you know perfectly well I could be taking pains [to] do a little better towards writing straight. But were I writing to some fair dulceniea [Dulcinea] I assure [you] I would not write on unruled paper. And what is more [I] would not write on letter or fools cap paper.

Now when you take every thing into consideration I am not so much to blame. In the first place I generally get in from the road perhaps a few hours before the mail goes out. Then I have to sit down on some old box and scratch away as fast as possible in order to send a letter off in that weeks mail. I am generally tired and dusty. Now after all this explanation can you blame me so very much for not writing straight on unruled paper[?]

I just returned in Camp last night after six days hard riding on the road. Have been in the saddle from morning till night and even now I feel a little sore from sitting in the saddle.

Last Wednesday I was one of ten to excort Genl. Frank Wheaton, Col. Foster the quarter Master and Dr. Middletin [Middleton] to Williamson Valley where they were going to lay out a new Camp.[16] Left here about ten o'clock A.M. Arrived at W. about three P.M.

Soon as [we] got there the Genl. told the Sergt. in charge of us that he had some important dispatches to send to Toll Gate. Said detail three men to go through with them. I knew very well I would be one of the three, although I had just returned from Toll Gate a few days before. And shure enough the sergeant came to me and told me to be ready to leave

---

16 Assistant Surgeon Passmore Middleton served with the volunteer forces during the Civil War, earning brevets to captain and major for faithful and meritorious service. He received a commission in the regulars on February 15, 1865, and was promoted to major in 1884. He retired in 1891 and died four years later. See Heitman, *Historical Register*, vol. 1, 708.

there after dark, for the Genl. would not let us start till after dark. About five o'clock it commenced to rain very hard, and for the first time since I came in to this Territory heard it thunder. About 7 o'clock we saddled up and went to report to his <u>Honor</u>. Found him sitting in the house by the fire enjoying a good smoke. Gave us the dispatches and said they were very important, and for us to go through quick as possible.

Don't think I ever saw a darker night. It still continued to rain in torrants, and oh how it thundered and lightinged. It was impossible for me to see the man riding along by me. I was the only one of the three that had ever been over that road, and as it was open Country most all the way, it was impossible to keep on the road. My horse kept on the road splendid, but the other two men were continually getting off. About every five or ten minutes they would ask me if I was on the road. I supposed we had gone about six or eight miles when Donally, the man that was in charge, called to me to know if I was in the road. I dismounted and felt on the ground till my hand went into a big wagon rut. Knew then I was all right. Told him yes I was in the road, said he was not. He rode down to me and found he had been off the road some distance. He stoped and proposed that we turn around and go back to the General, and wait till morning. I objected to going back as we had gone about half the distance, but had yet the whorst of the road to go over. The third party who had been riding behind was also in favor of returning and said his horse was completely played out. So you see there was two against one, so I had to consent to return.

I told them if we did return the Genl. would send us back again. Donally said if he did he would give us another man and horse in place of the one that was played out. Turned around and in course of time found ourselves in the Valley. We rode up to the house where the Genl. was in and ro[u]sted him out of bed, told him the circumstances. He did not seem to be very well pleased. Told us to get another horse in place of the one that was played out and go through.

We turned around to obey his order, when he called to us and told us to Unsaddle and wait till morning. But said we must be ready to start at day break. We found a little shed and concluded we would sleep in it. Got some Hay and went in. First thing I knew was lying on a litter of little pigs. One of the old ones had jumped up and ran against me, upsetting me, hay and all. We drove the poor little pigs out in the cold rain and spread our blankets in their bed, took off my Boots and turned in. Although the rain kept dropping on us all night soaking through the blankets, I slept sound as if I had been in a nice comfortable bed.

Soon as we saw the first dawn of day we were up. I pushed my foot in one of the boots, and found that it was half full of water. I had left my Boots sitting up when [I] turned in, and the rain dropping down had half filled them. Mounted our horses and went on a full run in to Camp Toll Gate in one and a half hours. Good sixteen miles. Got a good breakfast and returned to the valley where we found the Officers and men at work laying out a new Camp. We remained there till Sunday morning riding around the Valley. The Camp is to be called Fort Rawlins.[17]

Sunday Morning we started for this Post via Cheno [Chino] Valley. A round about way of getting back. Arrived in Camp sunday evening. Monday morning was in the Saddle again scouring the Country for a couple of Horses that had broke away from the Company. In fact the whole company was out. We found them in the evening. Tuesday I went to Williamson Valley again, escorting wagon loaded with lumber for the new post. Returned to camp Wednesday.

Sunday evening a man returning to Williamson Valley from Prescott City was jumped by the Indians and killed. He was known by the name of Oregon Jake.[18] He was an old hunter and before he left the Valley for Prescott some of the Citizens told him he had better not go by himself. He said he was not afraid, that he had hunted in this country for some years and had never been molested. He started out alone and arrived in Prescott safe. While in P. he received two hundred and fifty dollars in gold for a pair of mules he had sold to Mr. Bean.

Sunday he started back and was killed. A party of Citizens from the Valley started out in search of his body yesterday a little a head of the escort I was with. As [we] came down to the Valley tuesday we saw blood in the road. We told the Citizens where we saw the blood. Before we got to the place the Citizens had found the body and was returning

---

17 This was Camp Rawlins, a temporary cantonment established on the Prescott-Fort Mojave Road in February 1870. Named for Secretary of War John A. Rawlins, who had died the previous fall, the camp was maintained only until August 1870. See Alexander, *Arizona Frontier*, 99.

18 Jacob Smith, nicknamed "Oregon Jake," had migrated from Washington Territory to Arizona Territory some months prior to this incident. He was killed on February 28, 1870, while en route from Prescott to his home in the Williamson Valley. His body was discovered approximately five miles east of Lee's Ranch, on the road to Mohave. Smith was reportedly the third man killed by Indians in that area within a few months. His body was buried at nearby Bean's Ranch. See the *Weekly Arizona Miner*, March 5 and 12, 1870.

to the Valley. The body presented a terrible appearance. Every stich of clothing was striped from his person. He had two bullet holes in his breast, six arrow wounds and the most horrible of all, his throat was cut from ear to ear. They had pulled him some five or six yds. from the road and left him lying in the bushes.

That is the manner in which the demons mutilate a white person in this region. Who could have any sympathy for a race of barbarians like they are. They will never get any quarters from me should I come across any of the hostile Indians. There is no fear of them Jumping soldiers, unless they could catch one alone. They are afraid of our Spencer Carbines. They say soldiers shoot all the time. They mean a soldier can shoot seven times before reloading. Then when that is empty they have their Colts six shooting revolvers to resort to.[19]

We are expecting the pay master every day. Perhaps he will come in this evening. We leave here for New Mexico first of April. E and B Companys have started on ahead to repair the roads for us to go over.

I have just finished dinner, and now have to help sweep all around our quarters. We have about fifty seven men in the company, and out of that number there is only 12 or 15 for duty, the rest are on the sick report. Some belong to the Band. Some extra on duty, some on Herd. So that 12 or 15 have to do the escorting, Policing etc.[20]

P.S. Friday 4th. The Pay Master, General Wallace, and a number of other officers arrived yesterday. We will not get payed off till the latter part of this month when the other pay master arrives. This one is out of funds. I am detailed this morning to escort General Wallace and the Court Martial party to Camp Verdie [Verde], a distance of 55 miles.[21] Have to make it in one day. Must go now and saddle up.

---

19 Matthews was under the mistaken impression that he carried a Colt revolver, due perhaps to the widespread popularity of that company's products. Company L was actually armed at that time with the solid-frame .44-caliber Remington New Model Army revolver. See Farrington, *Arming the Cavalry*, 22, 24.

20 Matthews cites a pervasive problem in the army at that time, and one that prompted many men to desert.

21 Lieutenant Colonel George W. Wallace began his service as a second lieutenant in the First Infantry in 1839. He remained in that regiment, rising to the rank of captain, until he was promoted to major in the Sixth Infantry in 1862. Unlike many of his contemporaries, Wallace stayed in the regulars throughout the Civil War. In 1866, he rose to lieutenant colonel of the Twelfth Infantry, which was transferred to the Department of California three years later. At the time he visited Arizona Territory, Wallace commanded a six-company battalion headquartered at Angel Island. See Heitman, *Historical Register*, vol. 1, 998; and Rodenbough, *Army of the United States*, 567. Camp Verde was originally located in the

Camp Whipple, Arizona Territory
MARCH 11, 1870

I just returned to camp yesterday evening from Camp Verde. Was so Sayguine [sanguine] that [I] would receive a letter from home that [I] offered to bet with one of the company. But alas [I] was disappointed for there was none for me. Will commence from the first and give you a full detail of my six days on the road.

Last friday eight of our company and four of D Co. was detailed to go to Camp Verde, sixty five miles from this post to escort Genl. Wallace, Pay Master, & several other Officers. Left here 12 N and arrived at Bowers Ranch 3 P.M., distance 25 miles, remained there till next morning. Stood one hour guard that night, each man on one hour.

Left B[ower's Ranch] 8 A.M. After riding some 20 miles saw Indian signs, rode on very cautious for sometime. I was in advance with the Sergt. in command. As we came around a little bend in the road we saw one <u>poor</u> Indian on a run to get away from us. The Sergt. and I made for him on a full charge, also four others of the escort. Ran him some distance. When he found out he could not get to the hills before we would catch him, he turned around with his Bow and Arrow and pointed it in the direction of the Sergt. and myself. We were only about fifty yds. from him. As there was no trees around to dart behind we were in a quandary.

I crawled off my little Horse, turned him broad side towards Mr. Indian, expecting every minute to see an arrow stuck in him, by this time we were all pretty close togeather. We concluded the performance had lasted long enough. So all pulled up our Carbines and fired and down came Mr. Indian. Rode up to him and on examining him found four bullets had struck him out of the Six. He had his Bow and some Arrows, no cloth[e]s on except two old shirts. His Bow was unstrung, so he could not shoot. Had his bow been strung perhaps some of us would have got an arrow stuck into us.

One of the boys took out his Knife and clipped a lock of the Indians

---

Rio Verde Valley thirty-five miles east of Prescott in 1864 to protect the local mining district. In 1871, it was moved to a more healthful location about four miles south and a mile west of the river. It was originally named Camp Lincoln, but its name was changed to Camp Verde in 1868 to avoid confusion with another cantonment bearing the same name in Dakota Territory. Fort Verde, as it was known after 1879, was abandoned by the army in 1890. Today it is a state historic site. See Frazer, *Forts of the West*, 14.

hair with a small piece of his scalp. Left him there and resumed our Journey. Had gone I suppose five miles, when we heard the Indians howling at us from a high mountain. Went on a little further when we had a good view of them. Also shot, dismounted and fired a volley into them and down came one of them. The rest ran off. That was the last we saw of them during the trip.

By this time we came to what is called Grief Hill. It was named that because so many parties had come to grief by the Indians jumping them there. "Jump is a word used in this country instead of attackted." The hill reminds me more of the Maryland Heights than any other place I know. Only the M. H. is not as bad as this Hill. It is about one and a half miles down. Some places almost perpendicular. Dismounted and walked down, for it is too steep to ride down. Got down safely and in a short time was at the Verde.

Went into Camp on a flat where there was nothing but sand, and the wind blowing a perfect gale. Our eyes were full of sand all the time.

Left there Wednesday to return to this Post. Came to Bowers Ranch and stopped for the night. Had to stand Guard again. Next morning came in here. Had orders then to get everything ready to be inspected today, by Gen. Wallace.

Last night the wind blew a perfect Hurricane and during the night a snow storm came up. This morning when got up found the ground covered with snow, about six inches deep. Had to go to work shoveling the snow off the parade ground where we were going to be inspected. Soon as that was over, dinner was ready. Soon as [I] downed my ration of roast beef [I] perched myself on an old box to write a line home, a line really it is, for I do not feel much like letter writing.

This Pay Master is not going to pay us one cent. We expect the other Pay Master in a few days. I am mustered for five months and three weeks pay. Am just six months and three days in the Army today. And to say that I was sick of this kind of living would [not] fully express my meaning. But the time rolls along slowly. Sometime ago I had five years to serve, now I have only four and a half. It is very near time to go to the stables so [I] will have to close.

Enclosed find those shirt buttons Lec sent me when I was home. Give them to Clellie. I have no use for them out here, they don't look very well in an old Government shirt.

Fort Whipple, Arizona Territory
MARCH 15, 1870

Todays mail brought me your welcome missive of the 15th inst., with a line from George Winters. And as I am detailed on an escort to leave here for Camp Toll Gate with a Court Martial party tomorrow morning, will have to answer tonight.

The Indians have been showing themselves and committing depredations, quite frequently here of late. Last Saturday evening one of the early Settlers of this Territory got filled full of <u>arrows</u> by the Indians a few miles from his Ranch. He was very mean to Soldiers, and had on several occasions taken the bucket away from the Well to keep them from getting water. But he never made anything by doing so, for in every case the Soldiers went in his Ranch and compelled him to give them the Bucket. I have not heard one person say a sympathising word for him. It was also supposed he had some trading with the Indians as he was never molested by them before. And at the same time his Ranch was some eight or ten miles from any other. Another Ranch man lost some twenty head of Cattle few days ago, they were run off by Indians. A Scout of ten men went out, but failed to recover them.

I was out several days ago on escort. Killed two of them, but I believe I told you of it in my letter to you last week. During my trip to Camp Verde week before last we visited the Montezernia [Montezuma] Cave's, they were occupied by that tribe of Indians more than a century ago.[22] They are some five or six miles from Camp Verde. To enter them you have to climb up three ladders, then you find yourself on a small platform. To enter the cave, you have to crawl thru a hole about the size of a door to a dog house, then you find yourself in quite a large room and you find several doors or holes leading into other rooms. It also has a second story. The second story was made by the Indians, the other is natural with the exception of a lot of mason work put up by them to close the cave up. It would surprise some of our mason's to see how well those stone[s] were placed on each other, and the manner they plastered

---

22 Preserved today as Montezuma Castle National Monument, this structure was built by prehistoric farmers over seven hundred years ago. It consists of a five-story, twenty-room pueblo, and represents one of the best-preserved cliff dwellings in the United States. It is located five miles north of Camp Verde, Arizona. See *The Complete Guide*, 29.

them. Don't think any man that had served five years in the business could have made a better wall, or done it neater with the same material. They certainly must have been a very ingenious race.

After entering the rooms you find quite a number of pieces of broken crockery were manufactured by them. And also any number of bones of Birds and small animals that died in there. Scarcely anything else. I collected a few little things to remember the Cave by. It was quite a tiresome job ascending the ladders, as the opening to the cave is about two hundred feet high, almost perpendicular.

Many thanks for your compliments on my Cooking. It does not require a Pastry or French Cook for a lot of Soldiers, for they are never required to make a Plum Pudding [or?] fix some fancy dish. All that is necessary for a company cook is to know how to make a Kettle of Coffee, make a hash in the morning and a few other little things like that. But I must say I am not an aspirant for any such situations as that. Or do I wish to become familiar in the art of cooking.

During my six months in the service I have learned quite a number of little things, such as washing a shirt, putting a button on my cloth[e]s and even putting a patch in the seat of Pants. You would laugh to see them after I had finished with them. I do claim they looked ten times better with the hole in them, than they did after I put the patch in them. It was done about as neat as you would were you putting a patch on some old gunny bag. Well they will do to go on the road with. Riding so very much is very hard on clothing. And more especially on Pants.[23]

Some talk of the other Pay Master coming soon. The one I went with to the Verde is still here, but is going to leave tomorrow morning for Camp Toll Gate. I guess there is no doubt but the next one will pay us.

We had another exciting Horse race here today for One thousand Dollars. The horses that ran on Thanksgiven day for five hundred dollars ran today. And the horse that lost then won today. I think there was some sell in the affair. Considerable money was lost and Won. One man even bet the horse he was riding. He sang out, "Who wants to walk home[?]" An other man near by said he did not mind doing so, they bet

---

23 The woolen army pants for mounted men featured a double layer of fabric, called a saddle piece, over the seat to prevent chafing. At that, riding long distances wore out the seats. Some soldiers patched them with whatever material happened to be available, as Matthews herein describes, while others replaced the woolen reinforce with one made of more durable canvas. See McChristian, *U.S. Army in the West*, 19–20, 63.

horse against horse. And the man that proposed the bet, had the pleasure of footing it home.

In my letter to you last week I enclosed a set of screw buttons, one little pin and a little shell which came from the Mexican Coast. I had been carrying them in my pockets long enough. Give the buttons to Clellie, the Pin to Arthur and the little shell to Johnny [Johnnie]. And tell them to see if they can keep them till I come home. Guess Johnny [Johnnie] will not think he has an equal share, but you know I gave him my Skates when I was in Carlisle, and they are worth five times as much as the others. Tell them I have never received an answer from them to my letter to each of them some time ago. If they have not already written tell them to write and give me an account of their doings since I left.

Must close for want of something to write about. I have never missed writing to you one week since [I] came here. I send a letter, whether I have anything to say or not.

Oh how I would love to see you all. It seems an awful long time since I saw you all. I want Father and Mother to send me their pictures. Then I will have you all to look at. If not you in person, it will be some consolation to look at your pictures. I will have mine taken and send [it] to you the first opportunity.

It seems very strange that I never receive any paper. The Post Master must take them out of the mail.

Wednesday 16th, 8 o'clock A.M. Will have to add another P.S. to this. Last night just as I had closed my letter to you I heard the cry of fire. Looking out the door I saw the Officers Quarters in a blaze. I cryed fire as loud as possible, and ran down to the fire. The Bugler sounded the Assembly when all hands had to turn out. Reaching the scene of [the] conflagration I found the building occupied by Lieut. [Frederick H.] Dibble in a full blaze. It did not take long for the boys to get to the fire and mount the roof. A row of men was formed to pass buckets of water up to the roof. The Quarter Master Stores were opened and about fifty blankets were wet and layed on the roof. After some two hours the fire was extinguished. The loss is not very much. But had the fire occured the night before when a strong wind was blowing the whole buildings would be in ruins now, Q. M. buildings and everything else. I worked like a good fellow up on the burning roof. Would not have gone on the roof, had I not been one of the first at the fire.

Will now have to go and Saddle up to go to Toll Gate. Write to me every week.

Fort Whipple, Arizona Territory
MARCH 30, 1870

Lizzie's long and very welcome letter was received last week, but for the first week since I came to this post I missed writing to you. No fault of mine though. Was ordered out same day the letter came and did not get back to Camp again till Saturday, after the mail had gone. I also received Capt. Byers letter of eight sheets and a splendid letter from Lec. the same day. Tell you it made me feel good to read all those letters. They were all real nice.

I got in Camp Saturday and was on the road again Monday morning and returned this evening to find Fathers splendid letter and three papers. I must certainly be in good luck, am commencing to get letters every week.

I am getting very tired of this Kind of life, and especially so much riding. I use to imagine I could never get tired [of] riding, but at that time had little idea of entering the Army. Since I came here, I have averaged four days out of six in the Saddle riding from twenty to sixty five miles a day. My <u>unmentionable</u> at times is so sore that a cushing [cushion] would seem hard to sit on. But that does not keep me in Camp, sore or not I have to go.

Last week I was on excort to Camp Toll Gate with Col. Young. The Officers out here are all confirmed drunkards and he is no exception. On the way he produced the bottle and after drinking himself, he passed it around to us. He was pretty drunk and when he handed it to me, and I refused. You ought to have seen the look he gave me. He said, "What you won't drink with me[?]" I told him I did not indulge. He said G____ D____ M_____ you, the first time I catch you drunk I will tie you up. That's the kind of men we have over us in the regular Army. It would be more proper to call it the regular mob.

Col. Young commands K Co. of our regiment and in less than three years he has had over six hundred men for his own Co. The men desert soon as [they] come to the Co. and see what kind of a commander he is. His men say he is a perfect tyrant. But if he waits till I get drunk, before he ties me up he will wait a long time. Let him hold his breath till I get drunk or take a drop of liquor, think the Coroners Jury that would sit on his body would have to bring in verdict of Death from want of breath. If I was only out of this miserable mob and home they would never catch me in it again. If the Lord will forgive me for enlisting this time I will never do so again. All I ask is to be home once more.

> Give me my home where Kindness Seeks
> To make that Sweet which seemeth small
> When every life in fondness speaks.
> And every mind has care for all.

I mistook my calling when I entered the Army. I am a Poet instead of a common Soldier. Perhaps [I] might follow that profession when [I] get out.

    I am perched up in a second story bunk trying to write this while the men are [word missing] all around me. Before I sit down to write my head was full of something to write to you, but I declair I can think of nothing now, but I will finish writing tonight for I am just as liable to be ordered out tomorrow as to stay in.

    Next week I think will find us on our road to New Mexico. E Co. is waiting here till the 6th of next month to go with F D & L. We are all going togeather. From all account[s] I think I will like New Mexico much better than here. But I dread riding there. It will be a long and tiresome journey.

    Father, in his letter spoke of my feelings when in sight of those Indians. Well I hardly know how I did feel. I did not get excited very much. Not half as much as [I] expected too. But I assure you my feelings were not the most pleasant when they first gave the yell. I knew they were cowards and would not stand, so [I] took things cool. The only thing they are good at is to lay in the little scrub oak bushes about ten feet from the road and fire on one or two men when they are travelling alone, and even then they become so excited they scarcely get either of the men. If they don't strike you the first time, they won't strike you at all. But when you get one cornered so he has no avenue of excape then he makes a desperate fight. But what human or brute in the world will not make a fight when he knows he will be Killed. I would fight a thousand Indians till I was Killed, sooner than be taken by them, for it would be certain death anyhow.

I am so very sleepy that can with difficulty keep open my eyes. Have been doing so much riding at night lately, have lost a great deal of sleep. Will have to turn in and finish in the morning.

Friday 31st. Have just come off <u>drill</u>, this morning. After being out on <u>Herd</u> all morning. It seems that the Officers at this Post cannot see the men idle one hour. They have always something for you to do. Either Scouting, excorting, fatiguing, herding or drilling.

Genl. [Thomas C.] Devin arrived here yesterday to take us through to New Mexico.[24] One hundred new horses will be here on the 4th of April. And we are supposed to leave on the 6th. I will have to stop writing again and go to the stables and groom my horses one hour. And as the mail goes out this evening will have to close this miserable written and composed letter. You will have to excuse the writing on account of me having to write up in my bunk on an old blanket. Had I a desk or table to write on perhaps [I] could do a little better. Will write again next week, and will try to do better.

As a clerk in the L Company orderly room, Eddie was in a position to learn the local news and rumors almost as soon as his officers. Early in 1870, the Eighth Cavalry was directed to exchange stations with the Third Cavalry in New Mexico Territory, which was encompassed within the Department of the Missouri. A battalion of five companies, including Eddie's, assembled at Camp Whipple in April to begin a two months' march via Fort Wingate to Fort Union, the strategic western anchor of the Santa Fe Trail and supply depot for all posts in the territory.

Fort Whipple, Arizona Territory
APRIL 5, 1870

This morning had orders to pack up all our cloth[e]s and take them to the 1st Sergt's room where there was a large box made expressly for

---

24 At this time, Devin was lieutenant colonel of the Eighth Cavalry. He had served through the Civil War as a volunteer cavalry officer, being mustered out in January 1866 as a brevet major general. Devin remained with the Eighth until 1877, when he was promoted to the command of the Third Cavalry. He died less than a year later in April 1878. See Heitman, *Historical Register*, vol. 1, 370.

them. Even emptied our bed Sacks and will have to sleep on hard boards tonight. We had two Corporals to desert night before last, both of them nice young men. One had two years and the other three and half to serve. Both told me they were going to leave that night. A citizen in Prescott gave them one hundred and forty dollars in coin. They had about two hundred dollars. They told me they were going only a few miles from here and stay till we left the Territory. Then they would take the stage and go in to the States. I don't blame any man for deserting out here. We are fed and treated very badly, especially our Company. The Corporals took their Carbines and Revolvers with them. The morning following they were reported missing and the first thing was to see if their Arms were gone. When they found they were the Capt. knew they had deserted. Did not send after them, guess they thought it was no use. "A guess it wouldn't be." Well can't say am sorry they have gone, So much better chance for promotion. There is five non commissioned officers short in the Company and I think when the Capt. appoints those five, W. E. Matthews will be found among the five. But I aught not be so certain, for I have not been in the Company very long, and it is not so easy to get stripes in the <u>Regulars. Trust to luck</u>.

    I am going down town tomorrow if the weather is fine and have my photograph taken for you. I have been promising to do so long enough. You ask me to have a large one taken, but I cannot have it taken this time must wait till [I] get payed. Perhaps when [I] get to New Mexico [I] will have a large one taken.

    Don't write or send any more papers after you receive this till you hear from me again. Don't know yet where abouts in New Mexico we are going. It will take us about one month to go there.

    In 21 more days I will be 20 years old. I am sliding along in years. Don't seem long since I was fifteen, will be longer till I am twenty five, or will at least seem much longer.

    Wednesday Morning. I have just returned from Town. Got a mounted pass this morning and went down to Town to have my Photo taken. Found the Room locked up and a card on the door saying the Proprietor was at work at the Livery Stable. Rode over to the stable and found the "Photographer." Told him [I] would like to have my picture taken. Said he could not take any today. So [I] had to return to Camp without my Photo. Perhaps when [I] get to N[ew] M[exico] will have a chance to have one taken. That is the way people work out here. For instance in passing through town you see an old shop and a card stuck on the door "Judge Penny" Blacksmith & Attorney at Law. That is the Judges name and occupation in the City of Prescott.

Fort Whipple, Arizona Territory
APRIL 10, 1870

Everything is confusion this morning. We are all packed up ready to say "farewell" to "Whipple" and in three or four days will say the same to the "Terty"[Territory]. I say "God" be praised for taking me out of this——.

I have something <u>less</u> than two <u>tons</u> of luggage packed on my poor little <u>Horse</u>. The waggons are packed to overflowing and still a great deal will have to be left behind.

After we are out a few days we can lighten our saddles by putting part of our traps in the wagon that hawls the rations. Eighty four new Horses came here yesterday. We got 15 very good horses. Did not see any that I would trade my little horse for.

Five Companies move from here today. D. E. F. K. and L. We go by the San Francisco Mountains. The 3rd <u>Cavalry</u> that is to relieve us are enrout for this <u>Trity</u> [Territory].

I must now get ready for the move. Don't write till you hear from me again.

Matthews may have misdated his last letter from Fort Whipple. The official record indicates that the battalion embarked on the march on April 9, following the established overland mail route used by the Santa Fe Stage Company. From Fort Whipple, the column marched north to Bill Williams Mountain, where it turned northeast past the San Francisco Mountains to Walnut Creek, which it followed almost to its confluence with the Little Colorado River. There, the road crossed Canyon Diablo near its mouth and paralleled the river along its left bank southeast to Sunset Crossing. From that point, the route traced the north bank of the Little Colorado upstream into New Mexico Territory before diverging northeastward to Fort Wingate, a total distance of 325 miles.[25] At length, the route

---

25 After reaching Walnut Creek, this overland road approximated the route surveyed by Lieutenant Amiel W. Whipple in 1853. Whipple had been charged with laying out a feasible route for a transcontinental railroad generally along the thirty-fifth parallel from Fort Smith, Arkansas to the Colorado River. See Goetzmann, *Army Exploration*, 287–89. For accurate representations of this route, see

intersected the Santa Fe-El Paso Road, formerly a segment of the ancient Camino Real, at Albuquerque.

Companies E and K took station at Fort Wingate while the rest of the northern battalion continued eastward. Those companies of the Eighth Cavalry that had been posted in southeastern Arizona Territory concurrently marched directly eastward from their former posts to occupy new stations in the southern regions of New Mexico Territory.[26]

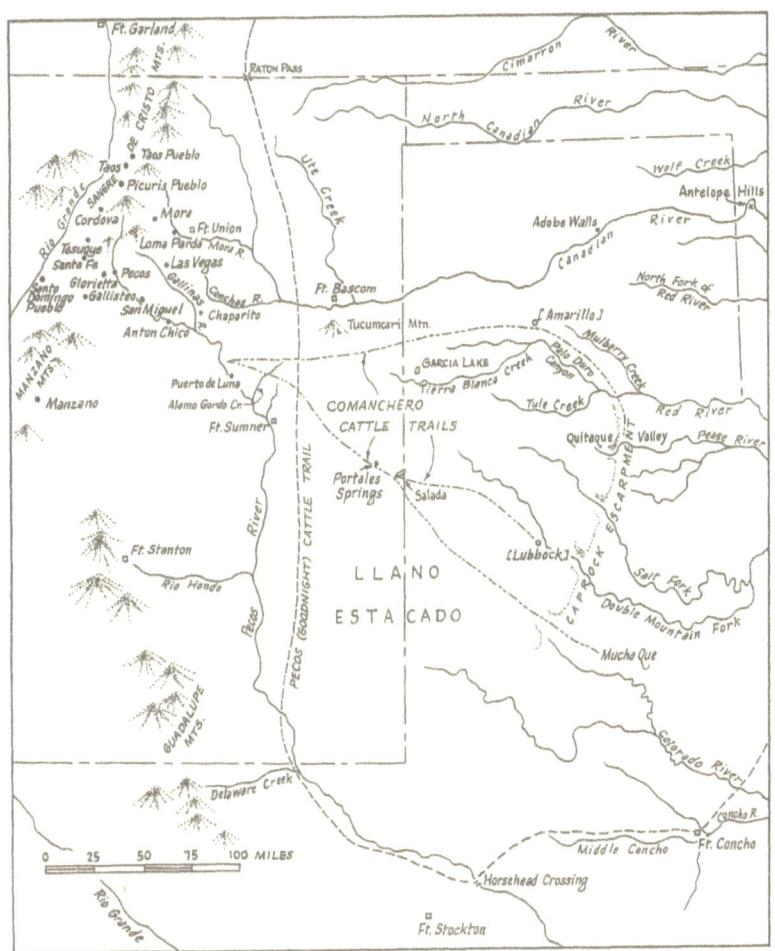

MAP 2. The Southwestern Frontier, 1865–1875.

"Map of the Military Department of New Mexico," Captain Allen Anderson, 1864; and "Map of the Territory of Arizona," C. Roeser, General Land Office, 1879. Not long after this, a new, shorter route was opened via Camp Verde to Sunset Crossing. See Hinton, *Handbook to Arizona*, 372, 374; Hodge, *Arizona As It Was*, 252; and Walker and Bufkin, *Historical Atlas*, 41.

26 See Eighth Cavalry Returns, April 1870.

CHAPTER THREE

"Wind, Wind, and Sand All the Time"

MAY—DECEMBER 1870

Upon the arrival of the Eighth Cavalry in New Mexico Territory, two companies, including Eddie's, drew a comparatively plum assignment at Fort Union, with the remainder of the companies parceled out among smaller stations ranging from Fort Garland, in southern Colorado, to Forts Craig and Selden, far to the south along the Rio Grande. Others found a new home at Fort Stanton, in Mescalero Apache country, while one unfortunate troop was condemned to occupy Fort Bascom, a primitive post on the Canadian River far out on the desolate eastern plains. It was a place Eddie Matthews would come to know all too well.[1]

---

1 Located approximately ninety miles southeast of Fort Union, Fort Bascom was established in 1863 to protect the road from Fort Smith, Arkansas to Santa Fe, New Mexico, and to defend the eastern approach to the territory from any possible invasion by Confederate forces. That threat never materialized, yet the army found Fort Bascom advantageously situated to protect the growing number of ranches along the Canadian River. The post also served as a staging point for military expeditions into the Texas Panhandle region, notably against the Comanches and Cheyennes in 1868. It was abandoned in 1870, but continued to be used as a summer campsite for cavalry patrols from Fort Union. See Frazer, *Forts of the West*, 95.

Fort Union had been established in northeastern New Mexico Territory in 1851 to contend with Indian troubles inherited with the territory ceded by Mexico following the conflict of 1846–1848. Early U.S. military posts initially followed the Spanish-Mexican custom of placing garrisons in villages and towns to protect the inhabitants from marauding war parties. Trouble arose, however, with soldiers living in such close association with civilians, resulting in corruption of the troops by alcohol, gambling, and prostitution. More importantly, the troops were not where they were most needed—in proximity to the various warlike tribes to serve as a protective buffer for the settlements.

Accordingly, the garrison at Santa Fe was removed to a site near the lower junction of the main branches of the Santa Fe Trail, the so-called Mountain and Dry Routes. The longer though better-watered Mountain Route also served as the principal U.S. Mail route into the territory, further justifying the need for troops at that point. For the next four decades, Fort Union would play a key role in the Southwest, protecting the northeastern New Mexico frontier and the vital route from Missouri, as well as serving as a base for offensives against Indians in the region.

Its strategic location ideally suited Fort Union as a supply base for the entire territory. By the late 1860s, it represented a sprawling installation embracing three facilities: the military garrison, a huge quartermaster depot, and the Fort Union Arsenal, each with its own commander. All manner of supplies came down the trail by wagon to be deposited in the enormous adobe warehouses at the depot. Several capacious corrals served as a central transportation pool with repair shops for wagons and harnesses.

Another of the army's missions in New Mexico was to contend with a practice that had persisted for decades—the Comanchero trade. This mutually lucrative intercourse was rooted in a tradition dating back to the eighteenth century, when Hispanic New Mexicans and Pueblo Indians along the Rio Grande valley found that the Kiowas and Comanches roaming the Staked Plains of neighboring Texas presented a ready market for corn meal, tobacco, blankets, cloth, and other goods. In exchange, the plains Indians offered cattle and horses taken from Mexican ranches in Chihuahua and Durango and Indian captives stolen from opposing tribes. Initially, these prisoners were sold as either domestic servants or slave labor for the mines of New Mexico. However, a new dimension in human trafficking unfolded when the New Mexicans conceived a moneymaking scheme whereby Mexican hostages were ransomed back to those families that were willing and able to pay. In either event, the Comancheros benefitted.

The practice continued unabated until well after the American acquisition of Texas and New Mexico in the mid-nineteenth century. The proliferation of white settlement into western Texas during the 1860s provided the Indians with more readily convenient sources of cattle, thereby altering the character of the trade. Parties of Comancheros from northern New Mexico, accompanied by pack trains or wagons loaded with goods, made regular rendezvous with the Indians, bringing them guns, powder, and later metallic cartridge ammunition, in addition to the traditional staples.[2] In a feeble attempt to bring about a measure of control over the traders, and at the same time derive revenue from the commerce, the territorial government instituted a licensing procedure that was quickly corrupted and rendered largely impotent.

After years of occupying New Mexico, the U.S. Army had been only partially successful in curtailing the Comanchero traffic. In fact, the trade burgeoned during the two years following the Civil War, due in part to the vacillating policies of Brigadier General James H. Carleton, commanding the District of New Mexico, who at times warred against the plains tribes and at other times encouraged the trade by issuing his own trading permits to the Comancheros. Attempting to impose a more forceful, consistent policy, General William T. Sherman, commanding the Division of the Missouri, penned an edict in 1867 authorizing army officers to intercept the trading parties and to confiscate all livestock found in their possession on the presumption that it was stolen. However, the Comanchero trade was so entrenched, with so many benefactors within the territorial government, that the civil judicial system could not be relied upon to back the army's actions. Even when the troops managed to arrest illegal traders, the courts usually acquitted them. Moreover, the officers executing the order fully appreciated that they might well be legally vulnerable, considering the bias of the local courts.

Little changed, therefore, until the army appointed a new commander for the District of New Mexico in 1867. George W. Getty, colonel of the Thirty-Seventh Infantry, then posted in New Mexico, was an 1836 graduate of West Point and a veteran of both the Mexican-American and Civil Wars. Getty pursued a more aggressive strategy by creating so-called picket posts on the territory's eastern frontier. Using Fort Bascom as a supply base, he assigned a detachment of the Third Cavalry to the strategic intersection of the Fort Smith Road with the north-south route connecting Forts Bascom and Sumner. He posted another detachment farther south to operate from Hubbell's Ranch.

By early fall, Getty's troopers had captured several unpermitted traders, impounding their goods and over eight hundred head of cattle. Despite the fact that the brands of the cattle were published in Texas newspapers, however, most went

---

2 See Kenner, *Comanchero Frontier*, 93–94, 155–56.

unclaimed, and those distant ranchers who did bother to file often could not produce adequate proof of ownership. Subjecting the army to further embarrassment, the U.S. District Court in Las Vegas freed a number of Comancheros after their attorneys argued successfully that federal trade laws did not apply to New Mexico Territory. The court subsequently ordered that the cattle and other property be returned to the traders. In the end, though, the army's stepped-up patrols along the Canadian and Pecos Rivers, interfering with the primary corridor to the Staked Plains, discouraged the traffic to such a degree that the problem largely subsided for the next two years.

A second and perhaps more influential factor combined with this to hinder the trade successfully. Lieutenant General Philip H. Sheridan, heading the Division of the Missouri, launched a campaign against the winter camps of the Southern Cheyennes, Arapahoes, Kiowas, and Comanches, suspected of preying on settlers and transportation routes in western Kansas. The Kiowas and Comanches, moreover, raided ranches in northern Texas, stealing cattle they subsequently traded to the Comancheros, and then took refuge on the reservations in Indian Territory.

Sheridan's strategy called for three columns to converge simultaneously on the upper Texas Panhandle. Two of these forces, one from Fort Lyon, Colorado, and another from Fort Bascom, were to serve as beaters to drive the scattered bands into the hands of the strongest expedition, composed of eleven companies of the Seventh Cavalry and five companies of infantry, plus the newly recruited Nineteenth Kansas Volunteer Cavalry, thrusting southward from Kansas.

Lieutenant Colonel George A. Custer, one of Sheridan's pets from the Civil War days, led the Seventh Cavalry in a dawn attack against Black Kettle's Cheyenne village on November 27, 1868. Despite Custer's initial success in destroying the camp and most of the Indian pony herd, a spirited counterattack by the Cheyennes, augmented by Arapahoes from previously undetected camps farther downstream, forced the cavalry to withdraw.

A month later, the Fort Bascom column, consisting of six companies of the Third Cavalry, discovered and attacked a Comanche village at Soldier Spring on Christmas Day. Following an all-day skirmish, the troops managed to destroy the camp, including the Indians' winter food supply, thereby forcing some of these Indians to seek protection at Fort Cobb, Indian Territory, and others to eventually surrender at Fort Bascom.

Custer's column remained in the field all winter, pressing the recalcitrant bands that refused to go in to the agencies. Thus, for months during 1868 and 1869, troops from the three columns scoured western Indian Territory and the eastern portion of the Texas Panhandle south of the Canadian River. The presence of many soldiers in the region, coupled with the uncertainty regarding when or where they might appear, made the New Mexican traders wary of venturing into the Staked Plains, even if the plains tribesmen were in a position to rendezvous with them. Hounded and kept on the defensive by Sheridan's troopers, the Kiowas and Comanches were also prevented from pursuing their usual occupation of plundering the Texas frontier.

The situation reverted, however, just when the Eighth Cavalry traded places with the Third, arriving in New Mexico in the spring of 1870. With troops absent from the Staked Plains and its environs for some months, the Comancheros had again begun plying their trade. Getty had already begun posting cavalry detachments on the Fort Smith Road with some success, in addition to dispatching patrols from Fort Bascom to scout the area from the Canadian River southward along the Pecos. It would now be up to Colonel John I. Gregg and his Eighth Cavalrymen to assume the thankless task of carrying out Sheridan's order to "break up and punish the bands of New Mexico traders who have been and are still trading for captured stock with hostile Indians."[3]

Fort Union, New Mexico

MAY 19, 1870

Arrived here yesterday morning. And I was at once put on Guard but not untill I had received and per[used?] two welcome letters from my dear home. Also one each from Jennie Zepp and Clara Wampler. I had no idea of receiving any letters for some time therefore the surprise was more agreeable.

It is now over eight months since I entered the house of God or listened to his teaching of the manner in which we should live. The last time was in Cincinnati, after I had enlisted, I spent one Sabbath there. Walking down town I saw a number of people entering a very fine edifice, and as I had not don[n]ed the Blue's yet, followed them in, and found I was in an Episcopal Church, and a very fine one too. In all my travells through Arizona I never saw a Church, Minister or Christain that I know of. So different from this Territory. Every Mexican town we

---

3 This quotation appeared originally in the *Republican Review*, July 30, 1869 (quoted in Kenner, *Comanchero Frontier*, 183). A useful contemporary overview of the illegal trade is found in Brigadier General John Pope's annual report, *ARSW*, 1871, 43–44.

passed through, there was a church in and it was in every instance the finest building in the Town. Let the town be ever so poor they had a place of worship, all are Catholic's though.

I have not found out yet whether there is a Photograph Gallery.

Fort Union, New Mexico
MAY 22, 1870

In my letter of the 18th inst. I promised to write to you on Sunday, but owing to a miserable <u>Diarreah</u> I was compelled to wait till today.

Monday, I have just this moment come out of the Cook House. For I have been elected for a turn in that disagreeable business. Assumed control of the business this morning, supperceeding Corpl. Mitchell of our company.[4] Two other Privates and myself propose to run the machine the coming ten days. I am very much opposed to working in the Cook House, but under the present circumstances am better off than would be were I in the company for duty. Out of 56 men, we have only 12 for duty. Those twelve have to go on Guard every other day, only get one night in bed. And it will be that way for two months, and perhaps more till the two (2) other companies of our Regt. arrive here. They have come here from Cheyeene on the Union Pacific Rail Road.[5] This thing of only one night in bed would Kill the oldest man living.

Another advantage I have in the Cook house, is I always get enough to eat. An[d] can always make some fancy little dishes to coat the appetite. At least something better than Hard Tack and Pork. But I must say we are living very well since we came here. In the morning have Beef Steak, Bread and Coffee. Dinner Beef, Bean Soup and Bread, Supper, Coffee, Syrup Bread and Pickles. Splendid cucumber

---

4 John J. Mitchell, a native of Tyrone County, Ireland, enlisted in the army on May 11, 1867, at Philadelphia, Pennsylvania. He was twenty-one years of age and had been employed previously as a gardener. Assigned to Company L, Eighth Cavalry, Mitchell served out his full term and was discharged as a sergeant at Fort Union in 1872. He must have remained at Fort Union, perhaps as a civilian employee, following his discharge because he reenlisted there in the Fifteenth Infantry on March 31, 1874. That he was discharged as a private without character in 1879 suggests that he was an indifferent soldier during his second term. See entry 991, p. 216, roll 33 and entry 51, p. 75, roll 39, ROE, RG 94, NA.

5 New Mexico lacked a rail connection at this time. Consequently, the regimental headquarters and Companies H and M, still in Nevada, were transported by rail to Cheyenne, Wyoming Territory, whence they marched overland to Fort Union. See Rodenbough, *Army of the United States*, 269.

pickles. The 1st Sergt., Quarter Master Sergt. & three Cooks, mess by ourselves. We always have something extra such as Eggs, Milk, Butter, Bread Pudding, Doughnuts & etc. How is that, don't that make your mouth water[?]

Eggs are worth 25 cts doz., Butter 50, Beef Steak 10 cts. lb., Milk 10 cts Qt. Prices here for everything is very reasonable. Very much the same as prices in the States. So different from miserable Arizona. How thankfull I ought to be for coming out of that place alive. In my letter of the 18th I said I believe to be concluded, me[a]nt continued, so will try to finish in this one, or at least give you an account of the March.

We left Fort Whipple at noon on the 9th Inst. only marched seven miles that day, to where the other three companys were waiting for us. D Company of our Regt. left Whipple same time as we. On the tenth we left Browar's Ranch with General Alexander our senior Major, in command of the 5 companys D, E, F, K, & L. We never marched more than thirty miles [word missing], broke Camp early in the morning, sometimes as early as 2 o'clock so as to get in Camp early in the day. If we would break camp at 5 o'clock would get into camp about 10 or 11 o'clock. Sometimes [we had] to make dry Camps. I suppose you don't know what a dry Camp is. It is where there is no water for men or animals.

At other times would have to Camp where there was no wood. Would geather little sage brush, and <u>Buffalo</u> Chips to make fire with. Suppose you don't know what buffalo chips are. Well it is Buffalo Manure. It when dry makes a splendid fire. People on the Plains burn it altogeather, for they can get no wood. I[t] would make you laugh to see us geathering it up in our blankets, and putting it on a pile at the Cook wagon. But if you were along and as hungrey as us, you would feel more like crying.

Saw no signs of anything civilized till we came to the little Colorado [River], where there was a wagon train loaded with Flour going to Prescott City, Arizona. The little Colorado like the Big, is a very muddy River. There is no rain, and when it rains it is worse than muddy. It is mud itself, is just as thick as good thick cream, but not one third as good. For four days we were compelled to drink that stuff. Was so thick that it would most choak you when you drunk it. You have to be very carefull where you water your horse along that river, there is scarcely anything but Quick Sand. Your horse would sink over his back some places. I saw several horses in over their backs, had great difficulty to get them out again. If they were to stay five minutes in such a place they would sink out of sight altogeather.

One place we camped where there was not one bit of water as every person thought. You could see nothing but huge rocks on all sides. The day had been very warm and we were nearly famished for water. Some of the men climbing around among the Rocks found holes in some of them where it had rained and the water was in these holes and would have to remain there till the sun would dry it up. It was reported in Camp that water could be found in small holes in the rocks. It created a panic, men run in every direction with cups and canteens, and in the course of an hour or so the Camp was supplyed with water, dipped out of the rocks, gill by gill. I never in all my life knew what it was to suffer for want of water, till that march. For two days, I had to do without water, not one drop could be got, except Alcoli [alkali] water, which was so strong that it would make you sick to taste it. Alcoli water is worse than salt water some times.

Three days from Fort Wingate we saw the first Indians we had seen since [we] left Arizona. They belonged to the Navaho tribe. They are at peace now. Have been since 1855.[6] They number some eight thousand. They are on a reservation all around Fort Wingate. They seem to be industrious, have any amount of sheep and Goats. Rais[e] corn, barley & C———, besides they get rations from the Government.

Two days out from Wingate [we met?] a Soldier mounted on a mule. He brought the Regimental mail from Wingate. Also the order for the distribution of the companys. We were in ignorance where we were going till then. We supposed our company would stop at Wingate. We were very agreeably surprised when the order was read out, for us to go to Fort Union. The order was for E & K companies to stop at Wingate, D at Fort Bascum, and F & L [to] go to Union.

We stoped three days at W——[Wingate], from there till we got here it seemed like we were in Civilization. Most every day [we] would

---

6 Matthews is in error here. Although the army had clashed with the Navajos on the eve of the Civil War, the most notable campaign occurred in 1863–1864, when troops under Brigadier General James H. Carleton invaded their homeland. Defeated at Canyon de Chelly, the Navajos were removed and forced to endure a miserable existence at Bosque Redondo in eastern New Mexico Territory. In 1868, the government relented and permitted them to return to their native country in northeastern Arizona and northwestern New Mexico. See Utley, *Frontiersmen in Blue*, 168–71, 237–47.

pass through some small Mexican Town. The water and wood is more plenty full here than in Arizona.

All went well till we came to the Rio Grand River. We came very near having quite a catastrophe there. The river is about three hundred yds. wide at the point where we had to cross. The river runs quite rapid, quite, is not the word, it is <u>very</u> rapid. There is two Boats at the crossing, one a Gov't boat the other a citizen boat. The boats are large enough to hold one wagon and six mules. When we got there the boats were in use. Quite a large Citizen Wagon train was on the bank waiting to be ferried over, but everything had to be droped and our men and wagons taken over first. The horses had to swim over. We took everything off of the horses and turned them loose. All hands got around D Co's. horses and drove them in, for one Companys horses were to be sent over at a time. One of D Co., a private, voluntered to ride his horse over in front of the others, so they would follow. All went well till the horses got in the swift current and then away they went down the stream at a rate that would [out?] distance some of our Rail Roads in a little while. They swam down the river about half a mile and came out on the same side that they went in on. The Soldier and his horse in the mean time made the other bank, but not togeather, for as soon as they struck the swift current the Soldier was washed off the horse. He had quite a struggle in the water and was pretty well exausted when he reached the other shore.

The horses were brought up and once more drove in with a Mexican which was along with us for herder at their head, mounted on a splendid little horse. He took the lead and we drove the horses in after him. This time they got across safe. One or two of the horses were washed down stream a considerable distance but got out safe.

Our horses were to cross next. And while D Co. horses were crossing our Capt. stuck a new idea. It was this, there was several small Boats on our side of the river. Three men got in one of them and took three horses by their halter straps and pushed out in the river and our horses after them. They no sooner struck the current than away they went down the river at a two forty rate. They looked quite pretty holding on to the horses. The horses in front made it look like they were pulling the boat, all you could see of the horses was their heads. The men in the boat saw there was no use in holding on to the horses, so they left them go and paddled to the shore. All got over some distance though down the river. My little horse was one of the three first to reach the shore.

"Wind, Wind, and Sand All the Time" 81

Now all the horses were over except F Companys. F Co. is commanded by an Irishman, Lt. [Robert] Carric[k], he was like the officers generally are, about half or a little more.⁷ He made a bet of five dollars that he would swim his own horse across. He went to his company and said all men that could swim step to the front. Five men stepped forward, he told them to undress and mount their horses.

When all was ready he took the lead and the men followed him. Then the loose horses were drove in after him. Soon as the horses got in over their heads the excitment commenced. The loose horses got among the men that were mounted, then commenced a scene I never want to witness again. First you could see the men a clinging to their horses, next thing the riders would be underneath the horses. They keep up continual back summer salts for ten minutes. It was hard to tell whether the men would ever come out alive. Finally one of them, a Corpl. more dead than alive, reached the other shore.

In a short time, after all the rest in the same state as the first, except the Lt., made the bank of the river. All was safe then but one and he had washed down stream with his horse a considerable distance. And for ten minutes more he and the horse struggled in the water. By this time he had got out of the swift current, and as a Boat could get to him there, a couple of Mexicans started to his rescue and brought him and his horse to the Shore. I don't think any of them got much sympathy, for there was no necessity for any such foolishness. Don't think any of the party would like to repeat the dose.

We went into Camp on the other side and stayed one day. It took 1 1/2 days to cross over the wagons. I visited the town of Alburquerque while we were in Camp on the river. It is one of the oldest towns in the United States. It has a population I suppose of three or four thousand inhabitants. The houses are all built out of Doby's. A doby is the same as a brick before they are burnt. They are made much larger than bricks and left to dry a considerable time. All the houses in this country are built of that material. Quite a fine Church and a very large one I saw in the town. Plenty of stores. Business I was told was very dull. We passed

---

7 Robert Carrick was born in Ireland and joined the U.S. Army in 1851 as a private in the Regiment of Mounted Riflemen. He later served as a noncom in the Second Dragoons. During the Civil War, he was commissioned as an officer in the Third Missouri Cavalry, from which he resigned in 1863. Returning to the army in 1867, Carrick was commissioned as a lieutenant in the Eighth Cavalry, but he remained in the service for less than four years thereafter. See Heitman, *Historical Register*, vol. 1, 285.

through a number of towns on the march. Alburquerque, Los Vegas, Sandersa, and Looma were the largest.[8]

I have only a few moments to write before taps goes, when all lights have to be put out. The third Cavalry leaves here tomorrow. Two of the 7th Cavalry from Colorado arrived here with dispatches today. They came two hundred and fifty miles through an Indian Country alone. They travelled in the mountains and out on the Prairie all the way. Bring news of a number of tribes of friendly Indians breaking out again. More work for the poor Cavalry men.

Fort Union, New Mexico
JUNE 1, 1870

Lizzie's and Susie's letter of April 12th just came to hand few minutes ago. From the long time it has been on the road, suppose it must have gone to Fort Whipple, and then sent here. It is very pleasant for me to receive letters from home & friends. And it is also a pleasure to write. But often I find it quite difficult to get a spare moment to do so, here as well as in "Arizona."

We have our time almost completely taken up with the duties of a Soldier. In "Arizona," if at any time we were in Camp one or two days, we would never be surprised to have the 1st Sergt. tell us to Saddle up immediately, with 1, 3 or 5 days rations to go on escort, Scout, or some such duty. Here you get one night in Bed. For instance tonight you are on Guard, tomorrow morning at 8 o'clock you get relieved. At nine, one hour after coming off Guard, you have to Saddle up and go on <u>Herd</u>. Come in with the Herd at 11 P.M. [4 P.M.?] Spend one hour grooming

---

8 Matthews's reference to "Sandersa" is unresolved. No town by that name, or a phonetically similar pronunciation, has been identified. This may have resulted from an error in translating the original typescript, or it could be a corruption of Sandia, a pueblo lying north of Albuquerque on the east side of the Rio Grande. It may seem odd that Matthews failed to mention Santa Fe, the territorial capital of New Mexico, yet the shortest route to Fort Union bypassed that town several miles to the south, via Galisteo. "Looma," used elsewhere by Matthews, refers to Loma Parda, a village located approximately seven miles southwest of Fort Union. Supported wholly by the soldier trade, cowboys, and the criminal element, Loma Parda was a den of saloons, gambling halls, and brothels, commonly referred to as "hog ranches." Post commanders placed it off limits from time to time, attempting to discourage the men from patronizing the place, but with little success. See Hart, *Old Forts of the Southwest*, 149–50. The total distance marched by the Eighth Cavalry during the regiment's change of station was 605 miles. See Eighth Cavalry Returns, April and May, 1870.

your horse, then get your supper. At sundown the Bugle calls you to "Retreat" to answer your name, and hear who are detailed for Guard on the morrow. As there is only 12 men in the company for duty and six on <u>Guard</u> each day, you are not surprised to hear your name called to be ready for Guard at 8 O'clock tomorrow. From Retreat till Tattoo, "2 hours," you have to Shine your belts, Clean your Gun, and Brasses so they shine like a dollar gold piece in the dark. Next morning at break of day, you fall in Ranks for <u>Reveille</u>, answer your name, and then march to the stables, spend half hour on the old bunch of horses, come back, swallow your Breakfast, and then put on all your good cloths, comb your hair, pull on white gloves that after one wearing will streach large enough to pull on your feet instead. Put on all your Belts, Shoulder your carbine, and then you are ready for Guard Mount. With all a Cavalry Man's traps on he would make any pack mule, or dunkey, blush to see a poor man carrying more than they could.

At the first sound of the Bugle, you rush in ranks to be inspected first by your first Sergt. In case he should find a speck of dust on your belts, or in your gun, you are hurried back in quarters and through the aid of numerous brushes assisted by a Spy glass you are able to see and remove the troublesome speck. You then rush back in ranks, all in a perspiration, and then are marched over to the Sergt. Major. He stands as a marker, for you to dress by.

Soon as all the details arrive on the ground and form a line, he Sings out, "right dress." You all cast your eye's to the right. If you can see the second button on the second man's jacket, on your right, you are Hunky dorey. But if by accident you should get one foot over the alinement, you're liable to have it cut off by the Sergt. Major's Saber falling on it with considerable force. The S[ergt.] M[ajor] then brings his saber up in front of his face, which is called a present, and sings out to the "Adjutant, who stands some thirty paces in front," "The detail is correct, Sir." The A. then draws his Sword and says, "Very well, Sergt., Take your Post." The Sergt. finds a Post on the left of the detail and hangs up there, till his honor the A. inspects your Gun, Belts, then opens your shirt collar to see if that bit of apparel has been to the Laundresse's in the course of a couple of months. When he is satisfyed that you are not, to use a soldiers expression, "Crumby Louzy," he goes to the next man, and so on till the guard is inspected. The cleanest man is chosen Orderly for the commanding officer.

The A. then marches to his Post and brings the guard to a present arms, then he salutes the officer of the day, that worthy says at the same time raising his hat, "March the Guard in review to their Post." The <u>Band</u> strikes up those patriotic tunes, "Who's been here since I's been gone" or "Yanky Doodle," which ever suites the band.

You are then marched to the guard house. During the day you escort prisoners around camp, emptying swill Barrels etc. At night you are put on guard over a stable, lot of wagons etc. with these orders: take charge of this post, and all Government property in view. In case of <u>fire</u> put on <u>more wood</u>. If the fire don't burn very fast, fire your gun off, then after waiting some time if it still persists in not burning, fire your gun off a second time. That is Soldiering in a nut shell.

I have spent some time and perhaps wasted some paper foolishly, but that is about as fair a discription of our duty here as I can give. The duty will not be so hard after while, when the other two Company's get here. My ten day's in the Cook House will be up tomorrow morning. But I can stay in longer if I wish to, under the present circumstances. I think will remain in it, till the duty gets lighter. This thing of Standing Guard every other night, is not very pleasant.[9]

The only objection I can find here is the miserable wind. Talk of March wind in the States, why it is not a comparison to this place. Wind, wind, and sand all the time. This Post is built on a plain. There is nothing to break the wind, therefore giving it full sway. It is very pleasant to walk down to the Post office every evening and see the Stage come in bringing the mail and passengers from the States. It seems so strange to have a daily mail.

I would be perfectly happy under the circumstances, in which I am situated, if I could only send you one hundred dollars. I know you need money. And had I not been so unfortunate [I] could have sent you that amount, soon as [I] got payed. The Pay Master payed off here a couple of weeks before we got here, so we will not be payed till next month.

---

9 Even though Matthews had previously complained about serving as company cook, a little exposure to guard duty changed his view. Sentinels were obligated to walk an assigned beat for two hours, then have four hours off before resuming the beat. During the daytime, the guards not walking post often supervised the prisoners on work details. At other times, they hung out at the guard house, getting what rest they could on an uncomfortable wooden dais while fully clothed and equipped during their twenty-four-hour tour of duty. Even after being relieved the next morning, the members of the old guard, as Matthews describes, performed light fatigue duties. Accordingly, a man was awake and active for approximately forty hours. See Rickey, *Forty Miles*, 91–92.

There is an Express Office here. Just as soon as I receive my pay I will send you every cent, except what I owe the Laundress and a few other little debts which will not amount to a great deal.

I have some little news to tell you, which I know will be gladly received by you although it is not much. The Post Baker here is not as smart as he might be. He cannot read, write or figure any, and it was necessary that some person should be there to look out for things. Keep count of what Flour comes in, and what Bread went out. In such a position there is more or less money to be made, from the sale of surplus Flour, flour sacks etc., besides you would have a chance to learn the trade, which would be a great thing to me. I was, recommended to Lt. Carrick for the situation by one of his F Company. The party that recommended me came and told me what he had done. I was delighted with the idea, if only [I] could get it. And [I] was in hopes of getting the place, till [I] told one of our Company, a fine young fellow he said, "Ed, I don't think you will get it." When I asked him why, he said, "You are going to be promoted in a few days." I then asked him how he Knew I was. Said Billy Thomas, the Adjutants Clerk told him. Said my papers were made out. Tell you what, it made me feel good, but would much soon have the former position, although it might not last very long. Promotion in the regular Army is slow, and one cannot raise very much or in other words, not very high. Still it speaks well for one, and more especially one in the service so short a time. Most Non-Commissioned Officers in the regulars are old Soldiers, but perhaps I should not speak so fast. I have not been promoted yet, hope though in my next to give you something more definite.

I have commenced one undertaking too Sister, and although I have so many times failed in others, yet I think with great care and watching in the course of time, "I will have as fine a what do you suppose[?]" Can you imagine[?] MUSTACHE. It is very young and tender, yet I think it will grow.

Fort Union, New Mexico
JUNE 4, 1870

Sunday evening [I] have just finished cleaning the Kitchen and have nothing else to do. Concluded [I] would spend a few minutes writing to you dear ones. Have nothing new to tell you, and suppose I will find some difficulty in finding a subject to write about.

Spent most of today sleeping, as had nothing else much to do. We have a Post Chapel here, but no person to fill the pulpit. Perhaps we will get a Chaplain after while. It has been a long time since I attended Divine Service. How strange not to have a minister at such a Post as this one that was in use during the Mexican War, and has been occupied by the U. S. troops ever since.

A couple of weeks ago, while on Guard I was sent in charge of six prisoners over to the Cemetry to dig a grave for a poor soldier who accidentaly shot himself while on duty. In looking at the number of graves and reading the names and epitaphs ("is that spelt right[?]") on the head Boards with the dates of burial, I noticed the majority of them were buried in 1848 & 50. I also counted over forty graves marked Unknown. It did seem hard to see so many graves without anything on the Head boards but Unknown.

We have turned in our Spencer Carbines and have drawn in place the Sharps improved. Don't like them half so well as the seven shooters. The Sharps are more dangerous than the Spencer. They are much easyer cleaned though. We have also drawn new saddles covered ones, they are very nice.[10]

You said your last letter, you wondered if I wore White Shirts. Yes I have worn them off and on ever since I left home, but have only one now. It is one that opens in the back. Carryed it from Arizona, washed and ironed, put it on last night with a Shakespere Collar. One that Lizzie made for me. The Shirt is one that opens in the back. When you have time Sister

---

10 Late in 1867, the Ordnance Department contracted with the Sharps Rifle Manufacturing Company to convert approximately thirty-one thousand Model 1859, 1863, and 1865 percussion carbines left over from the Civil War. They were to be chambered for the new army standard .50/70 center-fire metallic cartridge. Many cavalrymen, like Matthews, lamented the withdrawal of the Spencer repeater. However, the Sharps "improved" carbine, despite being a single-shot, had considerably greater power and range. It would be replaced by the Model 1873 Springfield carbine in 1875. See McChristian, *U.S. Army in the West*, 33, 116, 129. The "new" saddle he mentions was the same Model 1859 McClellan pattern the cavalry had been using, except that these were covered with fair (russet) leather. The Ordnance Department responded to widespread complaints about the original rawhide covering of the seat, which dried and split open in western environments. The cracked hide wore out trousers and rubbed a trooper's skin raw. The army issued experimentally one hundred recovered saddles to each regiment in 1870. See Steffen, *U.S. Military Saddles*, 81. Company L probably received the experimental saddles because it happened to be stationed virtually next door to Fort Union Arsenal.

"Wind, Wind, and Sand All the Time" 87

Lizzie, wish you would make me a couple of Shakespere Collars, long points to them, size 14 inches, or a little bit larger won't make any difference. Can take a paper one and measure by. Also some Kind of tie or beau, and send them to me in a paper. Suppose papers will come all right here. Would not ask it of you, if had any money to buy them with. But will prize them very much because they come from my dear home.

You must excuse the dirty appearance my letters present. I am using some paper I got while in the <u>Adjutants</u> Office in Fort Whipple and carrying it so far and handling it so much has made it quite dirty.

Will have to close and take this to the Post Office.

Fort Union, New Mexico
SUNDAY, JUNE 12, 1870

Have just finished devouring a <u>Suptuouse</u> [sumptuous] repast composed of <u>tough</u> roast Beef and burnt beans. Have nothing to do this evening, but write home. We have been here now nearly one month and no letter from home, yet, except those that were directed to Fort Whipple. I have most come to the conclusion that it takes a much longer time for a letter to go inside than what I had supposed. Every evening I ask the Adjutants Clerk, a young man of our company, if there are any letters for me, and invariably meet with the same answer, "No." But I will not despair. Know it is no fault of yours. They will come after while.

I am out of the Cook House. My twenty days were up Friday evening. Quite a large <u>Boil</u> made its appearance on my left cheek. It was not very painful, but felt very unpleasant. Went on the Sick report yesterday morning. Was excused from duty and marked [for] Quarters.[11] The Dr. gave me some kind of linament to put on my face. Helped to take away conciderable of the swelling. Was excused again this morning.

I hear that an act has passed Congress for the reduction of the Army to thirty thousand men.[12] Oh how I wish they would discharge

---

11 Being "marked for quarters" meant that a soldier had an affliction serious enough for him to be excused from duty and temporarily confined to his barracks.
12 He refers to the act of July 15, 1870. During the previous year, the army had been consolidated from forty-five to twenty-five regiments of infantry, while maintaining ten of cavalry, and five of artillery. The 1870 measure called for the army to be further reduced from about thirty-two thousand enlisted men to thirty thousand by decreasing the authorized strength of companies. See Heitman, *Historical Register*, vol. 2, 610–11.

the 8th Cavalry. But there is little prospect of them doing anything of the kind.

Two prisoners under charge of the poor Sergt. escaped Friday. They slipped their shackles over their feet and made good their escape so far. All our horses were out on Herd and before any person could drive the herd in, the prisoner's had got across the plain and into the mountains.

With this will send you a pattern for a Collar, which I would like for you to make and send to me in a paper, it is just the size. I was going to send you a pattern for collar, but made such a miserable one, concluded would not send it. You can get a No. 14 Shakespere and make them for me.

Excuse this little scratch of a letter, have no news to write you. Expect will hear from you next week.

Fort Union, New Mexico
JUNE 15, 1870

Just came off Guard this morning, and have nothing to do till this evening, so will write you a few lines although wrote a short note Sunday. No letter yet from home. Oh how anxious I am to hear from you and know you are all well. Don't know why I do not receive a letter from you, for know you have written to me long ere this.

Well I have bought a revolver for twenty dollars, that will save thirty for me. I saw a discharged Soldier offering it for Sale, and finally got the money from one of our Sergeants and bought it. Have turned it in now to the 1st Sergt. so will be in no danger of loosing another one. The loss of $20.00 is conciderable to me, but still I congratulate myself on saving $30.00.

No Pay Master has yet made his appearances around this locality. Would like very much to see one, and get some money once. Suppose [we] will not be payed till last of this or first of next month.

A Garrison Court Martial was held here last week tryed seven Soldiers and four Non-Commissioned Officers. Our 1st Sergt. and one Corporal of our Company was tryed. Charges against the 1st Sergt was using disrespectful language to Lt. Carrick, the Sergt. pled not guilty to the charges, and the Court found him not guilty, and restored him to duty. The Corpl. was charged with absence with out leave while on the Sick Report. He pled guilty and the Court found him guilty, and therefore reduced him to the ranks. But from the testimony of Lt. Wells, he giving him such a good character, his sentence was remitted, and he [was] restored to duty. One Sergt. belonging to F Co. was reduced, and another one fined $10.00 for being drunk.

If these officers would only Court Martial themselves for being drunk, it would consume all their time sitting on each others cases. A more drunken set I never saw. The more I see of their drunkeness the more I become disgusted with liquor and stronger my resolutions are to abstain from using it.

About two hundred men laborers, and Mechanicks are employed at the United States Depot at this Post. For some cause about fifty or seventy five are to be discharged today. Don't know what they will do, there is nothing else around here for them to do. And don't suppose a third of them will have money enough to take them to the Rail Road. A Soldiers life at the most is a very rough one, but is much preferable to me in this [territory?], or Arizona. Those employed by the Government do very well, as long as they can Keep their situation, but when they loose that, they have it very rough.

The weather has been very fine here lately, occasionally a wind and sand storm passes by sufficiently strong to un roof a house, but that is concidered nothing here. Most every person wears a pair of Goggels to protect their eye's from the sand.

Well I can write no more as I have nothing to write about. If I don't get a letter soon will give up to dispair.

Fort Union, New Mexico
JUNE 17, 1870

The young Ladies & Gents of Westminster must be more than loving, from discription. And there seems to be any am't [amount] of births. Must be trying to fill the Scriptures. I though[t] all those fine Churches would do some good in W[estminster]. Lizzie said after telling me of all the Births and forced marriages, says she does not know if such subjects are interesting to me. Of course they are. Anything from home is read with pleasure, even if it is an account of such a pretty young Girl like

Allie Walker, having a <u>child</u> five months after marriage. The workings of <u>providence</u> is <u>strange</u>.

Well I hardly know what to write. Nothing new going on, plenty of Guard duty. Am on Guard every other day, & night. Stand Post 2 hours and have 4 off. There is twenty nine general prisoners in the guard house, most all for desertion.

Has Jennie Z____ got home yet[?] She has written me two or three very nice letters. She is a very good correspondent.

Fort Union, New Mexico
JUNE 22, 1870

I am sitting in the Guard Room and will try to pass an hour away writing to you.

I came off Guard last Sunday, and was sent to report to Major Wilson, "Indian Agent here" for Orderly, to go with him to the Indian Reservation, fifty-four miles from here.[13] Went with him in his Buggy drawn by a pair of fine fast mules. Had a delightful trip. He is the only Gentlemanly Officer I ever met since [I] enlisted. Was just as familliar as if he had known me all his life. Would help to hitch and unhitch the mules, and in fact he helped to do every thing that had to be done. Lived splendid on the trip.

Went <u>trout</u> fishing Monday evening. The Major caught twenty three in a short time. I had the misfortune to loose my hook the first thing, had to content myself reading a paper while the Major fished. I would love dearly to have a week to myself to go fishing in that stream, they were splendid trout. First I saw since left Old Oakland. We went down to ishue rations to the <u>Apatche</u> and <u>Ute</u> Indians, there was about five hundred of them. They had just come in from the Plains, where they had been hunting buffalo. Returned to Camp yesterday, tuesday evening.

---

13 William P. Wilson had served with the Pennsylvania Volunteers during the Civil War, being brevetted twice for gallantry. After the war, he was commissioned in the regular Twenty-First Infantry, but the 1869 army reorganization left him without an assignment. In the interim, he was placed in charge of overseeing the distribution of rations at the Ute and Jicarilla Apache agency at Cimarron, New Mexico. Because the quarters there were inadequate for his family, Captain Wilson requested and received permission to reside at Fort Union. See Heitman, *Historical Register*, vol. 1, 1049; and Oliva, *Fort Union and the Frontier Army*, 511.

General Gregg with Major Manakin and Lt. Wheeler, the Q.M....[14]

[line missing]

... that McKellip arrived here last week know. He is a fine looking man, and is Officer of the day today. Gregg is in Command now, and from all accounts is a very fine man to soldier under. He is about seven feet tall.

It will not be very long now till pay day. I understand the Pay—Master generally gets here about the 4th of the month.

I have had a suit of cloths altered by our Company tailor, to wear on Inspection and Guard Mount. I am going to inquire of the Express Agent here what the Expressage would be on a small box sent from Balto. And if it is not to much, after I send my money home, I want several articles. Could get them here, but they would be inferior quality. First I want a fine pair of Boots or Gaiters. Yingling & John's made to wear only on the occasiones mentioned above. Next want two or three shirts, and several other things, which [I] would appreciate more because they come from home. And Lizzie, if the expressage is not to much, I will take you at your word and let you make the promised Slippers. They would be very acceptable to wear in the Quarters.

Received long letter from Thompson last night, was surprised to hear from him. Wrote me a real nice letter. I have no less than eight correspondence [correspondents] in Westminster, find it somewhat difficult to find subjects to write on. Cannot write the same in two of them, for know they show each other my letters.

Have just inquired what the expressage would be on a small box and find it will cost much more than I supposed. The Agt. says it will cost seven or eight dollars. So will have to dispense with the pleasure of a box from home.

---

14 Both of these men were members of Gregg's headquarters staff. First Lieutenant (bvt. major) John H. Mahnken served through the Civil War, initially as an enlisted man and later as an officer with the Sixth New York Volunteer Cavalry. He was mustered out in 1866 and was appointed to the Eighth Cavalry the following year. Mahnken served as the regimental adjutant from 1868 to 1878, when he was promoted to captain. He earned brevets to captain and major for his conduct in the Battles of Cedar Creek and Five Forks, respectively, during the war. He died in service in 1881. See Heitman, *Historical Register*, vol. 1, 684. Mortimer M. Wheeler had a varied military career, beginning with his commission as a second lieutenant in the Fifth Iowa Cavalry in 1861. As a captain, he resigned from the army in 1863 to serve as an ensign in the U.S. Navy from 1864 to 1867. After the war, he was appointed as a second lieutenant in the Eighth Cavalry. In 1869 and 1870 he was the regimental commissary of subsistence before he was honorably discharged at his own request in October. See ibid., 1024.

Fort Union, New Mexico
JUNE 27, 1870

Received two papers this morning. Harpers and Mercury.

Friday evening I was detailed with two of my company to go to Los Vegas distance 29 miles, after three Government horses, that were stolen sometime ago by deserters. Left here Saturday morning, went there in little over four hours. Hung around town till Sunday morning, when [we] got the horses and returned to Camp. Los Vegas has about two thousand inhabitants, principally all Mexicans. Some Jews and Americans. There are some very fine Stores there. It is a kind of supply depot, for Country Merchants. They can buy what they want there cheaper than [they] could have it brought from St. Louis.

There is quite a large Sale here today, selling off two or three hundred mules, wagons etc. Some very nice Stock among them.

The Indians are getting troublesome in this Territory. The troops at most every post except this are out Scouting. Would not be surprised if we were sent out soon. I would not mind taking a little turn over the Mountains and plains. It is so miserable dull here, that a trip for a month would liven us up a little. In Arizona we got too much of that Kind of work but here, we never mount our horses except when [we] get a Mounted pass. That is very seldom, and I believe that is done away with since Genl. Gregg arrived here. He is Lt. Col. of our Regt. and Bvt. Brig Gen'l.

Our Band have an invitation to go to Los Vegas on the 4th of July, they are going to have some kind of a Parade there. Guess the Band will go, prospects for any excitement here on that day look dull.

Will have to stop writing for want of something to write about. These letters are not so long as those written while in Arizona. There I was continually on the go, and there was always something new. Did I ever tell you about getting several pieces of Petrified tree, and some Lava on the march from A[rizona] here. Am going to keep them till [I] come home. Will try to write you a better letter next time.

[The following letter fragment appears to have been written by Matthews on approximately July 1, 1870.]

... Bridle, and Arms. His sentence came here [a] few evenings ago, and was read at Retreat. It was two years at hard labor, wearing a twelve lb.

ball, with a chain four feet long attached to the left leg, to be dishonorably discharged from the service and branded on the left hip with the letter D one and a half inches long. Hard sentence aint it[?]

He was at once put in the Guard house and the ball and chain put on him. I have since learned he is back clerking in the Q. M. office. Don't know if he is on parole or not, one thing the ball and chain cannot be taken off. He is quite an intelligent young man and at one time was first Sergt. of his company.

Corpl. Mitchell of our Company who was Court Martialed and acquitted few weeks ago, is again under arrest, and this time will be reduced. He was out on Herd and left it and went to <u>Looma</u>, a Mexican town seven miles from here. The private that was on Herd with him came in and reported him to the Captain. Mitchell did not come back till away in the evening long after the herd had been drove in. Was at once put under close arrest. This is the second time he has done the same thing since we came here, he will be tryed for both times soon. Nothing will save him this time, and he will not get off only with being reduced to the ranks. Will get imprisoned undoubtedly. I was told he intends to <u>desert</u> after pay day, which will be in a few days.

The bill for the reduction of the Army to thirty thousand, which has been passed will make a big change in the Army. It has reduced the Clothing allowance conciderably, price of clothing also, Non-Commissioned Officers, and after 1871, monthly pay.

A company of Cavalry use to be allowed 8 Sergt's. & 8 Corporals. We had seven Sergts. and four Corpls. Two Sergts. will have to be discharged or transfered to some other Company and one Corpl. will have to be made after Mitchell is reduced. They cannot reduce the Sergts. There would have been 1 Sergt to be made and five Corpl., now there will only be one Corpl., who will that be [I] would like to know.[15]

The 4th of July will soon be here, and from all appearances will be a dull one at this Post. There will be a National Salute of 37 Guns fired

---

15 Matthews was under the mistaken impression that the number of sergeants would be reduced. The organization table of March 3, 1869, authorized each cavalry company one first sergeant, one quartermaster sergeant, five duty sergeants, and eight corporals. Thus, prior to the order, his company had the allowable maximum of seven sergeants, but only half the number of corporals. The only change made in 1870 was a reduction in the number of corporals to four. See Heitman, *Historical Register*, vol. 2, 608–11.

here. Have been drilling men today that are to fire the salute, they are men that have been in the Service "<u>Artilery</u>" before.[16]

It has been raining here off and on for the last two weeks, every day more or less rain. Just what is wanted in this country. Will write again in day or two, by that time the Pay Master will be here. He left Fort Bascom, one hundred and some miles from here, yesterday morning, for here.

Lizzie, please make longer points on those collars you are making for me than those paper one's you sent me, and oblige.

Fort Union, New Mexico
JULY 10, 1870

I have received no letter from home for nearly two weeks. What is the reason[?] For the last two or three days no mail has come to this Post from the East. Mail comes daily from Santa Fe. We were payed off yesterday. Enclosed find 20.00. Not much I know, but after paying for my revolver, laundress, taylor, and several others found myself run pretty short. Am most ashamed to send so small an amount, but have only kept 5.00 myself to have some pictures taken. Will have them taken this week.

Nothing new at the Post except conciderable drunkeness among the Soldiers. One Company of Infantry came here today, and will remain till the other two Co. of Cavalry get here. F Co. of our Regt. that was here with us left day before yesterday for Fort Bascom, one hundred miles from here. The Indians have been committing depredations down there lately. They scalped one Mexican Woman and left her, but she came to and walked about two miles with the top of her head cut off. She is still living and doing well under the circumstances.

I will have to close and take this down to the Post Office in order to send it this evening. Excuse hast[e] will write again in a day or two.

---

16 All military posts had at least one piece of artillery for firing the traditional morning and evening guns and any special salutes, such as on Independence Day and Washington's Birthday. Because the five artillery regiments were distributed principally along the seacoasts, infantry and cavalry soldiers had to be trained to properly fire the guns. Sometimes, as Matthews points out, former artillerymen could be found serving in these other branches and were pressed into service.

Fort Union, New Mexico
JULY 24, 1870

It seems most an age since I wrote to you, but it was no fault of mine. Was sent out with five of my Company ten days ago after three mule thieves and six mules. The first hundred & 25 miles we made in 29 hours. That was not very bad going was it[?] For sixty hours we only had two meals. We were out ten days and travelled four hundred and twelve miles. Succeeded in getting two out of the six mules. We came on the thieves about dark in a deep Canon. Soon as they saw us coming they fired on us, but done no damage. Of course we returned the compliment and as we had two men to their one, we made it most to oh hot for them. They retreated, but kept up a continual firing at us. We followed them at a distance of course we were not going to run much danger. They droped two mules, but kept on with the other four. We picked up the two and went into Camp in the Cannon. In the morning we started back to Camp. We were out of rations and could follow them no farther.[17]

Got back here last night feeling rather tired, found one letter here for me. I have only received two or three papers since [I] came here. It is hardly worth while for you to send me papers as they never come to hand.

H Co of our Regt arrived here about one week ago, the duty is not so heavy now.

I got my pictures when [I] came in yesterday, and think they are very good. My suspender shows to good advantage. I did not notice it was so conspicuous, or would have put it out of sight. Enclosed find two for yourselves. I have one each for Mrs. Roop, Mrs. Gorsuch, Mrs. Dunegan, Jennie Zepp, Lec Payne, Mollie Birkett, Clara Wampler, J. W. Perkins, and Thompson, the Butcher. When I send all of those around I will be pretty well represented around Home.

Thompson and Jennie Zepp's letters and Photographs came to hand the day we went after the horse thieves. Did not get time to read them till [I] got many miles on the road.

Did you get the $20.00 I sent you[?] Hope it arrived all right.

I bought myself a very fine pair of Gaiters, fit me splendid and are

---

17 No mention of this event was found in the Regimental Returns.

only No. 5. Foot is getting smaller instead of larger. I am 5 feet 9 inches high and weigh 144, not bad is it[?]

While we were after the thieves, we went down to Fort Sumner. The Fort has been abandoned, but is the prettyest Post in the Territory. The Navaho Indians use to be on a Reservation down there. They left it some time ago, and went to Fort Wingate.

I will close now, as [I] have nothing more to tell you. Will only send one Photo in this. Will send one each for Mrs. R, G & D in letters to you. Excuse writting, pen is miserable.

Fort Union, New Mexico

JULY 30, 1870

Fathers kind letter of the 21st inst. came to hand few minutes ago. Acknowledging the late arrival of the little money I sent you. It seems so strange I receive so very few letters lately. I am sure you write often to me. I have not been receiving letters as often as [I] did in Arizona, when the mail only come once a week.

I was "Orderly" for Genl. Gregg, Commander of the Post, yesterday. Have been taking "Orderly" every time I Mount Guard lately. Would just as soon stand my Post, only it looks a little better to take Orderly, and you have all night in Bed. Where if you stand Guard you are on duty 2 hours and 4. off, but have to sleep with your cloth[e]s and belts on. If you should take your belt[s] off and the Officer of the day catches you with them off away to the Guard House you go.

Some talk of a Scouting party going out soon, don't know if it is true or not. The Indians are getting very bold lately in this Territory. Would not object to a little chaise after them.

So Mollie and Ida are coming up. Guess they are in W[estminster] long ere this reaches you. One year ago I was home when Mollie was in our little town. Today see where I am at. I have a picture for Mollie. Tell her if she writes for it she shall have it. I think if it is not worth writing after, it is hardly worth having. And as I wrote once to her and did not receive any answer, cannot write again. Enclosed find picture which you can keep or give to either Mrs. Roop or Gorsuch. I had one dozen taken and have them all promised. What do you think of them[?] Are they good or not[?] Sent one to "Lec."

Now [you] have a boarder have you[?] What does she do[?] Is she young[?] Tell me all about her. Would like ever so much to be at home, am tired of Soldiering and Soldiers life. Well one fifth of my time is very near in.

I can find nothing of interest to write you, this is not like Arizona where I could alway's find an item to write, but here it is the same old routine, every day.

Tell the children to write to me. They have stoped writing. I hope my absence is not making them forget me. Write often to me for your letters make me feel better all the time, even though some of them may be short. You may say sometime, "Well I will not write to Eddie, because I have nothing new to tell him." I want you to write if you only say you are all well, that is a great consolation to me to know you are all enjoying such good health. Please send me a few postage stamps. Am out. Remember me to those that inquire after me. Love and a Kiss for you all. <u>Mollie</u> and <u>Ida</u> included, for if I was there they both should have one though it would make <u>Ida</u> blush. "If it use to make her blush when I Kissed her," what would it do now, when this <u>Mustache</u> of mine would come in contact with that pretty little mouth of <u>hers</u>[?]

Fort Union, New Mexico
AUGUST 5, 1870

Father's kind letter of July 27th came to hand this morning. Don't know what I should do lately "in fact ever since I came to this Post" for <u>news</u> from <u>home</u> were it not for <u>Father</u>, He is the only <u>member</u> of the family that I receive letters from now. Of course I am as glad to hear from my <u>Honored Father</u>, as any member of the family. But [I] think some of you young folks could find time to drop me a line once in a while. I am shure you can find more to write about than I can, for it is the same old routine every day here. Am glad to hear that you are all well, and business is improving. May it alway's continue to do so.

I am getting two nights in bed this time, first two successive nights that [I] have had <u>in</u>, for some time. First [I] have had since [I] came back from Fort Sumner, when [I] was after the Mule thieves.

We had a Variety Theatre performance here few nights ago. Given by members of H & L Company's. Done very well, they took in about one hundred dollars, not so bad was it[?] They are going to have a performance once a week. Don't think I shall go soon again.

Sympathy for either side viz <u>France</u> or Prussha, among Soldiers is not very great. All say it is no money in their pockets or will they loose any Relations on either side. For myself I, like Father, are for P[russia].[18]

Enclosed find another picture for Mrs. R. or G. Have you received those two I sent you some time ago[?] I want Fathers and Mothers pictures, then I will have all of the family's. Can't you have them taken and send them to me. What do you think of mine, are they any thing like what your imagination pictures me[?] If you put your hand over the picture and leave nothing show but the <u>bust</u>, it looks much better, I think.

Oh how I would like to be home to go Berrying with you. We have none here, except Rasberries. Some of those are brought in Camp by the Mexican's. Sell for 20 cents fet. Some little Apples size of a Plum, and Peaches same size are brought in every day. We trade old cloth[e]s for them some times, at least whenever we have any.

Lizzie, can't you make me some Kind of a <u>tie</u> or beau, <u>latest agony</u>, and send me[?] Can not get anything pretty here. Nothing but old fashioned things for sale in the Stores. No doubt you think I want a great many thing's from home. Well I do for everything from home is appreciated more if they come from home. Nothing else to write about.

Guard Room, Fort Union, New Mexico
AUGUST 10, 1870

Fathers letter with recommendation from self and Col. McKellip, came to hand this morning.[19] The recommendations are splendid. Much better than I am deserving of. But should they do me some good, which they certainly should do, I will do my utmost to proove worthy of the confidence placed in me. And never give Col. cause to

---

18 This is a reference to the Franco-Prussian War of 1870–1871. It resulted in a decided victory for Prussia, making possible the unification of Germany under King Wilhelm I and the downfall of France's Napoleon III.

19 William A. McKellip, a Matthews family friend, practiced law in Westminster, Maryland. He was a thirty-five-year-old veteran of the Civil War at this time, having served as an officer in the Sixth Maryland Volunteer Infantry. He was mustered out as a lieutenant colonel late in 1863. See *U.S. Civil War Soldier Records and Profiles*, Ancestry.com; and *1870 U.S. Federal Census*, Ancestry.com.

regret the Kindness done to a wanderer away from home and friends. Even should his letter prove no advantage to me, my gratitude will be equally as great, for his endeavors to procure for me, something better than the general routine of a private Soldiers life. If Lt. Wheeler cannot do anything for me him self, perhaps he would show the Cols. letter to Capt. Hobart, or some of the other Officers. And some of them do something for me. I will deliver the letter to him in the morning, soon as [I] come off of Guard. And will let you Know with what success in a few day's.

Lizzie's letter, paper and two Collars was received day or two ago, but sorry to say the Collars are too small, by two sizes. They are so small that I cannot button them over a thin shirt let alone one of Uncle Sams regulation one's with the Collar cut off. Lizzie says she will make me a couple more, please make them larger and longer points to them.

There was quite a battle at Los Vegas some thirty miles from here night before last and yesterday, between whites and Mexicans. A dispatch was sent here to Genl. Gregg for troops to be sent down to aid the whites. The Genl. dispatched back saying, fight it out between yourselves, you commenced it, and you will have to end it. I have not heard how the fight resulted. Of course the Mexicans had the majority in number of men, but one white man can whip half dozen Greasers any time if he has any kind of a show. They are awfull cowards.[20]

Saturday night in a town six miles from here a fight was raised in a dance room.[21] Three women and two men were cut very badly. None but Mexicans were engaged in the fight. Fighting seems to be the order of the day, for my part I don't care how much they fight among themselves, for I have no more love for a Mexican than [I] have for an Indian, there is scarcely a pins choice between them. If there are any choice, the Indian [gets?] it, for he makes no pretention towards civilization. While the Greaser does, but seems to make the pretence mearly to hide his treacherous disposition. Their style of living is similar to the Indians.

---

20 "Greaser" was a derogatory term commonly applied to people of Hispanic decent. Although various theories have been advanced for the origin of the word, it may have actually derived from the Spanish word *gris*, meaning a mixture of white and black, sometimes resulting in a grayish skin tone. Hispanics of pure Spanish heritage sometimes referred to mixed bloods descended from early Spanish explorers and Aztec or Pueblo Indians as *los grisos*, i.e., those of mixed race. To the Anglo ear, this may have translated to "greaser." For a discussion of the term, see *ANJ*, Feb. 7, 1891, 410.
21 This incident undoubtedly occurred in the infamous village of Loma Parda.

And as to thieving the Mexican surpasses the noble red man.

I am sorry to hear of the disastrous defeat of the united Base Ball Club, the game seems to have been a one sided affair. May they be more successful in their next match is the wish of a lover of the splendid and healthy exercise. I noticed a few days ago the defeat of the supposed invincibles, "Red Stockings" by the "Athletics" of Phila. No doubt the Reds can get up some excuse for the defeat, like they did in the 11 ining game with the "Atlantics." I have no love for the City of Pork "bad luck to the day I set foot in the town."²²

More men enlist in Cincinnati, than any other [city] in the United States. If you once get straped in the miserable place you are bound to enlist, it is your only resort, let you be ever as willing to work, you cannot get it to do. They always have a full supply of hands, next thing you find a <u>home</u> in Uncle Sams mob.

Must close as have to go out with a prisoner to work.

Fort Union, New Mexico
AUGUST 15, 1870

I intended writing to you last Friday, But was taken with a Sick headache and had small vomitting spell, which caused me to go on the sick Report. Am feeling all O. K. this A.M., so don't get frightened, and think I am sick.

Well I gave those two letters to Lt. Wheeler, but don't think anything will come of it. He said he was out of the Q. M. Dept now and would go to his Co. soon as [he] could get his papers fixed up. Said if at anytime it was in his favor to do anything for me he would do so. And that was the end of it, and no doubt it will be the <u>end</u>. He will never think of the circumstance again. Or do I care, if such Letters as those wont do a forlorn <u>boy</u> any good I would like to know what would.

In twenty three more day's I will have my first year in. And if there is nothing better in store for me the remaining four years, than the duty of a <u>buck</u> Soldier, I hope they will give it to me the hardest they can. Even keep me fatigueing till Guard Mount, the last day of my time in this

---

22 In 1869, the Cincinnati Red Stockings, today's Cincinnati Reds, became the first regular professional baseball team in the United States. See "Baseball," *Dictionary of American History*, vol. 1, 419.

miserable outfit. Like the old Mexican [saying], a burnt Child is afraid of the fire. Same with me, when I would think in after days, of the hardships, and wages, I had gone through in day's gone by, it would make me remember the day I left my good home, to enlist in the R[egular] U[nited] S[tates] A[rmy]. If I have no good qualities or anything else, to secure for me something better than the common duty of a Soldier, I will try to make the best of a bad bargain. And do my duty like a man.

One thing I am proud to say, and that is, I have never been confined in the Guard House, or have never had one harsh word spoken directly to me by an Officer since I enlisted. I know if I had made myself liable any time I would have been sent to the Guard House very soon. But I am not afraid of Soldiering five years as a buck Soldier. Good qualities and deportment will show itself. Perhaps it will be some time, but it is shure. This may have a <u>slight</u> touch of <u>vanity</u>, I have most regretted ever giving those letters to the Lt. I have thought over it many times since, and have looked at it in this light. If I cannot rais[e] myself in the esteem of my Officers, I ought not to rais[e] at all. And if I had those letters now, [I] don't think Mr. Lt. W[heeler] would ever have the pleasure of perusing them. He will see that there is some person who is anxious for the welfare of <u>this</u> poor Soldier.

A Soldier in time of <u>Peace</u>, is not looked upon as one of the noblest <u>beings</u> of the land. Knowing then the opinion of them by Citizens. I have been trying as Col. McKellip, say's to <u>rais[e]</u> and prove myself superior to the majority of them. I think I have <u>Spouted</u> quite enough of my <u>good</u> quallities, Don't you[?]

We have a new Laundress in the Company. Her husband enlisted few weeks ago, he was raising stock in the country, and was doing very well till last fall when Indians ran away six hundred head of Cattle for him. He was going to Colorado with them, to market, was going to sell them and then take his family home to the States, But had his calculations spoilt by the noble red man.[23]

---

[23] This man was Private John L. Hawkins, age twenty-seven, who enlisted in Company L, Eighth Cavalry on July 11, 1870, at Fort Union. He gave his previous occupation as wagoner. Army regulations prohibited the enlistment of married men not already in service, so Captain Hobart must have overlooked that technicality in the interest of getting a laundress for his company. One wonders if Hawkins, a native of Fredericksburg, Virginia, might have been an ex-Confederate soldier who wound up in New Mexico after the war. Hobart obviously found Hawkins competent, if not experienced, because he promoted him to corporal within a year. Hawkins was discharged for disability on August 31, 1871. See entry 811, p. 50, roll 36, ROE, RG 94, NA.

They have been very kind to me, have taken several meals in the house. While I was sick, made Tea and toast for me, and sent it to me. Am to take some Ice Cream with them soon as [I] finish this, they are both young and have two children. They have just sent after me again to come and partake of some Ice Cream. As I have not tasted any since [I] left the States, will have to go. "Of course have no <u>taste</u> for Ice Cream." <u>Don't I write awfull since they mentioned Ice Cream to me</u>[?] Told them [I] would come soon as [I] finished this.

Fort Union, New Mexico
AUGUST 23, 1870

Fathers letter came to hand yesterday. Was ever so glad to receive it, had not heard from you for more than a week previous to yesterday. Lizzie's letter with the stamps failed to make its appearance yet, though [I] hope it may come yet. Am so very glad to know you are all enjoying such good health, and that business continues so good. May it exceed any expectations you may have, is the earnest wish of Eddie.

Am glad you think, my picture good. How many have you received[?] I sent three home hope you rec[eived] all of them.

About one dozen <u>Ute</u> Indians came into Camp yesterday, and had a big pow wow with the Indian Agent and General Gregg. Supposition among Citizens and Soldiers is that they will go on the war path soon, if they have not already done so.

Heavy arguments among the Soldiers about how the [Franco-Prussian] war will end. Prussia though has the most sympathisers. Those that argue the most on the subject care less which side wins, than those that are silent.

Capt. Hobart, our Captain, left here first part of last week with his wife, bound to Fort Levenworth, Kansas. His wife will go to her home in Nevada. Report says there will be an addition to the family shortly. Don't know how true it may be. The Captain will return with Recruits, and Horses. Our little Mustang Horses are to be turned in to the Q. M. and we will get the American horses, in their place. Our horses will be sent back to Arizona or to some of the out Posts of this Territory. The American horses are the best for level country, but when it comes to rough mountainous Country the Mustang are far superior. I would much sooner keep the little horse I have than run chances of getting a good little American horse.

There are a regular theatrical or Varriety Troop here composed of Soldiers. They give an entertainment once a week, have been twice. Don't think [I] will go soon again, the performance is very poor.

Ten men and a leader arrived here some time ago for the Regimental Band. We have much better music now. The ten men of our Company that composed the old Band have all been taken in the new one. Am glad to get rid of them. We will get duty men now in their place. Before they were carried on the rolls as daily duty men. We had to do the same amount of duty as though they were in the Company. When we had to cary them on the rolls, we only got every other night in Bed. Now we get two and sometimes three nights in.[24]

Must close and get ready for stable.

Fort Union, New Mexico
AUGUST 28, 1870

Lizzie's Letter of the 15th inst. written at Camp meeting received yesterday. We leave here tomorrow morning, for the "Indian Reservation" fifty four miles from here. The "Ute" and "Apache" Indians have been having a big fight among them selves. And we are going down to straighten affairs. Genl. Gregg will go in Command. He says we will try to stop the fighting by words. But should that not be forciable enough, we will try what virtue there is in our new Sharpes Improved Carbine. Each man carryies Sixty rounds of Amunition. Will remain there till M Company of our Regiment arrives there, which will be in fifteen or Twenty days. All our horses are being shod, today, though it is Sunday.

---

24 Even though regimental bands were authorized by regulations, musicians could not be specially enlisted for that purpose. With the exception of the chief musician, or band leader, bandsmen had to be drawn from the companies. The regimental commander was supposed to establish a tariff for each company, but in this instance it seems that all ten were taken from Company L. The vacancies thus created were to be filled by recruits, so long as the total strength of the regiment did not exceed the legal maximum. Matthews indicates that replacements had not been forthcoming, which consequently imposed a hardship on the remainder of the men. See *Revised Regulations*, 19.

Do not be alarmed for me. I will look out for No. 1, should we be compelled to quiet the disturbance by force.[25]

I can only write few lines now, as [I] am busy packing up, and turning in what we cannot take with us. Direct your letters here as usual. Perhaps I will write to you from the Reservation.

Would write more but have not the time. No doubt by the time we get down there every thing will be quiet. At least I hope so.

Fort Union, New Mexico
SEPTEMBER 11, 1870

Returned to this <u>Fort</u> yesterday evening, and was happy to find Maggie's long and <u>very</u> interesting letter here for me. Now little Maggie I will never take an excuse from you again for not writing to me. Any person that can write such a nice long letter as you did, can do the same anytime. And in the future if you do not write to me often, "I'll fix you when <u>I</u> come home."

I cannot find words sufficient to express my praise of Sue's picture. Suffice it to say it is perfectly beautiful and <u>grand</u>. I have showed it to every or nearly every man in the company, and all say it is a very beautiful picture, and that she favors <u>me</u> very much. One of the Corporals of the Company said when I showed it to him, "My God aint she pretty." What do you think now Lizzie, tell you what you and I are away in the back ground, since these young Matthews have begun to show their plumage. At one time I was under the impression that you and I could pass inspection in most any company, but since our big Sisters and brothers have grown up we are completely in the dark.

All I want now is my dear Mother and Father's picture's, then [I] will have the finest collection of any in this garrison. And Maggie, you have yours taken single for me, think your other does not do you justice.

---

25 The agent, Captain William P. Wilson, reported that the Indians were trading their government rations to the local populace in exchange for whiskey. Additionally, there was growing unrest among the Indians caused by the pending sale of the Maxwell Grant (there was no defined Ute-Apache reservation) to British investors, who wanted the Indians removed. See *Annual Report of the Commissioner*, 1870, 622–23. In obedience to instructions from district headquarters in Santa Fe, Gregg left Fort Union with thirty-eight men of Troop L, Eighth Cavalry, on August 29. Hospital Steward Edward B. Keller accompanied the command. The mere presence of troops must have been enough to quell the disturbance since there was no further trouble. See PR, Fort Union, NM, August 1870.

Must try and give you a little account of our scout. We left here on the 28th of last month. None of us was certain where we were bound for, but supposed we were going down on the Indian Reservation to quiet a disturbance between the Ute and Apache Indians. When we got down there found everything quiet. Stoped there one day, and resumed the march.

Next day we arrived at Red River Station, a notorious place for horse thieves.[26] We went in to Camp out of town a short distance and put a Guard on the picket line, where our horses were tired. About ten o'clock the Sentry caught a man close to the line in some high weeds, brought him in to camp and questioned him. Said he was a driver and road a herd of Cattle there, and that he had lost his way. The sentry took him up on a hill and showed him a fire where the herd of cattle were, and told him not to come back there again. In less than fifteen minutes the sentry caught the same man creeping up to the picket line. He was brought up again and could give no reason for being in Camp. The Sergt. in charge told the Sentry to take him out of camp again and if he caught him or any person else prowling around to shoot him.

He was taken out a second time, in about half an hour I woke up and heard the Sentry say, "Here you are again," and he brought the same man up to the Camp fire, questioned him again. Said he had lost his way again. Sentry said, "Come on with me. I am going to shoot you." Took him on a hill close to where I was sleeping and told him to run. The man did not do it and the Sentry fired his Revolver to the right of him. Soon as he fired the man started to run, but had not got more than four or five steps when the sentry fired the second shot, which struck him in the back, the ball passing through his body and coming out at his breast. He ran about one hundred yards and fell down close to a house, where he layed and groaned for fifteen or twenty minutes.

When Genl. Gregg, who was in charge of us, come up and inquired what the shooting was about, the Sergt. told him the Sentry had shot a citizen. The Genl. said, "Is that all[?]' [He] started to go back to the

---

26 Red River Station lay on the Mountain Branch of the Santa Fe Trail at the crossing of the upper Canadian River, which, during the Spanish and Mexican periods, was known as the Rio Colorado, or Red River. The location was approximately twelve miles south of present-day Raton. The station, also known as Clifton House, was a three-story adobe edifice that served as a home station for Barlow, Sanderson and Company, the U.S. Mail contractor. See Taylor, *First Mail West*, 148; and Riddle, *Records and Maps*, 44.

hotel, turned around and called to some of us to come with him where this man was still lying.

Went down and carried him in the house. The Hospital Steward who was with us, dressed his wounds. The fellow is doing very well, so I heard last night. Found out he was a notorious horse thief. Every body of Soldiers that ever passed through that place alway's lost some horses or mules, except us. Guess they will not bother the 8th Cavalry now quite as much as they use to the 3rd, who we relieved.

From Red River, we went to EmoryVille, that took us two more days.[27] It was there we found out for certain what we were after and where we were going. Took a rest for one day and thirty of us were detailed to take three days rations and leave next morning. The Sergt. told us we were going sixty five miles from there into Colorado Territory to what is known as the Stone Ranch, where a regular organized band of thieves stoped, under charge [of] one notorious kid Arbuckle. Said band have, "to use a Soldiers expression," felt the fear of God, "in all peaciable and law abiding Citizens," if there are any in this and Colorado Territory. A lot of stolen property, Cattle, horses, etc. was supposed to be there.

We rode all day and part of the night. Went in to Camp about 11 o'clock, with orders to be ready at the first peep of day, to go in on a charge. The Ranch was not more than five miles away. We were all ready in time and away we went as fast as our horses could carry us. Saw the Ranch and made a gallant charge with carbines drawn and loaded. Surrounded and took the Ranch without firing a shot or loosing a man, but on entering the building found it full of emptyness. Not a living thing could we see, the Bird had flown. So we had to return as empty handed as we come, had there been four or five men in the Ranch they could have made it warm for us, for the place was a perfect strong hold. The walls of the building are four feet through, solid rock. It is about fifty feet long and thirty wide. And history enough connected with it to make a very interesting dime novel. Something like Ned Buntling

---

27 Matthews refers to a place more commonly known as Emery Gap, named for Madison Emery, who settled on the Dry Cimarron River in 1862. Emery and his family raised vegetables and freighted them to Denver via a convenient canyon leading north into Colorado. Emery's Ranch developed into an isolated settlement bearing his name, as does a nearby peak. The pass is labeled on modern maps as Toll Gate Canyon and is located northeast of Folsom on Route 551 in the extreme northwest corner of Union County, New Mexico. See Julyan, *Place Names*, 123.

[Buntline] writes.[28] In my next [I] will tell you the story of it as told to me by a recruit of our Co. who has been in this country a long time.

The paper and Collars come all right. They are very pretty, little large but will do very well. Now if you send me a <u>nice</u> tie. Will promise not to bother you for some time. Am waiting with patience for the arrival of the letter with Mothers Picture.

Fort Union, New Mexico
SEPTEMBER [N.D.], 1870

Lizzie's letter with my darling Mothers picture came to hand this morning. Oh how glad I was to receive it. I think it a splendid picture, but Mother looks most too sad. Sue's picture has created quite a havock among the young men's hearts of our Company. Not less than half a dozen have fallen completely in love with it. Our Second duty Sergeant, is carried away with it. Say's he has only one year more to serve and then he is coming to Westminster to see Sue. He lives in Baltimore when he is home. He is quite a nice looking young man, about 5 ft. 10 or 11, weighs about 175, has black hair, black eye's and black <u>Moustache</u>. How is that for a description, Sue[?] Think you would like to take him for better or worse[?]

Now Father have your picture taken for me, then I will have the whole family.

In my last said [I] would give you the history of the <u>Robers Cave</u>. Will give it to you as it was told to me. Some four years ago, a Band of Robers, Commanded by a man named <u>Coe</u>, came to this place where the Stone <u>ranch</u> now stands, in Colorado Territory. They found a very large Cave in the hills, large enough to hold two thousand head of stock. They went to work and built this stone Ranch close by, and built it strong enough to resist most any person that come to drive them out. They dug a well in the house, and filled the house with provisions, so they could stand a siege in case it should be necessary.

Then they commenced business. I forgot to tell you how many men

---

28 Edward Z. C. Judson was a pulp novelist writing under the pseudonym "Ned Buntline." In his articles and popular dime novels, he sometimes seized upon real frontier characters like Buffalo Bill Cody, making them national celebrities. By 1869, Buntline was a household name throughout America. See Lamar, *New Encyclopedia*, 306.

belonged to this band. Well as far as I know they numbered one hundred and thirty one. They would go to the Ranch and run off all the horses and cattle they wanted. They would even come up here and stampede the horses and mules and run them down to their cave. Soon as they got several thousand head they would take them in the States and sell them.

Citizens were afraid to molest them. And several times the soldiers went down there and were driven back. At last the Commander of this post took eight Company's of Cavalry and went down determined to break the band up, and succeeded after six days hard fighting. In making them come out of the Stone Ranch, their well gave out, and they were nearly famished for water, and had to show themselves. Had it not been for that "no doubt they would have been there yet." On the sixth day the robbers opened the door of the Ranch and made a rush for the stream of water that run close to the ranch. Most of them was Killed or captured. Some though got away.

The Robber Chief, with his wife and child, a boy about nine years old, was among the captured. Coe was taken to St. Louis and tried, found guilty and hung. And now comes the exciting and interesting part. Mother and Son were at the Execution. After it was over and the body taken down, the Mother made the little Son stand over the body of his dead father and take an oath that he would avenge the death of his father, by killing the twelve jury men that convicted the father. The boy took the oath and up to the time of writing this has succeeded in Killing Seven of the twelve, and is not done yet. And so ends the story of the "Robbers Ranch."[29]

Some time after some persons, "I don't know who" found the cave where these robbers kept the cattle and horses, and found the dead

---

29 Although Matthews's version is embellished and somewhat confused, the story is founded in fact. Stone Ranch, the thieves' headquarters, was located on the Purgatory River approximately seventy miles below Trinidad, Colorado. This gang had been stealing stock throughout the region of southeastern Colorado, northern New Mexico, and Indian Territory. Some thefts of government animals from Fort Union were also attributed to this gang. Samuel Coe, (also known as Samuel Cole) occupied a large stone building with loopholes in the walls located on the Cimarron River near Camp Nichols, which was situated on the Dry Route of the Santa Fe Trail. Apparently, this was not Stone Ranch, as Matthews thought, but rather an unnamed hangout used by the robbers when they operated in the area. A thirty-man patrol of the Third Cavalry from Fort Union found the place in 1867 and arrested Coe, but he was later released for insufficient evidence. Troops from Fort Lyon, Colorado took over the investigation and assisted the sheriff from Trinidad in capturing a dozen members of the gang at Stone Ranch in February 1868. See Oliva, *Fort Union and the Frontier Army*, 354–55.

bodys of some fifteen hundred head of cattle, that had been shut up and left to die.

And now I have a little news to tell you which occured at Louma Padra, a Mexican town seven miles from here. There are several drinking saloons and two dance halls in the town and plenty of Mexican Women in the town to dance. The third Cavalry had two or three men Killed over there by Mexicans. Few nights ago a couple of Mexicans beat a Bugler of D Company. He came over to Camp and reported it to the men.

After Tattoo, about forty Soldiers out of the three companys here, went over to Louma, all armed with Revolvers, with the intention of taking the two Mexicans that whiped the bugler out and hanging them. When they got over there they could not find the men at first. In going down a street they saw a number of mexicans in a house, and in goes some of the boys and found it was a "Wake," a small child was dead.

In this house they found the two Mexicans. They were taken out and marched off in the direction of this Post. The Sheriff interfered and drew his Revolver. A couple of the boys caught him and took his revolver away and marched him off with the other two men. They took them to the reservation Post, and held a consultation. Some were in for hanging them while others wanted to whip them.[30] The latter was agreed upon. One of the boys made a small speach to the three Mexican[s.] He said, "We did intend to hang you, but as this is your first offence, at least the first time any of you have ever injured one of the 8th Cay., we will let you off giving each of you fifty lashes on the naked skin with our belts." They then striped them and gave each fifty lashes with their waist belts. The belts have a large brass buckle on, and every stroke would raise the flesh, they even give the Sheriff, who is a mexican also, fifty lashes for interfering. After it was over the boys told them, that if any man of the 8th Cavalry was ever touched again by any of them, they would come over and hang every Mexican in the town. I don't think there is any danger of any of the boys being hurt again in that town. They only gave them a little foretaste of what they need expect if anything of the Kind occured again.

The Officers saw the men going over, and about 10 o'clock they all went around to their Companys and had a check Roll Call. In that way

---

30 By "reservation post," Matthews means a marker designating the boundary of the Fort Union Military Reservation. Loma Parda was situated just beyond the southern perimeter of the fifty-one-and-a-half square-mile tract, and was therefore outside military jurisdiction. See ibid., 347–48.

they could find who was out of Camp. Next morning all those that had been to Louma were put in the Guard House, but were let out again during the day. Four Sergeants are under arrest for being over there. I was not in that party, but have always said if even one of our company should get Killed or injured over there or by any of the Mexicans, I would be one to go and clean the town out, for I have very little more love for a Mexican than [I] have for an Indian. Can see but little difference between them.

The paper with the handkerchief has not come to hand yet. The letter with ten Stamps come safely [a] few days ago.

I am in the Cook house again, not exactly in the cook house, but in the dining room, have to take care of the queens now.

Have only, "to use a Soldiers expression," got 3 years and a <u>but</u> to serve, more, though the <u>but</u> is nearly as large as the year.

Fort Union, New Mexico
SEPTEMBER 27, 1870

I feel as though I ought to write to you this evening, but what to write I'm shure [I] don't know, except our Company leaves here in a day or two for "Cimmerrone," the Indian Reservation, to remain one month.[31] My opinion though is, if they once get us down there we will not see Fort Union again very soon. If we have to remain there any time, we will have to build quarters for ourselves and stables for the horses. The buildings there now are in bad condition. And nothing would please old Capt Hobart more than to see the whole Company hard at work.

I understand the Citizens of Arizona have sent a petition to Congress, begging them to send or have the 8th Cavalry sent back to the Territory. They complain of the Indians being very bad, and 3rd Cavalry that relieved us [would?] do but very little with them. It would make but little difference to me if we were sent back, for I am getting sick of this miserable country. Guess you think I would get sick of any country, from the way I write. To tell the truth I am heartily sick of frontier life, and long for the day to come when I can set my foot in Civilization a free man.

---

31 Company L left Fort Union on September 30, 1870, to take station at Maxwell's Ranch near Cimarron. See Eighth Cavalry Returns, September 1870.

I can think of nothing else to tell you. Where we are going is only 54 miles from here. You can direct to me at this place till I see how long we are going to remain down there. Have not received letter from home for sometime. I am herding horses now, and have been this week. Not much to do except sit down on the grass and read, and now and then ride around the horses to keep them togeather.[32]

Camp near Cimarron, New Mexico
OCTOBER 4, 1870

Sues splendid letter was received few days ago. It will soon be drill call. So [I] will have only [a] few minutes to write to you, but guess [I] can write all that [I] have to say in those few minutes.

A lot of Recruits came to this place yesterday on their way to Fort Union. Last night one of them died.[33] No doubt from starvation. They left here this morning, leaving him here for us to bury. A party have been detailed out of our Company to bury him this evening. It don't sound very well for a Regular U. S. Soldier to die of starvation in a country where there are plenty, but it is actually the truth. Have seen more than one instance of the kind, when I was coming to my company on the Steamer Continental. When we were so hungrey and sick, in fact we were sick with hunger, we had to stand by and see our rations sold and carried away, and were not allowed to say one word. Little idea you at home have of the manner in which this disorganized mob, "for it is nothing more," is carryed on.

We have moved nearer the little town of Cimmerrone, than where first went into camp. We are now quartered in log houses, built by the 3rd Cavalry. They are much better than tents. We have had some few cold days since [we] have been out. Still have to drill twice a day.

Don't know of anything else to write, except that the "Saturday Night" with neck tie was received.[34] Accept my thanks for them. Sue

---

32 Matthews indicates that he was on herd guard. Cavalry horses not in use were taken outside the post to pasture on a daily basis when grass was available. Several soldiers from each troop were assigned to accompany the horses belonging to their unit to ensure their safety and to bring them back to the post at the designated hour.
33 Cimarron was located directly north of Fort Union on the Mountain Branch of the Santa Fe Trail. This party of recruits probably came from St. Louis, via Fort Leavenworth, Kansas.
34 A "Saturday night" is probably slang for a dress shirt.

ask Jennie if she received the letter I wrote to her after coming off that last trip, the time we went to the "Stone Ranch." Have not heard from her since then.

Excuse this writing, this pencil and old box that I am writing on are awful.

Camp near Cimarron, New Mexico
OCTOBER 5, 1870

Have not received a letter from home now for two weeks, seems most an age. We left Fort Union Sept 30th. The Ute's and few of the Apatche Indians on the Reservation at this place have been making some demonstrations of a general outbreaking carrater [character]. So much so that the citizens of this place applyed to Genl. Gregg for a company of Soldiers. And of course as we were the junior company, [we] had to go. We are a Senior company but have a junior captain.[35]

The English Company that bought the Spanish Grant from Maxwell, some sixty square miles for one million, three hundred and fifty thousand dollars have taken possession of the place, and have commenced to build a town. They intend to make a small colony of it, work the Silver mines and raise stock on a large scale. No end to the Johnny Bulls driving around in buggys drawn by a couple of fast nag's. The Indians don't like the Johnny's very well, they know soon as the English move here they will have to "Vamose," [*vamos*] leave the place.[36]

---

35 Duties and marching orders were frequently assigned according to the company commander's rank and seniority, based on the date of his commission.
36 After the former fur trapper Lucian B. Maxwell married Luz Beaubien in Taos, New Mexico in 1844, he and his new bride purchased half of the Beaubien-Miranda Land Grant. This enormous tract, extending from the present-day town of Springer into southern Colorado, had been given to Carlos Beaubien and Guadalupe Miranda by the Mexican government. Following Beaubien's death in 1864, Maxwell acquired title to the entire two-million-acre grant, making him the largest single landowner in the United States. Gold was discovered in the western part of the grant in 1867, prompting a flood of prospectors to invade the Maxwell estate. The community of Elizabethtown sprang up overnight. Faced with the overwhelming job of managing such acreage, Maxwell sold the property, as Matthews states, to foreign investors for $1.35 million. Thus the Maxwell Land Grant and Railway Co. was formed. Matthews correctly predicted that there would be conflicts with the Indians, since the Ute-Jicarilla Apache homeland lay at least partially within the grant. The new English owners lacked sympathy for American Indians, as well as the Hispanic people who had inhabited the area for centuries, and immediately tried to dispossess them of it. The Jicarillas were assigned a reservation northwest of Santa Fe and the Utes were removed to Colorado. The Maxwell Co., later acquired by Dutch bankers, survived into the mid-twentieth century, after a long and tortured existence, including some bloodshed. See Lamar, *New Encyclopedia*, 685–86.

For the last three days [I] have been living principally on wild Plumbs. I never saw such splendid or so many in my life. Some of them are as large as an egg. We have a first and second Lieutenant now both West Pointers.[37] Drill four hours each day. Mounted in the morning, dismounted in the afternoon. I like mounted drill very well, but have no taste for the dismounted.

We are living in tents, will not have to build quarters, as I at first supposed. Don't know of anything else to write about. You must excuse pencil and writing. Am lying down on my bed writing this.

Direct same as you have been to Fort Union, they will be sent down to me. There is no telling how long we will remain here.

Camp near Cimarron, New Mexico
OCTOBER 16, 1870

I wrote to you few days ago. This is Sunday, [I] have nothing else to do. So [I] will write you concerning what occured last night.

We are in Camp about 1 1/2 miles from the town of Cimmerrone. Last night the Mexicans gave what they call a Viley [*baile*], a "Dance." And as usual it broke up with a general row and fight. A number of our boys went to the dance and of course took their Revolvers with them. When the dance was about to break up a row was started. Pistols and Knifes were drawn and used. One of our boys was stabed in the back. The Knife penetrating to the shoulder blade, making a severe but not dangerous wound. One mexican was shot through the heart, and killed instantly. One of our Company was arrested on the spot, and taken by the Sherriff, "a white man," to Jail. Several Mexicans, recognized him as the man that Killed the greaser.

Two or three of the boys run up to Camp and reported the affair to

---

37 These officers were First Lieutenant Edmund Luff and Second Lieutenant Edmund M. Cobb. Luff, temporarily commanding the company in the absence of Captain Hobart, who was at Fort Lyon, Colorado, serving as a member of a general court-martial, began his military career as an enlisted man in an Illinois artillery regiment. He was commissioned in the Twelfth Illinois Cavalry in 1864, and was honorably mustered out as a captain in October 1865. About two years later, he was commissioned as a lieutenant in the Eighth Cavalry, with which he remained until he retired at the rank of captain in 1895. See Heitman, *Historical Register*, vol. 1, 646; and PR, Fort Union, NM, October 1870. Cobb was a native of Massachusetts and was appointed to the U.S. Military Academy from California in 1866. He joined the Eighth Cavalry following his graduation in June 1870. Cobb transferred to the Second Artillery the next year and remained with it until his untimely death in 1883. See Heitman, *Historical Register*, vol. 1, 312.

the Lt. in charge, stating that our boys were pined [penned] in a house, and not allowed to come out by the Mexicans. The Lt. ordered a squad of ten men to be sent down immediately with arm and ammunition, with orders to go to the house, and take the men out. If the Mexicans made any resistance, shoot every one of them. About two o'clock in the morning I was woke up, and ordered to dress, put on my arms and go with the men to rescue our misfortunate companions. The Corpl. gave me an account of the affair, while I was dressing. You may imagine how long it took me to make my toilet.

We did not take our horses but started on a trot march, "double quick," to the dance hall, and did not stop till we reached there. Got up to the house very quietly and surprised all in it. First object we saw was the dead Mexican, layed out on a board, with about forty candels burning around him and a number of men and women sitting around him. They were frightened considerably at seeing us enter with Carbines drawn and clicked [cocked?]. Some wanted to leave, but soon changed their mind when the muzzle of a carbine was stuck under their nose. The Corpl. asked for our man, and a woman that could speak English said they had all gone up to the Hotel where the Sheriff lived. We searched the house and found one Revolver, which we confiscated. All of us then went up to the Hotel and Jail which is all in one. We saw a light before we got to the house but they heard us coming and blew out the light. We went around to the window and called for the Sheriff, he answered us. We asked where our men had gone to. He said all of them had gone to Camp.

Just then Ford the man that was arrested called to us from the second story and said he was up there.[38] Most of our squad got so excited then they did not know [phrase missing]. The Corpl. demanded the prisoner. The Sheriff told him he would not give him up, said he had him in charge and would keep him untill he was tried. Said he had men and arms sufficient to protect him.

All this conversation was carried on between the walls of the house— the Sheriff and his posse inside, the Corpl. with his squad outside. We

---

38 William Ford enlisted in Company L, Eighth Cavalry, at Fort Union on July 23, 1870. He had previously been employed as a teamster. He was likely one of the employees Matthews mentioned in his June 15 letter as having been laid off from the quartermaster depot. Ford was a twenty-three-year-old native of Philadelphia. After the shooting incident at Cimarron, he deserted with the help of his comrades on October 16, and was never apprehended. See entry 432, p. 293, roll 36, ROE, RG 94, NA; and Eighth Cavalry Returns, October 1870.

held a consultation among ourselves. Some were in for making a rush, break open the doors, shoot everything before us, till we reached the prisoner. Others were in for setting fire to the house and burning them out. The Corpl. seemed to be in favor of that, then some other suggested to go to Camp and get more reinforcements. The Gentleman that suggested that was off about fifty yards behind a fence, and had to call out at the top of his voice, so as to be heard. He was a recruit that had just come to the company, and was looking out for No. One.

After all the rest got through talking I commenced, and told them my idea. It was this. I said, "Corporel, this man has been arrested by the Sheriff of the county. This Sheriff had to give Bonds to fulfill the duties of that office. He would by giving the prisoner up to us, forfit those bonds." Unless he made an effort to resist us, this man was in the power of the Civil law, said law rules [the] Military. And we were here to protect the Citizens and the Law, not to break it or molest the Citizens. And if we undertook to release that man we would make ourselves liable, and no doubt would have to suffer for it. If we broke in the house some of us would no doubt be Killed. Then I said to conclude with, we had better report the whole circumstance to the Lt., then if he wanted the man, we would take him, let the consequences be what they may. But said I, if the Corpl. in charge of the party say's bring the man out I will do my duty and help take him, let it be in any manner he wished. In less than two minutes we were on our road to camp, not one man said [remainder of letter missing]

Camp near Cimarron, New Mexico
OCTOBER 21, 1870

Here I have been twenty days and have only heard from you once. I cannot imagine why I receive so few letters from home. I am shure you have not forgotten you have a son and brother in this forlorn country. It is enough to be here when you can hear from home every week, but when it comes to one letter a month, is more than I can stand. If I can only hear regularly from you, I feel satisfyed with the lot the Almighty has given me.

There has been some very strong talk of these Indians breaking out. But I hardly think they will this week. We have had some snow and disagreeable weather, but it has cleared off again.

The young man that shot the man at the dance last Saturday night has made his escape. The Lt. brought him up to Camp Sunday to keep him till Monday morning, when he was to have a hearing. Sunday night we fixed him up as best we could. Gave him one [of] our best horses and started him off. And have not heard from him since. It was his own choice. Said if he was turned over to Civil Authority he would have to [word missing] it.

Monday morning I took the news of his escape down to the Sheriff. He did not like it very much. He came up to see the Lieutenant about it. L. told him he guessed the rest of us helped him off. Ford told us he shot the Mexican but said he had to do it to save his own life. Said the Mexican was coming at him with a large Knife, when he put his revolver to his side and shot him, Killing him instantly. In fights of those Kind the man that shoots the quickest always gets off the best. If you stand with your hands in your pockets, you are shure to be shot or cut with a Knife. For my part I stay away from those places. There's plenty [of] fighting to do with Indians without going to these dances to be shot, or cut up with Knifes.

Don't know whether we will stay here longer than this month or not. Am afraid though we will, see no preparation for going in yet.

It is pretty lonesome here. Nothing to see or do, except drill twice a day. It is blowing up pretty cold, guess we will have cold weather now for some time.

Don't know how you will make out to read this. I have commenced on the wrong side of the paper, and the old lead pencil is as hard as piece of iron.

Company L was ordered back to Fort Union on October 26, but a civil disturbance resulting from a local election at Elizabethtown, a mining camp near Cimarron, delayed its return for a few days. Lieutenant Edmund M. Cobb and a detachment of twenty-one soldiers accompanied a deputy sheriff to the town to quell the situation. Matthews makes no mention of this event, therefore we may assume he was not included in the detachment. That it was a minor affair is indicated by the official records.[39]

---

39 See Orders No. 140, HQ, Fort Union, NM, Oct. 26, 1870, Orders, Fort Union, RG 393; Luff to Mahnken, Fort Union, NM, October 28, 1870, LR, Fort Union, RG 393; and Jones to Gregg, Fort Union, NM, October 29, 1870, LS, District of NM, RG 393.

Fort Union, New Mexico
NOVEMBER 4, 1870

Your anxiously looked for letter came to hand this morning. First and only one I have received for one month, during that time I have written you four. While we were at Cimmarrone, I had almost given up the idea of hearing from you again. Sometimes I would imagine some of you were sick and you would not write to me on that account, but since your letter come to hand I am satisfyed.

Although am sorry business is so awfull bad. We arrived here first of the month, and mustered for pay. Will be payed off in a few day's, and will send you some [money?].

The young men of W[estminster] seem to be turning out rather bad. Guess I am about as well off here in this God forsaken Country as [I] would be back in W[estminster]. One thing certain I am better morrally than some of my old associates. I do not indulge in intoxicating drinks. My time is so much taken up with my duty, that [I] have little to spare for other purposes.

One of the Corporels is in arrest on several charges, which no doubt will be sufficient to reduce him. In that case some of the other Non Commisioned Officers have predicted that I will take his place should he be reduced.

F troop of our regiment come in here from "Fort Bascum" [a] day or two ago. There are four Company's here now, and all of them number 90 and 95 men. We have ninty five men in our company now. According to the number of men here, duty ought to be very light this winter.

I will have to close this scribble, but will write again in a few days. The paper and Stamps come all right. Many thanks for them. Write often.

Fort Union, New Mexico
NOVEMBER 14, 1870

Lizzie's letter of Oct. 27th came to hand [a] few days ago, containing the beautiful "tie." Every person admires it, and say tell your Sister to send me one, I tell them, will tell you to send one each for the company. I told one of our fancy boy's that you had another for me, and would send it to me soon as this was soiled. He said write at once, and say this is soiled already. Accept my thanks for this one, and send the other at your leisure.

Some talk in Camp of our Company going back to Fort Wingate soon. You remember of my speaking of that place being the first post we come to in the Territory. About ten thousand Indians are there on a Reservation. They belong to the Navajo tribe, pronounced in English Navawho. Should not fancy going back there. But no doubt this is no more than Soldiers talk, just started for a little excitement.

Another poor Soldier died here yesterday of Typhoied feaver. Just lately come to this Post. He belonged to the Regimental Band.[40] Is to be buried this evening. While am writing [I] can hear the Band practicing the funeral dirge. Oh how solemn it sounds. There is nothing that makes me feel so sad, and home sick, as to hear the Band playing in front of one of their comrade's, the Dead March. All the Soldiers in the Garrison have to turn out for his funeral this evening.

The Pay Master has not made his appearance here yet though are expecting him every day. Will send you some money soon as [I] am [payed.]

Know of nothing more to write you, this time. Will write soon again.

Fort Union, New Mexico
NOVEMBER 17, 1870

Will only have few minutes to write you a few lines. We were Payed day before yesterday. Only got two months pay $28.00. Enclosed find $20.00. It is all [I] can send this time. Use it for your own comfort. Am sorry that [I] have no more to send you.

Forty of our company principally old men of the company, myself included put in one dollar each, and bought a very handsome Saddle, Bridle, and Saddle Blanket, and presented it to our Second Lieut. [Edmond M. Cobb]. He is only from West Point [a] short time, and is the finest Officer I ever saw that came from that place. He received the present and thanked us very highly for it. Will have to stop and get ready for drill.

---

40 Musician Sigmund Weier of the Eighth Cavalry band died at Fort Union on November 13, 1870. See PR, Fort Union, NM, November 1870.

Write to me at once upon the receipt of this.

Fort Union, New Mexico
NOVEMBER 25, 1870

Four very welcome and interesting letters of 14th inst. came to hand few days ago. Will try to write you [a] few lines this evening, but what to write [I] am at loss to Know. Every thing is so dull here of late.

Spent "Thanksgiving" riding around the Country after a Deserter, but failed to find him. Another party went out this morning, and brought him in.[41] Since Pay day, the Guard House has been full of drunken Soldiers. I have yet the first time to get in.

Have been troubled for three or four day's with a miserable Diarreah. "How is that for spelling[?]"

Hope the letter with the twenty dollars came to hand, directed it to Arthur, thinking it would go with less danger of being opened.

You ask if [I] want any more collars, yes, when you have time send couple same size and style of the last you sent me. Have only those two good ones.

Can think of nothing more to write, guess you think I write very short letters since [I] came to this Post, but to tell the truth it is the hardest or most difficult duty I have to find something interesting to write you. Hope next time [I] will have some news to write you.

Fort Union, New Mexico
NOVEMBER 29, 1870

I have written two short letters to you, since [I] heard from you, this makeing the third. Have you received the twenty dollars yet[?] Hope you have, for it is very little I have to send you, and when I send that, [I] want it to reach you.

A young man that came out from the States with me in 69 is here

---

41 Private Michael D. Fulkerson of Company L had just enlisted on August 5, 1870, but deserted on November 16. Fulkerson, formerly a farmer from Illinois, was twenty-three years old. See PR, Fort Union, NM, November 1870; and entry 503, p. 295, roll 36, ROE, RG 94, NA.

with me now. He went to B Co. of this Regiment. Got tired of the service and wrote to his friends in Washington to get his Discharge for him. In less than three weeks he received a letter from them, and in it an order from the Secretary of War for his Discharge. He is waiting here to get his papers cashed and then is going home. He has promised me to go to Westminster and see you. His name is John M. Hurley [Hurly].[42] Thinks he has some relations there. I know you will be glad to see him, [he] is very talkative and can give you a good account of our travells in this and Arizona Territory. Also our trip from the States to Arizona. Hope he will be good as his word, and go to see you.

We are going to turn our "Mustang" Horses in to the Quarter Master tomorrow and draw American horses. All same color, "Sorrells." F Co. are going to draw all "Blacks," and D all "Bay's."[43] H Co. are not going to have any horses. It will look nice for all the horses are to be sent to the Company's in the Southern part of this Territory.

Well don't know of anything else to write you, "Except," would like you to send me a pair of "Pulse Warmers," you know what they are.[44] I think they would be nice to have when walking post, these cold nights.

Fort Union, New Mexico

DECEMBER 10, 1870

Have just taken my saturday evenings bath. And as [I] feel somewhat refreshed, [I] concluded [I] would try and write to you. The manner in which we get a bath now reminds me of home and my little brothers. We borrow a tub from one of the Laundresses, put on a large pot of

---

42 John M. Hurly enlisted at Philadelphia on August 6, 1869, at the age of twenty-two. He was born in the Georgetown district of Washington, D.C., and worked as a printer prior to joining the army. He must have had some well-placed friends in Washington political circles because he was specially discharged at Fort Stanton, New Mexico, on November 15, 1870, under SO No. 280, AGO, 1870, as a private. Hurly was en route home when he reunited with Matthews at Fort Union. See entry 632, p. 16, roll 36, ROE, RG 94, NA.

43 The mustangs he mentions were probably horses of Spanish blood obtained locally when the regiment was in California and Arizona. Assigning horses of like color to each company was a fairly common practice in the cavalry. It not only presented a uniform appearance on parade, but the respective companies could be identified at long distances.

44 This is probably a reference to a pair of knitted mittens.

water.⁴⁵ When it is warm enough [we] put it in a tub and jump in. Wash yourself as well as you can in front, then get one of the boy's to wash your back. That done you step out of the tub and walk forth a <u>cleansed</u> man.

We were all very busy today, unusually so, cleaning up our <u>Arms</u> and belts, for tomorrows "Sunday's" inspection.⁴⁶ Our Capt. has just returned to the Company. He has been absent on a Court Martial for some time. When the Lieutenant inspected us we were not very particular how we turned out. It is quite different when the Captain is here. You have to turn out clean as a new pin.

The weather is awfull cold here now, so cold that the ice on the pond where we water our horses has frozen so hard a horse could walk across without breaking in. Suppose the officers will soon have us out cutting ice to fill the two large ice houses here. You can judge how much ice it takes, when four Company's take turns cutting two day's each. There is a splendid Lake, about five miles from here where the ice is brought from.⁴⁷

We have drawn the new horses, and I have chosen a splendid horse. Don't know whether I will get him or not, as they are not ishued out yet by the Captain. He is, "the horse I mean," just the picture of the horse Jimmy Shearren, Adjutant of the 3rd Md. use to ride.

Lizzie in her letter received few day's ago, spoke of buying a Gold watch, If you do buy it, what will you take for the silver one, If you want to sell it, name your price, and if I can stand it, will buy it next pay day.

Know of nothing else to write this time though am very glad you received the money. Father write me a good long letter soon. One of the old style you use to write me when in Arizona.

---

45 Each company was authorized four laundresses to wash the men's clothes. These were the only women officially recognized and sanctioned by the army. The rates they were allowed to charge were established and reviewed periodically by a post council of administration. Each soldier's account was settled at the pay table. See *Revised Regulations*, 24.
46 Sunday morning inspection was a long-standing tradition in the army. Each company commander inspected his men on the company parade, or inside the barracks, at his discretion. He also dictated the uniform to be worn and whether or not the men would assemble under arms. See ibid., 46.
47 This lake, or lagoon, was directly south of the post, just inside the boundary of the military reservation.

Fort Union, New Mexico
DECEMBER 11, 1870

I just wrote you a short letter last night and will write you another one tonight. Was detailed for Guard last night for today, the details are always made out the night before. Took Orderly this morning as [I] generally do.⁴⁸

But that is not what I intend writing about. The Officers were all togeather in the Adjutants Office today, and held a big "pow wow." Immediately after they left the Office the Adjutant made out a detail of five men out of each Company warning the men on the detail, something that was never known of before at this Post. The order for the detail reads, "Five sober couragious men from each Company." I am one of the five out of our Company. Was detailed when on Guard, another thing that is seldom done in the Army. We are to hold ourselves in readiness to leave at a moments notice.

Conciderable curriossity is manifested by every body to know where we are going. I have a great curriossity myself, but can't find out what it all means. We are to go well armed and with plenty of Ammunition. Some say we are going after Horse thieves, others say we are going to Santa Fe to stay there. And others say we are going as an Escort for Genl. Pope, who is expected here every day.⁴⁹ The latter I think is what we are detailed for. He is Commander of this Department. And is going arround on an inspecting tour. If we go with him will have to travel all over the Territory, and visit every post in it. If I find out anything definite before we go, I will write to you and tell you what it is.

Fort Union, New Mexico
DECEMBER 16, 1870

Father's splendid [letter] just came to hand. It is a letter which does one good to read. My only regret is he don't write often enough to me.

---

48 Matthews would have been known as an "orderly bucker." A few individuals in each company, or sometimes just one man, vied for the honor of being selected as the commanding officer's orderly by presenting an impeccable appearance in his uniform, accouterments, and arms. See Rickey, *Forty Miles*, 92.
49 Brigadier General John Pope assumed command of the Department of the Missouri, one of three geographical departments comprising the Military Division of the Missouri, headquartered at Fort Leavenworth, Kansas, on May 3, 1870. Apparently, a rumor was afloat that Pope would be conducting an inspection of the posts within his department. See Thian, *Military Geography*, 15, 77.

But when he does write, they make up for the length of time between each other.

Well I am still at this Post though expected when [I] wrote to you last Sunday, to be on the road some where, which [I] did not know, or do I know yet. Although we are still waiting orders, have been issued fifty rounds of Carbine Ammunition, and eighteen of Pistol. They must expect us to do some fighting from the manner in which they are equiping us.

Winter has set in here. It is snowing quite fast now. It will not be very pleasant to be on the road [in] this weather.

On two occasions lately when we drill the Captain has taken me out of the squad I was drilling in and gave me a Squad of men to drill myself. It is no trouble for me to drill either with Carbine or Saber. And I can explain the drill to the men much better than the majority of our Non-Commissioned Officers. That don't look bad, does it[?][50]

Have nothing else to write this time. Will write again before we leave, if find out where we are going.

Next time you write please send me [a] few postage stamps. Am entirely out, and have no money to buy any with.

Santa Fe, New Mexico
DECEMBER 31, 1870

We "the escort of 20 men" left Fort Union last friday, two days before Christmas, Guarding Six Millions of dollars, for the U. S. Bank at this place. We brought it safely in four days, distance one hundred and ten miles. No wonder the Officials at Union were so very particular about the detail of men that was to escort the money. Talk of your Rich men, none of them ever slept on a more costly bed than I have. I spread my blankets down on the boxes of money and slept as sound as [I] would were I in my bed at home.[51]

---

50 The company commander was obviously considering Matthews for promotion by giving him a chance to demonstrate his ability to instruct others in drill.
51 This detachment was guarding currency intended for the U.S. Depository in Santa Fe. Three Treasury employees, S. A. Johnson, S. S. Gregory, and C. E. Coon, accompanied the shipment, which had been escorted in relays across the country. Captain James H. Gageby and a detail of the Third Infantry had come from Fort Lyon, Colorado Territory, to Fort Union, where they were relieved by First Lieutenant Edmund Luff and his detachment. This money enabled the First National Bank of Santa Fe to commence operations shortly thereafter. See the *Daily New Mexican*, December 28, 1870; December 30, 1870; and January 3, 1871.

Enjoyed my Christmas much. Dined on raw bacon and hard tack. Mrs. Hawkins, one of our Laundresses promised to save a chicken and enough Mince meat for a couple of pies for me till I come back. She is very Kind to me. Had two invitations to take dinner Christmas had I remained in Camp, but would have took dinner with the Company, had I been there. The Company had Chickens, Turkey's, Roast Pork, "fresh" pies, plum pudding etc. all in abundance. Twas too bad that [I] had to go away two days before C—mas.

Was quite surprised to find Santa Fe the dull and miserable place it is. It is situated in a small Valley, sourrounded on all sides by high hills. It lays so very low that the great part of the town is leveled with water. The buildings are very poor with a few exceptions. They have a state house about half finished, have been working on it fifteen years; and is only half finished now.

A few good stores in town, principally owned by Jews. Very few Americans in town. There is two little printing offices in town. Two or three very nice churches. Genl. Getty, commanding this district has his Head Quarters here.[52]

Have I think given you all the particulars of Santa Fe. Guess [I] will leave here tomorrow.

---

52 George W. Getty graduated from the U.S. Military Academy in 1840 and served in the artillery during the Mexican-American War, earning a brevet to captain for gallant and meritorious service at the Battles of Contreras and Churubusco. Throughout most of the Civil War, he served as a brigadier general of volunteers. After being mustered out of the volunteer service, he was appointed colonel of the Thirty-Seventh Infantry. He commanded the Third Infantry at the time Matthews encountered him at the Santa Fe district headquarters. That same day, coincidentally, Getty was transferred back to the artillery, commanding the Third Regiment and subsequently the Fourth before retiring in 1883. See Heitman, *Historical Register*, vol. 1, 452. Districts, often of a temporary nature, were subdivisions of military departments designated for administrative or operational convenience. The District of New Mexico was headquartered at the Post at Santa Fe (formerly Fort Marcy), adjacent to the Palace of the Governors. Construction of the headquarters building commenced in August 1870 at the corner of Palace and Lincoln Avenues. The complex also included six quarters for staff officers, immediately north of the office, and the district commander's residence, situated directly behind the Palace. See the *Daily New Mexican*, August 9, 1870 and August 15, 1870; and *Outline Descriptions*, 167–68.

CHAPTER FOUR

"We Only Shot to Scare Them"

JANUARY—DECEMBER 1871

*H*aving *dined on field rations to celebrate Christmas, Matthews was only too happy to return to the comparative comforts of Fort Union and routine duty. He had clearly become a veteran soldier by this time, having mastered the art of bucking for orderly at morning guard mounting. Taking such an honor required much time and effort beforehand to ensure that his buttons and other brasses glittered, that his leather was polished until it shone, and that his uniform and person were spotless. The rewards were immediate: escaping guard duty, having an easy day as an orderly, and being able to sleep in his own bunk that night, considerations not taken lightly by common soldiers.*

By early spring, however, Eddie was back in the saddle, following the Mountain Branch of the Santa Fe Trail into Colorado in pursuit of deserters. A short time later, he would participate in a patrol to Cimarron, some fifty miles north of Fort Union, to quell a disturbance among the Indians at the Jicarilla Apache-Ute Agency. It was likely his conduct on these missions that influenced his promotion to sergeant later in the year, not long after he celebrated his twenty-first birthday.

Fort Union, New Mexico

JANUARY 6, 1871

Returned from Santa Fe on the 4th inst. Was glad to find two letters & three papers from you. Also one letter from Mr. Thompson. Please accept my thanks for the two Handkerchiefs. Am only too sorry that [I] cannot send you all some nice present in return, but am not able to do so at present. Lizzie asked if I had a pair of sleeve buttons. No [I] have not, but have three or four pair of cuffs, of home made manufacture which [I] brought from home with me. I still stick to them.

In my letter from Santa Fe, I told you Mrs. Hawkins our Laundress said she was going to save my Christmas dinner for me. Got in here the evening of the 4th, dressed and went over to her house, and made a splendid supper off of Mince Pies and Tea. Am as fond of Tea as ever but seldom get any. When [I] do get it, it is at Mrs. H. I bought her a very nice pair of shoes from S[anta] F[e], payed 3.50 for them. She was highly pleased with them.

Will tell you what a Pedestrian I am. As you are alway's praising Lizzie's walking propensities. We left Las Vegas, which is 28 miles from here, on the morning of the fourth. As the morning was rather cool, four or five of us started on foot ahead of the wagons and walked about five miles, when the wagons come up, and we all got aboard. Had rode about eight miles when a young man, one of our party, said he had lost my pipe. It was one I brought from Arizona with me and prized very highly on that account. The young man would get off the wagon and go back on the road to look for it. I knew if he got off he would never catch up to the wagons again, and would have to walk into this place. He said he was bound to find the pipe if [he] had to go back to Las Vegas after it. Off he got and was left behind. After we had gone two or three miles farther I was thinking a good deal about him having to walk all the way in by himself, and all for an old pipe of mine.

I told one of the boy's to look out for my traps, that I was going to get off and walk in with Davis. Got off the Wagon, and sit down to wait for him to come up. Waited about half hour but no Davis to be Seen, got up and walked back two or three miles but could see nothing of him, though [I] could see his foot prints in the mud. Kept on walking back till [I] got within eight miles of Las V. and no Davis to be seen. Did not know what to do. Knew he could not pass me on the road or any where near it without my seeing him, as we were on the open Prairie. Come to the conclusion he had gone back to L[as] V[egas] and would stay there till [he] got an opportunity to ride to this place. So [I] turned around and had to walk in by myself.

Got in here about 7 o'clock that night. Had walked twenty three or four miles in less than six hours. Never stoped one second to rest. Was afraid to take a rest for fear [I] would not be able to get up again. My feet were all blistered, and [I] was in fact sore all over. When [I] got here [I] found that Davis had just come in ten minutes ahead of me, He had walked back some six miles, found the pipe and had taken a near cut across the Prairie and had passed me without me seeing him. He had no idea that I had got off the wagon.

This morning Mr. Hawkins, Mrs. H.['s] husband, come in the quarters and presented me with a very handsome Mersohaum [meerschaum] pipe, which cost him twenty dollars. It took me so much by surprise that I could hardly find words to thank him for it. He said that was my New Years gift. He has often told me he thought as much of me as he did his brother. And I believe it. I don't know how it is I meet with people where ever I go that are ever so Kind to me. I can't imagine what there is about me to cause them to fall in love with me, "Unless it is my good looks." I do not think there is one man in the Company but what likes me. I try to get the good will of everbody with whom I have to associate. And I succeed beond my expectations.

Was Orderly for Genl. Gregg today. Will write soon again.

Fort Union, New Mexico
JANUARY 12, 1871

Have not heard from you for some time. By that [I] mean one or more weeks. I received the pulse warmers in your last. They are very nice and comfortable.

We had a little excitement here few evenings ago. The Corporal of the Guard went in the guard house to lock the prisoners in their cells. One of them, a pretty hard case, ran by him and out the door. Knocked down the Sentry and away he ran at full speed. Sentry got up, fired at him, but missed him. The crack of the Carbine at the Guard House attracted all the Soldiers in the Garrison. We all ran to the Guard

House, found out what the disturbance was, and gave chase after the Prisoner. The race did not last very long as the Corporal was a very fast runner and soon over halled the prisoner. He was brought back and put in irons.[1]

Yesterday we had a race, "Horse," here, which resulted in our Captain loosing three hundred dollars. He picked out a horse in the Company, which he thought was fast, and had him trained by a Jockey in the Company. Made a race with Capt. McGonnigle, and got beat, not very bad though.[2] As the other horse only came out half leangth ahead. I did not see the race, was on Patrol after absent Soldiers in Loma Padra, about seven miles from here.

Don't know of any news to tell you, Will write soon again. Write soon.

Fort Union, New Mexico
JANUARY 19, 1871

Today [I] received the papers and Collars. All were very acceptable. Please accept my thanks for them. I really don't know what I am going to fill this letter up with, for this is with out exception the poorest place in the world to find anything to write about.

Some say in Camp that one or two of the Company's here are to be sent down to Fort Bascum, some two hundred miles [sic] from here.[3] The Fort was abandoned [a] short time ago, and the two company's brought up here, that were stationed there. This morning Genl. Gregg left here for that place to inspect it. Suppose when he returns [we] will find out who goes there if any Company's are to go.

In a few days Capt. Young, and Lt. Mahnken, "the latter our Adjutant," both of our Regiment, leave here for the States. Are going in on Recruiting Service, for two years. Don't know what part of the State[s] they are going to. Oh if they would only take some of us in with

---

1 Privates John Davis, Timothy Foley, Patrick Gartten, and Michael McGrath deserted on January 9, and Thomas Murphy on the following day. Murphy may have been the prisoner apprehended. See Eighth Cavalry Returns, January 1871.
2 Captain and Assistant Quartermaster Andrew J. McGonnigle commanded the supply depot at Fort Union. See Heitman, *Historical Register*, vol. 1, 666.
3 The straight-line distance to Fort Bascom is approximately 90 miles.

them for that length of time. I would give one years pay to go in with them, for there [I] could get a few day's off some time, and slip up to Westminster to see you all. Would'nt that be glorious[?]

I was Orderly again yesterday. Have taken what the boy's call the Cup, "Orderly," every time I have mounted Guard for the last three months. That don't speak bad, when it is given to the cleanest man out of twenty one. If these two officers that are going in would only say they would take two or three of the Cleanest and best <u>looking</u> Soldiers in with them, and set a day for us all to appear before them for Inspection, [I] think I would stand [a] tolerable good chance to go in with them, but no such good luck as that will ever happen. Especially to <u>poor me</u>.

Fort Union, New Mexico
JANUARY 19, 1871

My friend Hawkins that gave me the Pipe admired my pulse warmers very much. I knew he would like to have a pair. So told him I had a <u>nice Sister</u> at <u>home</u> who would, if I <u>asked her</u> [to], <u>make a pair</u> for <u>him</u>. And now dear Sister some time when you are resting from the tiresome work of "Teaching young Ideas how to shoot" [I] want you make another pair and send them to me.[4] And I will present them to him with your compliments. He and his wife are very Kind to me. Even last night the first Sergeant and I were in their house when they gave us as much as we could eat. Some of the <u>nicest Home</u> made bread and butter I have eaten since [I] left my Mothers table. It was just like the bread Mother and <u>you</u> Sister L. use to make. We also had a splendid cup of Tea to wash it down with. After the repast, [I] filled my nice <u>Moorschaum</u> [meerschaum], had a comfortable smoke, and retired to my witouse cinch [?] to dream of loved ones at home.

I made Hawkins a present of that nice Shakespere Collar which arrived today.[5] I only wear one, sometimes two a week, so [I] thought could spair it. Don't want you to think I give everything away you send me. I know a number of the boy's would love to have a home like mine,

---

4 This is a reference to Lizzie's occupation as a schoolteacher. She was twenty-two years of age and single in 1870. See *1870 U.S. Federal Census*, Ancestry.com.
5 A Shakespeare collar probably refers to a rather wide turnover detachable shirt collar.

where they could have such thing's sent too them. I have my friends in the Company, and when ever [I] get anything from you [I] show it to them. When all the boy's in the room come around to have a look at what ever it may be.

Guess [I] have written all that [I] can think of, and have not written much then.

Fort Union, New Mexico
FEBRUARY 2, 1871

Received [a] short letter from Father few day's ago. And one each from my little Brothers yesterday. Did not receive the papers yet which you said were mailed same day as your letter. Guess they will come to hand yet.

We had a severe snow storm here [a] few days ago. Drifted in some places six feet high. Mails were not running very regular on account of the roads being almost impassible. The snow is melting very fast now, makeing the roads awfull muddy.

Had quite a Stylish wedding here last monday night. A Miss Hoffman that was visiting Capt. Young was the Bride while Capt. Kauffman of our Regiment officiated as the Groom.[6] The wedding was large, but the Drunk after was much larger. The manner in which this young lady come

---

6 Captain Albert B. Kauffman, the regimental quartermaster, had seen considerable service prior to coming to the Eighth Cavalry. He enlisted in the regular infantry in 1847 and rose to sergeant by the time he was discharged at the end of the Mexican-American War. He subsequently served as an enlisted man in the Sixth Infantry on the Western Frontier from 1850–1859, being discharged as a first sergeant. In 1860, he enlisted again, this time in the Fourth Cavalry, and remained with that regiment as a noncommissioned officer until 1863, when he secured a commission as a captain in the Eleventh Missouri Cavalry. He was honorably mustered out as a major in 1866, and was immediately accepted as a first lieutenant in the Eighth Cavalry. Kauffman remained with the regiment until just a few months prior to his retirement in 1891. See Heitman, *Historical Register*, vol. 1, 586. The bride was Sarah F. Cofran, born in Boston, Massachusetts, in 1848. Her parents, George and Sarah L., migrated to California, where her father was engaged as a contractor, during the 1850s. As Matthews states, Miss Cofran lived with the Young family at Fort Wingate prior to her marriage. She was approximately twenty-two years old when she married Captain Kauffman, who was twenty years her senior. She is shown as "C. Caufron" on the Fort Union Chaplain's Record, but that entry was probably made from memory by Chaplain David W. Eakins after the record of marriages, baptisms, and funerals was made an official requirement in 1875. The date of the marriage is recorded incorrectly as "1872," and the captain's first name is lacking. The 1870 Census recorded her as "S. F. Coffron," but the family surname is spelled Cofran on both the 1850 and 1860 Federal Censuses. See *U.S. Federal Censuses*, 1850, 1860, 1870, and 1880, Ancestry.com; Chaplain's Record, in Fort Union Collection, NMHU; and GO No. 1, Department of the MO, January 11, 1875, RG 393, NA, Washington, D.C.

to share her fortune with a bold Captain of the 8th Cavalry may be interesting to you, so [I] will relate her history, or as much of it as I know.

Sometime in '69 Capt. Young and family left Arizona on a leave of Absence for a few months. And went to San Francisco. In Nov. 69 I was coming to my Regiment a recruit. When we went aboard the Steamer Continental, Capt. Young took command of us. It was then I saw this young lady. We had been out to Sea but a few day's when [I] found out this young Miss was a friend of Mrs. Youngs and was going to Arizona with her, expecting of course to catch some unsuspecting Officer by her sweet smiles and winning ways. She soon received the name of "Drum Major" from her size and weight. Weighed two hundred lbs. and was little less than six feet. We arrived all O. K. in Arizona, but this fair Miss failed to make a conquest while in that Territory, but had better luck after we come to this uncivilized Territory.

K & E Companys, commanded by Capt. Young and Kauffman, remained at Fort Wingate, first post in this Territory that we come too. As there was nothing to be seen there, except about ten thousand "Navajo" Indians it is no wonder the Capt. fell in love with this fair Miss from California. A short time ago Capt. Young come to this post and took command of H Company. And about a week ago Capt. Kauffman come after his intended, And took her for better or worse. And I guess he got the worst of it. They left here next morning after they were married for Fort Wingate. So my tale comes to an end. "May she live happy with the Captain,["] is my wish.

Father asked me a few questions in the boy's letter, will answer them now. There is five companys here, four Cavalry and one infantry. About four hundred men in all. We live in splendid Quarters made of "Adobes." Guess you don't "Savy" [sabe] as the Mexican says for understand.

Adobes are made out of mud, they are two feet long, one wide and six or eight inches thick. Are moulded like a brick, and put on a yard to dry. Don't burn them like you do brick in the States, [you] let the sun dry them. They get very dry and hard, and make a very warm house. All the houses in this Territory are built of them. I will try and make a rough drawing of the Quarters.

[We] burn wood, no coal used. Blacksmiths burn Charcoal. Have heard that Coal has been found in different parts of the Territory. One mine was found on the "English Land, Grant Co. Land."

Curency all paper, no specie. Prices of Grain and Provisions given here are the Government prices. Everything is ruled by the Govt. in the Territory. Wheat $8.00 [per] hundred, Corn $14, Flour $6, Potatoes $5, Beef $6, Pork fresh 20 cts lb. You can buy a Sheep for one to two dollars. Don't know the prices of Merchandise, though [I] guess they are much higher than in the States. It costs conciderable to freight goods from the Rail Road here. Nearest point to the Rail Road is Kit Carson, in Colorado Territory. Distance two hundred and eighty miles. The Kansas Pacific Rail Road, runs to that place, and from there to Denver in the same Territory where it ends. The Roads from here to Kit Carson in the winter is almost impassable. No Trains pass over it during some months in the winter, for fear of getting snowed in.

Must close this, but will resume the subject at some future day. Will try my hand on a sketch of this Post today.

Fort Union, New Mexico
FEBRUARY 10, 1871

Father's welcome letter received two day's ago. As [I] have the day to myself [I] will answer it.

Mounted Guard this morning and as usual took Orderly. Reported to the Commanding Officer. He sent me to my Quarters and said report at Retreat, "this evening."

Fathers account of Female Sufferage created some fun for a few of the boy's who I read the letter "or that part of it" too. All agreed with him in case they be allowed a vote, they should be allowed the Musket. We would all accept them with outstretched arms as "Bunky's. Let them come.

Capt. Young and Lt. Mahnken left here for the States, few day's ago. Did not take any men with them. Genl. Gregg has gone to Santa Fe and taken command of this District. Major Jewett, is in command here.[7]

---

[7] Gregg assumed command of the District of New Mexico effective February 1, 1871, replacing Colonel George W. Getty, Third Infantry. Gregg left Fort Union on January 31 to report to his new headquarters in Santa Fe the following day. See PR, Fort Union, NM, February 1871, RG 94, NA, Washington, D.C.; and the *Daily New Mexican*, February 1, 1871. Captain Horace Jewett was a career regular and company commander with the Fifteenth Infantry at Fort Union. In 1882, he was promoted to major in the Sixteenth Infantry, to lieutenant colonel of the Third Infantry in 1886, and to colonel of the Twenty-First in 1891. Jewett held two brevets for gallantry in action during the Civil

"We Only Shot to Scare Them" 133

One of the employese in the arsinal, shot and killed a Mexican man night before last. After he killed him [he] come up and offered to give himself up to the commanding officer. He would have nothing to do with the case. The man then gave himself up to Civil Authority and was taken to town for trial.[8]

About thirty of D Company left here this morning on a scout. Don't know where they have gone.[9]

Will try to finish the account of this post in this letter. Undertook to make a drawing of it [a] few nights ago, found it more difficult than [I] thought it would be. Gave it up as a bad job, but will try again sometime. Our Quarters are plastered inside. In each room are seven upright posts, and places around each post for eight Carbines and Sabers, also [a] place to hang belts on. In each room [barracks?], "two large rooms for each Company" are about thirty single bunks.

First thing after coming from stables in the morning, you roll your bed sack up place it at the head of your bed, fold your blankets up nicely and lay them on the bed Sack. All the bunks look the same. Have one large Leviathan Stove in the room, which will heat all parts of it.

In the rear of the Company Quarters, are the Laundress Quarters. A long row of buildings, called by the boy's "Soap Sud Row." In each Laundress Quarters, a card is tacked up with prices for each piece of washing. Done by order of Genl. Gregg. Will give you the prices, for one month's washing: Govt Cloth[e]s $1.00 for [word missing], 25 [cents] pants, white shirt 10 [cents], bed sack 10 cts. I wear white shirts all the time, but my laundress never charges me any thing extra.

In rear of Laundress Quarters are the Company's stable's, all walled in with [a] high wall ten feet high.

It is dinner time now, so will close.

War, the first for the Battles of Shiloh and Murfeesboro and the second for the Atlanta Campaign. See Heitman, *Historical Register*, vol. 1, 573.

8 Matthews refers to Fort Union Arsenal, also known as Fort Union Ordnance Depot, located about a mile west of the post on the site of and housed in some of the buildings of the first Fort Union, 1851–1862. The arsenal was composed of a commanding officer's quarters, a barracks, a clerk's quarters, a general repair shop, storehouses, magazines, and sheds for artillery pieces. In addition to a detachment of regular ordnance soldiers, who provided the skilled workforce, the arsenal employed a number of civilians as common laborers. See Oliva, *Fort Union and the Frontier Army*, 731–33.

9 This must have been a routine mission having no particular results because the records make no mention of it.

Fort Union, New Mexico
FEBRUARY 15, 1871

Received [a] good long letter from Father, and one from Clellie this morning. Also papers and Pulse warmers. Gave the latter to Hawkins. He was delighted with them. You must have taken great paines to send me some late papers, those you sent me short time ago were very late. One especially, The Harpers Weekly, was dated Dec. 11th, 1869. Had a big laugh over it.

I have been reading more lately than ever did before. And what I read now is of some benefit as well as pleasure to me. Have read "The Emperor Napoleon" Empress Josephine, Alexander the Great. And am now reading queen Victoria's memoirs of the Prince Consort, Prince Albert. I take great interest in reading those books now. We have a Post Library here. Can get books any time during the week. Have not much time for reading but devote all spare time mostly.

Know you will be pleased to know that I have a taste now for books of that standard. Some parts of the life of the Empress affected me very much. Once while reading tears rushed to my eyes, and my heart seemed to come up in my throat. Napoleon regretted the Divorce from Josephine, [to?] the last days of his life. On St. Helena, was there ever a more faithfull, loving, or devoted wife to man, than Josephine proved to be to Napoleon[?] And after all her fidelity to be cast off. Ever watchfull over his affairs, feritting out plots against his "Napoleon's" life, and did save his life more than once. And when Napoleon's jelouse nature imagined his wife was unfaithfull to him, and reproached her for it. She proved her innocence in every case. But had she reproached Napoleon for his infidelity to her, while in Egipt, when he almost forgot his Josephine, while living with his beautifull mistress "Madam DFomey"(that was her name I believe). How would he have exculpated himself of that charge, had Josephine spoken to him about it. No doubt he would have flew into a rage and dismissed her from his presence. Napoleon was great, but Josephine was the greatest. What do you think of your Son now[?] I must be improving when can spout so eleguently on the merits and defects of the great Emperor Napoleon. When I left [remainder missing]

Fort Union, New Mexico
FEBRUARY 23, 1871

Received Letter from Lizzie day before yesterday, expressing fears that I was sick as you had not heard from me for two weeks. Cannot imagine how such a long time could elaps with out you hearing from me. I am shure I never allow a week to pass with out writing one and sometimes two letters, to you. Last week I wrote two letters to you and a short one to each of my little brothers.

You seem to have a bad opinion of us boys, to think if I had not a stamp to write to you, [I] could not borrow one in the Company. I am seldom without them, thanks to your selves for sending them to me. If it should ever happen that I was out of stamps, and could not borrow one in the Company, [I] would go to the General and ask him for one, sooner than not write to you.

When we were at Cimerron for a month I got out of Envelopes and could get none in the company. So walked up to the 1st Lieutenant's quarters and asked for one. He only had one, and he gave that to me. You must not get frightened when a week passes without you hearing from me. If I ever [I] should get too sick to write to you, [I] would get some person to write for me. I never enjoyed better health in my life than since [I] enlisted, though [I] have like your selves a cold now. Caught it on guard two nights ago. Failed to take orderly for the first time in three months.

You may talk about wind and sand storms, but I never saw anything to equal the storm that has been blowing here today. You can't see one foot ahead of you for the sand, and wind blowing a perfect hurricane. It has blown part of F Company's stables down. And one or two large gates down. No person dairs go out of the quarters except are compelled to go.

Major Clendenin of our Regt is expected here every day to take command of this Post.[10] There will be two details of men leave here

---

10 Major David R. Clendenin rose from captain to lieutenant colonel of the Eighth Illinois Cavalry during the Civil War and received brevets to colonel and brigadier general by war's end. He was appointed to the Eighth U.S. Cavalry in January 1867 and remained with the regiment for five years. He subsequently served with the Third Cavalry and the Second Cavalry until he retired in 1891. See Heitman, *Historical Register*, vol. 1, 310.

soon. One party of seventy five or a hundred men are to go to Kit Carson after four hundred horses.[11] And another small party go to St. Louis Mo. with some prisoners that have to go there for four years. Would like to go on the latter trip, though [I] would not like the former [in] this weather, as it is my luck to go on all such details.

I had to suffer for several days with a tooth while at Cimmerrone before a Doctor could be found to draw it out, and when [I] did have it drawn the Dr. was drunk, and had to make two or three pulls at it. Hurt a good deal but [I] felt all right after [he] got it out. I have made up my mind not to suffer any more with the tooth ache if [I] can get them drawn out.

The young man Hurley that I spoke of has gone home. Left here nearly two months ago. I gave him a letter of introduction to Father. He promised faithfully he would go to see you all. Soon as [he] got settled at home, [he] promised to write and send several papers to me, but has never done it yet. Guess he will not visit Westminster before spring.

Don't know of any thing else to write this time. It will soon be pay day. Will send you some money then.

That Nec tie you sent me some time ago is soiled now. Send along the other one you said you had for me please.

Fort Union, New Mexico

SUNDAY, FEBRUARY 26, 1871

Four prisoners arrived here [a] few day's ago, from Fort Wingate. Will be sent from here to the State prison of Missouri. Or at least 3 of them will. As one made his escape yesterday. The cooks alway's carry the Prisoners meals to them in the Guard House, and leave the dishes till after they get through eating. So yesterday one of the four prisoners took up a lot of pans and walked out of the Guard House, past the Sentry on duty and has got away. The Sentry thought he was one of the Cooks, and let him pass. The prisoner had four years to serve in the Penitentary.[12]

---

11 This detachment was being sent to the railhead of the Kansas Pacific at Kit Carson, Colorado Territory, to receive a herd of remount horses destined for the regiment. Matthews, for obvious reasons, was not eager to make that trip in winter.

12 No record of an escaped prisoner was found. Presumably, the man was caught within a short time, and therefore the incident would not have appeared in the returns.

Major Clendenin of our Regiment, arrived [a] day or two ago, and has taken command of this Post.

I have a miserable cold in my head, in fact nearly all the Company have colds, caused by the changable weather. The day's are generally warm but the nights are quite cold.

I just wrote to you two days ago, so am at a loss for something to write about. Suppose [I] will have stop writing for this time, by thanking Master Clellie, for his very appropriate Valentine. And can truly say [I] would prefer charging a turky any time to a lot of Apatche Indians. Especially if It was nicely roasted, like Mother does them.

Fort Union, New Mexico
MARCH 3, 1871

Have just come in off a twenty five mile ride, and feel a little sore, as [I] have not been riding very much lately. Yesterday [I] was sent out to the Saw Mill with a Corpl. and another man after a load of lumber, twenty five miles from here. After one or two accidents, [we] arrived there. The Corporal was riding in front of the wagon and six mules. One of our company and my self was riding in the rear of the team. I noticed the teamster dismount from his saddle mule, and as he did so [he] fell to the ground.[13] His foot hung in the stirup and he was being drug along on the ground, the teem was going in a trot. He was in a very ugly predicment.

I took the whole thing in at a glance, jumped off my horse and thought I gave my horses bridle rein to the young man who was riding at my side, but instead of doing that let my horse loose, he no sooner found he was loose than he wheeled around and started for this place fast as he could go. I paid no attention to my horse running away, but ran myself fast as [I] could to the rescue of the teemster, and reached him in time. Got the mules stoped and his foot out of the stirup. He was very sore after [he] got loose, and was very loud in his praises of my presence of mind.

---

13 The six-mule wagon was the workhorse of the army from 1855 until well into the twentieth century. As the title implies, it was drawn by six mules and could haul up to about a ton of freight over the roughest roads, or cross-county when necessary. The driver did not sit on the wagon; rather, he rode the saddled left-wheel (rear) mule and controlled the team using a lead line to the foremost pair, a whip, and voice commands. See Lindmier, *Great Blue Army Wagon*, 33, 41–43.

Said I had saved his life, that he could not have keep his head from under the front wheel much longer. The Corporal and man run my horse about five miles, but finally run him up against some high rocks and caught him. Reached the mill without any more accidents.

Stoped there last night stood four hours guard over our horses and mules, and returned to this post this evening. Found all the men busy making ration sacks, mending cloth[e]s etc. for to go on, as the report says, a six months scout.[14] Three companys leave here in four or five days. D, F, & L. We are to Scout through this Territory and into Texas. Supposed to stay out six months. Object of the scout, to break up bands of thieves, Indian traders and annihilate all the Indians that we come across. Don't know what facilities [I] will have for writing and receiving letters. Major Clendenin will go in command of the expedition I suppose.

Will write to you again in a day or two. And can perhaps give you something more definite. Am on Guard again tomorrow. Excuse writing etc. for I feel quite tired and sleepy.

Sherman House, Trinidad, Colorado
MARCH 12, 1871

Just one week ago, I wrote to you. On the night of the 9th I was ordered to get ready, with eight day's rations, to go after Deserters. To report to Lieutenant Henisee of D Company.[15] For forty eight hours we rode as hard as our horses could carry us. During that time we traveled one hundred and thirteen miles (113).

We was told by Citizens all along the road, that we were only a few

---

14 A "ration sack" probably refers to the forage sack cavalrymen used for carrying a two- or three-day ration of grain for their horses. Strapped to the pommel of the saddle, the simple canvas sack measured about twenty inches long by about seven inches in diameter. The open end was tied off with a choke string. One design observed by the editor had another tie string at the midpoint to divide the ration in equal parts and allow the filled bag to bend more readily over the pommel. See Steffen, *The Horse Soldier*, vol. 2, 164.

15 Argalus G. Hennisee, like Matthews, was a native Marylander. He had been a company officer with the First Eastern Shore Maryland Infantry throughout the Civil War and was granted a commission in the regular army in 1867. He served as a lieutenant in the Nineteenth Infantry from 1867 to 1869, but was unassigned for a few months during the army reorganization until being appointed to the Eighth Cavalry. He served with the regiment as an adjutant and as a company commander until he was promoted to major with the Second Cavalry in 1898. He retired at the rank of colonel in 1903. See Heitman, *Historical Register*, vol. 1, 523.

miles behind these deserters. We did not get any sleep, till we arrived at this place. Here our Lieutenant gave us one nights sleep. This morning we caught two of the Deserters. I pitied the poor boy's, but could not help catching them. The Lieutenant took eight men out of the "twenty one" and followed after the other deserters. And gave me instructions to take charge of our wagon and traps, also the prisoners, and men, that were left behind. Said he would be back this evening.[16]

You must excuse such a short letter, would write more but have not the time.

Population of this town is one thousand Inhabitants. Considerable business done here.

We will go back to Fort Union from here. You must excuse such a short letter and poor writing, am very tired and sleepy.

Sherman House, Trinidad, Colorado
MARCH 13, 1871

Still at this place. Wrote you a few lines yesterday, but was so fatigued with hard riding and want of sleep that [I] could scarcely keep my eye's open. Did not expect to stop at this place so long or would have waited till this morning before writing to you. Our Lieutenant took four men e[a]rly yesterday morning and followed after the Deserters. Few moments ago the Guide that went with him returned, and said they had caught one more of the party. Said the Lieut's party had rode forty five miles yesterday, and their Horses were completely played out, and they would not get in here before night. You can imagine how a man feels after riding one hundred and fifteen miles in forty eight hours, horse back, without a wink of sleep.

We will remain here another day I suppose, to recruit our horses. And then return to Fort Union. Will take our time going back.

The people of this town think a great deal of a Soldier. And do all in their power to make our stay as pleasant as possible.

Don't suppose [I] will have an opportunity of writing to you again till [I] get back to Fort Union. Excuse loneity [?] as have not time to write more.

---

16 Matthews probably was a noncom by this time, though the date of his promotion is not known.

Fort Union, New Mexico
MARCH 26, 1871

It has been some time since I wrote to you. Not since the two [I] wrote from Trinidad. On that trip we were out twelve days. Captured eight Deserters, travelled four hundred miles during that time. Run out of rations and had to dispatch to this place for some to be sent to us. Returned to this place on the 21st. And found three letters here for me. One from Father, Jennie, & John Reese.

While we were out the Pay Master visited this post and payed off. Lt. Cobb who is in Command of the Company would not sign the Pay Rolls for us, and draw our pay.[17] So [I] will have to wait two months more.

I remained in Camp two days, when Lt. Cobb sent for me before breakfast, and said he wanted me to get ready soon as [I] got my breakfast to go on the road again. Said he knew I had had but very little rest after the bad trip we had just come off, but it could not be helped. Although we have about eighty men in our Company, fifteen or twenty of us have to do all the scouting, escorting, etc. The Officers are afraid to send any of the new men, "or as we call them" recruits, on the road for fear they will desert. And take horse, Carbine, revolver, and equipments with them. When they desert from the Garrison they can only take their carbines with them. As the horses are in the Corrall, and revolvers are in the 1st Sergeants room.

Had to take my horse and an extra one with five days rations and go to meet a squad of our men who were out on the road and had caught a deserter from our company. The deserter was sick and could not walk in.

Just returned to camp this evening, got something to eat, had a good bath in a big tub of warm water, like the children use to have at home, feel much better after it. Went to the first Sergeants room and found Lizzie's letter written from Shades School house, without a date.

Day before yesterday we had considerable fun at some Indians expense, on the road forty miles from here. We come to a ranch owned by a Dutchman; he and his spouse are very Kind to us poor

---

17 Although a company commander was permitted to collect the pay for absent enlisted men, provided it was witnessed by another commissioned officer, young Lieutenant Cobb was probably reluctant to be responsible for the money belonging to so many men. See *Revised Regulations*, 351.

Soldiers. When ever we stop there they give us as much bread and milk as we can eat. The Apatche and Ute Indians reservation is close by, and when ever they find the old dutchman is away from home they come down from the hills to the house and beg the old woman for every thing to eat she has. And if she gives anything to one she must give to all. When we come up to the ranch [we] found about twenty Indians there. We dismounted went in the ranch and found the old woman in a terrible excitment. She told us her husband was not at home. Said that the Indians were very angry with her, because she would not give them all something to eat. In fact the poor woman was badly frightened. We told her to keep quiet and we would soon send the Indians away.

We took our Carbines off our saddles and told the Indians to leave. They did not seem to care about going. One of our party raised his carbine and fired over their heads, that frightened them, and off they ran scattering out like skirmishers. We fired about twenty rounds after them. We would shoot all around them to see them change their directions. We were very carefull not to hit any of them, the life was nearly frightened out of them. And they never stoped running till they reached the mountains about three miles. The old woman was greatly pleased, took us in the house and gave us all the warm biscuits, butter and milk we could eat.

After we got through, went up the road four miles to the "Government Agency" and put up for the night. These Govt. Agency's are scattered all over the Territories, for Soldiers to stop and get forage. And if you are out of rations you can get it from them. During the evening the Chief of the Indians sent word down to the Agent, word that some soldiers had been shooting at his men, and wanted to know what his men had done to make us shoot at them. The Agent sent word back that his men had been acting very badly at the dutchmans ranch and that we only shot to scare them. After that the Indians could be seen all over the hill[s] in every direction, but they would not come near the ranch. The Agent told us we had better keep guard over our horses, for fear the Indians would come down and try to steel them. We kept watch over the horses all night and would have made it pretty hot, had any of them tryed to get a horse, but nary Indian made his appearance.

Strong talk of a big scout going out soon, against the "Commanche"

Indians. They are a hard tribe "or nation" of Indians to whip. And if we do get into a fight with them some person will get hurt.

I received a letter from my friend Hurley. He told me he was going to visit you in April. Just think of it, in one month from today I will be twenty one. I remember when I was quite small how I use to wish to be of age, it is just the reverse now. I wish to be a young boy again. And if such a thing could be, and I knew what I do now, what a different life I would lead. I am writing this in the cook house as it is after "<u>Taps</u>" when all lights in the quarters have to be put out. I rode thirty five miles today, so [I] feel a little tired, and will close.

Camp near Cimarron, New Mexico
APRIL 8, 1871

It is a shame, I must admit that I have not written to you now for more than a week, but when I explain to you why I have not done so, know you will pardon me.

On the morning of the fourth D and F companys of our regiment left Fort Union, on a big Scout. We, "I mean our company," were complaining because we were not going along, when lo about twelve o'clock the order come for us to be ready to leave in three hours. You can imagine some quick packing of changes of clothes, blankets, Tabacco, pipes, etc. In an hour we were ready to move. At 3 o'clock P.M. we rode out of Fort Union, and arrived at "Qkata," [Ocate] a mail Station 18 miles from the post at dark. Camped for the night and next morning started out and arrived at this place, three miles from <u>Cimmeron</u>, and fifty one from Union. We found out on the road that the "Apatche" and "Ute" Indians on a reservation here threaten an out break on account of the Government stoping issuing rations to them. They, the Indians, fired three shots at the Indian Agent here a few day's ago. So we were sent down for the protection of the Citizens. Don't know how long we will remain here.

Short time before we left the Post we organized a Base Ball Club in our company, I had the honor to be elected Captain of the 1st team. We brought our bats and balls along with us, and have been amusing ourselves and passing away the time playing ball.

We are camping in tents, two men in an A tent, so we can make ourselves very comfortable.[18] I have not heard from you now for more than two weeks, have received no mail since [I] came here.

I am lying down, writing this on my blankets, and it is getting so dark that [I] cannot see the lines, so [I] will stop for the night perhaps will add a line in the morning. So good night to you all.

This evening while sitting in my tent all alone thinking of you all, I took your pictures out of my <u>diary</u>, took a good look at all of them. Kissed you all and put them back. That is the only consolation I have when [I] get to thinking of you all.

My bunky just come in the tent and said the report was now that we were going back to Fort Union Monday 11th inst. Will say again good night, for [I] cannot see a line.

Sunday Morning 9th inst. You will perceive by the straight writing above that I was either frightually <u>drunk</u>, or was writing in the dark, the latter was the fact, the former is a stranger to me. As I still keep my word in referance to drinking intoxicating liquors.

This morning was spent in targate practice with our revolvers, fine manners to observe the sabbath in the Army. Have heard nothing either in reference to leaving here tomorrow. So will close, write to me at Union.

At this point the letters end abruptly, resulting in a gap of thirteen months. Because Matthews had proven a reliable correspondent with his family, the editor concludes that the original letters for this period were lost or destroyed. However, by relying on other available sources, we are able to generally reconstruct the activities of his company from mid-April of 1871 until the correspondence resumes in late June of 1872.

Company L returned from Cimarron to Fort Union later that month to resume garrison duty. The only event disrupting the tranquility of the post was the desertion of several soldiers in May, including four from Matthews's company. General Pope addressed this widespread problem in his annual report: "Desertions have been numerous since the passage of the law reducing the pay of enlisted men," he wrote. But that was not the only cause he cited. With the rapid development of the western frontier, economic opportunities abounded. Soldiers with initiative

---

18 The "A" tent derived its name from its similarity, in cross section, to that letter of the Roman alphabet. It measured about six feet high at the ridge and six feet in length. The floor area was approximately fifty square feet and it was intended to sleep four men, though it could accommodate six if necessary. Accordingly, Matthews and his bunky found it commodious for only two men. See Billings, *Hardtack and Coffee*, 39–41.

and a lust for prosperity found it difficult to remain in the service on a private's monthly salary of $13.00 when it was relatively easy to "go over the hill." Private Matthews, having demonstrated his reliability, was one of two men sent out with a sergeant on detached service, and it may have been his party that apprehended two deserters and brought them back to Fort Union to face charges.[19]

There may have been a tacit understanding between the traders and the Comanches and Kiowas that they would avoid molesting the New Mexico settlements. Yet Department Commander John Pope was of the opinion that "this traffic, which supplied the wild Indians with arms and ammunition to depredate upon the trains and the settlements, has always been injurious and dangerous to the security of the very people among whom these infamous traders live."[20] The Eighth Cavalry was thus responsible for interdicting the illicit traffic to and from the Staked Plains.

Major David R. Clendenin commanded a battalion based at Fort Bascom during the spring and summer of 1871. His pitifully small force of two companies (D and F), at times reinforced by additional detachments from Fort Union, attempted to scour the country east to the Texas state line, and thence ranged southwest until it intersected the Fort Sumner Road. Detachments also regularly patrolled south of Bascom and along the Fort Smith Road. Colonel Gregg likely understated the situation when he described it as "difficult and severe duty." We cannot confirm that Matthews participated in any of this field service, but the fact that thirty-five of the forty-four members of Company L were dispatched to assist Clendenin on June 6 suggests he may have.[21]

During one nine-day scout, F Company netted twenty-two illegal traders, seven hundred stolen cattle, and over a hundred ponies and burros. A detachment of Company D soon thereafter brought in twenty-one Pueblo Indian traders and almost two hundred head of cattle, plus over four dozen horses and burros. These accomplishments proved that despite the vastness of the district, the cavalry could in fact intercept and arrest trading parties.[22]

---

19 See Eighth Cavalry Returns, April and May 1871; and *ARSW*, 1871, 44.
20 See *ARSW*, 1871, 43.
21 See Randlett to AAG, District of NM, May 3, 1871, in LR, District of NM, RG 393, NA, Washington, D.C.; and Clendenin to AAAG, District of NM, June 6, 1871, in LS, Fort Union, NM, RG 393, NA, Washington, D.C. The return for that month lists only two members of his company as being on extra or daily duty, and both of them were assigned as the company cooks. See Eighth Cavalry Returns, June 1871.
22 See Eighth Cavalry Returns, May 1871; and Receipt by Nathaniel Pope, Superintendent of Indian Affairs, Santa Fe, NM, June 12, 1871, in LR, District of NM, RG 393, NA, Washington, D.C.

These successes nevertheless posed a problem for the military. What to do with the captured traders, goods, and livestock? For decades, the army had been allowed the latitude to serve as a *posse comitatus* as necessary to augment regular law enforcement, particularly in the sparsely populated territories where civil authorities were few or nonexistent.[23] Initially, Clendenin summarily destroyed at least some of the traders' illegal possessions, likely the arms, munitions, and liquor, but local New Mexican authorities objected. Although the prisoners initially were sent to Fort Union, a subsequent edict from Washington, D.C., mandated that they be turned over to the appropriate civilian jurisdiction. Colonel Gordon Granger, who had replaced Gregg as commander of the District of New Mexico on May 1, consequently directed the officers at Bascom to send all prisoners, under guard, directly to Santa Fe for trial. The troops impounded the cattle and other stock until the lawful owners, usually Texans, could claim them.[24]

The detail escorting prisoners from Fort Bascom was to accompany them as far west as Whittemore's Ranch, situated near the Pecos River at the junction of the Fort Smith Road. There, the escort was relieved by a detachment from Fort Union that would take the prisoners on to Santa Fe. Granger stipulated that two or three reliable soldiers who had participated in the arrest were to accompany the prisoners all the way to Santa Fe to serve as witnesses for the grand jury.[25]

Company L's stint of field service was brief, only through the end of June, and by early July, it was back at Fort Union, where a draft of new recruits bolstered its strength to more than seventy men. This influx of new men, combined with the loss of some of the noncommissioned officers, resulted in Matthews's promotion to sergeant. For the remainder of the summer, the noncoms occupied much of their time with showing the new men the ropes of army life and instructing them in basic cavalry tactics and guard duty to develop them into useful soldiers as quickly as possible.

---

23 This loose interpretation of the U.S. Constitution was curtailed in 1878, when a new law prohibited military forces from assisting civil authorities, other than in instances specifically authorized by the president or Congress. See Tate, *Frontier Army*, 93–94.

24 See GO No. 11, HQ, District of NM, April 30, 1871, in Orders, District of NM, LR&O, Arrott Collection, NMHU; AAG, Department of the MO to Granger, June 14, 1871, in LR, ibid.; AAAG, Dist. of NM to CO, Fort Union, NM July 15, 1871, in LS, Fort Union, NM, ibid.; Gregg to CO, Fort Bascom, NM, July 15, 1871, in LS, Fort Union, NM, ibid.

25 See *ARSW*, 1871, 43; Caraher to CO Detachment, Eighth Cavalry, Fort Bascom, NM, May 14, 1871, in LR, Fort Union, NM, LR&O, v. 25, Arrott Collection, NMHU; and Hennisee to Post Adjutant, Fort Union, NM, May 22, 1871, in LR, Fort Union, NM, ibid. These events resulted in a temporary change of scenery for Matthews near the end of August, when he was detailed as a member of one of the escorts from Whittemore's to Santa Fe. See Eighth Cavalry Returns, August, 1871.

Matthews's company continued to carry out routine activities as part of the Fort Union garrison for the remainder of 1871. But Eddie ended the year on a sour note. Despite his repeated pledge to his parents to shun alcohol, the self-proclaimed "great advocater" of temperance went on a drunken spree early in December along with his friend Corporal Clinton C. Harlan. Whether this binge occurred at Loma Parda or at the soldiers' bar operated by Post Trader John C. Dent, it had serious consequences for both men. Undoubtedly disappointed by the conduct of noncoms in whom he had placed his confidence, Captain Hobart had little choice but to set an example by demoting them. Acting on Hobart's recommendation, Colonel Gregg promulgated an order on December 8 stripping Matthews and Harlan of their ranks and reducing them to privates. That Eddie lied to his family about this embarrassing incident is revealed in his letter dated August 27, 1873, in which he claims to have resigned his position as quartermaster sergeant because he felt he could not master the paperwork.[26]

---

26 See Orders No. 114, HQ, Eighth Cavalry, December 8, 1871, in G&SO Issued, Eighth Cavalry, RG 391, NA. One might question why Eddie had to tell his family anything, considering that they were far away and would not have been the wiser. However, it is clear that relatives and friends were addressing their letters according to his current rank. Had he not fabricated an excuse, those letters would have continued to come to "Sergeant W. E. Matthews," and that would have been noted by his superiors.

CHAPTER FIVE

"Have Had All the Indian Fighting I Wish"

JANUARY—DECEMBER 1872

*M*atthews's demotion to private apparently had no lasting effect on his reputation. At frontier posts where recreational opportunities were few, many soldiers drank, often to excess, to offset boredom. Eddie's abilities, personality, and soldierly bearing worked to his advantage, for the very day following his reduction, Gregg detailed him as a clerk in the regimental headquarters at Fort Union.[1] There, he worked under the direct supervision of the adjutant and sergeant major, tediously copying by hand correspondence and orders, and consolidating company morning reports into monthly returns for his regiment. Still, it was better than regular troop duty. Matthews was to continue on this detail through April, when orders came down directing Gregg to make another concerted effort to curtail the illegal Indian trade on the Staked Plains.[2]

---

1 It was not uncommon for some noncoms to intentionally violate regulations in order to be reduced, thereby extricating themselves from the responsibilities of command. One wonders if this was such an instance. See Orders No. 115, HQ, Eighth Cavalry, December 9, 1871, in G&SO Issued, RG 391, NA.

2 See AAG, Department of the MO to Granger, District of NM, April 13, 1872, in LR, Fort Union, NM, RG 393, NA, copy in v. 27, LR&O, Arrott Collection, NMHU; and SO No. 61, District of NM, April 21, 1872, copy in v. 27, LR&O, Arrott Collection, NMHU.

Of the three cavalry companies then at Fort Union, only Captain William McCleave's Company B was prepared to march immediately to old Fort Bascom to reestablish a summer camp on the Canadian River some 90 miles southeast of Fort Union. McCleave's vanguard left the post in mid-May, while Gregg inexplicably dawdled, to his superior's frustration.

Shortly before finally leaving Fort Union with the other two companies, Gregg reiterated a suggestion he had made the previous year to Colonel Gordon Granger, commanding the District of New Mexico. Since the Comanchero traders and the Indians were meeting on or near the Staked Plains, and posted lookouts to carefully scan the table-like plains for signs of approaching troops, it was almost impossible to catch them in the act of conducting their illegal commerce. A more effective strategy, he urged, would be to place his battalion "in the very centre of this illegal traffic and if [they were] not strong enough to force the refractory Indians back, [they] could at least hold any position and intercept all traders." His request had fallen on deaf ears, perhaps because such a plan would entail authorizing troops belonging to the Department of the Missouri to operate within the boundaries of the Department of Texas. However, in the meantime, his superior must have obtained a nod of approval because Granger immediately fired back a telegram instructing Gregg to "break up all the camps of illicit Indian traders and take their stock," thus granting him wide latitude to accomplish the objective.[3]

A problem arose, however, when Gregg reconnoitered the Canadian River valley for fifty miles east of Fort Bascom without finding a place he considered suitable for a semi-permanent cavalry camp, "nor [one] affording facilities for operations on the Llano Estacado [the Staked Plains]." Gregg therefore settled temporarily upon a site he christened, "Summer Camp on the Canadian River," which was only five miles from the old post. From there, he intended to launch a scouting expedition to the headwaters of the Red River.

Gregg's scout was to be a cooperative though uncoordinated effort with troops from the Department of Texas. Marching westward from Fort Richardson in late June, Colonel Ranald S. Mackenzie led three companies of his Fourth Cavalry to the Freshwater Fork of the Brazos River, where they were joined by three

---

3 See Gregg to AAAG, District of NM, July 3, 1871, in LS, Fort Union, NM, RG 393, NA, copy in v. 26, LR&O, Arrott Collection, NMHU; Gregg to AAAG, District of NM, June 4, 1872, in LS, Fort Union, NM, RG 393, NA, copy in v. 27, ibid.; Gregg to AAAG, District of NM, June 7, 1872, ibid.; and Telegram, Granger to Gregg, June 8, 1872, in LS, District of NM, ibid.

additional companies from Forts Concho and Griffin. The united command then proceeded on a reconnaissance through the heart of the Staked Plains.[4]

By late July, Gregg had concentrated five companies of his regiment at the camp (Company C had come all the way from Fort Selden), and soon thereafter, he left Fort Union to take personal command of the battalion. As we shall see, Private Matthews, still attached to the regimental headquarters, was pressed into service as a teamster for one of the big six-mule wagons loaded with supplies for the coming expedition.

Camp near Fort Bascom, New Mexico
JUNE 25, 1872

Father's letter with two papers came to hand yesterday evening.

Was ever so glad to hear from you, especially, that you were all well. You say the $10.00 sent you failed to arrive, but perhaps the letter had been mislaid, and has come to hand before this. It was enclosed in a letter addressed to Clellie.

Well, you see we are still in Camp at this place. Have been working constantly ever since [we] arrived, Putting up shades over our tents, and fixing up as comfortable as it is possible to make ourselves.[5] Suppose about the time [we] are fixed up nicely [we] will have to leave and go after Indians. Several rumors of Indians committing outrages some distance from here has been afloat, but it seems they were all false alarms, as no scouts were sent out after them.

I have not had the opportunity to send you the "buffaloes" tail yet, as his "buffaloeship" has to be caught before his tail can be cut off. And I have not seen one since [I] proposed sending you one.

---

4 See Fourth Cavalry Returns, June–September 1872; *ARSW*, 1872, 55–56; and Carter, *On the Border*, 376–83. The Fourth Cavalry conducted a similar operation in the Texas Panhandle in 1871, when it engaged the Comanches on several occasions. For a detailed participant's account, see ibid., 156–212.

5 Troops serving in the Southwest commonly erected ramadas over their tents when they expected to be in camp for any length of time. A *ramada* was a shelter constructed "at a small expenditure of labor in erecting a few additional upright saplings and cross-pieces, and a covering of cottonwood foliage, [that] secured a modicum of shelter from the fierce shafts of a sun which shone not to warm and enlighten, but to enervate and kill" (Bourke, *On the Border with Crook*, 4). This simple shelter, used by Indians and Hispanics for centuries, broke the sun's intense heat and provided a generous air space beneath to keep the tents more comfortable than if the rays of the sun had fallen directly on the canvas.

Fifteen of our Troop have just been ordered out, with 15 days rations. Dont know where they are going. My name was on the detail, but Capt. Hobart had it taken off. And am now detailed to do a lot of writing for one of our Lieuts.

Will keep me busy for 20 or 30 days, this I know will suit Mother, as there will be no danger threat[en]ing her big Son. It was not my wish that I be detailed for if wanted to Clerk, would have remained in the Adjutants Office in Union. And I told the Lieut. as much, but he would not let me off said he knows of no other person who could do it. Will be excused from all other duty. And perhaps the Gentleman will give me a $5 or $10 when [I] have finished. Commence work in the morning, but as the mail leaves here earlier tomorrow morning, [I] will have to pencil you these few lines tonight.

Camp near Fort Bascom, New Mexico
JUNE 25, 1872 (continued)

Well loved ones, I dont like to send you this short letter, but am afraid [I] will have to do it as I can think of nothing else to write you. Unless [I] give you a description of our Camp.

The Camp is situated in tolerable low bottom land within one hundred yards of the Canadian River. M Troop's Camp is on the right, as it's Captain is the Senior Officer of the troop commanders. B Troop in the center. And L on the left. Each troop has two lines of tents with a company street of forty feet wide. As the sun shines very warm this season of the year, down here we are putting up shades over the tents, and as B troop has been here some time they have their shades finished and not only looks well, but is very comfortable to lounge. The shades are twelve feet high, and covered over with brush.

Genl. Gregg (our Colonel) has his tent "or rather tents" pitched in a nice shady grove about two hundred yards to the right of the Troops.[6]

---

6 During the nineteenth century, the army offered only one decoration, the Medal of Honor, to recognize bravery in battle. Officers exhibiting courage not rising to that level, or performing other meritorious deeds, were frequently bestowed with brevet rank higher than their normal grade. While this entitled them to be addressed by their brevet rank, the title was merely honorary, and regular army officers exercised command only at their permanent rank. The brevet came into play only in the unlikely circumstance that two officers of the same permanent rank happened to have identical dates of commission. In such an instance, the one having the higher brevet rank assumed command.

And [he] is fixed up so nicely that one would suppose he was out on a pleasure excursion. And in fact that is all it is to him. He has one large wall tent for his sleeping apartment, adjoining which is another large tent for his dining room and in rear of that is his Kitchen, [it] has a nice board floor (and in fact all the officers have board floors in their tents). He has a man to ride five miles every morning for milk. A four mule team is sent the same distance each morning after spring water for the officers. And an other team is sent ten miles once each week for ice. With all this comfort, and plenty of Whiskey to drink it is no more than a pic-nick to him.

Will try to have more news to tell you in my next, for there is no danger of my going out scouting for twenty days.

Summer Camp on Canadian River
JULY 1, 1872

Tomorrow morning a wagon leaves here for Fort Union. I cannot allow an opportunity to pass for sending you a few lines, if only to say that I am well and still retain my <u>hair</u>.[7] Nothing of special interest has transpired since [I] wrote to you. No new Indian outrages have been committed so far as heard from. And the watch word is "all quiet on the Canadian." Good news, especially for my honored Mother.

Have been quite busy since last I wrote you. Getting up a lot of Proceedings of Board's of Survey's for our Lieutenant.[8] Don't suppose any of you (excepting Father) know what kind of proceedings those are, but he can explain the nature of them for your gratification if you are qurious [curious]. Today I made out one set [of] four copies, consuming

---

In Gregg's case, he had earned two brevets during the Civil War, first to brigadier general and a second to major general of volunteers. Therefore, Colonel Gregg, commanding a regiment after the war, as was proper for that rank, was commonly addressed as "general." See McDermott, *Guide to the Indian Wars*, 23–25.

7 This is refers to the possibility of his being scalped by Indians.

8 The purpose of a board of survey was to assess the amount and nature of damage to, or deficiency in, public property that may have resulted from some cause beyond normal wear and tear. The board also affixed responsibility for the damage, or rendered a determination that it was beyond anyone's control. The clerk had to reproduce, by hand of course, the required multiple copies. See *Revised Regulations*, 150.

six sheets of legal cap paper. And as the Lieut wanted them as soon as I could possible have them done. Finished them by dinner time, and then commenced another set this evening.

Have been offered a Clerkship in the Commissary and Subsistence Department at this Camp but declined the situation. Have at last got tired [of] doing an officers work who receives $200.00 per month, while I only get $13.00. It is too much like Pat carrying the <u>brick</u> up three or four flights of ladders while the man on top of the house does all the work. I would not be making out these proceedings for the Lieut. could he have got another man.

I weighed myself this evening, and only weigh 138 3/4 lbs, am 5 ft 9 inches tall, and going on 23 years old, black eyes, black hair (what there is of it), had it cut short for the occasion, dark complexion.[9] (At the time of writing darker than [I] would care to be were I on my way east.) Am very badly sunburned, but taken all in all [I] am a pretty fair piece of human nature. <u>And my worthy parents deserve great credit</u>. [I] Imagine Lizzie saying vanity personafide.

And now that I have reached and passed the age when a boy is not supposed to be a boy any longer, I have failed to experience the feeling that when quite a boy [I] imagined [I] would feel upon the arrival of my 21st year. And [I] am now just as big a boy in thoughts etc. as [I] was five years ago. And if I was home this night [I] would be hanging around my loved Mother, and like as not would want her to spread my bread with butter and syrup (that is if my stomach felt as it does now). Dont think I am hungry from the above, it is only said in a jest, for we get plenty to eat of the kind, but it is a very poor kind.

Father speaks of being a local preacher when he was my age. What a vast difference in the occupation of Father and Son at the age of 22, but then you was not Father then, or was I son. Nevertheless it dont alter the great contrast between two occupations. The one seeking to save, the other paid to destroy human beings souls. One prepared if called to appear before his maker, the other with scarcely a hope. Shurely there can not be a greater contrast. Especially in one family. A christian in the Regular Army, excepting the few Chaplains, and they

---

9 Eddie exaggerates his height. His enlistment record gives his physical description as: brown eyes, black hair, fair complexion, and five feet six and one-quarter inches tall. See entry 214, p. 202, roll 36, ROE, RG 94, NA.

are even doubtful, would be as great a curiosity as one of Barnimes Canibals.¹⁰

The heading of this is the name of our Camp. But you can direct to either place. You might direct to the latter just for a change, as our mutual friend [the] P.M. [postmaster] of W. [Westminster] will think I have taken a five years lease of Ft. Union. It will be Taps in a few moments, and my candle is just about the sixteenth past of an inch long, so had better say Good night to you all.

The Buck-board (mail express) will be here in a few days, will write again then. Taps has just gone.

Fort Bascom, New Mexico
AUGUST 3, 1872

I now take advantage of my first opportunity to account for my self since [I] last wrote to you. I left Union the 21st of July in charge of six mules and a big Government wagon loaded with forage for this Camp. And after spending seven days on the road with plenty of rain each day [I] arrived at our destination (this Camp). And it is with gladness in my heart that I can say "I am still alive," for mules without exceptions have great propensities for using their hind feet on all occasions, without a thought of where they are going to strike you.

Upon our arrival in Camp [we] found the place had been visited by a flood which had made great distruction in Camp. Nearly all the Q. M. and Subsistence stores were washed away or damaged so as to be unfit for issue, causing a loss of a number of thousand dollars to the Government. One man of M Troop was drowned and one horse of our Troop shared the same fate.¹¹ We have now moved camp to this place.

---

10 Matthews refers to P. T. Barnum, the renowned American showman of the latter part of the nineteenth century.

11 Cavalrymen began using the term "troop" informally when referring to a company at least as early as the Civil War. However, it did not become official nomenclature until 1881. The infantry continued to use "company" and the artillery "battery" after that time. See ANJ, October 29, 1881, 278. The soldier who drowned on July 21, 1872, was Private Gilbert Rollins of M Troop. He was a twenty-seven-year-old veteran, having begun his second enlistment on December 14, 1871, at Fort Garland, Colorado. A Canadian by birth, Rollins had worked as a laborer prior to his army service. See entry 534, p. 85, roll 40, ROE, RG 94, NA.

C and D Troops have arrived and we now have five Troops of our Regiment here. It is rumored that we will move to the front and commence hostilities in a few days.[12] We expect to be joined by some Troops of the 4th Cavalry soon as we get into Texas. But, my opinion is we will have very little fighting to do. And the less we have the better it will suit me. I am still in charge of my mule team geting my 20¢ extra per day.[13] And to tell you the truth I dont care if I have to drive it all summer, for duty in the Troop is not as easy as it might be.

The Troops was paid while we were in Union. Our Lieutenant drew pay for us. I have some money to send you, but will have to wait until some Officer goes to Los Vegas (28 miles from Union), and then send it with him. Can get a money order now at that place.

We are having some of the warmest weather I ever experienced. It is impossible to make ones self comfortable any place during the day. The perspiration is running off me in great large drops.

I know you will complain of this poor letter, especially of the bad writing, but it is the best I can do. My hands are so sore and rough from handling the dirty harness. I will write to you again by the next opportunity.

Fort Bascom, New Mexico
AUGUST 4, 1872

Since [I] come to take my present situation into consideration [I] should not be particular what kind of letters [I] received, for [I] am now about five hundred miles from no place with a certainty of going farther. I dont know by what conveyance your letter came from Union. Lieut. Boyd, the Q. M. of the expedition sent it to our Camp this evening. It could not have been delayed long on the road. Capt B's letter has not reached me yet, hope it will come safely. The $10.00 [I] sent you for the boots [I] have long since given up as gone to foul hands. I was talking to the Post Master in Los Vegas when I come down this last time and

---

12 Company C, having already marched from Fort Selden, on the Rio Grande in the southern part of the territory, was left at Fort Bascom to guard over the supply base and to conduct local patrols. See Eighth Cavalry Returns, July 1872.

13 Men assigned to "extra duty," such as skilled laborers and teamsters, were paid twenty-five cents a day, in addition to their regular pay. See *Revised Regulations*, 127.

spoke to him of the circumstance. And he told me that the mail was lost about that time. So suppose that was the mail I was unlucky enough to send my money by. No use to cry about spilt milk but it will never occur again, for now the P.O. in Los Vegas (28 miles from Union) is a money Order Office, and when ever [I] want to send money, can send it down there by some Officer and let him get an order. I have some money to send you now but will have to wait until an Officer, or I go to Union and then send it.

You can tell Yingling, if he has not already made those boots for me to have them done for certain by the 1st of October as that is the time we are supposed to return. I will correct my order as to the kind of boot [I] want on a slip of paper and enclose in this. And [I] will send you another ten dollars to pay for them. (Not in this)

Dear Sister you speak of my getting married, and say [I] must not before I am 30. Now I will say to you what [I] have never done before, and that is I have never yet met the young lady who I could <u>love</u> better than "my loved ones at home." I mean you all, taken as one, or as a whole, and have long since given up the idea of ever getting married until you all are comfortable provided for. It is <u>you all who</u> is entitled to my love and help. And if God spares me to reach you in good health you shall have that undivided help which you are so justly entitled too, and have it with the most cheerful heart. So dont ever think of me getting married before thirty, if [I] do then. I believe I am the broken link that can be repaired or connected on this earth. So when that broken link is once more connected let us do our best to keep it in its place for the future. And not allow another link to be lost from its place.

And if it is your wish we go to England, we will go, provided the requisite is forthcoming. As for myself, [I] cant say [I] have particular desire to go, but [I] will do all in my power to have your wish gratified. I have thought a great deal about what [I] can do when my time is out, and some how have fixed upon Rail Roading. Think I would like the life. And since you speak of Mr. Meredith being conductor on the Hagerstown Road perhaps he could get me a place, for have only got <u>2</u> years <u>1</u> month and <u>4</u> days more to serve. And it is time I was thinking of an occupation. I am content to do anything so that I can be with and assist you all I can. What do you think of my choice, perhaps by the time I come home there will be something better for me to do. And something that will allow me to be with you more, that is what I want never to be separated again.

I am strong and healthy. Never enjoyed better health. And could you only see me now, seated in my tent, saddle stirup for a candle stick, pillow and poncho for a desk, collar of my shirt unbuttoned, sleeves rolled up and the perspiration running off me at the rate of 40 knots an hour. Know you would say I look fat, saucy, ragged and dirty. And you would say what is no more than the truth, for I am the whole with one exception, namely saucy. And that I am not for am always respectful to every person whom I come in contact with, and for that trait I am liked by both officers and men. It is a common rule for men in the Army to call each other by their last name, but I notice I am an exception to the rule, for when [I] am addressed it is as Eddie.

We are still in Camp at this place, but [I] think will leave in a few days. I spoke to Lieut Boyd Q.M. about being relieved from driving the mule team. And he told me the General said he was not to relieve any of us teamsters until the other train which is on the road comes in. And it was expected in to-day. I am not particular about being relieved. If anything [I] think [I] would prefer the team on the scout, but then [I] would not have such a good chance of sending Father the buffalos tail. This is the wrong season of the year for buffalo or would have Killed one long ago. Just for the tip of his tail. So [I] could send it to Father, to prove that I am a better shot than [I] use to be. But just you hold your breath until you get that buffalo's tail. And guess you will feel like taking a long breath.

I wrote you a bit of a letter yesterday which will go by the same conveyance as this, so with them both perhaps you can make one letter. I know you will have some difficulty in deciphering the meaning of this, but it is really the best I can do under present circumstances, half the time I cannot see the lines.

Taps has gone so [I] will have to put out my candle but [I] will first give you the instructions for the boots, and then perhaps will add a line in the morning.

Fort Bascom, New Mexico
AUGUST 6, 1872

We have every thing packed up to move tomorrow. I have been relieved from driving mules and will go with the Troop. The Command will number about three hundred and fifty men. We also take one 12 lb Howitzer along, and if [we] have an opportunity of fireing at the Comanches with that there will be some fun.[14]

Our Camp presents an appearance this evening which reminds me somewhat of cleaning up day at home. Every thing is packed up ready for the move. All our surplus property will be left here until we return. Are only taking along what is actually necessary. We will be out forty days, or at least we are taking that number of days rations. Don't suppose I will have an opportunity of writing to or hearing from you during that time. But if should have an opportunity will shurely take advantage of it and will write when ever I possible can.

I dont want you to worry because you do not hear from me every week, and imagine everything that could by any means happen me. I have too much to live for to unnecessairily run into danger. You can rest assured loved ones, that I will take good care of myself. I think the scout will amount to but very little.

This makes my third letter to you this week, and they will all go in the same mail, dont think you can complain of number.

Have had no opportunity to send you the money, so will give it to the Captain to take care of until we come back.

Cant think of anything more to write you, so [I] will bid you all good bye until [I] can write you again.

Fort Bascom, New Mexico
AUGUST 6, 1872

We leave this Post tomorrow on a forty day Scout and as it will be

---

14 The model 1841 twelve-pounder mountain howitzer was the most popular artillery piece used on the frontier prior to the advent of the Hotchkiss 1.65-inch mountain gun in the late 1870s. Almost every post had at least one, and sometimes several, of these small bronze howitzers. Having a total weight of approximately 583 pounds, the piece was relatively light and easy to maneuver for the six-man crew. The tube had a bore diameter of 4.62 inches but a length of only about twenty-eight inches, thus limiting the range to approximately nine hundred yards, according to the type of projectile used. The howitzer could fire explosive shells, spherical case shot (shrapnel), and canisters, tin cylinders containing 144 lead balls of .69 caliber. The latter had an effective range of about two hundred yards. The original gun was designed to be quickly dismantled and carried by two mules equipped with special packsaddles. More popular in the West was the "prairie" carriage, which had a wider wheelbase than the mountain version and was therefore more stable when being drawn overland. Ammunition was transported in a special two-wheeled ammunition cart drawn by one mule or horse. See *Ordnance Manual*, 54–56, 75, 271, 281, 386.

impossible for me to communicate with you during that time I have concluded to keep a small "Journal" of events. I know it will partly make amends for the long silence.

August 7, 1872—Our Command numbering about three hundred men of our Regiment, composed of B. D. L. and M. Troops with forty days rations, left Bascom at 10 o'clock A.M. As General Gregg, (our Colonel) was not ready to leave at that time, he gave Capt. Bankhead (Senior Captain) Orders to move the Command, and he would join us soon as he could complete his business at the Post.[15]

We moved off marching in an eastern direction over the prairie (not on any road) until about 2 o'clock when [we] came to a road. Close by [we] found wood and water and went into Camp. Pitched the Officers tents and was preparing supper, when Genl. Gregg came up and gave orders to move forward. Tents had to be taken down, wagons repacked, horses caught and saddled. After an hours work, with no end to growling we were all ready to resume the days march. Only marched four miles farther when [we] went into Camp, found plenty of water, but very little wood. Distance marched 12 miles.

August 8, 1872—Left Camp at 7 A.M. [We are] still marching over the prairie. Learned that we were taking a short cut to get on the old Fort Smith road, which runs from Fort Smith, Arkansas to Santa Fe, N.M.[16] It was L Troops turn to fall in rear of the wagon train to act as rear guard. Whenever more than one troop marches together the troop starting out in advance falls in the rear next day. In this way each troop takes its share of what is considered the disagreeable duty of marches viz: guarding the wagon train.

The day was very warm. Saw nothing of interest during the days march. Went into Camp at 2 P.M. [and] found plenty of wood and water. The latter not being very good and had the appearance of coming from a brick yard, distance marched 14 miles.

August 9, 1872—Our Cooks (Kind hearted fellows) thought they would treat us to some soft bread. So last night they baked. At breakfast

---

15 Henry C. Bankhead transferred from the Fifth Infantry to the Eighth Cavalry in December of 1870. He was an 1846 graduate of the U.S. Military Academy and had served with the Fifth through both the Mexican-American and Civil Wars. He was promoted to major in the Fourth Cavalry in 1873 and retired six years later. See Heitman, *Historical Register*, vol. 1, 189.

16 This was the route from Fort Smith, Arkansas, to Albuquerque explored by Lieutenant James W. Abert in 1845. Abert's map and detailed report represented the first reliable information on the Canadian River region of the so-called Staked Plains. See Goetzmann, *Army Exploration*, 123–27.

this morning I was handed something which from its color and weight I presumed must be part of a brick, but was told by the cook that it was my ration of bread. Now I believe my digestive organs are about as strong as the majority of the white race and I would no more attempt there powers on that piece of bread, than I would on a 12 lb solid shot.[17] I politely thanked our gentlemanly cook, but declined eating any of his fresh bread, prefering "hard tack" which had been baked in some mechanical bakery in the first year of the late Rebellion.[18]

We brought some beef cattle from Bascom with us[. D]uring the night they became frightened and stampeded. Half the men of our troop was sent after them returned with the cattle about 9 A.M. The Command (excepting our troop) left Camp at 7 o'clock. We soon caught up with them after our men came in with the Cattle. After a short march of 6 miles [we] went into Camp, near the old Fort Smith road. The road looked as though it had been considerably traveled on some years ago, but none at all lately. Found plenty of wood and water. Suppose you will wonder why we are making such short marches. The marches have to be regulated by the water. And as there is no certainty of finding water at the same place it was a year before, the General prefers camping where ever he is sure of the water to running any chances.

August 10, 1872—B. L. and M. Troops left Camp at 8 A.M. leaving D Troop behind to search for the Cattle, which had again stampeded during the night. It is singular how these cattle will become frightened and run off, although guarded on all sides by sentrys.

During the day saw numbers of Antelope, first game [we] had seen since leaving Bascom. They were very wild and it was impossible to get a shot at them. It rained some during the past night, also a little this morning.

The General rode horseback from the time we left Camp this morning until 2 o'clock P.M. when he returned to his Ambulance. Dont think he is much of a horseman, but like Father, prefers lying off in an Ambulance to horse back riding.

---

17 A solid shot was a cast-iron cannonball used primarily for battering fortifications.
18 Hard bread, called hardtack by most soldiers, was a plain cracker made of flour and water. The crackers measured approximately three inches square and one-half inch thick. Nine or ten constituted a day's ration for each man. They were packed fifty pounds to a wooden crate. Virtually all of the hardtack issued to the army for more than a decade after the Civil War had been produced during the war years, much of it by a mechanical bakery in Baltimore not far from Eddie's hometown. See Billings, *Hardtack and Coffee*, 114–16.

Something resembling a drove of cattle was seen at a distance. The command was halted until the General examined it through his "field glass" and pronounced it dust which had been raised by the wind. Marched thirty miles when [we] found water sufficient for the Command, but no wood. Had prepaired ourselves before leaving our previous Camp for such an emergency by putting plenty of wood on the wagons. D Troop has not come up yet, but will perhaps before dark.

August 11, 1872—Still in Camp. D Troop failed to arrive last night. Our wood has run out. All hands took sacks and scattered over the prairie picking up "buffalo chips" (buffalo manure) to cook by. These chips make a very good fire, but the odor arising after they burn sometime does not smell as sweet as "new mown hay." But then Soldiers are not particular about the smell, somthing to appease their appetites is more in their minds than any thing else, and little difference to them it makes whether their victuals are cooked by coal, wood or buffalo chips. D Troop came in at 10 o'clock.

The Command left camp at 11 A.M. marched four miles and went into Camp again. Short marches there, but I suppose the General knows his business. Anything to put in the forty days. We may meet some Indians on the road but unless we increase our gait, we will never overtake any.

I have just returned from standing two hours herd guard. Supped sumsstiously of stewed Antelope, killed by one of our troop, fair coffee. (I only drink one quart each meal) and some splendid biscuits. The latter had no resemblance to the bread baked at the Camp a few days back. I have filled and lighted my old friend and companion [his pipe], and will soon close my days diary.

We are now in splendid hunting ground. Antelope are as plentiful as flies in harvest time, but are much harder to Kill. They are very wild, more so than a person would expect, as they seldom see a hunter. One of our troop succeeded in Killing one [a] little while ago. Their meat is very nice eating. Soldiers prefer it to Army bacon.

August 12, 1872—Broke Camp at 6 1/2 A.M. Found plenty of Cedar Wood [and] loaded our wagons, for this will be the last wood we will find for some days. We ascended a high hill when [we] found ourselves on the "famous staked Plains" of Texas. Famous for wild game of all Kinds including Kiawa and Comanche Indians. It is the hunting ground of these tribes. Two of the most desperate tribes of

Indians on the American Frontier. As far as the eye can see is nothing but the bare plain, not the least hill or anything to obstruct ones view.

What a great pity some <u>poor man</u> could not own about forty miles of this land <u>in</u> some Eastern City. It would then be worth something, but as it is, it is not worth one cent an acre at the present time. And it never will be worth anymore.

The first buffalo was Killed by one of D Troop to-day. From the quantity of meat I saw in the wagon which brought it in, I would judge they must weigh about one thousand pounds. One quarter of the animal was given to us and will be cooked for breakfast tomorrow. I just saw another buffalo, about one mile away, too far to go after. Am feeling confident that [I] will be able to send you the tip of my first buffalo's tail. We went into Camp at 3 P.M. distance marched 20 1/2 miles.[19] Found plenty of good rain water in holes in the plains. No wood "excepting buffalo chips." The General had pickets stationed on all prominent look outs to watch for Indians, for we are now on their hunting ground and may have a visit from them any moment.

August 13, 1872—Left Camp at 6 A.M. marching almost due east, in fact have been marching nearly in that direction since [we] left Bascom. During the morning we saw at least five hundred Antelope, but nary buffalo, or red man. The former [we] are anxious to see but no particular desire to meet the latter. Unless we could have a little time with them without danger of loss on our side, and that is one of the few impossibilities. About 4 o'clock [we] came to halt, and went into Camp. Found plenty of rain water in holes, but nary stick of wood. Scattered over the prairie and in a short time had procured a sufficient quantity of the indispensible material for cooking purposes for the night and morning. Miles traveled 30 1/4.

August 14, 1872—We all woke up this morning rather early from sound slumber by the patter of rain in our face's. We had not sufficient transportation leaving Bascom to carry tents for the men, and would not have brought them if [we] had. So we had no roof over our heads,

---

19 When military columns in the field were accompanied by wheeled vehicles, marching distances could be accurately measured by use of an odometer. Typically, this instrument was a small circular brass box containing a series of gears regulating an index on a dial plate affixed to the exterior. The odometer was calibrated to the circumference of the wheel to which it was attached. It recorded the number of revolutions made by the wheel, and this number, multiplied by the wheel's circumference, was used to calculate the distance traveled. See Lord, *Civil War Collector's Encyclopedia*, 97.

excepting the broad canopy of Heaven. And as our Father wished to water his wild animals of the plains, he opened his flood gates allowing the water to pour down on us poor tired and weary Soldiers, who were trying to rest from a days hard ride. We had two alternatives, one to lie and take the wetting in our blankets or get up and put on our boots (the only part of our clothing which is taken off upon retiring when scouting), roll up the blankets and stand the storm. We chose the latter, standing out taking the rain with mutterings of "hard times." Eat our breakfast in the rain.

Saddled up and left Camp at 6 A.M. in the rain. For four or five hours we rode in a cold and chilling rain, however it cleared up at last, when Old Sol came out in all its glory. Making many a heart glad. We are still marching over the level plain without a hill or mound of any Kind in sight. Nothing to see except the sky above and a broad plain below, devoid of vegetation of any Kind.

Saw no game of any Kind during the day's march, something unusual. Went into Camp at 2 P.M. distance marched 21 miles. Plenty of water and buffalo chips in abundance.

August 15, 1872—Struck tents and left Camp at 7 A.M. marching due east. About 9 o'clock we came to a small stream, the water was clear and excellent. We marched along and went into Camp on its banks at 1 o'clock P.M. Only saw one deer in the shape of game and from the way it jumped and ran off, [I] suppose we frightened the life out of it.

Our Guides and pickets report Indians at some distance, but [we] have seen none very close. Dont know what truth there is in the report, as I spent the evening sleeping. Stable Call has gone so I must go and take care of my horse. Marched 17 miles to-day.

August 16, 1872—Little did I dream when [I] closed my days diary of the 15th inst. that before the rising of another sun, the most important and dangerous event of our seemingly useless scout would transpire. A Soldiers life on the frontier is one of danger and vicissitude. When he lies down to rest at night he has no guarantee of a peaceful nights sleep, and so it proved last night.

Yesterdays march brought us to the commencement of very rough looking country, and our Camp was located in a splendid place for a surprise, and night attack by Indians. Danger was not anticipated and was the most remote thought in our minds. Before turning in for the night we as usual squatted around in groups to have an hours smoke and talk on the progress of the scout, and the probabilities of seeing an Indian. Many were the ludicrous remarks made by the boys. After smoking and talking ourselves tired, all turned in to sleep, excepting the guard, who paced too and fro his lonley beat, probable thinking of absent ones at Home, and little dreaming of the near approach of our dangerous foe.

About 1 o'clock A.M, I awoke from a sound sleep by the report of several Carbines, connected with the most unearthly yelling it has ever been my misfortune to listen too. It sounded to me like all the Devils incarnate, and all the Demons of Hell had issued forth in that one lonley spot to make the night hideous with their orgies. No pen is capable of describing my feelings at that moment. I of course knew that we were "jumped," (attacked) by Indians, and from those blood chilling yells, I imagined we had been totaly surprised and that the Indians were right in our midst, dealing death on all sides. But that was not the time for thought, immediate action was required from all.

Again there was two alternatives before us, but what a vast difference from that spoken of in another part of this "Journal." One victory and life, the other failure, only to meet a most horrible death. I was only a moment getting a cartridge in my carbine, and with revolver in one hand and carbine in the other, with only my shirt and pants on, I ran to the right of our troop and on a line with B Troop where the firing and yelling was the loudest. I could see the Indians by the light of the moon riding in a circle near our lines, firing at us as they charged by. I discharged my carbine at the first Indian I saw, and never taking time to notice with what effect, I reloaded and fired as fast as I possible could. By this time our whole Command was up and the firing became more general. The Indians seeing that there was no hope for them, commenced to withdraw.

At this stage of the fight a detail of 10 picked men was made from each troop to form a line and advance about one hundred yards from Camp and take station as pickets.[20] I was one of the number from our

---

20 Pickets were sentinels of an advance guard. Their purpose was to maintain vigilance over the country in front of or around the perimeter of a friendly body of troops. When in the immediate presence of the enemy, as in this instance, pickets were deployed as a line of skirmishers with the men positioned at five-yard intervals. At other times, especially at night, pickets were grouped in threes at strategic points, the men taking turns staying awake and alert. In the event of an attack, pickets would open fire and hold their ground for as long as possible. If forced to retire, they were to give ground slowly as they fell back on the main body so as to retard the enemy's advance. The manual states, "courage and common sense are the principal requisites for a picket," which speaks well of Matthews. See Kautz, *Customs of Service*, 46.

troop. Forming a line in a moment, we advanced at a double quick step, firing at the retreating Indians as we ran. When we reached the prescribed distance from Camp, we came to a halt, and kept up a fire from our Carbines, as long as we could hear a yell from an Indian. Finally all became quiet, when we deployed as pickets. And there remained until daylight relieved us from our unpleasant watch.

I would like to be able to pen my thoughts during the short engagement, and while keeping guard until morning. But such a thing is impossible. Suffice it to say that thoughts of you, loved one's, was more prominent in my mind than the danger I was in.

When morning dawned, we found that our loss was very slight. One man, a Sergeant of Troop B, wounded in the leg, and two mules Killed.[21] A number of the wagons bore bullet holes in there canvas, showing that the Indians fire was too high. It is impossible now to tell the loss of the Indians, as they left none of their number behind. We are satisfied that from the number of shots we fired more than one of their number was hit. Our Mexican Guide, told us that he heard more than one of the Indians cry out that they had been shot. Perhaps there will be some way of finding out their loss later.

These Indians I learn are fastened to their horses with straps, during engagements, and unless you Kill their ponies it is impossible to dismount them. It is strange to me that none of their ponies was Killed during the fight, but I suppose we like them fired too high.[22] There is not much accuracy in firing at night, and more especially firing mounted. I almost forgot another part of our loss. Our beef cattle again stampeded at the first

---

21 General Gregg's report of the battle reads: "At this camp [No. 9] the Indians attacked the command at 1 A.M. 16 Aug. but were promptly repulsed by 'B' Troop, on whose front the attack was made. The attacking party numbered about 40 mounted Indians ('Kiowas') whilest quite a number kept up a scathing fire from the surrounding bluffs. The beef cattle that were being driven along for the use of the command were stampeded and lost. The Indians however did not get them as they were followed back on the road we came as far as Pinto de Agua, a distance of 36 miles. Great credit is due to both officers & men of the command and particularly to Capt. McCleave ('Troop B') for promptness & coolness with which the sudden & unlooked for midnight attack was repulsed. Casualties: 1 enlisted man (Sergt. O'Neal of 'B' Troop) wounded, 2 mules killed & 1 horse wounded and 8 head of cattle lost. From subsequent information received the Indians seem to have suffered severely, having lost 4 killed & 8 wounded" (Gregg to AAAG, District of NM, September 17, 1872, in Box 32, LR, Department of the MO, RG 393, NA).

22 Matthews was probably correct in his assumption. Because of a shooter's inability to see his sights clearly, nighttime firing tends to be high, with the bullets passing entirely over the intended target. The officers and noncoms should have directed the men to fire low, a military rule of thumb

shot and we have never seen them since. But this loss, we consider our gain. As we had to guard them every night and had trouble enough with them. We are happy now [line missing].

We left the scene of our late encounter at 7 A.M. by getting out of the Cañon and up on high ground. About 10 o'clock we saw an Indian rancharee and charged it, but found that it had only been vacated a few hours before our arrival.[23] Saw no other signs of Indians during the day's march. Went into Camp at 2 P.M. Camped upon high ground. Guess the General has had enough of Camping in Canons for some time. Took more precaution in forming our wagon train so as to form a better stockade against the attack of Indians. Camp was laid out in a square with one troop to guard each side. B Troop had been left behind in the morning to search for the missing cattle, as they were in charge of them when they ran off. And as they had not returned yet, ten men from each of the other troops was detailed to guard their side of the Camp.

Our troop has only 23 Privates, for duty, and out of the 23, 19 was on guard. The Officers had been so badly frightened the previous night that they are determined not to be surprised again. Every Camp before we were attacked the Officers all pitched their tents as far from the men as they could possible do with safety, but to-night, all with the exception of Capt. Randlett and Lieut. Hennisee of D Troop, have had their tents pitched in among the Quarter Master's wagons and mules, prefering the dust and smell from the mules, to the danger of Camping on a line with the men.[24] The two Officers above alluded to had their tent pitched as close to the line where their men sleep as they possible could during the evening. As night approached the tent was lowered to the ground and the officers bed made upon it. I will be on guard again to-night, but there is no room to complain. My own doings brought me on

---

whenever the range was unknown because a bullet striking the ground short of the target probably would ricochet and might still inflict a casualty. See Heth, *Target Practice*, 37.
23 *Rancheria* is a Spanish word meaning a collection of huts. In the American Southwest, the term was widely used to mean an Indian camp.
24 James F. Randlett served with the Third New Hampshire Infantry throughout the Civil War and was mustered out in 1865 as its lieutenant colonel. He was assigned to the Thirty-Ninth Infantry in 1867 and transferred to the Eighth Cavalry in 1870. From 1886 until his retirement in 1896, Randlett served as a field officer in the Ninth Cavalry. See Heitman, *Historical Register*, vol. 1, 815. Officers who shared hardships and dangers with their men gained their respect, though one must question why the officers dropped their tent. Perhaps they did so to reduce its visibility as a target.

this scout, and the whole troop is on guard to-night. Every precaution has been taken to avoid another surprise. Distance marched 17 1/2 miles.

August 17, 1872—Still in Camp. B Troop has not arrived, and the night did not pass without another alarm of Indians. Our troop was in Camp in rear of the main Camp. We had three posts to guard during the night. One on the picket line over the horses, and two outposts about five hundred yards from our Camp. With orders for all the guard to sleep at the out post, and if attacked to fall back on the main Camp.

I was first relief over the horses, and having stood my three hours guard went to the out post and turned in to sleep the remainder of the night. Being very tired and from the loss of sleep, slept unusually sound, and failed to hear a shot fired by one of D Troops sentrys with the cry of Indians. But suppose my mind was on that one subject the most, that I awoke with an indistinct recollection of hearing the cry of Indians. I looked around from right to left where there had been [a] man sleeping when I turned in, but could not see a single man, not even the sentrys who's beat was right along our front.

I confess that I was not a little frightened for the moment. I could not account for the sudden spiriting away of the remainder of the guard, but when I looked in the direction of Camp I saw by the light of the moon, numerous heads sticking up above the mens saddles, which had been arranged in a line to form a Kind of fortification for the men when lying down. Catching up my arms and blankets I made as fast time getting over those five hundred yards which intervened between our picket post and Camp as ever "Hary Bassett" made at any of the Saratogo Races, the same distance.[25] I croached down behind my saddle and soon learned what all hands were on the alert for.

Two mounted Indians had been seen approaching Camp in a stealthy manner, supposed for the purpose of reconnoitering our Camp. From the position our men were in sleeping at the out post in case of an attack from that side and a charge by the Indians, we would very

---

25 Matthews refers to Harry Bassett, a celebrity three-year-old thoroughbred racehorse that was the undefeated eastern champion and the winner of both the 1871 Travers and the Belmont Stakes. In a July 1872 race at Saratoga, New York, Harry Bassett came in first ahead of the projected winner, Longfellow. See Hotaling, *They're Off*, 93–99.

probable be cut off and be subject to the fire from both our own men and the Indians. Not a very pleasant situation by any means.

Soon as the shot was fired all hands (excepting myself) ran in. I would have been in soon as any of the others, had I only heard the shot. I talked pretty plain to those men who slept near me, for running in and leaving me sound asleep. They were all so badly frightened that they could not take time to see that all guard[s] were awake. I am not very courageous, but if [I] dreaded the name of Indians as much as a great number of our Command, I would never Soldier a day on the frontier. My idea of and what little knowledge of Indian fighting I have, shows conclusively that a white man is far superior to an Indian in a fight. We have all the advantage of improved Arms, abundance of ammunition to expend at will. In fact all the advantage is on our side. But the dread of the savage, and his unearthly yells (to use a Soldiers expression) "puts the fear of God in the white mans heart."

The shot fired by the Sentry had no effect, but to drive off the two Indians who retreated in quick order, and failed to put in another appearance. B Troop arrived in Camp about 8 A.M. reporting that the Cattle had gone back in the direction of Fort Bascom, and had not as we supposed fallen into the hands of the Indians. It made little difference to us whether the Indians got them or not as we had no desire to recover them. The General sent our Guides out this morning to recomwiter [reconnoiter]. They returned in an hour or two with the information that Indians in great numbers had driven them back and that the Indians were within five miles of our Camp.

We were in Camp on the level plain, while the large Canon in which we were attacked ran to our right and about three miles away. This Canon I suppose is full of Indians, it being their home during the winter. It was impassible for our wagon train even if we wished to follow through it, something none in the Command wished to undertake. And if we had have undertook such a thing, many of our number would never return, so "loved ones," perhaps I might have been one of the number. No person can fortell.

Imagine yourself wending your way through some deep chasm, on your right and left huge mountains rise almost perpendicular, and who's sides are one mass of solid rock. You look up and find that the top's of these mountains rise hundreds and hundreds of feet above you and you have "Canon Blancho" (White Canon) before you.²⁶ Had we have undertaken to pass through this Canon We could have been Killed by the Indians rolling stones down the sides of the Canon, and at the same time would have been powerless to harm a single Indian.

When our Guides returned with the information of the close proximity of a large body of Indians, orders were issued to form the wagons in such a manner as to be impossible for Indians to get in. And while a few men could keep a large body of Indians off, soon as this was done D, L, and M Troops were ordered to saddle up at once. Ammunition in abundance was issued to each man.

We then mounted and formed in line, when General Gregg rode up in our front and made a short speech, the substance of which was that we were now in the country of a sleepless and untiring foe, who's nature was one of treachery, and who when least expected attacked the white man, and if successful tortured their victims in the most brutal manner. He wound up by telling us, Indians were reported in large numbers near our Camp, that we were going out to meet them and possibly some fighting a foot would have to be done, and in that case he wanted every man to be ready for any emergency.

Soon as the General had concluded his brief remarks, the Adjutant rode to the front and gave the Command "Attention to Orders." He then read an Order from the General, thanking the Officers and men for the gallant manner in which we met and repulsed the Indians in our late encounter with them. This was more to inspire us with confidence in our self than anything else. And I believe it had a good effect with the men of the Command. For myself I did not derive any great inspiration from the Generals remarks or from the Order read by the Adjutant. I knew what had to be done in case we met the Indians. My own life was at stake as well as the Generals or any of the Command, and I was willing to risk that life with the rest, but not foolishly. I have too much to live for. Too many bright hopes for the future to recklessly run myself into danger.

---

26 Blanco Canyon was formed by the White River (formerly Catfish Creek) eroding into the eastern face of the tableland known as the Staked Plains in the Texas Panhandle. The canyon lies north-northeast of the city of Lubbock and extends some thirty-four miles from Hale County, through southwest Floyd County, and into the southeastern portion of Crosby County. See Carter, *On the Border*, 151–52.

We then marched off in a direction parallel with the Canon. As we rode along I occupied my mind for a time by scanning the faces of the greater part of our Troop. Some looked stern and resolute, while others were wreathed in smiles called forth no doubt by some humorous remark of some of the wits of the troop, but taken all in all a kind [of] stillness prevailed throughout the entire Command. As regards myself, [I] cant say that I felt very rejoiced at the prospects of a fight with the Indians, $13.00 a month is not an incentive to throw ones life away. And as to my patriotic feelings, I candidly say, I have none. I have never been blessed with the inspiration. And while riding along my thoughts went back to little Maryland, to green fields, friends, Loved parents, Brothers and Sisters, and the day I would be free to enjoy the pleasures of my home and the company of those "loved Ones at Home."

My mind was so occupied with these pleasant thoughts, that I forgot for the time the mission we were on. And was only brought back to reality, by the Command, coming to a halt and the exclamation "there they are." Looking in the direction the Command had been marching in, I saw at the distance of about a half mile some twenty Indians, they looked at us for a few moments. And then turned their horses heads and galloped [away?]. In this way we traveled about a mile, seeing no other Indians, or getting any closer to those before us. The Command came to an other halt. The Officers held another consultation and the conclusion come to was the Indians were drawing us into an ambush. With this conclusion came the Command "Left About wheel March" and we turned and marched back to our Camp. Many were the countenances which brightened up and many were the hearts made glad by this Command. I also experienced a feeling of relief when [I] saw we were marching back to Camp, for [I] have had all the Indian fighting I wish for the remainder of my life. And I have also seen sufficient of frontier life to satisfy any roving inclination I could possible have in the future.

When [we] reached Camp, every precaution was taken to avoid loss of life should the Indians attack us during the night and we fully expected they would. Nine men from each troop was detailed for guard. Again I was one of the number, making my third guard in succession, without a nights rest. Pretty hard on a fellow to stand guard every night, ride twenty miles during the day, herd horses until darkness sets in and then while resting, do several little odd jobs which military necessity requires to be done. But I have the least ground to complain, [I] had no business to leave Regimental Head Quarters.

Sunday, August 18, 1872—The night passed without an attack and I am sure none in the Command regret it. But had the Indians put in an appearance, they would have met with a warm reception. Every person in the Command slept with his clothing on, and Carbine loaded. All we would have had to do in case the Indians attacked us, would be to discharge our Carbines and re-load.

We left Camp at 6 Am. After an hours ride we come in sight of at least one thousand buffalo. A party of men was sent out to Kill sufficient for the Command. The men started off in a gallop in the direction of the buffalo. In a short time they were in among the huge monsters firing shot after shot into them. Every person became excited with the chase, which was in full view. Not a hill or mound of any kind to abstruct our view. The chase lasted about fifteen minutes and during that time twenty one buffalo were Killed. Three were put in a wagon for our use, the remaining eighteen left on the plains to be devoured by Cayotes and other small animals which live in this part of the country. It seemed a shame to Kill those large Animals merely for the sport. The meat of those eighteen buffalo left to waste on the plain would have been sufficient to keep that number of families for one year. But little did the men think of wastage, so excited were they during the hunt. Oh how I wished to be one of that hunting party, just for the sake of fulfilling my promise to you. But I have no fears but there will be plenty of opportunities to make good my promise before [I] return from this Scout.

Saw a few Indians during the day, but too far away to go after. Went into Camp about 4 o'clock, in a Canon, which connected with the Canon in which we were jumped. Found plenty of wood and abundance of excellent water. And above all a splendid place to be jumped again by Indians. In fact we could hardly find a worse place to Camp in. But we had either to Camp up on the plain without wood or water, or decend the Canon and chance an attack by Indians.

We are now seemingly at the end of the Staked Plains, before us is nothing but baren hills, small valley's and miserable looking Canons. In fact about as unprepossessing a piece of nature as a person would wish to see. Will take chances for a nights undisturbed rest. Distance marched to-day 29 miles.

August 19, 1872—Morning dawned without an incident to chronicle. My sleep was as sound last night, as any part of old Rip Van Winkles. It was my first "all night in" for five consecutive nights.

Leaving D Troop to guard Camp. General Gregg took the remaining three troops at 8 A.M, on an inspecting tour of the largest Canon. We rode down the Canon about six miles following an Indian trail. Rode in single file the greater part of the way. As the trail was very rough and narrow, [we] dismounted and climbed to the top of the Canon, leading our horses. Found the country open, but much rougher than the plains we had been traveling over. I cant see how we are to get our wagons out of the Canon, unless [we] go out the way came in. The General sent our troop to scout along the top of the Canon until [we] returned to Camp. He took B and M Troops and rode off in another direction. At this time of writing he has not returned. We saw but few signs and no Indians on our way back to camp, and got back in time for dinner, traveled about twelve miles.

August 20, 1872—Still in Camp in the Canon, The General and party returned about 4 o'clock last evening. His party saw no Indians. Sent B Troop after buffalo. They returned late in the evening bringing in five buffalo. They report seeing plenty of Indian signs, but no Indians.

August 21, 1872—Broke Camp at 6 A.M. [and] found a place to get out of the Canon north of the point which [we] came in at. Had some difficulty getting our wagons up to the top of the Canon. Marched during the day in a north eastern direction. Saw so many buffalo, that [I] actually got tired [of] looking at them. And wished a thousand times that they would keep out of sight. Saw at the least estimation three thousand in one herd. Did not Kill any as [we] had fresh meat on hand. The Country over which we traveled was rather rough. Camped near water at 4 o'clock, having marched 24 1/2 miles.

August 22, 1872—Left Camp at 7 A.M. Marched over very rough ground. So rough as almost to be impassable for the wagons. Went into Camp at 11 o'clock, after a march of 7 miles. The General took D Troop and marched five or six miles farther to examine the country. Returned to Camp about 3 o'clock. We are Camping on the banks of a small stream, the water has an alkali taste, and Is not much relished by either man or beast.

August 23, 1872—Broke Camp at 7 A.M. Our troop was sent to

Scout along the banks of the stream. We were to follow the stream for six or eight miles and then to rejoin the Command, which was marching in another direction. Saw a few wild turkeys and deer, but no Indians. After marching about ten miles down the river, we started to search for the trail the Command had taken, but failed to find it until [we] had nearly returned to the place we started from. Had then to follow up the trail until [we] came to Camp. The Command had marched about fifteen miles, while we had ridden fully thirty.

For the last few days we have been traveling over some of the roughest country I ever saw, country that a <u>Maryland</u> farmer would not risk driving his Cattle over. While we have to get thirty eight wagons and Ambulances over it. Some places look to be impassable, but we find ways to drag the wagons and mules over.

August 24th, 1872—Before leaving Camp this morning three men from each troop was detailed to hunt buffalo. I was one of the three from [the] troop and rode out with great anticipations of having fine sport and at the same time fulfill my promise made to you. We left the Command to our right and after a fruitless hunt of an hour a messinger joined us from the Command saying the General wanted us over near the Command, where there was plenty of buffalo, and some Indian Ponies, and perhaps some Indians. We soon galloped over where the Command was marching. B Troop was left back to help us in case we should be jumped by Indians and it was the general opinion we would be, if we rode over the rough ground where the buffalo and ponies were seen.

Capt. McCleave, Commanding Troop B and who is considered one of the best Indian fighters on the frontier, told us to ride fast after the buffalo and if the Indians jumped us, he with his troop would jump them. So off we started as fast as our horses could run. A young, reckless, and daring man of our troop and myself soon found ourselves ahead of all the others, and regardless of danger we dashed in among the frightened buffalo, who were running as fast as their legs could carry them. If I was excited when watching a buffalo hunt, I was a hundred times more so when engaged in it, and now that I was in among the huge looking monsters, I had some trouble to manage my frightened horse. I rode almost on top of a large bull buffalo and with the muzzel of my carbine within five feet of his back, fired and over rolled my first victim.

I was too much excited with the chase to stop, dismount and cut off the promised trophy, but dashing after the other buffalo, loading as I rode. I soon rolled another over, and then taking my revolver out I rode along side of a powerful looking one, and fired four shots into his side before [I] succeeded in Killing him. Without checking my horse I rushed after the flying buffalo. Again I was in among them firing as fast as I could load. Loading my carbine I rode [as] close as [I] could get my frightened horse. (And who by the way was showing signs of distress) to a handsome buffalo Calf and succeeded in shooting him through the spine. He immediately fell and died in a few moments.

I stoped my horse, dismounted and examined my meat, and while looking at the buffalo I thought of my promise. I took my Knife and cut off the "tip of his tail." And now loved ones, you see I have fulfilled my promise. This instead of my first buffalo, is my last one, and perhaps the last one I shall ever Kill. For now that I am composed and look at the danger I so rashly run into, it almost unerves me. I had always given myself more credit for better judgement than I displayed to-day. And had little idea that through excitement [I] would foolishly ride into imminent danger.

Rowalt, the young man from our troop who was near me, and who lead his horse over to where I was standing, said "Ed we have ridden too far away from the balance of the party and the best thing we can do is to rejoin them soon as possible."[27]

We mounted our horses and just as we done so, a man from D Troop who had followed us joined Rowalt and I. We were taking a survey of the country to see which was the quickest way of getting out of the rough country, when I saw at a distance of about a thousand yards five Indians riding towards us. I showed them to the two men with me. And as we did not know how many more there might be, we concluded to retreat.

So loading our Carbines, we retraced our way as best we could. The Indians continued to follow us, but did not appear to gain on us. We

---

27 This was Sergeant John F. Rowalt of L Company, an Ohio native who enlisted at Cincinnati on May 11, 1868. When he joined the army, Rowalt was a twenty-one-year-old farmer. He proved to be an exceptional soldier, distinguishing himself during a fight with Apaches at Lyry Creek, Arizona, on October 14, 1869, for which he was subsequently awarded the Medal of Honor for gallantry in action. See entry 147, p. 246, roll 35, ROE, RG 94, NA; Rodenbough, *Army of the United States*, 279; and *Medal of Honor*, 212. For another instance of Rowalt's conduct, see chapter 6 herein.

rode slowly back keeping our eyes open and Carbines ready for immediate action. After riding a couple of miles through the most miserable looking country I ever saw, we were joined by Lieut. Williams, of B Troop, who was in charge of us.[28] We reported the Indians to the Lieutenant, who thought the best thing we could do was to get on open ground soon as possible, as we were in danger of being jumped any moment. If we could only get out of the rough country we could stand the Indians off in case they attacked us. All the way back we found dead buffalo Killed by Rowalt and myself. In this way we were able to retrace our trail until we saw B Troop, who becoming uneasy were looking for us. You can rest assured I breathed a sigh of relief when [we] had come up to the troop.

From the time Rowalt and myself rode away from the party, we were in danger of being Killed any moment. I know there was plenty of Indians in the hills through which we rode. And I would no more think of riding over the same ground with one man again than I would of attacking a whole tribe of Comanche Indians.

This is my first buffalo hunt. And it will be my last. I almost broke my neck during the chase, with out the aid of the Indians. I was riding as fast as my horse could run, one hand holding the bridle reins, my loaded Carbine in the other. When my horse jumped in a Cayote hole and stumbled for twenty yards before recovering himself, the fall threw me out of the saddle and almost over his head. My spur catching in my lariat was all that held me up, and had I have fallen very likely I would have been Killed or badly hurt. And now that I have come out of this hunt safely, I have made up my mind never again to tempt providence by engaging in another.

We found that B Troop had loaded the wagon with hind quarters of buffalo killed by themselves, without touching one we had Killed. Got into Camp about 5 o'clock. Suppose we must have ridden forty miles during the day, while the Command marched 15. I feel very tired this evening, and have concluded never again to go on another buffalo hunt. "Although it is so exciting."

And now after writing about my exciting buffalo hunt and the

---

28 Richard A. Williams graduated from West Point in June 1870 and was assigned as a lieutenant to the Eighth Cavalry immediately thereafter. He rose to the rank of captain and served with the regiment until his death in 1890. See Heitman, *Historical Register*, vol. 1, 1042.

dangers escaped, I have the most sad and painful event of our scout to chronicle. Upon the arrival in Camp, of the Command this evening, pickets were stationed on all the prominent points to keep a lookout for the approach of Indians. It was our troops turn to furnish the picket guard. At each station three men were posted. One man had to be mounted all the time, while the two off duty at the time could lie down and rest.

One of the men named Hannan, very likely feeling tired, carelessly tied his horse with a lariat and then made it fast around his body, remarking at the time that in case he went to sleep his horse could not get away from him, little dreaming of the truth of his words. We had just finished eating supper, when one of the pickets galloped into Camp, reporting that Hannan's horse became frightened at a buffalo approaching, and had ran away draging Hannan after him, and that when found he was dead. The Doctor went out in an Ambulance and returned with the body, life was extinct, and the supposition was his neck was broken at the first jump of the horse. The men on picket with him say that he never cried out, or made any effort to check the horse, this confirms our supposition. We undressed and washed him and then put him into a wagon, there to remain until the morrow.[29]

I will be on guard to-night and can my feelings be imagined when walking back and forth in rear of the wagon which contains all that remains of a brother Soldier, who had been so suddenly taken from us. I am sick and tired of this kind of living, but believe if [I] was to die and be buried in this God forsaken country, [I] would never rest easy in my grave. This thought is to horrible to dwell upon.

Sunday, August 25, 1872—Remained in Camp to perform the last sad rites of our brother Soldier and comrade. His horse, which sent him to appear before his God, is now being saddled up for the purpose of following his master to the grave. I will attend the funeral with the troop and when [I] return will finish my remarks. At 10 o'clock A.M. the Command formed into line. The remains [were] placed in an Ambulance. On each side walked four pall bearers. In rear of the Ambulance, his horse was lead by one of the troop, following came the

---

29 The man who died so tragically was Private John Hannan, a laborer who had emigrated from Canada and enlisted in the U.S. Army at the age of twenty-two on July 25, 1870. The place of his death was recorded as "Rio Cibolo, Tex." See entry 786, p. 49, roll 36, ROE, RG 94, NA.

firing party. As the Ambulance came in front of the troop on the left of the line the troop presented Arms and soon as the remains passed by the troop would wheel and march by Company front to the grave.[30] Arriving at the grave, the body was lowered, when Lieut. Boyd read the Episcopal burial service.[31] This finished, three volleys was fired over the grave, and soon as it was filled up one of the trumpeters sounded "Taps" over the grave. This last performance in life means "put out your light." And I suppose in death it means that "your light is already out." This I think is a proper interpretation of the meaning of "Taps." Poor Hannan's light had been put out, never again to be relighted on earth. This death has cast a sadness over all in the troop, and in fact over all the Command.

August 26, 1872—Struck tents and left Camp at 7 A.M. The whole Command, wagons and Ambulances passing over poor Hannans grave, the object of this was to leave no trace of a grave for Indians or Coyotes to rob. And after all had passed over it, there was nothing to show that one of our number had been left there.

We marched for six hours in the bed of a dry sandy creek. The mules were almost worn out draging the wagons after them. And no wonder as our horses and mules were only getting two quarts of corn a day, besides what little grass they got while in camp.

We also were not living very high. Our flour was all gone, and we were put on three quarter rations of hard bread, by an Order of General Gregg's. Had the hard bread been good we would not have complained, but it was all full of worms. Old hard bread which undoubtedly had been baked in some mechanical bakery during the first part of the late war. We were getting as much buffalo meat as [we] could consume, but this meat has very little nutriment in it. And besides we were all tired of

---

30 Here Matthews describes a basic military funeral, though a somewhat informal one considering that the command was in the field. The troops rendered honors by presenting arms as the deceased soldier's body passed by. Then they reversed arms, and finally they wheeled by company fronts to follow the remains to the gravesite. The firing party was composed of eight privates, commanded by a corporal. After the body was lowered into the grave, the party fired three volleys. See Upton, *A New System*, 359–60.

31 Orsemus B. Boyd, a native New Yorker, was a corporal in the Eighty-Ninth New York Infantry during the first two years of the Civil War. In September of 1862, he secured a commission as a second lieutenant in the One Hundred Forty-Fourth New York Regiment. He entered the U.S. Military Academy the following year, graduated in 1867, and was appointed to the Eighth Cavalry. Boyd was promoted to captain in 1882 and died three years later. See Heitman, *Historical Register*, vol. 1, 236. Boyd's wife, Frances Anne, published her memoirs, *Cavalry Life in Tent and Field*, in 1894.

seeing it set before us. Lieut. Luff of our Troop, took me and another young man to search for water. We rode to the left of the bed of the creek for a distance of five miles, but failed to find any but Alkali water, plenty of that could be found in parts of the creek through which the Command was marching.

We were retracing our way back to the Command along the bed of the creek when we saw where nine ponies and one dismounted Indian had crossed the creek a short time ahead of us. The trail was quite fresh, and as we rode along we kept a sharp look out on both sides of the creek. When we saw the Command they were in Camp. And to tell the truth I was glad when we were there also. I have not forgotten my late buffalo hunt yet, and have no desire to run any more chances with a couple of men.

The Command had marched about twelve miles while we had riden seventeen during the day.

August 27, 1872—Our troop with the General left Camp at 7 A.M. to examine the country. Rode about 12 miles, as the country was very rough. The General concluded we had gone far enough. And acting upon the thought he turned around and returned to Camp.

At 1 o'clock P.M. tents were struck, when we left Camp, taking a direction which looked very much like going <u>home</u>. If this be the case, none will regret it, for I know the Officers, as well as the men have all had enough of Scouting for some time. For myself, [I] dont think I will go to any unnecessary trouble to go on an other one. Two of our horses gave out and were shot this evening. Went into Camp at 6 P.M. distance marched 15 miles, while our troop has traveled 27 miles.

August 28, 1872—Left Camp at 9 A.M. We now are "homeward bound." The country over which we are passing is not as rough as some we have traveled over. Still it is of no earthly account for anything except for buffalo pasture. We rode until 3 o'clock and then went into camp in a very pretty cotton wood grove. The prettiest place I have seen on the scout. The water was excellent and convenient, while the wood was scattered all around. There was also an abundance of wild grapes. Distance marched twenty miles.

August 29, 1872—Remained in Camp to recruit the stock. Our troop was sent out buffalo hunting. And as my horse had a sore back, I was left in Camp in charge of the extra horses. And indeed I am not sorry to be left in Camp for a days rest, for I have done a great deal of extra riding. The troop returned after three hours riding, having failed to see any buffalo, the first fruitless hunt on the scout.

August 30, 1872—Left Camp at 7 A.M. Crossed an old wagon trail supposed to have been made by the 3rd Cavalry some years ago. Went into Camp at 12 M. [meridian] near a pretty running stream. Washed my cloth[e]s and person in it and feel considerable better since [I] relieved myself of the surplus dust. Distance marched 12 miles.

August 31, 1872—We mustered for two months pay this morning. And left Camp at 8 o'clock. Marched until 4 o'clock when [we] went into Camp on an other small stream. The water is very good, with plenty of wood convenient. Marched twenty one and a half miles.

September 1, 1872—Remained in Camp to rest and recruit our Animals, who need it very much. B Troop are out buffalo hunting. We have now only fifteen days to complete our Scout. How I wish they were up, for [I] am sick and disgusted with this Scout. But I am not the only one in the Command that is sick of the trip. Both Officers and men are loud in denouncing this aimless wandering, for we have accomplished nothing so far, and are not likely to during the remaining fifteen days.

B Troop have just returned from their hunt, bringing in twelve hind quarters [of] buffalo. It has been divided and each troop is now busy "Jerking" the meat. Jerking beef or buffalo is I believe of Indian or Mexican origin. The object is to keep it from spoiling. When it is properly dried, it will keep for a great length of time. The mode of curing is very simple. The meat is cut in thin strips and then hung on lariats in the sun to dry. It will dry out thoroughly in one day. It is then taken and packed away in sacks with out salting. I like the meat much better this way than when cooked.

September 2, 1872—Left Camp this morning at 7 o'clock. Come onto our old road made going down. Since leaving Fort Bascom, we have formed a figure 6 in marching. Suppose [we] will follow our old trail back. Camped at 12 o'clock in the same Canon as [we] did going down. Are about 7 miles north of our previous Camp. Only traveled ten miles this morning.

September 3, 1872—Broke Camp at 7 A.M. Left the Canon and ascended to the plain. Are now on our old road, "Homeward Bound." Oh what ecstasy there is in the word. If it was only "homeward bound" in reality the ecstasy would be a thousand times greater. But as uninviting a place as "Union" is, we are all rejoiced at the prospects of soon returning to it. And when I once more return to it, never again will I want to go from it in any but an eastern direction.

Camped at 12 o'clock near plenty of water. Distance marched 10 miles.

September 4, 1872—Left Camp at our usual time this morning. Killed several buffalo near the road during the day. Went into Camp at our old Camping ground, after marching 18 miles.

September 5, 1872—Broke camp at 7 o'clock. D and M Troops were sent to examine the Canon in which we had been attacked going down. We marched steadily until 1 o'clock when [we] arrived at and went into Camp at the same place we were jumped. The two troops sent out returned in about an hour reporting that they saw a large and fresh Indian trail in the Canon, that the Indians could not have passed more than an hour before they got down in the Canon. I was on picket during the evening, but saw no signs of Indians. Every preparation was made to give the Indians a warm reception in case they put in an appearance during the night. I will be on guard again to-night and you can rest assured I shall keep a sharp look out. Distance marched to-day 20 miles.

September 6, 1872—Leaving D Troop to guard Camp. General Gregg, with the remaining three troops started out at 6 A.M. to search for Indians After traveling fifteen miles we came to a trail made by a large party of Indians, a day ahead of us. Examined and crossed the trail. After marching seven miles farther we came to the main Canon, "Canon Blancho." The General examined the Canon with his field glasses, but saw no Indians. Took a short rest and then started to return to Camp. When [we] come to the Indian trail, [we] changed our direction to follow it. The General thought we would find something more definite in regard to the number of Indians and the where abouts of their Camp. Followed their trail five miles but gained nothing by it and was only going farther from Camp. Even now it will be impossible to reach Camp before night overtakes us. Changed direction and set out for Camp.

Several horses of the Command showed signs of giving out. One of ours had to be shot as it was impossible to drag him along.

Marched until darkness set in without striking our trail. Rode along in hopes of seeing something that would give us an idea of the whereabouts of Camp. After wandering around for a couple of hours the Command halted and we realized that we were lost on the plains. The probabilities were that the farther we traveled the farther away from Camp we would wander. To make our situation more disagreeable, a cold rain commenced to fall, while the dark clouds hung between us and the sky, enveloping us in a darkness impossible to penetrate. So dark did it become that I could not see the man riding by my side and who was within two feet of me all the time.

About this time several shots were fired in quick succession in rear of the Command. We halted at once, when Captain Bankhead, M Troop, dashed up and reported to the General that a number of the men of the Command were back with played out horses, and he thought it was them firing to find out where the Command was. The General ordered several shots to be fired in the air, and sent some men back with orders to shoot what horses had given out, and for the men dismounted, to join their respective troops. Another of our troop came walking up showing that he had left his horse to bleach on the plain.

When all the men caught up with the Command, we moved forward only to become more confused. In this way we continued to wander until near midnight, when the General, becoming satisfied that it was impossible to find our Camp, halted the Command and gave orders to unsaddle our horses.

Wraping up in our saddle blankets, half the Command turned into sleep, while the other half held the horses. "My bunky," and I drew lots for choice of the guard. I won and took first watch. I threw my saddle blanket over my shoulders to keep warm. (I had foolishly left Camp without my blouse and was in my shirtsleeves). While the rain continued to fall, I sat perched on my saddle holding two horses, who from hunger were pawing the ground in hopes of finding something to eat, for neither man or beast had eaten anything for eighteen hours.

It was then I realized the horror of being lost on the plains. I had frequently read of people being lost on the prairie and plains, but little imagined I would ever realize the reality of the situation. My thoughts wandered back to my earliest recollections, and as I traced my eventful career up to the present time, I was filled with remorse. Some thoughts brought pleasant recollections, but these were soon overshadowed by thoughts that were not pleasant to dwell upon. In this manner I spent my tour of the guard, and soon as [I] was relieved [I] rolled up in the saddle blanket and soon was sleeping soundly.

At the first dawn of day all were up and in the saddle. After an hours ride we came in sight of Camp. We had marched beyond it during the night. If there ever was a lot of happy men, it was us. And not only our party who had been lost, but the men who had been left to take charge of the Camp. After eating & big breakfast, we all turned in to sleep, for both men and horses are badly in need of rest. During the day and night we marched fully fifty five miles.

September 7, 1872—Have just woke up from my sleep and feel very well considering everything. The rain continues to fall making it rather disagreeable for us, as we have no tents. All we have to do is stand out and weather the storm. Some of the men are still sleeping although their blankets are wringing wet. I imagine that I feel the effects of this exposure in my bones, but suppose it will soon pass away.[32]

Sunday, September 8, 1872—I was awake and moving around earlier than usual this morning, and am feeling splendid. No doubt "loved ones" you wonder what has occasioned this wonderful feeling. This morning completes "three years" of my bondage in the service of the United States. Only two years yet remain and when that time rolls around and I receive my freedom papers, my happiness will only require one thing more to be complete and that is to be home with you "loved ones."

We marched eighteen miles to-day. Nothing of interest occuring.

September 9, 1872—Left Camp at the usual time. Killed several buffalo during the day. While riding along my thoughts went back to little "Maryland" and to the time that I shall return [to] "loved ones," who are ever foremost in my mind. Pleasant thoughts they were and when we went into Camp at 3 P.M. after a march of 20 miles, I felt less fatigued than [I] have [on] any days march since leaving Bascom.

September 10, 1872—Marched twenty nine miles to-day.

September 11, 12, and 13, 1872—Marched respectively twenty seven, eighteen and fifteen miles. Nothing of interest occuring. Only one days ride yet to Fort Bascom. Should I find from your letters that danger is all passed, hardships all over and the experience of scouting will teach me to remain in a good place in the future, if I should be fortunate enough to have one.

---

32 Even though the army issued shelter tents, field commanders frequently ordered their commands to be in light marching order, leaving behind tents, ponchos, and all other superfluous equipage. See McChristian, *U.S. Army in the West*, 102; and King, *Campaigning With Crook*, 57–58. Such exposure to the elements often caused veterans to suffer from rheumatic afflictions while still in service, or later in life. See Rickey, *Forty Miles*, 132.

September 14, 1872—Broke Camp at 8 A.M. Have only fourteen miles to make before reaching Bascom. As mile after mile was traveled, you could see the men cheer up. While an animated conversation was carried on until we rode up to the post.[33]

Matthews added the following material as a postscript after returning to Fort Bascom.

When the Command went into Camp the mail was distributed to the men. How anxiously I waited for my share but instead of receiving a letter, I was sent out on picket. Never in all my life did I feel so sad and disappointed. Was this the welcome I was to receive upon my return from forty days and nights spent on a barren and desolate plain[?] Sometimes suffering the pangs of hunger, at other almost famished for a drink of water, and during all this time "you loved ones" were constantly foremost in my mind, both night and day. I had anticipated spending a happy day persuing your letters, but alas what a disappointment. There is no use trying to describe my feelings as I rode out to the picket station, for it is impossible to do so.

I arrived at the station and seated on my horse, I gave way to my feelings. Could not control them any longer. And although I am a man in years, I am not ashamed to cry on such an occasion. A half hour passed in this way when I saw one of our troop approaching, (the young man [Rowalt] with me on the buffalo hunt, spoken of in another part of this diary). He had both hands full of something, but I could not tell what the something was. He soon reached me and said, "Here Ed is a lot of mail for you. I thought you would like to have it as soon as possible, so I brought it out." My heart was too full to thank him for his kindness, but instead I broke open your letters, devouring the contents like one that had been starved and then set before a repast. In fact I was starved for want of the nourishment your letters afford me.

When I found that you were all alive and nothing serious anticipated, my happiness knew no bounds. I was at peace with all mankind. I had received payment with interest, for all the hardships [I] had to

---

33 The column marched 260 miles from the North Fork of the Red River back to Fort Bascom. See Eighth Cavalry Returns, September 1872.

endure on the scout. My disappointment on arrival at this post has been forgotten and to you "Loved Ones" do I owe my undying love for all this happiness.

Little more remains to be said. The Scout as a "failure," was a decided "success." We accomplished nothing, and the cost of the expedition will greatly add to the "National Debt." But this will only be a few more dollars added to the overburdened tax payers of the country. And now "loved ones" if you can derive any pleasure from the perusal of these pages, I shall feel happy.

This trophy dangling to the first page, is to show that I have fulfilled my promise, "only this is the tip of the last buffalo's tail I Killed." Dont take this last sentence as it is written, it is a mistake which [I] have not time to correct.

It was reported to General Gregg at Fort Bascom before we left there, that in our engagement with the Indians, four were Killed and eight wounded. He entered this number in his Official Report.

From his perspective as a soldier in the ranks, Matthews may have viewed the expedition as an utter failure by its lack of tangible results and encounters with hostile tribesmen. Gregg did, however, locate the trunk line trail used by the Comancheros from New Mexico and confirmed that "it has not been used as a thoroughfare for illicit cattle trading within the past two years, yet previous to that time there can be no doubt a very large trade must have passed annually over it."[34] Gregg's New Mexican guide led him to a place he claimed to be Quitaque, the reliably watered canyon featuring a high lookout point on its rim, frequently used by the Indians and the traders as a summer rendezvous. Unbeknown to Gregg, Quitaque actually lay about forty miles south of that point. Whether the guide was mistaken, perhaps confused by a similar place, or intentionally misled the troops, is open to question.[35] Nevertheless, the scout was the first thorough exploration of the area embracing the headwaters of the Red River, and the detailed record of distances, water sources, and topography kept by Gregg's engineer detachment would prove to be a valuable supplement to the army's knowledge of the region. Importantly, General Nelson A. Miles would use it in his final campaign against the still free-roaming Comanche and Kiowa tribes in 1874.

---

34 Gregg to AAAG, District of NM, September 17, 1872, in Box 32, LR, Department of the MO, RG 393, NA.
35 See ibid.; and Kenner, *Comanchero Frontier*, 197–98.

The summer's operation, along with other factors, had significant ramifications affecting the Comancheros' operations. Gregg's penetration of the traders' haunts, coupled with Mackenzie's simultaneous crisscrossing of the Staked Plains, served notice to the traders that the region no longer afforded them sanctuary.

Then too, Texas ranchmen, disgusted with being the long-suffering victims of cattle thefts, took matters in their own hands. During the summer of 1872, a party of ninety heavily armed Texans invaded New Mexico and systematically reclaimed cattle and horses bearing their brands. The sheer size and determination of the group were usually enough to intimidate the New Mexicans into relinquishing the stock without a fight, but violence sometimes erupted nevertheless.[36]

Eddie Matthews and his comrades could not have appreciated it at the time, but these events influenced many former traders to give up the business as being too risky. Even though illegal commerce with the Indians did not end entirely after 1872, the Red River War two years later brought an end to the Comancheros by finally removing from the plains their former partners, the Kiowas, Comanches, and southern Cheyennes.

FIGURE 1. William E. Matthews. (Courtesy of Fort Union National Monument.)

FIGURE 2. Cavalry recruits being introduced to mounted drill at the Carlisle Barracks depot. (Courtesy of the U.S. Army Military History Institute.)

---

36 Perhaps the most notorious of these incidents occurred when some sixty Texans raided the unsavory village of Loma Parda, near Fort Union, shooting up the town and killing the police chief and another man. The Texans claimed the inhabitants had resisted them in their attempts to inspect cattle on two previous occasions. See Kenner, *Comanchero Frontier*, 194–96.

FIGURE 3. Double- and triple-tier army bunks accommodated four and six men, respectively. (*Harpers Weekly*, July 18, 1861.)

FIGURE 4. Fort Whipple, Arizona Territory, with the town of Prescott, the territorial capital, visible in the left background. (Arizona Historical Society, no. 1210.)

FIGURE 5. Fort Union, New Mexico Territory. (Courtesy of the Palace of the Governors Photo Archives, NMHM/DCA, 009174.)

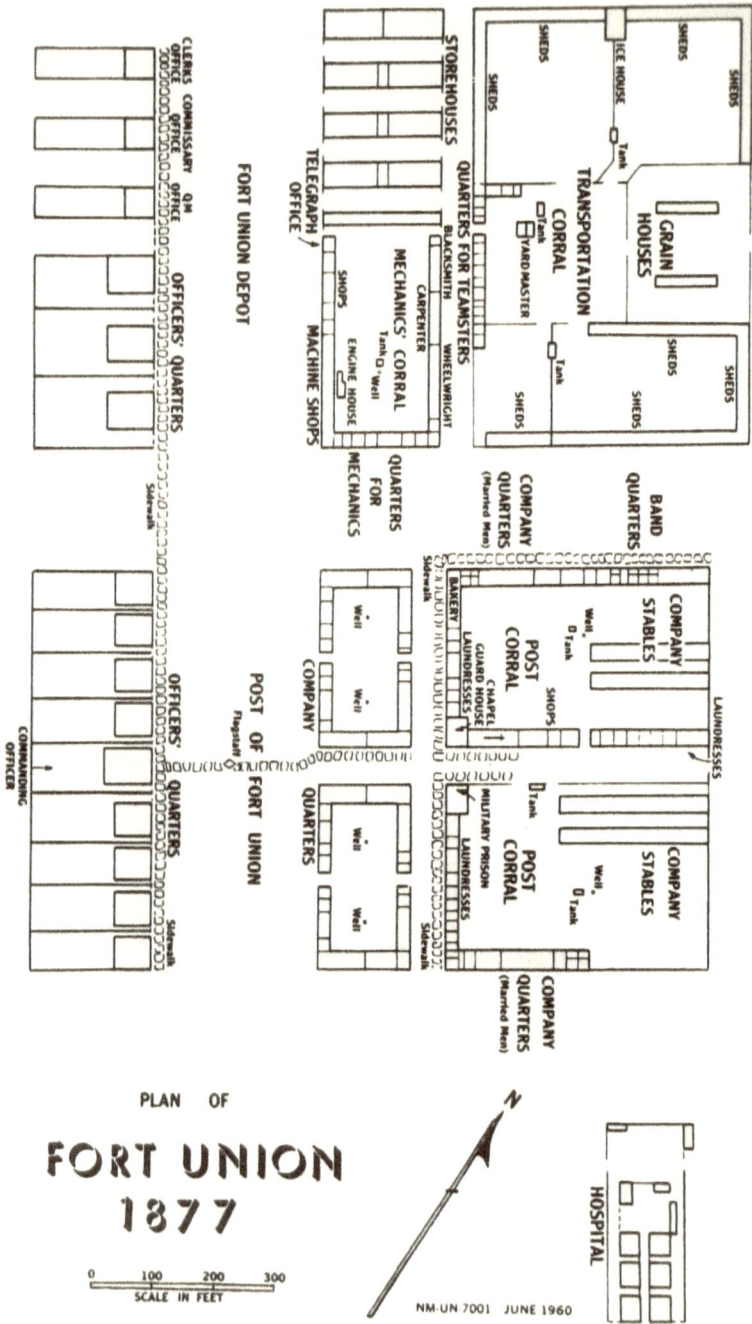

FIGURE 6. This plan of Fort Union illustrates the juxtaposition of the post with the large supply depot adjacent to it. (Courtesy of the National Park Service.)

FIGURE 7. One of four identical barracks at Fort Union, each housing a company of cavalry or infantry. The fronts of the U-shaped buildings faced inner courtyards, which explains the lack of visible doors. (Courtesy of the Palace of the Governors Photo Archives, NMHM/DCA, 014549.)

FIGURE 8. The Fort Union Sutler's Store, which also housed a bar, was a popular place with soldiers, though they resented the merchant's high prices. (Courtesy of the Palace of the Governors Photo Archives, NMHM/DCA, 014544.)

FIGURE 9. This 1867 image shows Las Vegas, New Mexico Territory, much as it was when Matthews was stationed at nearby Fort Union. (Courtesy of the Trustees of the Boston Public Library, Print Department.)

FIGURE 10. The interior of the barracks at Fort Union would have mirrored this infantry squad room at Fort Leavenworth, Kansas, photographed in 1873. The only major difference would have been that Sharps carbines would have occupied the circular racks, rather than the Springfield rifles shown here. (Courtesy of the Frontier Army Museum, Fort Leavenworth.)

FIGURE 11. Matthews and his comrades would have presented an appearance much like these Third Cavalrymen photographed in New Mexico in 1867. (Courtesy of the Trustees of the Boston Public Library, Print Department.)

FIGURE 12. Eighth Cavalryman in the regulation full dress uniform worn for guard mounting and other formal ceremonies. He has followed a common custom of having the standing collar on the jacket shortened for greater comfort. Soldiers occupied much of their leisure time preparing for inspection by cleaning their arms and polishing the twenty buttons on the jacket, the brass shoulder scales, the belt plate, and all the brass insignia on the hat, in addition to blacking their boots and belts. (Author's collection.)

FIGURE 13. Matthews visited the District of New Mexico Headquarters in Santa Fe in December of 1870, soon after it was constructed. The building stood off the northwest corner of the Plaza. Buildings of Fort Marcy are visible immediately behind the headquarters, with the officers' quarters fronting on Lincoln Avenue. (Courtesy of the Palace of the Governors Photo Archives, NMHM/DCA, 001715.)

FIGURE 14. Colonel Gordon Granger, shown here as a major general of volunteers during the Civil War, commanded the Fifteenth U.S. Infantry and the District of New Mexico in the early 1870s. (U.S. Army Military History Institute.)

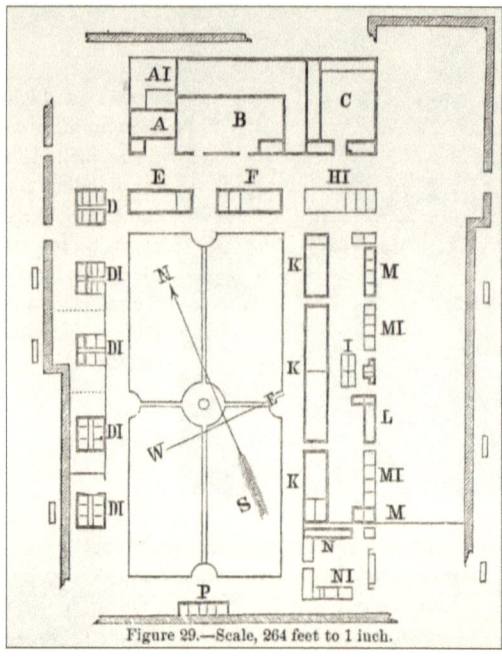

FIGURE 15. Plat of Fort Bascom, New Mexico, ca.1870. A and AI, cavalry stables; B, cavalry corral; C, quartermaster corral; D and DI, officers' quarters; E, quartermaster storehouse; F, commissary storehouse; HI, storehouse; K, barracks; L, mess hall; M and MI, laundress' quarters; N, old hospital; NI new hospital; P, guardhouse. The buildings drawn with single lines and marked "I" were incomplete. (*Circular No. 4*, Surgeon General's Office.)

FIGURE 16. Colonel John Irvin Gregg began his military career as a private during the war with Mexico and rose to the rank of Brevet Brigadier General of Volunteers during the Civil War. He commanded the Eighth U.S. Cavalry from 1866 to 1879. (U.S. Army Military History Institute.)

FIGURE 17. First Lieutenant Edmund Luff, Eighth Cavalry, was one of the company officers assigned to L Troop. He was one of the few officers for whom Eddie Matthews expressed genuine respect. (U.S. Army Military His-tory Institute.)

FIGURE 18. An Irishman by birth and a U.S. Dragoon for ten years prior to the Civil War, William McCleave was appointed captain in the First California Cavalry in 1861. As a member of the California Column sent to intercept Texas Confederates invading New Mexico in 1862, McCleave was captured during the march across what is now Arizona. McCleave survived the war and later received a commission in the Eighth U.S. Cavalry. He retired at the rank of captain in 1879. (Courtesy of the Palace of the Governors Photo Archives, NMHM/DCA, 009152.)

FIGURE 19. Cavalry trooper wearing the new dress uniform adopted by the army in 1872. The style of both the black felt helmet and the coat reflected contemporary British and German influence. (Courtesy of Montana Historical Society.)

FIGURE 20. The Fort Union hospital not only served the local garrison, but also provided a higher level of care for sick and injured military personnel from other posts throughout New Mexico Territory. It had six wards and a capacity of one hundred patients. The two surgeons usually assigned there were assisted by enlisted hospital stewards and soldiers detailed from the companies. (Courtesy of the National Library of Medicine.)

CHAPTER SIX

"Soldiers Are Not Given to Shedding Tears"
JANUARY–JUNE 1873

*S*ometime after returning from the scout on the Staked Plains, Matthews was again promoted to the rank of quartermaster sergeant and was obviously content to resume garrison duty. The lack of mail from home, however, continued to annoy and depress him, even though he apparently had not communicated with his family since shortly after the expedition concluded. Frigid winter weather restricted the troops' activities, but a rumor was already circulating that they might have to take the field again in the spring. It was not something Eddie relished, but he resigned himself to accepting without complaint whatever he had to endure for the remainder of his time in the army. Meanwhile, he continued to count down the months and days he had left to serve while considering his options for making a living after being discharged the next year.

Fort Union, New Mexico
JANUARY 28, 1873

I hardly know how to write to you this evening. Or do I remember when I ever felt so disheartened. The first mail from the East we have had now for more than a month arrived this morning. I was all excited and could scarcely wait for it to be opened and distributed so anxious was I to hear from you. But alas for great expectations, for when it was distributed there was nothing for me. Not a word. I tell you "loved Ones" it is hard to be shut off from everything that is dear to me on earth, without so much as knowing whether you were sick or well.

Could I only feel satisfied in my mind that, you were all well, I could rest contented, but this living in suspense is killing. I understand there is another mail on the road but don't know when it will be here. Hope though it will not be long coming. And when it arrives it will bring to me words of your welfare. I believe we are to have weekly mails until the stage animals are well of the Esizootic [epizootic]. Every horse and mule at this post, numbering about one thousand, are sick with the disease. The necessary work of the Garrison is done with Ox Teams. Our horses have the disease very badly, but none have died so far.[1]

The mail arriving has enlivened the Post a little. Still it is very dull. We have had two of the coldest days just past that I ever felt. Could scarcely stick our nose out without having it frozen. It has moderated a little today.

I was quite sick two days last week, but nothing serious. Am quite well now.

Well "loved Ones" as usual I will have to close with another short letter. But I think a short letter is preferable to none at all. Write to me soon and often.

Fort Union, New Mexico

JANUARY 30, 1873

Oh but don't I feel happy this evening. You have no idea how good I feel. Can you imagine what has wraught this wonderful change[?] Or what has occasioned this extroadinary happiness[?] Will not keep you in suspense, but will tell you at once. It had been more than a month since

---

1 Epizootic catarrh was an epidemic disease afflicting animals throughout the United States during 1872 and 1873. It became so prevalent among army animals that the Quartermaster Department distributed instructions for the treatment of the disease. See *ANJ*, November 2, 1872, 181; and Bourke, *On the Border With Crook*, 208.

I had heard one word from you. Or in fact received a letter from any person. And as you can imagine [I] was dying for a letter. But this morning brought the mail from the east, and with it came three letters from home. One from Ida White, and a very nice one from Snider Noel. Also received three papers. Now I suppose you can imagine how good it made me feel to sit back and read letter after letter. I felt something like I did when reached Fort Bascom last fall, after the "forty days scout," when [I] had all those letters and papers to read.

My three little brothers have added greatly to my happiness by writing to me. Their letters were all good. And they are deserving of great credit for their rapid improvement.

I am going to take your letter and comment on any subject that [I] think will assist me in writing you a readable letter.

Father you dwell a great deal on "thanks for money." And I must say I hardly understand your motive for doing so. I am lead to believe that you have misconstrued the meaning of my remarks on "thanks and many letters," in a letter written to you some time ago. I think the best thing for us to do is to drop the subject until I come home, and then I will be better able to explain the matter. What say you "My honored Father" shall it be peace or war with the pan. If you choose the latter, I shall be compelled to decline. As the match would be too unequal.

One year seven months and nine days remain yet for me to serve Uncle Sam. You speak of there being great rejoicing when I return. And why should we not rejoice[?] Five years separation from home and all that is dear, besides being isolated in a country who's inhabitants make no pretentions to civilization, but live and look like the murderous savage who roams this part of God's creation. I have pictured our meeting more than a thousand times, since [I] have been absent. And how none of us will ever forget that reunion. All I ask is that God will spare us all to meet once more around the family hearth, to talk of the past present and our plans for the future.

You acknowledge the receipt of my Christmas present in your letter of Dec. 30. And also say you have received the money from the Post Office. I feel very proud to be able to assist you a little. My only regret is it is not more. You say you are afraid I am depriving myself of necessary comforts. No I am not, Uncle Sam supplies me with clothing and food. It is true they are both rough, but one does not want very fine cloth[e]s in this country. And it would not do for one to become too fond of eating good things in my present situation, for next spring when we go down on another campaign it would go hard to fall back on Government straight in the line of grub.

And as to your regrets that you are unable to put it away until I come home, so that I will have something to start upon, I do not send it to you for that purpose. Or do I wish you to feel badly because you have to use it, for I assure you it does my heart good to be able to send it to you. You only make me feel too happy with your kind words. God bless you for them. And speed the day that will bring us together. Oh what a happy day that will be.

Lizzie gives me to understand from her note in the boys letters that she purposes writing me a long, long letter soon. I hope she will.

Yes indeed I will imagine myself in Heaven when I return and hear you all sing "Home Again." And it will not only be imagination, but will be to me Heaven in reality.

I am satisfied now that I know you are all well, with the exceptions of having colds. I was quite sick a couple of days last week. Guess [I] had (like the Horses) the Epizootic. Am feeling as well as usual now.

Our Horses are still very sick, not one in the stables but has the disease. Ox Teams are doing all the hawling to be done in the post.

Will have to close for to-night.

Fort Union, New Mexico
FEBRUARY 5, 1873

Fathers short letter, both boots and a Democrat came safely to hand this evening.[2] The boots are a perfect fit. And Harlan is highly pleased with them.[3] Sends you his thanks for all trouble. And wishes to know the price, cost of expressage to Baltimore and return, and amount of postage. In brief he wishes you to send in your bill an be paid.

I suppose you have received my letters long ere this. Old Epizootic has caused considerable trouble and anxieties during the time it has been raging. The horses and mules at this post show little signs of

---

2 The *Democratic Advocate* was published in Westminster, Maryland, from 1865 to 1972.
3 Clinton C. Harlan enlisted in the army on May 30, 1870, though his name was omitted in the Register of Enlistments. He passed through the Cavalry Depot at Jefferson Barracks, Missouri, and was assigned to Company L, Eighth Cavalry, on September 13, 1870. See Eighth Cavalry Returns, September 1870.

improvement. My horse was the worst case in our troop. Although he has always had the best of care, and choice of feed. What is more he shall always have it so long as I am Q.M. Sergeant. By the way in writing the word Sergeant, I notice both you and the Editor of the Democrat spell it Sargeant, or Seargent. Now if either of you see proper to give me my military rank just spell it as I have, and you will be O.K. But I am not particular whether you put the rank or not.[4]

There is strong talk here now, that we are going scouting next month or early in April. I don't like the idea one bit, but suppose there is no other resort. Would rather give two months pay than go on another expedition like that of last year's. Still if Uncle Sam says go, go we must. They can keep me going until the 8th of September 1874, and then I will go on my own accord until I arrive at a little City in Maryland. There I'll pitch my tent, and give up fighting Comanche Indians, eating salt horse, hard tack, and all that kind of foolishness. If we do go on another campaign this summer I will have an easier time. Will not have any of that disagreeable guard duty to perform. And will have every night in bed.[5]

This thing of crouching down on the ground of a dark night all alone, expecting every moment to be startled with the yell of a war party is not a pleasant situation by any means. And is more disagreeable when you have to repeat the dose four nights in succession, as I had to do last summer. If I can possible keep clear of that duty for the balance of my enlistment I intend to do so.

Harlan says he has not lost any Indians and dont think he will look for any this summer. Our troop has lost ten men by desertion since we returned from last summers campaign. And will loose that many more if we start on another expedition of the same kind. I know one though who cannot be frightened into desertion, no matter how many campaigns the regiment goes on. My time shall be faithfully served to the last day. And then when I get my discharge, I'll bid farewell to the Kiowa and Comanche's.

---

[4] The company quartermaster sergeant was responsible for the accountability and care of all camp and garrison equipment, quartermaster and ordnance property, fuel, forage, and the wagon assigned to his company. In garrison, he was in immediate charge of the company storeroom and its contents. He also maintained the records of such property. Although the quartermaster sergeant normally was excused from routine drills, he nevertheless had to be familiar with tactics so that he could fill the role of duty sergeant as necessary, particularly in combat. See Kautz, *Customs of Service*, 170–71.
[5] As a private during the 1872 summer expedition, Matthews was subject to standing guard, whereas he was exempt from that duty as long as he held the rank of quartermaster sergeant.

I see in the papers where the Modoc Indians are making it warm for Uncle Sams boys. And also where General Crook is doing the same thing for the Apatche's in Arizona.[6]

Lizzie's promised letter has not yet come to hand, although I am anxiously looking for it. Now my dear good Sister if you have not already written to me, do so at once. If you was out in this uncivilized country as a missionary I would never tire of writing to you. You can write and I know it. If you could not, I would not ask it of you. Mother, cant you wake those Sisters and brothers of mine up a little[?]

I have been doing lots of letter writing lately. In the last three days [I] have written to the following persons. One home, to Ida White, Jennie Zepp, John Reese, Snider Noel, and one to John L. Hawkins, who use to belong to our troop. This may not be very interesting but then it helps to fill up this sheet.

Fort Union, New Mexico
FEBRUARY 13, 1873

Last evening your letter dated Feb'y 3rd came to hand, also a paper. And I now feel just as happy as any boy could who had one and a half years to serve Uncle Sam.

Long ere this reaches you, you will have received my several letters and will know what has caused the long silence on my part. I had the advantage of you in the present case, I knew the reason I did not hear from you. While you have been conjecturing every thing imaginable as to the cause. But I hope after this we will hear from each other more regular. Mails come and go three times each week now, before the Epizootic we had daily mails.

---

6 The Modoc War occurred in 1872 and 1873 along the California-Oregon boundary. It is best remembered for the callous murder of Brigadier General Edward R. S. Canby by the Modoc leader Captain Jack and a party of his followers during a peace talk. The campaign degenerated into a frustrating siege of several months during which troops assailed the Modocs in their sanctuary in the rugged lava beds. For a complete history of the Modoc War, see Murray, *The Modocs and Their War*. See also Utley, *Frontier Regulars*, 198–206. Matthews also refers to Brigadier General George Crook's campaign against the Tonto Apaches and Yavapais in northern Arizona Territory during the same time period. See ibid., 194–98.

Old Ep[izootic] is now letting up on the poor horses and mules. Out of [the] great number of cases at this post, not one proved fatal. Us boy's were in hopes some of our horses would go to the happy hunting grounds, so [we] could get some new ones, but old Es. fooled us. And we were oblieged to doctor the old ones. The report here now is our regiment is to go to Texas in the spring, and relieve the 4th Cavalry. Don't know where the boy's got their information from.

Lizzie tells me of the parties and sleigh rides she has had this winter. I have had nary a sleigh ride, but have attended two troop "balls" this winter. Our troop started off with a grand ball on Thanksgiving day. Had a splendid time, danced until 3 o'clock A.M. The Officers with their ladies honored us with their presence, and opened the ball. M Troop followed us with one New Years, but I did not attend that although [I] had an invitation. Understood they had a very pleasant time, but had very few of the female sex.

Next on the programme came B Troop with a grand ball and supper. They, the members of B Troop, took plenty of time to get every thing ready, indeed their ball and supper room looked splendid. I did not intend going to their ball, but Capt. McCleave their Captain came over to our Orderly room the night of the ball and insisted upon the 1st Sergeant and I going. Dressed and went over and danced until Reveille, 6 o'clock in the morning.

And now to wind up the ball season we "Good Templers" are going to have a little private one on the 21st inst. We have an Order of Good Templers at this post numbering about fifty members principally all Soldiers.[7] Some twelve or fifteen women also belong to the order. Have very pleasant times on our meeting nights. Will tell you all about the ball after it is over.

Harlan asks to be remembered to you all. Sends thanks for the boots, and wants to know the damages. The Democrat comes all right.

---

7 The Independent Order of Good Templars, a temperance society, originated in New York in the early 1850s, and lodges quickly proliferated throughout the United States and Canada. Within twenty years, the organization spread to England, Europe, and beyond. Alcoholism was prevalent among both officers and enlisted men in the army. The isolation and boredom experienced at western posts were significant factors contributing to the problem during the post-Civil War era. Men at a number of posts organized local chapters of the I.O.G.T., which served as wholesome social outlets and an encouragement for men to abstain from liquor. See Rickey, *Forty Miles*, 161–62.

Fort Union, New Mexico

SUNDAY, FEBRUARY 16, 1873

Susie's more than welcome letter, with Democrat came to hand this evening. I had been sitting in the office for more than an hour wishing for a letter or some word from you. When in walks a man from the Adjutants Office with the Troop mail. And in it one letter and a paper for me.

Now if I only had something to write about this would be just the time. A quiet Sunday night with no place to go. And even if there was some place, [I] would not go until had acknowledged the receipt of your letter.

I am glad you have heard from me at last, and are satisfied that I am well. We are only receiving mails three times a week now, but [I] suppose [we] will have a daily mail in a short time.[8] It is singular some of the eastern papers did not speak of the discontinuance of our mails during the prevalence of the Epizootic. All the Colorado and New Mexico papers censure the "Stage Contractors" in strong terms for withdrawing the Stages.

What little snow fell the other day has all disappeared. And now the ground is as bare as it was before the storm. This has been one of the most pleasant winters I ever saw. Am afraid there will be no ice to fill our "ice house." Whether we have any or not will make but little difference to us enlisted men, for we would get but little of it any how.[9] The water at this post is good enough without ice.

Have no fears dear Sister, that I will become discouraged or lose hope of returning to you again. I have been away too long, and have passed through too many vicissitudes to lose hope now. When the day of liberty, and in which I am to return to you "loved ones," is so near at hand. There is too much happiness in store for us all to become discouraged now. September 1874 in all its glory, will usher in in due time. And then we will meet once more. Won't we all be happy then[?] We will all

---

8 Matthews should have considered himself fortunate to be stationed at a post on a primary mail route, the Santa Fe Trail. Many frontier posts at this time received only one or two mails a week.
9 Most of the ice collected during the winter was saved for use in the hospital during the summer. But, as Matthews implies, a considerable portion of it went to the officers for their ice boxes and toddies.

sit around the fire at nights and have a big talk. You can tell me what has happened during the past five years, and I will tell you what I have seen and passed through during the same period. It makes me feel so happy to think of our reunion, that I hardly know what to do. Harlan is here bothering me by his gab that I can hardly write. I just threatened to throw the Mucilage bottle at him if he did not shut up, but its no use, you might as well try to stop the world from revolving on its axes, as to stop his tongue.

I will have to close for to night, but will try and add a few lines in the morning. Good night, and happy dreams to you all.

Monday morning, February 17, 1873. After a good nights sleep, and after eating a large plate of "hash" for my breakfast I resume my place at the desk to put the finishing touch on this. Have not an idea what else can write about. Under stated circumstances guess it would be a good idea to close. Some of these days [I] will be able to write you a better letter.

Fort Union, New Mexico
FEBRUARY 26, 1873

Your Sunday letter written by Father and Lizzie came to hand yesterday evening. Since its reception I have experienced feelings I never felt before. Can you imagine what has caused this strange feeling[?]

Sister says "Well Eddie, probable I shall become Mrs. Hart, and move away to Pittsburg. When you come home in '74 you can stop into see me." I suppose most brothers would feel proud at the prospects of becoming a "brother in law," but strange to say no such elated feelings have come over me. The very idea of you getting married and leaving us seemes to me that I shall never see you again, and that you will no longer be my own darling Sister. It may be selfishness in me to want you to remain as you are and not become Mrs. Hart, or any other Mrs. Still I cannot help wishing such could be the case. Don't think me selfish, unreasonable and unjust to desire you to remain simply my sister Lizzie Matthews for I am not. The expression of my feelings on this subject is only brought out by the devoted love I have for you. And if it were possible for our family circle to remain as it now is, I would cheerfully devote my life to the object of increasing your happiness. But such things have been decreed otherwise by an "Almighty God." And we should be content to abide by it. This is enough on this subject.[10]

There is nothing in the shape of news connected with this post to write you.

The weather still continues fine and pleasant. Very different from what you seem to be having. I will write to you again soon. Excuse brevity, and let me hear from you often.

Fort Union, New Mexico
MARCH 2, 1873

Sunday evening, [I] have finished my dinner composed of roast beef, bread, coffee and plum pudding. Had my after dinner smoke and am now sitting at my desk for the purpose of giving you some Indian news.

We have had a small party of men stationed at Fort Bascom for some time as escort to a party of surveyors. The survey having been completed the detachment was ordered to return to this post, but before they left Bascom, an incident occured which will do honor to all engaged. On the 24th of last month about one hundred and twenty five Indians put in an appearance at a ranch, some twenty miles from Bascom. Captured a wagon, took every thing they wanted and left the place with out Killing any person. This is owing to the fact that none but Mexicans were about the Ranch. And the Indians seldom Kill them.

It was reported to Sergeant Rowalt who was in charge of the detachment of our troop, the close proximity of the Indians. That day Rowalt, Corp. Foos, Privates Davis and Wilson (all of our troop) in company with six citizens started out after the Indians and came up on them in a Canon some nineteen miles from Bascom. A fight at once took place and in a short time three Indians were obliged to withdraw leaving five of their number Killed. It is very probable more of them were either

---

10 Eddie's reaction to the possible marriage of his sister reveals traits of possessiveness and selfishness. As it turned out, Lizzie did not marry Hart. She remained single for seven more years, marrying Andrew R. Thompson on January 7, 1880. They afterward resided in Newburgh, New York, where Andrew was employed as a directory compiler, probably by a publishing house specializing in city and county directories. See *Maryland Marriages, 1667–1899*, last modified 2010, Ancestry.com; and *1870 U.S. Federal Census*, last modified 2010, Ancestry.com.

Killed or wounded. And you can rest assured our boys pushed them pretty hard or the Indians would never have left their Killed behind. None of our party was hurt.

This morning a citizen from Bascom arrived here with the news. And brought a letter to our Lieutenant signed by a number of citizens praising our men for the manner in which they fought the Indians. The Lieutenant brought the letter over to the Troop and read it to the men. After he had finished reading, three cheers for our little party was given by all hands. The citizen who brought the letter was one of the party in the fight and he said he never saw men behave better in a fight than our boys did. Said they were no more excited than they would have been had they been hunting rabbits.

M Troop leaves here tomorrow morning. And L has orders to be ready to leave at a moments notice. Are to go down to Bascom.

It is my opi[ni]on now we will go on another campaign, and will start earlier than we did last summer. If I hear anything more about leaving here [I] will tell you at once. No other news to write about.

Fort Union, New Mexico
MARCH 7, 1873

Your ever welcome letter dated 26th inst. with a Democrat came to hand this morning. And as [I] am doing nothing this evening [I] will devote an hour in the pleasant duties of writing to you.

Our Indian fighters returned to the Post yesterday laden with a great quantity of trophys such as blankets, revolvers, ammunition, bows and arrows, and a handsome lock of hair of a defunct Indian Chief. Several of the trophys were presented to me by my friends and when I come home are to be transfered to my little brother Arthur, who I see solicits curiosities for his cabinet.

Sergeant Rowalt with three men of his detachment and five citizens left Bascom on the 26th inst. (the day your letter was written) in pursuit of a party of marauding Kiawa Indians who had been commiting depredations in that part of the country. Our party overtook the Indians in a "Canon" 19 miles from Fort Bascom. The fight was short but decisive. The Indians numbered 17, five were left dead on the field and several wounded. Their Camp, accoutrements etc., etc., captured; the citizens accord great praise to Sergeant Rowalt and his men for their prompt action and gallant bravery. This is the first time for years that any of these marauding parties have been caught and chastized. An account of the fight with mens names attached who were engaged in it have been forwarded to the War Department and I suppose they will all receive "Medals of Honor."[11]

M Troop left here during the week for Bascom, and we are held in readiness to move at a moments notice, [we] have been quite busy for the past two days packing up the surplus property belonging to the Troop.

The Sergeant Major was telling me to-day there would be no campaign this year like last. Said General Gregg intended to send one troop out scouting at a time, who would scout for a month and return to this Post, and then another troop start out and so on until the summer is over. That will be a very good idea. Will like it better than going out all summer.

At our "Good Templers ball" a young lady and I eat a "Philopena." A few evenings after, I caught the young lady. Night before last I received the following note with a very handsome present.[12]

> To Eddie Matthews
> One who loses and will not pay.
> I think none could be meaner.
> And as I've lost, I can but say
> Enclosed you will find your Philopener.—E.L. Williams.

The present was a handsome "slipper" to hang up on the wall to put a

---

11 Rowalt, leading a detachment composed of four soldiers and a half-dozen civilians, distinguished himself in action against Kiowa Indians on February 26, 1873. He pursued and overtook a band of seventeen warriors, killing five and wounding three. Sergeant Rowalt, Corporal John Foos, and Privates A. P. Davis and John Wilson were cited in GO No. 5, Department of the MO, March 17, 1873, for gallant and meritorious conduct. See entry 147, p. 246, roll 35, ROE, RG 94, NA; and Rodenbough, *Army of the United States*, 279. This fight was officially recorded as occurring at Angostura, New Mexico, some eighteen miles from Fort Bascom. It should not be confused with the present town in Mora County having the same name. Indian casualties are listed elsewhere as five killed and seven wounded. See *Chronological List of Actions*, 53. Sergeant Rowalt had previously been awarded the Medal of Honor for gallantry in action in a fight at Lyry Creek, Arizona. At that time, L Company, Eighth Cavalry was stationed at Fort Whipple. The medal was presented on March 3, 1870, but strangely, Matthews makes no mention of the ceremony. See Chapter 5 n. 20.

12 A philopena is a party game in which two people, usually male and female, share the two kernels of a nut. If one fails to fulfill a given condition, that person pays a forfeit, usually a nominal gift or favor, to the other.

watch in. I will take good care of it and bring it home with me September 8th, 1874.

I will have lots of nice things to bring home with me. Am collecting everything that will be a curiosity to any of you.

There is three young friends sitting in the room doing all in their power to make me wind this up and talk to them. I told them to hush for a moment as I had an "idea." Harlan spoke up and told me to put it down as it was the first one I had had for a long time. Guess he is about right. By the way he told me to tell you when you spoke of him in your letters not to Mr. him, as it did not sound natural. There are no Mr. in the Army.

Harlan has made a lot of very nice frames for pictures (photographs) and if you can send me any pretty young ladie's pictures I wish you would do it. Have all of yours in one large frame and do not want to take them out.

Well this is enough for this evening. Write to me soon and often.

P. S. March 8th. To-day is Mothers and Lizzie's birthday, and for a birthday present I send you a Son and brothers best love. It is all I have to send you. May you both live to see many more birthdays is the prayer of your Son and brother.

Fort Union, New Mexico
MARCH 14, 1873

Intended writing to you last night, but [I] was feeling too tired, so [I] put it off until this morning. Have been hard at work all week packing up Company property, drawing necessary stores etc. We received marching Orders to be in readiness to move Monday 17th inst. Are going to "Fort Bascom" and will be rationed to May 1st. Dont think we will be gone any longer. I think soon as we arrive at Bascom M Troop will return to this Post, and then B Troop will relieve us about the 1st of May.

You must not feel uneasy about me in case you should not hear from me every week. The mails from B[ascom] may not leave more than once each two weeks, but I will write to you by every mail. I have not heard from you now for more than a week. Father's long letter of which you speak about in a letter received three weeks ago has never reached me. So [I] suppose it is lost. Cant you write me another just like it[?]

There is considerable excitement in Camp caused by the report that our regiment will change stations with the 2nd Cavalry this summer. The 2nd is stationed along the Union Pacific Rail Road. Wouldn't that be tip top if it should only prove true[?] I understand General Gregg is expecting marching orders to that effect by every mail. Am afraid it is too good to be true.[13] Four of our troop whose time of service expires next month will be left here to be discharged. After them I am next on docket for the honor. That is some consolation any how, even if I will not be discharged until September 1874.

The Lieutenant will soon come over to finish packing up, so I will have to close this. Will write to you Sunday. Hope by that time [I] will hear of something more definite about going to another station. Excuse short letter. Write to me as often as you can. Kind regards to all my friends who inquire after me.

Fort Union, New Mexico
MARCH 16, 1873

Before this reaches you, I will be at Fort Bascom. Every thing is packed up ready to move to-morrow morning. And I have only left this sheet of paper out to write to you. Am afraid this will be the last letter you will receive from me for at least one month, but you must not become uneasy on that account. Rest assured "loved ones," you will not be forgotten by me, or will I neglect writing to you by every opportunity. [I] Dont think we will remain away longer than the 1st of May.

Sisters letter with picture of Mr. H[art] reached me last evening. Had just returned from the Q.M. Depot, where [I] had been turning in forage and some extra horses. Was delighted to receive a letter once more from my "darling Sister" who so seldom writes to me.

The gentleman who's picture I herewith enclose is fine looking, this is all I can say or would say for any gentleman who would take my sister from me. Mother, you say, dont want you to become an old maid. Neither do I, but I will tell you just what I do want you to become, and that is a "young maid." I will be nothing but a bachelor, and we will live

---

13 This proved to be a false rumor. The Second Cavalry remained in Wyoming and Montana Territories for many years. See Rodenbough, *Army of the United States*, 181–90.

to-geather. Won't that answer better than getting married and leaving all the rest of us for good[?] But as you have decided to rest the matter here until September '74, when I shall return, I will say no more about it, for [I] cannot write half so well on the subject as [I] could say verbally.

I have almost forgotten to thank Father for his production on cold weather, which you seem to be having in abundance. It is quite different here with us. I never saw a finer winter than this has been. We have had no cold weather, and very little snow. Have no ice put up for next summer should we remain in this territory, but ice or not it makes little difference to us so long as we remain at this Post. The water here is very good and plenty of it.

Well I will now have to say "good bye" as [I] have some private property to turn over for Lieut. Luff this evening. Turn it over for safe keeping in the Q. M. Department.

Write to me as often as possible for I shall expect a letter by every mail, which comes to Bascom.

Fort Bascom, New Mexico
MARCH 24, 1873

Have only been in camp about half an hour. Am feeling quite tired but as M Troop leave here to return to Union in the morning [I] want to send you a line to say I am well, and that [I] arrived safe. Nothing of interest occured during our march from Union. We will remain here until the 1st of May and it is probable B Troop will then relieve us.

No Indians around here, though the citizens seem to anticipate a rade by them soon, to retaliate for the loss they sustained in the fight with Sergeant Rowalt and party.

I will have to say good bye, for a day or two as [I] have a lot of business on hand which must be attended to. I will write you at more length soon. Excuse writing and mistakes, for [I] am very tired this evening.

Fort Bascom, New Mexico
MARCH 26, 1873

My inclination this blustry morning is to commence a letter to you. I say commence for the reason there is no telling when an opportunity will afford itself to send this off. I can write all I want to this morning, and finish when [I] have a way of sending it to Union. I wrote you just a line the night we arrived here, and sent it to Union by M Troop, who left for that place next morning.

The men of our troop are all busy this morning trying to fix up bunks etc. for their comfort. Harlan and I are quartered in a snug little room by ourselves. We are fixed very comfortable. And [we] can stand a month or two of this kind of life very well. And if we could only hear from home, [we] would have no reason to complain.

I have my store room in another building. Will have to commence my quarterly papers tomorrow. So [I] will be kept busy for four or five day's.

Our Lieutenant is either very much frightened, or is apprehensive of danger, for he is using every precaution. [We] Have only to ride three or four hundred yards to water and [we] have to carry our revolvers with us. [We] Have also to fall out under arms at all roll calls. In case of attack we will certainly not be taken by surprise. It may all be very well to provide for any immergency, still it looks as though we were all frightened at our own shadow.[14]

The citizens down here seem to think the Indians will come back to avenge the death of five of their number, who were killed by Sergeant Rowalt and party. So far as I am conserned, I have no fears of them attacking this post so long as there is any soldiers about.

[I] Dont think we will stop here more than one month, or will have to come down again this summer. Guess B troop will relieve us about the 24th of next month.

A citizen who keeps a store at this place came up to me yesterday and said: "You are Sergeant Matthews, aint you[?]" Told him that was my name. Said Sergt. Rowalt had spoken very highly of me and that Rowalt was a great friend of his. And if he could accomodate me in any way, I should not hesitate to call on him. I thanked him for his kind offer and told him I would certainly do so in case he could help me any time. Rowalt has gained many friends down here by his

---

14 Some of the enlisted men may not have appreciated how quickly Indians could sweep in and cut off an inattentive and vulnerable party. In this instance, warriors might have surprised the soldiers and driven off many of their horses, leaving the cavalrymen dismounted. Lieutenant Luff had probably been instructed by his superiors to maintain vigilance at all times.

prompt action in pursuing and killing those Indians [a] short time ago. And as he and I are such good friends the citizens are anxious to do anything for me they can.

Had another kind offer from another citizen yesterday evening. I rode out to a ranch about half a mile from the post to get hay for our horses. Made the necessary arrangements and was about to return to camp when the ranch man said, "Sergeant, I will bring you in a cow in a day or two, so that you can have plenty of milk while you remain down here." Told him [we] would be very glad to have the use of a cow while here, and would promise to take care and feed her well for the milk. Am expecting my cow every moment. If the citizens continue to show their generosity in this way, I shall be sorry when the time comes for us to pack up and pull out.[15]

If we only had plenty of reading matter, [we] could spend a month or two quite pleasantly down here. Our library consists of part of a Democratic Advocate, two or three New York papers and a small volume entitled "The House of the Seven Gables," by Hawthorne. I have not read the latter yet, but will commence it soon as [I] put this aside. This composes Harlan's and my library. And I flatter ourselves that our's is the most extensive in the troop. Our's is a very literary troop, when any ten cent novels are to be had.

I think it is about time to close for this morning. Am brought to this conclusion by the fact that [I] have run out of a subject to write about. Will put this aside until such a time as the "Spirit" moves me, or should there be an opportunity to send this off before the "Spirit" moves me to write more, will do so. For the present will bid you ideose [*adios*] (Mexican, for good by).

No. 2
Fort Bascom, New Mexico
SUNDAY, MARCH 30, 1873

I have written to you twice previous to this since our arrival at this post. My letter dated March 24th telling of our safe arrival [was] sent to

---

15 While the presence of an army post was always an economic boon to the area, citizens in the West were inclined to view the regulars either favorably or unfavorably, depending on the proximity of Indian trouble at any given time. When hostilities occurred in the immediate area, as in this instance, civilians went out of their way to curry the favor of the troops. See Rickey, *Forty Miles*, 27.

Union, with M Troop. My second bearing date March 26th is still in my possession. Will send both to Union next week by a citizen, who leaves here Wednesday.

Oh had I only the muse of a poet for one half hour, so as to be able to describe the fulsome smell which is wafted through my little room by the "gentle breezes." This post is infested by that little animal called the "skunk." Last night one took possession of our cook house and helped him or her self to Soldier straight. (hard tack and bacon). And I imagine he or she must have been fonder of the said delicacies than us $13.00 a month chaps, for this morning when the cooks entered the room for the purpose of getting breakfast, Mr. or Mrs. Skunk was found in full possession, and could not be coaxed to vacate. The cooks knew gentle means had to be resorted to or else suffer the consequences.

So breakfast was prepared in the quietest manner possible. When breakfast was announced, men moved around as quietly as though death were in the room. And all this time the skunk lay quietly in one corner seeming indifferent to what was going on, but this state of affairs had to be settled in some manner sooner or latter. And the case resolved it self into two alternatives. The skunk had to be ejected quietly, for if violence was used he would certainly sprinkle his "cologn" water over all in the room, or else the cooks and Kitchen would have to be moved. The latter would cause considerable trouble and inconvenience, so the former plan was decided upon.

After several attempts to coax his or her highness out gently and all proving fruitless, sticks and stones were pelted at the animal until finally it took refuge in a Camp Kettle. One of the cooks then procured a shovel and placing it under the Kettle both were safely carried out doors. The animal was then Killed, but not before he or she had ladden the atmosphere with the quintessence of his or her cologn water. If I only had another skunk to write about, [I] think [I] could be able to send you a long letter, but unfortunately I have not. So you must content yourself with this.

This much of my letter has been taken up by the rediculous but, now I have a sad and painful subject to write upon. The day M Troop left here for Union, several of the men had been drinking too much. Twelve miles from here one of the party was thrown from his horse and fatally injured. The Ambulance was sent out after him, and he was brought back to this place. Everything was done to save his life; but to no purpose. He died on the 28th inst.[16]

Yesterday his remains were buried in the grave yard at this place, followed by our troop. The buriel service was read by the Hospital Steward, military honors performed over his grave, and then the dead was left with the dead. The living to return to the duties of life. And to think or try to think how soon their time would come. How sad it is to see one die and be buried in this uncivilized country, with out a friend to shed a tear over ones grave. For soldiers are not given to shedding tears over a fallen comrade's grave, no matter how dear a friend he was in life. His fate should certainly cause every soldier familiar with the circumstances to pause before taking a drink of intoxicating liquor. It has been a long time since I tasted the poison. And with God's help it will be a much longer time before I do.

All is quiet at this post. Indians have been reported as seen below here some thirty miles, but none have shown them selves around the post. And I don't think they will so long as a Troop of Cavalry is stationed here.

I would give most anything for a letter from you to-day. I can hardly wait until such a time as the mail is sent down to us. One consolation I have and that is the longer I have to wait the more letters I will have when the mail does come. Perhaps [I] will have something else to tell you before the mail leaves here.

Fort Bascom, New Mexico
APRIL 2, 1873

Father's ever welcome letter dated March 11th came to hand about 4 o'clock this evening. Oh how glad I was to hear from you. It seems most an age since [I] received a letter from you previous to this. And still

---

16 Private John Taylor was a Scotsman who had enlisted at the age of thirty-two on March 10, 1866 at San Francisco, California. He was a butcher by trade. Taylor was assigned to Company C, Ninth Infantry, in which he served out his three-year term until discharged at Camp Bidwell, California. He enlisted a second time on June 28, 1869, again at San Francisco, and was assigned to Company M, Eighth Cavalry. Matthews reveals the real reason for the accident, although the official record states only that Taylor was "killed March 28, 1873 by being thrown from his horse at Fort Bascom, N.M." See entry 180, p. 193, roll 32 and entry 104, p. 197, roll 37, ROE, RG 94, NA.

it is not so long. Still the less time I have to serve and remain away the more anxiously I look for your letters. My time of service is gradually growing beautifully less, but very slowly seemingly. Only one year, five months and six day's.

The mail from Union was brought down by a Surgeon, who was ordered to this place. And all mail will be sent to Union on the 4th inst., when the wagon that brought the Surgeon down will return. I have two other letters written to you and will send [them] with this. Hope they will all reach you.

My dear Father accept my sincere thanks for your compliments found in your letter. They are double acceptable for coming from you, suppose I must be deserving of them for [I] know you are not given to bestowing praise where it does not belong. It shall always be my aim to improve morally and intellectually, as much on your account as my own. And I hope I shall never be guilty of any action which I think would not meet with your approbation. There was a time I regret to say when I forfeited your love, by my bad conduct, but how happy am I to night to know that a Father and Mother who's love for their ering son is so great and who's prayer is for the safe return of that son. God bless you all, and grant the prodigal son to return to those loved ones. It will be my chief aim to promote your happiness in all things.

I am very proud of Johnnie, he certainly is doing splendid and is a good boy. Wait until we are all togeather and then we will see what we all can do. I have no fears but every thing will turn out all right after all, us four boy's can certainly do something to earn a decent living for the family. And I [am] sure none will hesitate to do all he possible can. Only wait patiently for the 8th of September 1874. Time on its slow axes will soon bring it here, and then to meet you. Oh what happiness for all. Five years is a long long time, but to look back five years does not seem to be such a long time either.

It is about 10 o'clock now, time I was in bed. And as I have not an over plus of news [I] will just put this on the shelf until morning. And perhaps after a nights rest, [I] will find something to fill up this sheet. So good night and happy dreams. And a hope also that I may have all night in bed without being awakened by the yell of the Comanche or Kiawa. Don't anticipate anything of the kind, although they are prowling around the country below here. In case they should put in an appearance I think they would meet with a warm reception. I just issued out plenty of ammunition to the men this evening, not because I anticipated danger, but for the reason it is always better to be prepared for any immergency. Time to turn in. So good night again.

Wednesday April 3rd. I have now returned to finish my letter begun last evening. And [I] am happy to say [I] rested undisturbed last night.

It is blowing a perfect hurricane out doors and the sand keeps blowing over my paper so fast that it keeps me busy blowing it off. (Small boy wanted at small wages to blow it off for me).

I was greatly amused at Fathers lengthy account on the advantages of tactics. But in reply [I] will have to say the only tactics used in fighting Indians are the same as used by them. These summed up would make but a small volumn. And are easily explained. The first thing to be done starting out after Indians is to strike their trail, follow it [and] come upon the enemy to fire into them. And then every man get behind a tree, stone or in fact anything that will protect him from the return fire of bow and arrows. And then fight for his life, using any tactics which will give him the least advantage. These are the only tactics I know of as used on the frontier in fighting Indians. We do not charge the enemy by divisions, regiments, troops, or even by sets of fours, but each individual charges on his own hook when ever he thinks his hair is safe in doing so.[17]

It is true we have a great advantage in fighting Indians, but the greatest is to be found in improved arms, with an abundance of ammunition. And still the advantage is not so great as one would imagine, for these Indians are well armed, and a great number of them have the latest improved arms. The bow and arrow is used more these day's for killing game, and seldom used in an engagement with the white man.

It may seem very strange to you how these Indians procure these arms and ammunition, but to us it is as plain as rolling off a log. These territorys are infested with a lot of scoundrels who trade with the Indians. And I have no doubt for one gun, twenty head of cattle would be given in exchange. These parties are citizens of the territorys doing some legitimate business to keep up appearances. And who at the same

---

17 "Sets of fours" refers to the basic tactical formation used during the late nineteenth century. Lieutenant Colonel Emory Upton devised a new system of tactics, adopted by the army in 1867, calling for all movements to be based on sets of four soldiers. On being formed, the members of a company were numbered off accordingly. See Jamieson, *Crossing the Deadly Ground*, 9–10.

time have a lot of "Mexican greasers" to do the dirty work for them. The Indians seldom kill a Mexican, and it is just for the reason that they would cut off all resources by doing so. These white scoundrels are too cowardly to do this trading themselves, so therefore they employ these black rascals to perform this business for them.[18]

The Hospital Steward and a Sergeant of the troop are in my room arguing on the justice of General Court Martials, desertion etc. and are bothering me some little by their chatter. And besides I have about exhausted my budget of news. You must write to me as often as possible, for your letters are a source of great pleasure.

Fort Bascom, New Mexico
APRIL 13, 1873

I never was happier but once since [I] have been away from home than [I] am now. This morning news was received of the close proximity of Indians. Ammunition was at once issued to the men. And a detail of men saddled up to leave. About this time the Mail arrived from Union. Was brought by a citizen.

All thought of Indians or danger, vanished like a flash from my mind. My one thought was to hear from you, and I was not disappointed for [I] was handed six letters and two papers. Two from home, one from Ida, one from the Ex. Q.M. Sergeant of our troop, who is now in Texas, and two from Fort Union. The men in the troop can always tell when I receive a letter from home, for [I] am then always laughing and generous to a fault. Would give the shirt off my back if [I] was asked for it. Where ever I went could hear some of the boys remark, "I'll bet Ed has heard from home, see how he smiles." I don't want you to think I never laugh or smile except when [I] hear from you.

Suppose you will want to know all about the Indians. So [I] will commence on that subject first. Yesterday three men and a guide from Union arrived here with dispatches for the Lieutenant to the effect that a number of "Cheyenne Indians" had left the Reservation at Camp Supply, Indian Territory and the supposition was they were bound for this place and for us to be on the look out for them. This news created

---

18 He refers to the Comanchero trade.

some little excitement but not much, for we are secure enough here. Every precaution has been taken and everything been done to strengthen the post, that it would almost be an imposibility to drive us out.

The Lieutenant concluded not to send a party of men out to-day. So we are waiting for the morrow, and the news it will bring. The party from Union will return to-morrow, and I will send this up with them. We are having more facilities for sending letters than expected when [we] came down here, but [I] am very glad of it for [I] know how anxious you are to hear from me. You must not be alarmed on my account for I am in no danger of being hurt. Or will I expose myself unnecessarily.

Another months rations has been sent down to us. Suppose from that we will have to remain here longer than we anticipated. It is true I would sooner be in Union, but [I] do not mind stopping here another month. I am having splendid times. Nothing to do but eat and sleep, very different from what [we] had it last summer.

Soon as we return to Fort Union I am going to tender my resignation again as Q.M. Sergeant. You will be surprised at this I know, but not so much after I have explained matters. Last year Congress made an appropriation increasing the present pay of the Army. Before the increase a Sergeant received $17.00 per month. Now they receive $17.00 per month for the first and second years, $18.00 per month for the third, $19.00 the fourth and $20.00 for the fifth year. This increased pay [is] to be retained until the expiration of the Soldiers enlistment. This bill through some cause deprives a Company Quarter Master Sergeant from the retained pay, although it allows a man to hold the position. I suppose the men who got up that bill thought from the opportunities a Q.M.S. would have he could appropriate enough Q.M. Stores to make good his pay. Or else they must have thought a man would be satisfied with the rank, without the pay, but I assure you I am not one of those kind of men. It is not the rank that I am after, but the dollars and cents, that is what I want.[19]

---

19 Company quartermaster sergeants were authorized for all line regiments in 1866. However, as a means of reducing the size of the army only a few years later, further promotions to that rank were prohibited, and the rank was eliminated from the pay table effective May 15, 1872. Incumbent quartermaster sergeants were allowed to retain their rank until the end of their current enlistments, thus 430 positions were eliminated by attrition. Thereafter, each troop of cavalry was authorized only a first sergeant and five duty sergeants. The wording of the order was ambiguous regarding the salary of incumbent company quartermaster sergeants, since they were not included in the current pay table. If Matthews's interpretation was correct, the intention was likely to motivate incumbents to take vacancies among the duty sergeants. The elimination of the position notwithstanding, the need for the

I have no fears but what [I] could make good what Congress had deprived me of. And not do it either through dishonesty, but even if I could make a hundred dollars a month more than my pay, I don't know that I would be satisfied. It is certainly an unjust bill. And one that would induce a man holding my rank to be dishonest, but there is one way of getting around the bill and that is to hold the rank of duty Sergeant, and perform the duties of a Q.M. Sergeant. The only difference in this would be the rank. And that don't amount to anything in my estimation, so long as there is no pay attached to it.

Soon as we received the Order to that effect I took it to the Lieutenant, showed it to him, and told him what I thought about it. He did not understand the bill to read as I thought, but said he would inquire into it. He has been waiting for the pay master to come and then will find out from him, but it will be some time yet before we are paid. Will have four months pay due us last of this month.

The Q.M. Sergeant of B Troop has already been relieved or reduced to duty Sergeant at his own request, but is still performing the duties of Quarter Master Sergeant. Will let this matter rest until [I] get back to Union.

In regard to the thirty days furlough each year [I] have only to say it is the same as every thing else connected with the Regular Army viz; "a fraud." It is intended only to deceive. A man enlists with the expectation of receiving that furlough whenever it is due, but in case he applied for it, ten chances to one he would be put in the "Guard House" for having the presumption to ask for that which was promised him when he enlisted. It would be no more than a Soldiers right to allow him the full time promised at the expiration of his enlistment, provided he had not had thirty days furlough each year, but the Government disallows a day, let alone five months. You can make up your mind that you will not see me until I have served my full five unless something miraculous should come to pass in my case.[20]

---

function continued, and one of the duty sergeants was invariably delegated those responsibilities. The special chevron for company quartermaster sergeants, having three stripes surmounted by a single tie, was eliminated with the adoption of the 1882 uniform regulations. See Heitman, *Historical Register*, vol. 2, 600, 604, 608; *ANJ*, June 27, 1872, 796; GO No. 61, AGO, April 23, 1873; and McChristian, *Uniforms, Arms, and Equipment*, vol. 1, 179.

20 The "guarantee" of a thirty-day furlough annually was held out as an inducement to attract recruits. Army regulations permitted commanding officers, *at their discretion*, to grant furloughs to enlisted men. Company commanders similarly were authorized to grant furloughs of not more than

I have only "One year, four months and twenty five days to serve." And when it has been served Uncle Sam will have received all the service he need ever expect from me, for nothing could ever induce me to serve again under this Government, no matter what inducements they would offer me. Every man in the Regular Army would be justifiable in deserting. Reason, the Government has broken its contract with us in more than one way. And I think when the contract has been broken by one party, the other should not be obliged to fulfill its part. But enough of this as my idea on this subject does not amount to a straw, no matter whether right or wrong.

Susie dear, allow me to compliment you for your last production in the shape of a letter to me. It is I think the best letter you have ever written me, "perhaps this is because you speak of Joe so Kindly." And then you ask me to be honest and candid and say whether I entertain a fond regard for her still, these are not just exactly your words, but amounts to the same meaning. This is rather a personal question I must admit, and when I think of years passed and gone in which I was the subject for considerable amusement on account of my devotion for that fair and perhaps fickle one, I don't know whether you are entitled to a full confession or not, but as you seem so anxious, and have given me credit for being very forgiving I will be candid in the matter, for [I] know of nothing connected with my intimacy with Joe that [I] have cause to feel ashamed of. And (to use your expression) so far as her using me ugly, I dont know but what I deserved all I got. <u>Yes</u>, "little inquisitiveness," I do still think a great deal of Joe. More than I do of any other young lady I ever Knew. (My Sisters of course excepted). You with the rest of the family often laughed at me for thinking so much of her. And will laugh at me when you read this, but as there is nothing to cause me to blush in loving one so fair, you may laugh all you wish too. And I shall not feel hurt. And if I knew what you have written me in regard to her was true I would feel much happier tonight than I do now, although I am feeling very happy as it is. You can thank Mrs. Hurley for me for her good opinion of me as expressed in your letter.

---

twenty days within a six-month period. As Matthews discovered, furloughs were rarely approved in practice. Regulations specifically prohibited soldiers from taking furlough when "about to be discharged." In other words, there was no legal means for him to get out of the service early. See *Revised Regulations*, 34, 487.

And as far as Jennie and I are conserned, I don't know that I ever wrote or said anything to her in which she could sue me for "breach of promise." She has been very kind to me since [I] have been away from home. More so than some other's of my professed friends, and her letters were always read with pleasure. I care but little how much she thought of Mr. Long (or Short) for that matter, for [I] never had any pretentions in that quarter, but had I known she received both letters and was waiting for a third from me before answering, I dont think I should have written the second or would I have answered hers when [I] received it. My reason for writing a second was through the belief that my former one had been lost in transit.

You can rest assured that I have no desire to correspond with any person where the pleasure derived from the correspondence was not mutual. Writing and receiving letters are two of the few pleasures I have in my present situation, but I could feel no regret in giving up those pleasures if I knew I was deriving pleasure from a source distasteful to the other party. You speak of a Rachael Smith speaking of knowing me, and also of her speaking well of me. I know a good many Smiths, but Rachael I don't know. Perhaps I knew her in my younger days, and when she was in better circumstances. It is too bad to forget one because she is poor. Nevertheless if Rachael says she knows me, I guess she does. Hardly think Rachael would tell a "no such thing" about a little thing like that.

Well here I am writing away this time of the night 10:30, while out doors the wind is blowing a perfect hurricane. You must excuse writing etc. for the wind finds its way through the cracks in the wall and keeps my old tallow candle flickering all the time. I dont know but what [I] could write a good deal more, but it is getting late, and besides [I] guess have written about enough.

I wrote Ida a good long letter about a week ago, but will answer the one received to-day soon.

Fort Bascom, New Mexico
APRIL 18, 1873

Two or three men of the troop will start for Union on the 20th inst. to bring down some "pay rolls." I have very little news to write you, but will send a few lines anyhow.

Have heard nothing more about Indians, and the report brought in a few days ago has proven untrue.

I had a talk with the Lieutenant yesterday evening in regard to the pay and rank of a Quarter Master Sergeant. When the Circular from the War Department in regard to my case was received, I took it at once to the Lieutenant for his opinion. He did not understand it to read the way I did but said he would refer it to the Pay Master, as he would be the best authority to go by. And as we have not been paid since that time he has had no opportunity to have the thing settled. He told me yesterday that he could not believe Congress would pass a legislation which would do an injustice to one class of Non Commissioned Officers, which this bill would certainly be if it proved as I supposed. He said a Quarter Master Sergeant was responsible for a great amount of property, and if anything his pay should be increased instead of decreased. And if the Pay Master should decide the bill to mean as it surely reads, he (the Lieutenant) will do anything in his power for my interest. Said he thought the Pay Master would be down here by the 15th of next month. And then the question would be decided. Lieutenant Luff has always taken a greater interest in me than any officer I ever met. And I know he will do what is right. So [I] intend to wait for the decision of the Pay Master.

In eight more days I will be "twenty three years old." And [I] am just as much a boy as [I] was eight years ago. It seems strange that I cannot imagine myself a man in years, growth, and feeling, but it is true I only think of myself as a "big boy." And when my time of service is out you will find me almost the same as [I] was five years ago. No doubt I will look a little older, but that will be about all.

I will have my picture taken first opportunity and send [it] to you, [I] have no idea though when that will be. I wish some of you would find out if Joe has had any pictures taken since I left home. If she has and you can get one for me, I wish you would do so "just for curiosity." You need not tell everybody I asked you to do so. Or need you make fun of me for asking you such a question.

The Sergeant who is going up to Union just came in my room, and told me he was going to start in the morning instead of on the 20th as supposed. He will bring the mail down with him. Hope there will be lots of mail for me.

Well "loved ones" I have nothing else to write you this morning. I am well and able to eat my ration. That is pretty good ain't it[?]

Fort Bascom, New Mexico
APRIL 20, 1873

This is Sunday morning, and [I] will have to attend "Inspection" in about half hour, but as the mail leaves after inspection [I] want to send you some late news by it.

Yesterday our 2nd Lieutenant [Cobb] arrived and has relieved our 1st Lieutenant [Luff] of the command. The latter leaves here to-day for Fort Union, where he will receive supplies etc. for a "four months scout." He is to act in the capacity of a Q.M. B and M Troops are enroute to this place and will arrive here this coming week. General Gregg is also expected here some time during the week. I hardly think the command could start on a scout for at least one month, as the grass is very poor yet, and our horses could not stand the trip on half rations of grain. It is my opinion only one troop will go out at a time from this post. And they will only go out for 20 or 30 days, and then return. But this is only my own opinion [and I] have nothing official to confirm it.

I will write to you by every mail that leaves here. And I want you to write to me as often as possible. I have had no reason to complain of negligence on your part since [I] came down. And hope you will continue to write to me as often for the balance of my enlistment, for the nearer the time of my discharge the more anxious I become to hear from you. Father's letter written on the 2nd inst. was welcomed by me yesterday. Rest assured loved ones, I will take the best care possible of my self. And will not unnecessarily expose myself to danger. My ambition for "Military glory" is not so great as to risk my life to gain it. All I want when my time is out is a character which will prove to you that I have faithfully fulfilled my contract with the Government. Although they have broken theirs with me.

I have not time loved ones to write more this time, will enclose this in one written on the 18th and which I thought would now be on its way to you.

Fort Bascom, New Mexico
APRIL 25, 1873

I have just this moment finished washing the dishes, and policing the room, was elected to perform those duties this morning. First time for eleven days.

Five or six men of M Troop arrived here last evening from Stone Ranch 28 miles from here, where their troop is stationed. They brought in a small mail, but nothing for me, but I will not complain for [I] have received as many letters from you as [I] could expect. These men came down to see the Doctor, and will return this morning. They report "all quiet in that quarter," and it is the same with us. Have heard nothing more definite in regard to the scout.

Tomorrow I will be 23 years of age, a Quarter Master Sergeant in the Yankee Army. And three thousand miles from home, nice predicament for a young man. I must admit they are not such qualifications as I would wish for, but [I] still cannot better myself.

Gus Valoise (your old Quarter Master Sergeant) is now a 1st Lieutenant in the 9th cavalry and is stationed in Texas. I saw his name in the "Army and Navy Journal" the other day. The 9th is a Negro regiment, but suppose you are awair of that fact.[21]

I really do not know what to write you, and if [I] have to send this short scrawl, know you [I] feel disappointed. So what can I think of to write you is the question which agitates my mind.

I weighed my self the other day and weigh 146 lbs. As heavy as I ever weighed I think. Am feeling well and am enjoying excellent health. In fact [I] was never in better health.

I have half a notion to destroy this, but upon second thought, [I] will send it to you, for a poor letter will be better than none. Will do better next time. Write to me often.

Fort Bascom, New Mexico
APRIL 27, 1873

Fathers welcome letter dated April 10th [was] received about an hour ago. Was brought down from Union by Captain Young (of our

---

21 In 1866, Congress authorized the creation of two new cavalry regiments, the Ninth and Tenth, composed exclusively of African American enlisted men commanded by white officers. Two of the standard works dealing with the black regiments during the Indian Wars are Dobak and Phillips, *The Black Regulars*; and Leckie, *The Buffalo Soldiers*.

regiment) who has assumed Command of this post.²² The escort that came with him will I suppose return to Stone Ranch twenty eight miles from here where M Troop is stationed tomorrow. Will write you a few lines and send it that far by them, hoping an opportunity will soon afford itself for sending it from there to Union.

I have no idea what is going to be done down here this summer. We hear so many different reports that it is difficult to know which to believe. Have heard no late reports of Indians being near this place. And even if they were near [I] would have no fears of them attacking us, unless they caught one or two men alone. These Indians are more afraid of us than we are of them. And they are not coming around here so long as there is a troop of Cavalry on the lookout for them.

One of our boys was out hunting yesterday, and returned to camp with the news that he had Killed a "bear." Three or four of the men took their horses, went out with the one that had Killed the animal and brought it in. It was a small black bear weighing about 250 lbs. We have been eating bear meat all day. And have enough bear's oil rendered out to last me the balance of my enlistment.

Yesterday was my "birthday." I have now been a pilgrim in this world 23 years and one day. And at this age what a desirable situation. I find myself holding, a "Q.M.S. in the Regular Army." And three thousand miles from any place.

In your calculation of the time I have yet to serve when your letter was written, you made a mistake of one month. I had then one year four months and 28 day's instead of one year, three months and 29 day's. My time of service expires September 8th, 1874. I have no hopes of getting my discharge a day before my full time has expired. Although when I enlisted I was promised a thirty day's furlough each year. As this would be impracticable while stationed on the frontier it would be no more than justice to allow me the full time promised on my last year. And discharge me when I had served four years and seven months. This like

---

22 Samuel B. M. Young began his military career as a private in the Twelfth Pennsylvania Volunteer Infantry in 1861, but gained the rank of captain, followed quickly by a promotion to major, in a cavalry regiment that fall. He was mustered out of the volunteer service in 1865 at the rank of colonel. He served a little more than a year as a lieutenant in the Twelfth U.S. Infantry before gaining promotion to captain in the Eighth Cavalry when it was organized in 1866. He later served in various cavalry regiments, rising to colonel of the Third in 1897. The Spanish-American War saw him elevated to brigadier general and major general of volunteers. By 1901, he was a major general in the regular army. See Heitman, *Historical Register*, vol. 1, 1067.

all other inducements held out to young men to get them into the Army is a fraud. But what more could be expected from a Government, controlled by a gang of thieves as this is.

Our legislators goes to work to lessen the present expenses of the Government by reducing the pay of enlisted men of the Army from $16.00 per month for private soldiers to $13.00. At the same time they increase the Officers pay. And to make themselves good for their trouble they stick their own hands into the public Treasury and add two thousand five hundred dollars to their own pay. A noble deed they certainly have done. And instead of lessening the expense they have increased it.

The Government has broken its contract with me in more ways than one. And if it was not for you loved ones at home, I should never fulfill mine with it, but I have never allowed the idea of desertion to enter my head. And the only thing that has induced me to serve my time faithfully has been my love for you. I could never be driven to disgrace you by having the name of a deserter attached to that name of a Matthews.

I am sorry you have gone to the trouble of writing to the Secretary of War in regard to the furlough question, for I have no doubt your letter will be thrown into the waste paper basket and that will be the last of it. My term of service is not so long now, and when it has expired I will bid adieu to the service of Uncle Sam. And if by chance at any time in the future my services should be needed in the Army "why of course my Government should have it," but enough of this.

I celebrated my birthday by cutting or rather shaving off my mustache. And washing my cloths, that being the only thing I could think of to do to remember it by. My face tonight is free from hair as it was twenty three years ago.

The boys in the troop have given me the name of Jimmy lately and I am called by that name all the time now, even the citizens around here have taken it up. I rode out to a ranch the other day to order some fresh beef, when the ranchman said, "Jimmy will you want a whole one[?]" I asked him who told him my name was Jimmy, and he said he heard all the men calling me that name, and supposed that was my name.

Well here I have filled this sheet, with what, I hardly know, but if you can find any pleasure in reading it, well and good. If not you can throw it in the fire, and I shall not feel hurt.

The Democrat comes regular and affords me much pleasure I read every advertisement and everything else in it. And had I to serve my time over again, I would not be without it.

Fort Union, New Mexico
MAY 7, 1873

Have just arrived from Fort Bascom. Rode one hundred and seventy three miles in two and a half days. So perhaps you can imagine whether I feel tired or not. I have no particular desire to sit still long. And [I] enjoy eating my meals standing. Will feel all right though in day or two. I came from Bascom in charge of the mail party. Also brought some dispatches up for the Commanding Officer. I will start back on the 9th or 10th inst. Will go back in three days.

Every thing was quiet when I left Bascom. I mailed a letter to you from Los Vegas. One that I had written a week or more before and sent as far as the Stone Ranch. Picked it up when [I] came to that place and brought it along.

B Troop left here yesterday for Bascom, and General Gregg left for the same place in Company with the Pay Master to-day. I will return to Bascom in time to receive my pay. And [I] will send a part to you if [I] can find an opportunity.

Lizzie's letter dated 29th inst. received few minutes ago. Also a Democrat. You can imagine what a fright you gave me, when I opened the letter and read the first three lines, "I really ought not to begin a letter to you, or any one, feeling so sad and distressed as I do tonight." As I read these words my heart commenced to rise up and almost choak me, for [I] was sure something terrible had happened to some of you. And when I read a little farther and found out what you ment by those words, I could not help giving out to a sigh of relief. Your letter contained some very sad news, and although being unacquainted with the young lady I felt sad to think of her sad[?] taking off.

Only 16 months and 1 day, time is passing away splendid.

You need not be in any hurry sending those shirts you have so kindly promised me, for so long as I remain at Bascom [I] will have no use for them. Wear only old cloth[e]s down there and as I have to do my own washing [I] would have no use for white shirts. Dont think I could do them up very well. An old government shirt is just the thing I can wash and do up. If you have not already commenced those for me or have not bought the material. If you have no objections and will pardon the begger for being the chooser, I would just as soon you would send me a couple colored shirts. Nearly all the men around here wear those kind now, but whether white or colored they will be very acceptable.

I saw another new Order in regard to Qr. Ms. Sergeants to day. They are done away with altogeather and those holding that position now will be reduced to duty Sergts. I suppose there will always be a Sergeant acting in the capacity of a Q.M.S. but as soon as I return to B[ascom] and am reduced will try to get rid of all the duties pertaining to the Q.M. Dept. Since there is to be no more Q.M. Sergeants, the 1st Sergt. will be supposed to perform those duties in addition to those at present. And as our 1st Sergt. has more to do now than he is capable of doing, I dont see how he is going to get along.

I will tell you all about it soon as [I] return. You must please excuse this for [I] am feeling very sore, tired and nervous.

Will write again perhaps before [I] leave here.

Fort Bascom, New Mexico

MAY 11, 1873

I returned to this place yesterday evening, having rode one hundred and thirty two miles in two and a half days. What do you think of that for horse back riding[?] I guess if you had to ride that distance you would not feel inclined to sit down for some time, but to tell you the truth I dont feel the least fatigued to-night.

When I was going up to Union I met Lieutenant Luff on the road and he told me he had a lot of mail for me but could not get at it without considerable trouble. He brought it down with him, and all the time I was in Union, I was anxious to return just to read your letters. And now that I have returned I am happy to say I was not disappointed by not receiving good news from you. Soon as [I] reported my arrival with the detachment under me, I hastened to the first Sergeants room and found one letter from Father, one from Ida, one from Snider Noel and two from Howard and Co., Jewelers—New York. Also received a Democrat and two papers Snider Noel kindly sent me. To say I was happy would not express my feelings.

All my letters contained the best of news. "All well" two small words tis true, but oh what happiness they convey to the absent one. Ida's letter was the best she has ever written me although all her letters are elegant. Perhaps the reason I consider this the best one is she spoke so well of me, and ended her letter with these words "But Eddie, I think what I will like best in you, is that you are no longer a wild heedless boy, but a <u>man</u> with the thoughts, experiences, and aspirations of a man. Am I not right[?] I often imagine what you will be like, and how you will do, have formed a very high estimation of you. And think you will not disappoint me." Her whole letter was written in that strain. Even had I not the aspirations of a man now, I would certainly be the most unreasonable boy not to strive to be all she hoped I would be. But "loved ones" I am proud to say Ida, or any of my friends who entertain a hope that I will return a <u>man</u>, instead of a heedless boy shall not be disappointed. Snider Noel is also a good correspondent, writes me good letters, and seems to find pleasure in the personal [word missing] of my letters. The letters from Howard and Co., who you remember I bought several watches from, informed me they had changed their place of business, and solicited orders from me in case I wanted anything in their line at any time.

Now you see I have spoken of all my letters except yours, because I have left it for the last, is no reason I think it the least. Father speaks in it of my account of the Skunks visit. If my charge against the skunk was good and justifiable, his defense was better. And should the two charge and defense go before a jury composed of "Skunks," I fear my charge would prove groundless, and the jury would decide that the subject of all these remarks was justifiable in entering the Troop Kitchen, and would bring in a verdict also against our Troop for Murder in the first degree, with the recommendation that we be put to death by being confined in a small room without ventilation, and have all the skunks in the country to sprinkle us with their "cologn water" until the <u>pleasant</u> smell would carry us to the "happy hunting grounds of the great spirit."

I would have written to you again from Union, but was unexpectedly ordered to return by <u>trail</u> to this place. Genl. Gregg and the Pay Master also arrived here last evening, and I suppose we will be paid tomorrow.

B Troop got in this evening, and I understood two more Troop's of our Regiment have been ordered here. The latest report is a reservation for the Ute and Apatch Indians is to be established here; or near here and that we are only here to keep them on it.

I see by the papers that the Comanche and Kiawa Indians have sued for peace, and have promised to go on a reservation, restore all captives, Cattle, property and forever live at peace with the "Pale face," provided their two great Chiefs, Satanta and Big Tree, now in custody, are released. The proper way to accept this prayer would be to introduce these two Great Chiefs to just enough rope to keep their feet from touching the ground. By this mode their soul would be wafted to the "happy hunting grounds" and both Citizens and Soldiers living on the frontier would be relieved from any fear of them ever going on the "War Path" again. Soon as this was done would be the time to listen to any terms of peace. The very idea of a Government like this allowing a few dirty, thieving Indians to dictate terms of peace is disgusting to every subject in it, except a few contemptible Quakers. And even these large hearted, meek and proud Sons of Adam, must be disgusted since the death of General Canby and Dr. Thomas, for I see none of them have applied for the vacant position of Indian Commissioner. I guess none of them want the position now, unless the contract would be for them to remain in Philadelphia and have Agents to perform any little dangerous duty that might occur, for instance holding "Pow Wow's" etc.

It is getting late so [I] will stop for the night. If I can send you some Money [I] will do so. Don't suppose the Pay Master would object to taking it to Los Vegas, and sending you a Money Order. I will ask him anyhow soon as we are paid.

Fort Bascom, New Mexico
MAY 14, 1873

The Pay Master leaves here this morning. His Son (Mr. Porter) has kindly promised to send you $60.00 by Money Order. He will either send this from Santa Fe or Los Vegas.

Fort Bascom, New Mexico
MAY 14, 1673

I sent you by the Pay Master Clerk this morning $60.00. He will send this by Money Order. Hope you will get this without as much trouble as you had the other time.

All is quiet here with no prospects of being enlivened by the "Noble Red." From the quantity of Supplies coming in every day I judge we are booked for all summer.

I am now a duty Sergeant, but am performing the duties of a Q.M.S. [quartermaster sergeant]. Captain Hobart is in Command of the Troop. Soon as he arrived here, he spoke to me in regard to the pay of a Q.M.S. and said it would be better for me to tender my resignation as Q.M.S., but said he wished me to continue in the office, just the same as before. The Company Order was published the other night and reads, "At his own request Q.M. Sergeant Wm. E. Matthews is hereby reduced to the rank of Duty Sergeant." I am now receiving $19.00 per month where as Q.M.S. [I] was only getting $17.00.[23]

I have not time to write you any more as the Pay Masters Outfit is ready to leave. Harlan's $10.00 for the boots is included in this $60.00. $25.00 of this is for Mother, the balance Father's. Excuse haste, Will write again in a day or two.

Fort Bascom, New Mexico
MAY 18, 1873, 10 P.M.

I have this moment finished answering Arthur's letter, if such a scribble is entitled to that name. And now [I] will try to say a few words to you all.

I received by todays mail Arthurs letter and a Democrat of May 3rd. There is little or nothing to write about. We have six months supply of rations here so [I] suppose [we] are booked for that time. No Indians around that we have heard of. Everything quiet and I hope it may remain so for the time we stop here.

The weather is very warm here, too warm for comfort, but [we] have to stand it. When is Lizzie going on her visit to Oakland[?] When I passed through O. in '69 the only persons I saw which [I] knew was

---

23 Beginning in the third year of his first enlistment, a soldier drew an extra $1.00 per month, and $2.00 upon attaining his fourth year, as an incentive to discourage desertion. Thus Sergeant Matthews was earning his base monthly pay of $17.00, plus $2.00. Because the rank of company quartermaster sergeant had been abolished, no longevity pay was authorized for that grade. This was the key factor causing Matthews to resign his position. See *ANJ*, May 18, 1873.

Mr. and Jim Daley and Owen Hart, and none of them knew me until I made myself known. The latter wanted to know all about Father, he rode eight or ten miles up the road with me. I told them I was going to Omaha, and I did go there, but in a different capacity than [I] had any idea of. But here I am now in New Mexico, with only one year three months and twenty one days to serve. I tell you what I will soon be home with you. The time seems to pass away faster now than ever before since [I] have been away. A year and three months will soon roll around and we will all be togeather once more.

I sent you $60.00 by the Pay Masters Son. Hope you will not have to wait as long for this as you did the last I sent you by P.O. Order.

Indeed I don't know what to write to you. And am ashamed to send you such a thing as this. It seems as though I ought to find lots to tell you about, but when [I] come to write [I] can think of nothing.

The Troops here are all quartered in tents, but I have a large room for my store and office.[24] And [I] have moved my bed in. Am fixed up real comfortable. And am surrounded on three sides with rations, forage and Company desk. Harlan rooms with me, and is now sound asleep. The money for his boots is included with the $60.00. Says he is a thousand times obliged to you for your trouble. Sends his kind regards to you all. Says it seems as though he knew you all. And has promised to pay me a visit when our time is out. He has eight months longer to serve than I have.

I don't think we will leave this post to go on a scout this summer. We may be sent out for ten or fifteen days some time but not longer. Have not heard anything lately about any more Troops coming down here.

Father haven't you any more old blanks you can write to me on[?] Some like those you filled up and sent me last summer. The men in the troop still talk about those big letters you wrote me, try your hand again.

I bought 680 lbs of Potatoes today for the troop, paid 7¢ per lb. Pretty good price, dont you think so[?] When we left Union a Sergeant and one man was left to make a garden for the troop, but as we have had

---

24 By this late date, Fort Bascom's buildings were quite dilapidated. The troops probably found tents to be cleaner and more comfortable, if not safer, than the crumbling adobe structures. Apparently the storehouse was in better condition, probably because it had been repaired to protect the supplies from the elements.

no rain yet, guess it will be a failure. Last year we raised turnips enough to feed a regiment for a year and when we left Union, this summer, we left enough in the Cellar to supply any number of people. Harlan says our gardners did not raise anything but burs and turnips, and he is about right. Potatoes only grow in some parts of this territory, the soil is too sandy. All farming and gardening in New Mexico is done by irrigation. And nothing will grow where it is impossible to irrigate except soap weed and cactus. By the way this soap weed is splendid for washing cloths. The roots are dug up and put in a tub of warm water and by shaking it up well a foam arises equal to any made from soap.[25]

Well I see by putting down soap weed etc I have filled up two half sheets of paper, better than I expected when [I] commenced. Haven't anything else to write about.

Fort Bascom, New Mexico

Oh, how can I thank you for your kindness to the absent one. Words are but poor excuses to express my feelings to-night. Your present was received safe this evening, and I thank you for it. Their value is nothing compared with the recollections brought forth. The time is not so far distant when I shall be with you and then Loved ones, I will prove by <u>deeds</u> my gratefulness for your kindness to me, but what is the use of my trying to write as I feel when I can't do it.

Father's welcome letter bearing date of May 8th was also received. He makes excuses of nothing to write, but I am sure he managed to fill up a sheet of letter paper with interesting news. Don't make any excuses my dear Father, your letters are all interesting and welcome. If you can only say "We are all well" I shall always be happy. I hope you may be successful in getting the appointment of Clerk, to that august body, (our City Council). I have made a mistake in the above I see, it is not a Clerkship, but a Collectorship you aspire to, but anyhow I hope you will get it, and I also pray Sue may get her school. Then our prospects would look favorable. Father a collector, Lizzie and Sue school marms, Johnnie a mechinest, Mother in charge of home affairs, Arthur and Clellie assistants and Eddie three thousand miles away keeping commissary stores

---

25 This refers to the root of a small yucca plant found on the plains.

from spoiling. How different are our vocations, and still we must be content. But I see no reason why we should not get along well, when we all work togeather.

You are not the only one glad that our Regiment is not in the Modoc Country. New Mexico has always been distasteful to me, and I have always been praying for a change of stations but rather than go to Oregon, I would remain here. I have no desire to risk my life at this day. There was a time when I would rush into danger without giving a thought for the consequences, but now each day life seems more dear to me. You need entertain no fears of our Regiment being ordered to that part of the country, for I think we are booked for New Mexico this year at least. The Modoc war can not certainly last much longer. And it is an outrage on our Government for having allowed it to continue this long.

Genl. Crook has brought the Arizona Indians to terms, and has done it with small loss on our side. Peace with the Arizona Indians is something never before known and from all accounts it is likely to remain so for the future. I read an account of the Modoc War in the "New York Herald" of April 30th. It spoke of the excitement occasioned by the attack and rout of Major Thomas' Command. And said there was a strong disposition evinced by a number of the old frontiersmen of the town of "Yreka, Cal." who were accustomed to Indian fighting to form a party that would meet the Modocs on their own ground and fight them in their own style, if any inducements were held out to them. And that they could accomplish the extermination of Captain Jack and his band with far smaller sacrifice of life than will ultimately be lost if the "regular troops" have to do it themselves.

I know there is lot's of red tape business carried on in the Army both in peace and time of war, but if a lot of destitute frontiersman would presume to undertake a thing of this kind and I had the authority I would as soon shoot one of them as I would one of Captain Jack's band. The very idea is a slur on the regular soldier. Talk about a lot of insignificant frontiersmen exterminating a band, or tribe of Indians, where a large Command of regular soldiers had failed is the greatest piece of presumption I ever heard of. Why the Indians in Arizona thought no more of "jumping" ten or a dozen citizens, and getting away with their hair than they would of eating a good breakfast, at the same time they would not think of attacking three Cavalry men. I know this to be a fact, for when I was in Arizona there was never a week went by with out the Apatches scalping one or more of the same kind of frontiersmen as are to be found in Yreka Cal. And during the time I was there we never lost a man by the Indians. Although we were constantly on the road in parties ranging from two to ten men.

The inducements these chicken hearted frontiersmen want is in the shape of a five hundred or thousand dollars greenback. If they are so positive they can exterminate the Modocs with but small loss on their part, why do they not volunteer their services without asking for any inducements from the Government[?] It would be no more than right, for they would only be fighting for their homes, but the truth of the matter is they are afraid of their cowardly cranium's, and only imagine they could exterminate the Modocs. But enough of this.

Captain Hobart with twenty six men of our troop left Camp this morning for Fort Union, they will travel across the country, not going by the road. The object is to comply with a Department Order to the effect that the country between here and Union shall be patrolled regularily. And also between here and Fort Sumner, the order also states that we are not to pursue any Indians, but only to protect the citizen.

I have been left behind in Command of the balance of the troop, and to look out for the troop property. M Troop leaves here in the morning for Fort Sumner, taking with them fifteen days rations.[26]

Everything is quiet here, an no apprehension of trouble from Indians. And in fact we dont want any.

I received a "Postal Card" from Baltimore today from some person signing himself "Old Soldier." I can't imagine who it can be from. The writing is something like Captain Byers, but not so good as he use to write. Do you know of any person sending me one[?] I suppose before this reaches you, you will have received my small favor, at least I hope so.

Well it is quite late and as there will be no chance of sending this on

---

26 Companies B, G, H, I, L, and M, Eighth Cavalry, rendezvoused at old Fort Sumner in May to seek out and restrict the movements of parties of Mescalero Apaches in the region. See Eighth Cavalry Returns, May 1873. Established in 1862, Fort Sumner was located in the Bosque Redondo region along the Pecos River in eastern New Mexico Territory. The place became infamous for serving as an internment camp for the Navajos, defeated at Canyon de Chelly in 1864. The post was abandoned after the Navajos were permitted to return to their homeland in the Four Corners area in 1868. The property was later purchased by land magnate Lucian B. Maxwell. See Frazer, *Forts of the West*, 104.

its road for a day or two I will close, and add another line before sending it off. Good night and happy dreams.

Fort Bascom, New Mexico
TUESDAY MORNING, MAY 27, 1873, 10 A.M.

I am now at liberty to do as I choose until 4 P.M. All my work has been done until that time. I know there is nothing I could do which would afford you or my self more pleasure than writing you a long letter and if I can only get myself properly started you shall have one.

I have read this morning what [I] wrote to you last night, and find I have expressed my sentiments in regard to the Modoc War, and frontiersmen of Yreka Cal. exactly. And the reading of it has only increased my disgust of the class known as "old frontiersmen." You have no idea what a disreputable class of people these same old frontiersmen are. And I can hardly find words sufficiently strong to describe them. Suffice it to say nine tenths of them are either horse thieves, murder[er]s, burglars, bigamists or something worse, who have fled from civilization to escape the punishment they so richly deserve. Here on the frontier they do almost as they choose. Committing murder or thieving with impunity. It is true now and then you will find a "<u>white man</u>," but you will invariable find him too poor to leave the country. He will tell you honestly that if he could only raise enough money to carry him to some part of the States, New Mexico or any of the other territories would never see him again. These men all had more money when they arrived in the territories than they will ever have again, and the final[e] of their career will be a resting place in the sandy soil of some of the territories. An honest man has no more business in a frontier country than a cow would in a "brokers office." And should I be so unfortunate as to be discharged [from] the service at a frontier post, I hope it will be close to some Rail Road where I can jump aboard of some lightning express, shake the frontier <u>sand</u> (for the soil is something that was but is no more) from my feet and get among civilized people soon as possible.

M Troop are ready to leave for Fort Sumner. They will remain about fifteen days. The party from Union yesterday who brought the mail, also brought the report that our troop would be ordered to return to Union, as a lot of Military prisoners had been brought to the prison there to serve sentence.[27] And that the Infantry Company now stationed there was not strong enough to guard them. I hope the report may prove true.

Although I have no reason to complain of my duties here. I have comfortable quarters, and am living very well. My duty is just heavy enough to give me an appetite for eating my ration. I bought about a thousand pounds of potatoes @ 7¢ per lb. the other day for the troop, also a lot of canned tomatoes, and forty pounds of dried apples. Gave the troop "plum pudding" for dinner Sunday, and apple pies the day before. Not bad living for soldiers is it[?]

Opportunities for making "Company fund," from which these delicacies are purchased, are better when stationed in the field than when at a post.[28] Here we are issued [a] full ration of bacon, and can sell it for 15¢ per lb. and can buy beef for 5¢ where at a post seven tenths of the meat ration is beef, and the men will eat more than their ration.

About a week or two ago I sent off to be sold over five hundred pounds bacon, two hundred pounds Sugar, one barrel Vinegar, one hundred pounds Rice, one hundred pounds Horminy, and one box Soap, savings of rations, but I tell you it keeps me busy at times to watch that nothing is Wasted. I also sent an order to Union for one thousand pounds of Middlings [coarse grain, probably corn in this instance] to be fed to some hogs we have there.

I see I am doing very well in regard to sending you a long letter and I have just found out what has moved the "spirit." I put on one of those elegant shirts you so kindly sent me this morning, and it feels so comfortable, and looks so nice I cannot help but write. And fear if I don't take it off I will use up the quarters supply of letter paper. Again allow me to thank you for the gift.

Has Lizzie given up the idea of visiting Frostburg and Oakland this summer[?] I know of but one place I am longing to visit, and that place is <u>home</u>. I can hardly think there was ever one who prayed more to be home than I do. And the nearer the time for my return the more anxious I

---

27 Fort Union's large complex included a military prison, apart from the post guard house, for housing military prisoners transferred from other posts within the District of New Mexico. Built in 1868, the prison's stone cell block, housed within an adobe building, contained ten cells. See Oliva, *Fort Union and the Frontier Army*, 357.

28 Matthews refers to being in the field because Fort Bascom was no longer an active post with its own supply line.

become and the more dissatisfied with the Army. "One year, three months and twelve day's." And then a free man, free to return to those I love so devotedly, and who are waiting to welcome me home. Perhaps our happiness will be so great when we are all togeather once more that we will forget the trouble and pain endured the past five years.

We are expecting another mail from Union to-day. If it comes there may be something more for me in it. At least I shall hope so, but will not feel very badly disappointed if there should be nothing. It is dinner time so [I] will put this aside, and will wait for the Union Mail before closing.

Fort Bascom, New Mexico
MAY 27, 1873 [CONTINUED FRIDAY MORNING, MAY 30]

Have just finished making out my Forage and Ration Returns for June.[29] And while [I] have nothing to do [I] might as well add a few lines to my now lengthy letter. Although I don't know that [I] have anything of interest to write about. The mail from Union has not yet arrived. Should have been here two days ago at least. Don't know what is detaining it.

We had a small shower of rain last evening but not enough to do any good. You complain of too much rain, while we complain because we have none at all. Perhaps the Good Lord has come to the conclusion that this part of his creation will never be worth anything, and intends to dry it up. If I was only out of it I would not care how soon he done so, but so long as I am obliged to sojourn in it I, of course, [I] will have to crave his indulgence to spare the country until I am permitted to depart with my buzzard (Discharge).[30]

I am having very easy times now, scarcely doing enough to give me an appetite for eating my rations. Will tell you what I have to do, although it may not prove very interesting, but still will have one virtue, that of filling up my letter. Roll out of bed at 5 o'clock, have ten minutes to dress, put on my Arms and get out on the parade. The

---

29 As company quartermaster sergeant, Matthews was responsible for completing requisitions for hay and grain for the company's horses. He also prepared a ration return every ten days based on the number of men present with the company.
30 The face of the army discharge certificate was surmounted by a national coat of arms having an eagle as the central figure, prompting soldiers to refer to it as a "buzzard."

assembly is then sounded where my detachment fall in ranks. I call the roll and report all absentees, dismiss my men, return to my quarters, put away my accoutrements. Then [I] issue forage and have the horses properly groomed. [I] Return to my quarters, wash and go to breakfast. That finished [I] return to quarters, clean up my room, dust off the desk, and then polish my boots, brush my cloth[e]s, wash again and dress my hair, put on a white shirt (one of those Mother so kindly sent me). During the time since breakfast I have my usual smoke (not pleasant for Mother to know) then sit down at the desk and make out the morning sick report.

At sick call [I] walk over to the hospital tent, give the book to the Steward, wait until the sick are examined and then bring the book back to the office. Then [I] make out the morning report and any other writing to be done, take it in the Adjutants Office and at 8:30 march on my Guard (when [I] have any detail). After this is over [I] water or turn our horses out to herd according to orders. This brings me to 9 o'clock A.M. (present time). Nothing to do now until 11:45, when [I] get my morning report from the Adjutants Office. And then [I] go to dinner. Then [I] take my usual after dinner smoke. That over I sometimes lie down on my bed and sleep until water call, 4 o'clock [I] ride to water (about three hundred yards), return [and then] issue forage and have the horses groomed. Take another wash, hair dress and go to supper.

At Sun down retreat is sounded by the trumpeters. The men fall in ranks under arms. I call the roll and make the details for the morrow. Nothing to do then until 8:30. Tattoo is then sounded when the men fall in ranks again [and] have their names called and then the day's work is over, at 9 o'clock P.M. Taps is sounded when all lights are put out and all noise (except the noise of nature) is hushed. And about this time your Son and brother is generally found under his little Government blankets sound asleep dreaming of "loved ones at home."

Here I have nearly filled up another sheet of paper telling you what I do day and night. It does not amount to anything, and still I believe it is no more than right I should tell you of my duties and how my leisure time is spent. I would not have you think I sleep every afternoon, for I do nothing of the kind. Whenever I have any books or papers to read, I read them. And [I] do any writing I feel like doing. I have a young friend in the Adjutants Office, at Fort Union, who sends me lots of papers, and sometimes a book. Reading matter is always in great demand when at a place like this. And most of our leisure time is spent in reading.

Friday Evening. Retreat is over, and I again bring forth my letter to add the finishing touch to my work. The Mail from Union came in about an hour ago. Was handed lots of mail for the troop, and supposed there would be lots for me. "See next sheet."

"This is what came to me," accompanied by a lot of envelopes, postage stamps and a letter from the sender, telling me these indispensables were a present from him and that I should use them in writing to my little affinity. I will cheerfully obey his instructions, and write the first to "you my only affinity."

Besides this present I received a Democrat and a Postal Card from our Ex. 1st Sergeant, who is now in the Adjutant Generals Office at Washington. These Cards must be becoming the rage in the States as this is the second I have received away out in this forlorn country.

Enclosed find photograph of my friend and ex room mate Clinton C. Harlan. It was struck off from a negative taken before he enlisted and [he] had just received some from his brother this evening. It is a very true picture, but he has grown older and stouter since that was taken, and besides does not wear as good cloth[e]s now as he did then. He gave it to me to send to you. He is now Clerking for the Quarter Master and rooms with another Clerk. I will now have to do all the company writing myself, although he has asked to be allowed to assist me when ever I need him as he wants his place back again when we return to Union. Guess though I can get along without his help. Have heard nothing from the mail about a Troop being sent back to Union for duty.

Eight of the General Prisoners just sent to Union to serve their sentence made their escape last Sunday. As there were no troops but Infantry at the Post, and very few of them, the prisoners had nothing to fear from pursuit. I would not be surprised but this will be the cause for ordering a troop up. If it should be the case I hope ours may be the lucky one.

Well "loved ones" I think it is time to close this. I will have one consolation in sending this off, and that is if I have not given you quality, I have quantity. Write to me as often as possible.

I forgot to enclose the picture, but the envelope has as much in it now as it will hold so [I] will enclose it in this. Let me know at once if the money comes safe.

I have written seven letters to go off in this mail which will leave Sunday or Monday. And may write two or three more before [I] finish.

Fort Bascom, New Mexico
JUNE 24, 1873

I had been thinking of you for an hour or more this evening. And allowed my imagination to carry me home. While in this state the mail from Union unexpectedly arrived. We were all very much surprised for [we] did not expect it until the 26th inst., but I assure you it was none the less welcome for being ahead of time. And now how can I express my happy feelings for [I] have again received nearly as much mail as the balance of the Troop put togeather.

Received two long, interesting and splendid letters from Father, who is ever thoughtful of the absent one. One from Sister Lizzie which was more than welcome on account of [the] long time intervening between letters from her. One from a Soldier friend. A postal card from an ex Soldier. A paper from home and two Watches from Howard and Co. New York.

These happy remembrances of the absent one fills my heart to overflowing with gratitude and love. And I find it impossible to express my feelings. I would be more than selfish were I to utter a complaint in this for being situated as I now am, when I am weekly the recipient of untold happiness, conveyed to me through the medium of letters from home. And while I am writing of my own happiness I cannot help thinking of some of my comrades who watch the arrival of every mail with a hope of receiving a letter from some one at home. And when the last letter has been distributed to find a sad disappointment in the place of the fulfillment of their expectations. No word from a loving Mother or Father. Nothing to remind them of the existence of one friend in the wide, wide world who had a thought for the welfare of the absent and unfortunate Soldier boy. These are the class of men who fill our Guard House and Military Prisons. They become disgusted with themselves, the world and every person in it. And the principle cause of all this is not having some loved one to give them a word of hope or encouragement.

Will change this subject for [I] am making both you and myself feel bad with other peoples misfortunes. Allow me my dear Father to set your mind, at ease in regard to your description of Westminster and its inhabitants. I find the greatest interest in the perusal of them. Your descriptions are admirable, and when you have exhausted Main Street, you can take up all the others, Court especially. So far, I am acquainted with nearly all the persons named. And this makes it all the more interesting. Accept my thanks for your compliments. But I fear you rate my letters to high.

It is getting quite late and as I have been doing a great amount of writing today [I] will put this up and finish in the morning. Good night and happy dreams to you all.

Wednesday Morning June 25. Before going to sleep last night [I] devoted an hour in the personal[s] of the Democrat. I find lots of interesting matter in them, and in fact every thing that tells of W[estminster] and its inhabitants is interesting to me.

The watches I spoke of as having received were for two men of our Troop. When ever any of the men of our Troop wants a watch they get me to order it for them. This makes the eighth Waltham Watch I have bought from Howard and Co. Sold five for $50.00 each, one $37.50, one $32.50 and one for $31.00, total amount paid me for the eight $351.00. Total amount paid Howard and Co. for the same $290.75, leaving a balance for my trouble of $66.25. Not a bad business where one has no Capital invested is it[?]

The men are always satisfied with their watches. When ever of them wants a watch they tell me the kind they want and I tell the just what I will charge them for it. They deposit the amount in the hands of some Officer until the watches arrive, and then hand it to me. I take their money and pay for the watches without any trouble whatever on my part and am always well paid for the handling of their money for a few moments. This is the way the old thing works. I shall continue in the business just so long as [I] can find a customer.

B Troop, or the greater part of them, left here for Fort Union last friday and this Mail brought orders for the balance of them to be sent up. They leave this morning. Suppose B will remain at Union this summer.

It was reported here that the Ute Indians who have been for a long time at peace have broken out and gone on the "War Path." Their hunting ground is up in Colorado near the Spanish Peaks, and I suppose B Troop will be sent there to see how matters stand.

Everything is quiet down here. Capt. Young, Commanding Officer of this place, went out with Troop M on a four days trip. Returned last evening bringing in with them as captives one wild rabbit and three crows being the only hostile enemy to be found in a radius of fifty miles of this camp. Guess if nothing larger than these animals and Birds are to be found our hair will be safe for this summer at least.

My Quarterly Papers are nearly finished. Made them all out by my self. Will have them ready to send off by next mail. Capt. Hobart complimented me for their neatness. No erasures of figures are to be found on any of them. Something seldom seen in Quarterly Returns. Harlan is a splendid clerk so far as writing and rapidness is conserned, but has one great fault "incorrectness." He can do as much work in one day as I can in two. But when the Rolls or Returns are compared three mistakes in his to one in mine will be found. He is rapid and inaccurate, while I am slow but pretty sure. I examined the clothing book the other day and found a number of mistakes in it. Some of them as much as $10.00. But $10.00 or 10¢ is all the same so far as the mistake is concerned. It is bound to be discovered by the authorities in Washington and notification of the existence of the mistake be sent to the Troop Commander of the Troop, with orders to make the necessary corrections.

I corrected them all and told Harlan of it. Said he could not imagine how he come to make them. Told him I knew how he done it, and if he would not get angry I would tell him. Promised he would not, so [I] told him he had too much confidence in himself, and was always too sure of being right. When if he had went over his figures, he very often would discover a mistake. Took it in good faith and has promised to be more particular in the future in case he should have anything to do with the Troop Books. I am not particular whether he ever comes back as Troop Clerk or not, or in fact whether we ever have another Clerk so long as I am in the Troop and have any thing to do with the Troop records. For when [I] attend to it myself [I] feel confident it is correct. Guess you will think I have a great deal of confidence in myself, and in fact I have, but it is for this reason: whenever I have anything to do which needs be correct, I take plenty of time to do it in, instead of waiting until the last moment and then do it in haste.

Only one year two months and thirteen days yet. This last year has passed away very fast, but none too fast for me. Will soon be home with you.

The weather is very warm here, and flies make it very disagreeable for every person. Something less than four million of them are now buzzing around my head, lighting on my hands & paper, and keeping me busy pushing them off the lines so [I] can tell you all about it.

Suppose now we might as well make ourselves comfortable here until the last of October. Don't think [I] shall mind stopping here until then, so long as we have a weekly mail.

Am in splendid health, but am melting all the flesh away from my bones. If the weather gets much warmer [I] will have to be put in ice if Uncle Sam wishes to carry me on his Muster and Pay Rolls, or else [I] will melt and vanish.

MAP 3. Fort Union Military Reservation.

CHAPTER SEVEN

"I Shall Never Soldier Again"

JULY—DECEMBER 1873

Summer at dreary Fort Bascom seemed to pass agonizingly slowly for Matthews as he endured the oppressive heat of New Mexico's eastern plains, combatted swarms of flies that stuck to the body "like wax," and contended with the never-ending paperwork incumbent upon a quartermaster sergeant. The mails, delivered irregularly to the summer camp via Fort Union, offered the only enjoyable diversions from an otherwise humdrum existence. Even the Fourth of July "left no impression," but an Indian scare would offer a welcome break in the usual monotony.

Fort Bascom, New Mexico
JULY 3, 1873

The mail from Union came in yesterday but [I] found no letter from you. Felt a little disappointed, but this was lessened some by the receipt of a very nice letter from Lec Paine. One from Captain Byers

"I Shall Never Soldier Again" 243

containing eight pages. One from Ex-Sergeant Rowalt (who was in Command of the detachment that Killed the five Indians last March) and who is now discharged and living at Cincinnati Ohio. One from Sergt. Walters of our troop at Union and a paper from W[estminster]. Ought not complain much had I[?] And still I would have liked a letter from you.

I can now breathe free for the next three months, have finished all my Quarterly Returns, Muster and Pay Rolls and all other papers pertaining to the Troop. I was complimented for my muster and pay rolls, both by Capt. Hobart, Troop Commander, and by Col. Young, Reviewing Officer. Capt. Hobart said my rolls were very neat and looked much nicer than Harlan's and that is saying a great deal.

The Capt told me last night to have seven days rations ready for twenty six of the Troop who are to leave here on the 5th inst. Suppose they are going up to Union after horses. We have more horses here now than men and are to have still more.

B Troop I understand is stationed at Sayers Ranch on the road leading from Union to Pueblo C[olorado] T[erritory] in the Ute Country. Have heard nothing since [I] last wrote to you of the outbreak by the Ute Indians. All quiet down here and likely to remain so this summer.

One of M Troop was drowned here four days ago while bathing in the river. His body was recovered next day after and was buried with the honors of War.[1] There is a strange fatality connected with that Troop. Every trip they have made to this place they have lost a man. Last summer one was drowned. In April of this year another was Killed by his horse and now still another meets his death while bathing. Three casualities in less than a year.

The Canadian, like the big and little Colorado River, runs very rapid and its bottom is composed of quick sand, so that when a man or horse once sets into it he seldom gets out again. When we were coming

---

1 William Hodges, Company M, Eighth Cavalry, drowned on June 27 or 28, 1873, while bathing in the Canadian River. A native of Rhine, Prussia, Hodges had been a blacksmith prior to entering the army at Louisville, Kentucky, on January 24, 1872. He died at age twenty-seven. There is a discrepancy in the date of death between the Register of Enlistments and the regimental returns. See entry 4, p. 29, roll 39, ROE, RG 94, NA; and Eighth Cavalry Returns, June 1873. Hodges was buried at the site of the summer camp. His funeral was conducted on the evening of June 28, and was attended by all members of the command not occupied with other duties. See Orders No. 17, Summer Camp, Eighth Cavalry, June 28, 1873, in Eighth Cavalry G&SO, RG 391, NA.

through from Arizona in '70 one evening I was riding my horse to water over what I supposed was hard dry sand, when all of a sudden my horse went down in quick sand until nothing but his head and back could be seen. And it took about a dozen of us to pull him out, which we finally succeeded in doing.

Lec writes me she has just parted from a young friend who has received a <u>Commission</u> in the Signal Service. I think there must be some thing wrong in Denmark.[2] The Authorities are not appointing or giving Commissions in the Service now from Civil life and are not likely to, especially in the signal branch of the service. She says he is allowed thirty days <u>Leave</u> of <u>Absence</u> each year, but I imagine she means "furlough," which will prove a fraud as all other promises made by U.S. Agents. I believe if the truth was known some young gentleman friend has discovered his cash account to be short with prospects of it becoming shorter unless he done something soon and that he has done as lots of other young men have in a like prediciment, viz: <u>Enlisted</u> instead of <u>being Commissioned</u> as he has informed Lec. Perhaps if she could see him to-day she would find him dressed in a suit of Uncle Sams blue, without rank or commission higher than private. Even Corporals or Sergeants are not made in the signal service until the men have served some time and are perfectly instructed in all branches connected with their duties, and are capable to teach those placed under them. I have not been thus candid in answering her letter, but I predicted she had seen the last of her friend for five years to come unless he happened to be serving in some part of the [East?], in that case he may get his <u>furlough</u> rather <u>Leave of Absence</u>, but I have my doubts. She need not be informed of this as it will not help the matter any.

Only 1 year 2 months and 4 days and then I will get a furlough which will exceed any this young man will [receive?] for the next five years to come.

The weather still continues very warm, and flies, the greatest pest imaginable, are buzzing around in swarms lighting on one's face and

---

2 Matthews's reference is to William Shakespeare's, *Hamlet, The Prince of Denmark*, in which Marcellus warns Hamlet not to go, for "something is rotten in the state of Denmark." Marcellus suspected that the death of Hamlet's father was not by accident, as reported, and he was concerned about Hamlet's safety. It is interesting to note the exposure Victorian-era students had to English literature. For the context of the quotation see Irace, *The First Quarto of Hamlet*, 46.

hands and sticking like wax. You have to push them off, as they are not the scary kind.

Well loved ones there is nothing left for me to write about. And as the mail leaves in an hour will close and send this off.

Summer Camp, Eighth Cavalry on the Canadian River, New Mexico
July 9, 1873

The mail from Union arrived this morning but brought nothing to me. This is the second mail (two weeks) since [I] heard from you. Can't imagine what can be the matter. Are any of you sick, and you are delaying writing to me on that account, or have you written to me and I have not received them[?] Will hope to hear from you for sure by next mail and will then know what has occasioned the long silence.

On the 5th inst. Capt. Hobart with 26 men of our troop left here for Union on a little scouting expedition. Will be gone about twenty days. I was left here again in charge of the balance of the Troop, horses, property etc. and indeed was not sorry, for a nice cool room is far preferable to sitting in the saddle all day under a scorching sun.[3]

The weather is warmer than I ever saw it in this country. And the flies are so bad during the day that one is kept busy pushing them off. Some of our horses are going blind on account of them.

The 4th of July has passed and like all other holidays spent in the Army left no impression to remind one of it. The same old routine of duty was performed, and the same old beans and bacon was set before us for dinner. With this and the usual growling by the men the day passed away. And when Taps was sounded at 9 P.M. none in Camp was sorry that the day was passed. I have only one more 4th of July to spend in the Army, and am very thankful, for if [I] had many more [I] dont think [I] would stay. One year, one month and twenty eight days, that will soon pass away, but not too soon for either you or I.

We had quite an excitment in Camp all day yesterday and last

---

3 Companies L and M, posted at Fort Bascom, mounted periodic scouting expeditions during the summer for the purpose of disrupting the illicit cattle trade. See Eighth Cavalry Returns, July–September, 1873.

night, occasioned by the report of Indians being seen about twelve miles from here. The Mexican that brought the news in was out herding cattle and said he saw the Indians coming in this direction. He started for Camp as fast as his poney could run and after riding some distance his poney stepped in a hole, fell and broke his neck, so the Mexican had to come in on foot.

Col. Young, who is in Command of Camp, issued the necessary orders to make preparations for the enemies reception. Our horses were out on herd at the time but were at once run in, saddled up and every thing made ready for an attack. Our force is not very strong now, only number fifty one including officers, sick, lame and lazy. Col. Young took our men and rode off to a prominent look out where with the aid of his field glasses he could see the country for four or five miles. He returned in an hour or two reporting that he could see smoke supposed to come from a Camp fire about five miles away. The mexican herders were sent out with orders to find out about the number of Indians and as they could not return before 11 or 12 o'clock, we formed our selves in small parties and discussed the all absorbing topic viz: would this prove an attack or would the report like nearly all of the kind prove a false one[?] There was nothing improbable in the Indians coming here, as there is plenty of water on the prairie and the grass is splendid, but we have been fooled so often that we hardly placed any dependence in this report.

About 9 o'clock I went to bed and was soon sleeping soundly, all thoughts of Indians had vanished from my mind for others of a more pleasant character when suddenly I was awakened by some one knocking at my door and calling, "Sergeant Matthews." I jumped out of bed and opened the door and found the Veterinary Surgeon waiting to get in. He told me the Mexican herders had returned and reported the Indians to have turned out Mexican traiders who were returning from a traiding expedition down the country. A detail of ten men under Command of Lieut. Rogers was ordered to saddle up, and take three days rations and go after the traiders. The party left about 12 o'clock and have not yet returned. Suppose they will capture the outfit and bring it in.

So the report has proven a mistake, and although the majority of the men were loud in their denunciations of the whole lying Mexican race, I have not a doubt but every one in Camp was glad the affair turned out as it did. For my part I would be in for hanging every greaser, or white man, that brought in a false report of Indians, for it is inclined to make men careless and sometime perhaps a true report might be brought in and no faith placed in it, and the result might prove a disaster on our side.

Col. Young just rode up to my room and told me to take half the night on Guard to-night. There is so few non Commissioned officers here that only one can be detailed each night. I have not been on Guard since we went up from here last October, so a guard will not hurt me any. Will have nothing to do but relieve the sentrys, but will have to keep awake half the night.

2:30 A.M. Have just posted the second relief, and as am obliged to keep awake until day break, will while away part of the time writing to you.

Guard duty is a Military necessity and has to be performed. It comes pretty hard sometimes especially at a time like this when the guard is doubled and men only get one night in bed. By this I mean being on guard every alternate day and night, but I have done more than this many times.

Last summer on our forty days scout [I] was on guard for four successive nights, would fall asleep as soon as relieved from post, and could not keep awake during the days march, but doze in the saddle. It is a miserable sensation to sleep riding horseback, your horse makes a mistep and awakens your drowsey senses for a moment and then to make him more careful you use your persuaders (spurs) on his sides regardless of the pain you inflict. This little exercise arouses your sleepy senses for a few moments and only makes matters worse, for your horse becomes so use to the spur that when he makes another blunder or misstep he naturally expects to be spurred and makes a sudden spring, almost dislocating your neck by the sudden jerk he gives you. And then if you fail to throw in your spurs he feels disappointed, but takes a long breath of relief. But I guess he is glad to be disappointed. It is always better in cases of this kind to treat your horse gently but it is not human nature, especially a soldier.

This Guard will not hurt me any, or will I feel the loss of a half nights sleep, as I have never been on guard since last October. A Q.M. or acting Q.M. Sergeant is not supposed to perform guard duty and is never put on except in cases of emergency.

Well I can think of nothing else to write you this time. You need have no fears for my safety, for should the Indians pay us a visit we will be able to receive them with all due honors, and as we are pretty well fortified will be able to stand them off. There is nothing improbable in them coming up here, but there is in them attacking us at this post. They may come on a thieving expedition and steel some of the Ranchmens stock, but it is not likely that they will bother us.

These Indians know what it is to attack a party of Uncle Sams Regulars. Although I have noticed in some of the Eastern papers they speak rather sparingly of the efficiency of the regular soldier, since the Modoc trouble. It is easy enough for these "Knights of the Quill" to sit in their easy chairs and tell the people how the thing should be done, but it is far from easy to do it when at the scene of action. I have no particular love for the regular Army, or do I advocate its efficiency, but I am not so predjudiced against it but can give it credit for what it deserves. And I say the regular soldier to-day is as brave; and can whip as many Indians as either the frontiersmen or Volunteer Soldiers. And could vanquish as many of these destitute Editors, who write so much about "what they know of Indian fighting and how it should be done" as could be put before them. I would like to have one of these chaps set before me about this time to see how near his chicken heart I could strike with one of Uncle Sams improved carbines. There never was a man that dispised the Army, especially the Regulars, more than I do to-day but still I give it credit for all it deserves. And know it can do; and does as much as any same number of people could under the circumstances.

And this Modoc affair proves my words. It is true it took some time and considerable loss to defeat the Indians, but when all the circumstances are taken into consideration it was accomplished as quick and as well as could be done by any other parties. And had it not have been for a lot of these hungry Editors in the East who's writings to a great extent influenced the authorities in Washington, the Modoc Indians would have been so eventually disposed of by the Soldiers (and these same Regulars who are so inefficient) that the Modoc War would have been a terror to all the Indians in the country. But in the way and long delay in disposing of the captured Modocs, which has been decided upon through the influence of a certain class, the war will only prove an incentive for other tribes of Indians to try a like war.

I have heard that the authorities have turned the two Indian Chiefs Santanta and Big Tree who were in Confinement in Texas loose, and have sent them on their way rejoicing.[4] And if this be the case we may expect a visit from them before the summer is over. But I must stop this for the subject disgusts me, and I would not attempt writing upon it could I control my temper.

Summer Camp, Eighth Cavalry
On the Canadian River, New Mexico
JULY 23, 1873

The Mail came in this morning and a good mail it was for me. Two long letters from Father, both mailed on the 7th inst. One from Lizzie, from Frostburg, one from Ida, one from Jennie Z. and one from John Reese, also two home papers. You can rest assured I feel happy tonight.

This place is as dull as usual, no excitement or anything else except "flies." The party sent out after the Mexican traiders returned without having seen anything of them.

Our Company returned on the 20th inst. and brought down eleven new horses, so that now every duty man has about four horses to take care of. Too many horses by far. I dont see what the Captain wants with so many when we have so few men, but then he has nothing to do with the grooming of them except bossing the job.

I dont know how I am going to fill this up. Ought to write you a good long letter I know for your good ones received, but when one has not a subject to write about it is pretty hard matter to write either a long or interesting letter.

Harlan wants another pair of boots, and I believe I do also. Have worn mine constantly ever since [I] received them, and this is the worst country in the world to wear out boots, so much sand and gravel. Will give full directions for both pair. And will send you the money by "Post Office Money Order" by the time they are done. Please go to Mr. Yingling

---

4 This was a false rumor. Kiowa chiefs Satanta and Big Tree had notorious reputations as a result of their frequent raids on northern Texas ranches. Following their attack on a government wagon train and subsequent capture at Fort Sill in 1871, both men were tried and imprisoned by the State of Texas. The Quakers, who wielded much influence over the Grant administration, pressured the government to negotiate with Governor Davis for the release of the chiefs. Those discussions finally bore fruit in October 1873. Following the Red River War of 1874, Satanta was returned to Huntsville Prison, where he committed suicide in 1878. Big Tree was later freed and became a devout peace advocate. A full narrative of these events is found in Leckie, *Military Conquest*, 151–53, 176–80, 218–19.

and ask him to make them at once. The sooner they are done the sooner he will get his money. This time we will be more liberal and send you the money for both the boots and the postage on them, for it can't be a very profitable business for you to only receive the price of the boots from us and have to pay the expressage out of your own pocket.

I have a notion to change my situation again. Dont know whether you will approve of it or not, but I know it is bettering my situation if I do it. It is to give up my present position for a Clerkship in the Subsistence Department. I think I can get the place as the Clerk now there has been appointed Sergeant Major of the Regiment, [I] will get six dollars and twenty cents extra pay, which will be two dollars and twenty cents more than I am now receiving. And besides [I] will not have to pay for any cheverons or stripes which takes nearly all the difference in the pay of a Sergeant from that of a Private. And now that my time of service is so near out I am after the dollars and cents, instead of rank. Anyhow will be able to tell you in my next whether I have made the change or not. Give me your ideas, but I can imagine what you will say in regard to it. And that will be for me to use my own judgment in the matter, and if it betters my situation you will be satisfied. Harlan is clerking in the Quartermasters Department and if I get the vacant clerkship will be in the same office with him.

You must excuse this hastily written letter for [I] have been doing a lot of Company writing to go off by this mail and it is now quite late.

Fort Bascom, New Mexico
JULY 30, 1873

Just received the Union Mail and was happy to find a good long Chapter from Father.

Am afraid this will necessarily be a short letter, for [I] am suffering with an "Ulcerated throat." Caught cold on the night of the 28th which settled in my throat. Went on the Sick Report on the 29 and am still on it. The Doctor burnt my throat with Caustic this morning. Not a pleasant operation to the patient I can assure you. My throat is very sore but [I] guess it will soon get well. It is so seldom I have anything the matter with me that when I do, I am as cross as a bear with a sore head.

Well I have made the change which [I] spoke of in my last. Am now Clerking in the Subsistance Department as a high Private. My pay now is $21.20 per month, where as a Sergeant I was only getting $17.00 and had to buy my stripes out of that. My duties are less bothersome now than they were as Sergt.[5]

The Captain did not seem to approve of the change, but he looked at it only in his own interest. Said he had no one else in the Troop who could make out his Company papers. I recommended one and told him I would give him all the necessary instructions. And would assist him at anytime he needed me. He would give me no satisfaction that evening but next day sent for me and said he would make the change.

Harlan and I will get along finely togeather, and guess I will keep this place until my time is out. Have only one year, one month and eight days yet to serve. My time is getting less very fast. Will soon only have one year to serve and then will almost imagine myself home with you.

A wagon from Union came in yesterday bringing some "pack Saddles." Would not be surprised if a Scouting party was sent out, have not heard of any, and everything is quiet down here. Suppose these saddles have been sent down so that small parties can be sent out with pack mules instead of having to take a wagon with them.

Dont expect the Pay Master will come here now until the last of next month. So that I will be unable to make good the proposition made in my last letter, but will do so as soon as [I] am paid.

This is an awful poor letter, and an ashamed to send it to you, but have nothing to write about and even if [I] had am not feeling much like letter writing. It hurts me so much to swollow that I have eaten scarcely anything the last two days.

When you write to me direct [to] W. E. M. Company L 8th Cavalry, as the word Troop is done away with.[6] And I have done away with my rank and title. I wish you would tell Mr. Vandeford, Editor of the "Democrat" of the change. And any of my correspondents you may see. I hope by the next mail I will be feeling well again and have something to write you.

---

5 Matthews's voluntary reduction to private became official on July 26, when Corporal Daniel G. Harvey was promoted to the rank of sergeant in his place. See SO No. 23, HQ, Eighth Cavalry, August 15, 1873, in Eighth Cavalry G&SO, RG 391, NA.
6 The term "troop," meaning a cavalry company, had become so common in the army that General William T. Sherman felt compelled to issue an edict prohibiting its use. See GO No. 5, AGO, June 20, 1873.

Summer Camp, Eighth Cavalry
On the Canadian River, New Mexico
AUGUST 20, 1873

Father's two long letters dated respectively July 27th and August [?] received to-day. Was ever so glad to hear from you but have had no room to complain for a long time. Why do you suppose some of your letters lately have not reached me in the order written[?] I have received the Chapters in there regular order so far. And hope [I] shall continue to be as fortunate.

The troops here have been scouting the country considerably here of late, but so far have accomplished nothing excepting the Capture of Mexicans and ponies of which I told you in a former letter. The Civil Authorities have taken the Mexicans, but the ponies are still in our possession. Our Company was out Scouting from the 10th to the 17th Inst. Killed one Buffalo, the only one seen on the trip.

Some thirty five or forty Recruits are on the road for the two Companies here. It will help the cause considerable as the companies are pretty small. Suppose though these will prove like all the rest sent to us since [we] have been in New Mexico viz: remain four or five months and then Desert. Our Company has had one hundred and three desertions since its organization, and I suppose we have had as few as any Company in the Regiment. I know K Company has lost fully three hundred men by desertion since the latter part of 1866. When you come to add the total number of the desertions in the Regiment since 1866, it would show a fearful large number. And the cause of this is easily told. Small and inferior rations, too much work, and rough treatment by Commissioned and Non Commissioned Officers. The Government issues a sufficient ration in the first place, but the great trouble is it has to pass through so many different Depot's and Commisaries and, like our Congressmen, each makes a grab. And by the time it is ready to be issued to the men there is nothing left.

I am doing finely in the Subsistence Department, and like it better than anything [I] have been at since [I] have been in the Army. I think Harlan will get a Clerkship at District Head quarters on General Service pay $73.00 per month. Out of this he will have to buy his own Cloth[e]s, and it will cost him about $10.00 extra to board. This amount with his rations he can live very well. The General Service Clerks all wear Citizen clothing. Harlan has a friend at Santa Fe who wrote to him saying if he would like the position he thought it could be got for him. Harlan answered at once saying get it if possible.

If my time was not so short I would make a desperate effort to get on General Service, but as it is I am very well content and can put the balance of my enlistment in in any capacity. And as I shall never Soldier again [I] dont want to know any more about Military matters than I do at the present time. Clint says if he gets on General Service, he wont rest until he get's me there also, but by the time this was accomplished if such a thing could be, my time would be out. He has nearly a year longer to serve then I have. It will be a good thing for him.[7]

Expect the Pay Master will be here in ten or fifteen days. Will then be able to send you some money.

I have now One year seventeen days and twelve hours to serve. Getting down pretty fine on one year, aint it[?]

Have exhausted my subjects, so will have to stop.

Morning of the 21st. Only one year and seventeen day's. News just received that Comanche Indians have visited Fort Sumner about one hundred miles from here and run off a lot of Stock belonging to a man by the name of Maxwell. Suppose one of the Companies here will be sent down. This man Maxwell is immensely wealthy and can well afford the loss, however great it may be. He is the man that owned the great track of land in this territory embracing the town of Cimaron. The whole track was I think some sixty square miles. His Agent, a Mr. Wadingham (an Englishman), sold this land to an English Company sometime in 1870 for about thirteen hundred thousand [one million three hundred thousand] dollars. The Company established a Colony at Cimaron and made quite a nice little town of that place. But it has proved a bad investment, and I understand the Company have failed. Fort Sumner had been abandoned by our troops and was purchased by Maxwell.

---

7 Soldiers not assigned to line units were attached to the General Service, which included clerks at the various headquarters above the post level and men in the permanent parties at recruit depots. Such clerks had a comparatively easy life, as Matthews points out, because they wore civilian attire, worked regular office hours, resided in cities, and performed none of the military duties expected of other soldiers.

Summer Camp, Eighth Cavalry
On the Canadian River, New Mexico
AUGUST 27, 1873

Your ever welcome letter of August one, mailed on the 13th inst., received this morning. I have done a hard days work today am feeling quite tired and my hand is kind of crampy, but as the mail leaves first thing in the morning will have to answer tonight in order to send it off.

The Captain came to me yesterday and asked if I would make out the "Muster and Pay Rolls" for him. Told me the young man who is now Company Clerk could not possible make them out. So I of course told him [I] would although [I] have lots of work to do in the office. Made out the first Roll in about six hours, but had to work hard to do it. Compaired it and found it correct. Can now easily copy the others from it.

If you remember I left the Company Office and gave up the position of Q.M. Sergeant in Dec. '71, for fear [I] would not Master the papers pertaining thereto.[8] And now in '73 I leave the same position to go in an Office where [I] have five times as much of the same kind of work to do. And then [I] have time to help do the Company writing. I don't pretend to be much of a Clerk, but [I] can always get a place in an Office. And [I] have no trouble in making out any of the Returns, posting books or writing letters. And where I have worked once [I] can go back again. This sounds a good deal like self praise, but it is not written for that purpose I can assure you.

I try to keep you posted of my doing, and this is part of them. Thirty three Recruits for the two Companies here arrived few days ago. 24 for M and 9 for our Company. They helped the cause considerable. But then I don't suppose they will remain long with us. Fifty men leave here in the morning on a 25 days Scout. Don't know where they are going. Haven't heard of any Indians being around lately. Guess that is the reason the scout is going out. Want to hunt them up.

A report has been started in Camp that our Regiment is to change Stations with the 1st Cavalry this Fall. The 1st is stationed in California and Oregon, up in the Modoc Country, but as the Modocs are defunct [I] don't suppose there will be any danger in going up there. Would be

---

8 Actually, Matthews was demoted to private for being drunk. See addendum to chapter 4.

willing to run [my] chances anyhow. I have not much faith in the report, although there is nothing impossible in it. And we have a right to expect a change. The Officers here seem to think we will change stations this year.

Only one year and twelve days now, and then I will be "homeward bound." Will promise you a full account of my trip when I get there. The days seem to pass away very rapid, but don't seem to total very fast, but I suppose the time will pass after awhile. And our meeting will only he the more happy for the long separation.

If Mr. Yingling has the Boots done before I can send the money for them you let him keep them or else you can get them and keep until I send the requisite and instructions for sending them.

I have just read this last part of my letter and find the word "them" is mentioned a few times more than the law allows. You can correct the sentences, and consider me "yours truly." News are scarce, and naturally command a high price. Modocs are in their Lava Beds in this part of the country and likely to remain so.

I don't know of anything else to write you this time. Write often for your letters are the greatest blessings I have, and without them I would be miserable.

Summer Camp Eighth Cavalry
On the Canadian River, New Mexico
SEPTEMBER 3, 1873

Sue's letter of the 13th and Father's of the 17th of August received at 10:30 A.M. I have read them over three times already and have no idea how many more times [I] will before [I] receive another one. Sue's letter was elegant, and her description of the habits, doings and appearances of my three <u>little</u> Brothers, afforded me both pleasure and amusement. Many and many a night I have when lying down to rest or when on Guard tried to picture you all as you appear now, but my mind would invariable carry me back to the days of '69 when I last saw you. And then commencing with Father and Mother I would scan each face and talk to myself until I have wound up with Clellie. I could then see you all as plain as though you were before me. And I have also spent many pleasant hours when on the days march under a burning sun, or when walking the lonely post of a Sentry at night when all around was quiet or sleeping, in thinking of the day of our re-union.

Oh, how pleasant would be my thoughts on these occasions. And I know I have never overdrawn the picture. I often think I would like to spend the first evening entirely with none but you. And then again I would think it would be nice for any of our friends if they should happen to drop in to see how gloriously happy we all were. This subject is so pleasant that I can hardly think of quitting it. We have not so long to wait now for that happy day. Only one year, four days and twelve hours until my discharge is due. And I might induce the Captain to give me 10 or 15 days on my time.

I came to the Company Office yesterday to add the "Record of Events" to the Muster and Pay Rolls. The Captain came in also while I was there, and all at once surprised me by saying, "Matthews, if you will remain in the Office and do my writing and learn all you can of Quarter Master papers until your time of service expires, I will give you a good recommendation and try to get you a place In the Q.M. Department, or I will use my influence to get you on Civil Service, and if I could do that for you, you would commence with twelve hundred a year."

He told me Col. McGringle [McGonnigle], who a short time ago was Q.M. at Fort Union Depot, was now stationed at Washington, and as they were particular friends he had no doubt Col. McG would do anything he possible could for me through his recommendation. The Captain complimented me for neat and clean work, and said I was correct and that amounted to more than anything else. I was completely taken by surprise, and hardly knew for a moment what to say, for I had never expected the Captain to evince any thought for my welfare after I am discharged from his Company. But I soon gained my speech, and thanked him for his consideration, and told him I would do all in my power to make myself worthy of any recommendation he might see proper to give me. It was through his influence our late 1st Sergeant got a Clerkship in the Adjutant General's Office at Washington. He is now receiving $1800 a year, and is not much better [a] Clerk than I am. This would be a good thing for me if I could only get it. You can rest assured I'll make a desperate effort to get it ever though I should fail. What do you think about it[?]

Col. Young, Lieut. Pullman, Lieut. Rogers and sixty men from this place are out on a 26 day Scout. They may find Indians, but I have my doubts, as no Indians have been seen around this part of the country for some time. We have Forage here for our horses until the 16th of next month, expect by that time we will leave for Fort Union.

My sore throat has long since ceased to he sore. And I can now swollow my rations as easy as ever. Have pulled myself up to my standard weight 145 lbs and there I stick. Don't believe my hide will hold an ounce more than that as [I] never caught myself weighing more. Think [I] will have to get one of these "Kid glove" stretchers and try to expand myself a little in order to weigh a few pounds more. Now when I come home I want to be properly fixed and want to weigh pretty heavy.

I read that portion of Sue's letter speaking so nicely of Clint to him, also the description of my little Brothers. He was very much pleased with it, and told me to say to you that the first thing he intended doing when he was discharged was to pay you a visit. He had long since planned visiting W[estminster]. Say's he imagines he knows you all now. And that you seem to him as old friends instead of strangers. Has not received his transfer General Service yet, but is expecting it.

You must write very soon to me again for your letter was a real pleasure. I would write more but [I] have some work to do in the Office.

Don't know when the Pay Master will be here, although he has been Ordered to pay the Troops here from Dept. Head Q[uarte]rs.

Summer Camp, Eighth Cavalry On the Canadian River, New Mexico
SEPTEMBER 5, 1873

Oh, but I've had a terrible time this day. And [I] feel that I cannot rest until [I] tell you the cause, although [I] need rest worse than any person you ever saw. The cause of all this trouble came about through our Laundress (as usual a woman at the bottom of the trouble) moving from the post. I had allowed my <u>soiled</u> (very dirty) under clothing to accumulate with the intentions of having it all washed at one time, thus avoiding some little trouble every week. Through this laziness I was brought to grief today.

It was just this. My cloth[e]s had to be washed, and as there was no person to do it except myself, I of course had to suffer. Soon as [I] had eaten my breakfast (fried bacon, dry bread and bad coffee) [I] got a Camp Kettle from the cook, spent half an hour scouring the grease out of it, filled it with water and put it on the fire. Then [I] got two tubs (half barrels sawed into) put my dirty cloth[e]s in one and poured some cold water over them and let them soak until water on fire got heated. Sit down and took a smoke to keep my courage up. Thought it was time the water was warm enough to commence hostilities.

Went to the kitchen and put my hand in the water to see if it was hot. If you could only have seen the oldest boy of the Matthews family hopping around that kitchen howling fire, you would have said that water was warm. Got my tub and filled it with some of that warm water. Carried it to a shady spot and commenced my work on one of those nice shirts Mother sent me. Forgot to tell you [I] had borrowed a wash board. Put lots of soap on that shirt and made a push down the board then a pull up, and then another down stroke, hand slipped off the shirt and the result, about one inch of bark off my knuckles, second accident. Finally got the shirt washed, hung it on a line and tried a second. Pretty warm by this time.

Got along with [the] second pretty well, not quite so dirty as first one. Hung it along side the first, perspiration rolling off in large drops. Soldiers commence to congregate and ask questions, "How much do you charge for washing Jimmy[?] Do you trust[?] Guess I'll get the Captain to have you detailed to do the Company washing." I told them if they did not leave and let me get through with my work, there would be a subject for a first class funeral. All this time I was scrubbing away on my third shirt and wishing for a Washing Machine.

Got through with my shirts finally, four in number, and then tackled a lot of handkerchiefs. They were not so bad, washed six of them and hung them up to dry. A little breeze came up and blew them off the line. Naturally I suppose they fell in dirt and had to be washed over. Was in a beautiful frame of mind about that time, inclination to swear, but as that would not wash the handkerchiefs didn't do it.

The handkerchiefs were followed by two pillow cases, and two collars. Got more hot water and pitched into five <u>very</u> dirty pair of white stockings. This was a hard job, back almost broke, and hands felt like I had just participated in a hard game of Base Ball. I was a long time trying to get those socks clean, but it was no use. Perseverance [and] army soap; no patience could do it. Hung them up to dry.

Took a rest and wished I was done. More hot water and commenced with a towel, was now through with the washing with the exception of three pair of drawers. My arms and back ached and I hated to tackle those drawers, but had to do it. Rubbed and scrubbed, put on lots of soap, perspired freely and at last shouted Eureka, and Fell back exhausted.

Received the congratulations of my friends and felt ready for dinner. Soon as [I] had eaten that meal (fried bacon, boild rice and dry bread)—don't mean by this that I fried bacon etc., this was what [I] had for dinner—had another smoke.

Then as I intended finishing in style, [I] borrowed our tailors iron, which weighed about thirty pounds, put it on the fire, and while it was heating brought in my clothes and sprinkled them. As I had never done any ironing before [I] had some doubts about the success of the thing. Thought I had better experiment a little before trying my hand on a white shirt, had no starch, but that made no difference. Spread out my towel, grasped the iron firmly, burnt my sore hand a little and made a lunge out. <u>Result</u>: towel looked like a yellow cat singed. Iron was too hot. Let it cool off, and tried a collar, got through with it but had more wrinkles in it than there was any use of. Tried my hand on a colored shirt; same result as with the collar. Concluded a man couldn't iron cloth[e]s unless he knew how.

Took the balance of the cloth[e]s and spread them out, passed the iron over them lightly making lots of wrinkles, folded them up and took an inventory of stock: four shirts, three drawers, five pair stockings, seven handkerchiefs, two pillow cases, two collars and one towel. Put them in my box and dont think [I] will do another washing while [we] remain at Fort Bascom. My back aches, my arms and hands are sore, and I feel generally fatigued. And I feel the greatest sympathy in the world for all poor creatures who have not a washing machine. I never did begrudge paying my Laundry bill, but will always pay it more cheerful for the future.

As I always tell you of my trials and troubles thought [I] would have to tell you of this. As a <u>washerwoman</u> I am not a success, and don't think [I] shall again go into the business.

Sunday, September 7, 1873

Have just got through with our Sunday morning Inspection. I have nothing to do in the Office today so [I] concluded to write a note to you. Have fully recovered from the effects of "my days washing." And [I] now think of it as one of the disagreeable things that has passed, never again to be renewed if it can possible be avoided.

On the evening of the 5th a number of my soldier friends congregated around my tent and for two or three hours quite an animated conversation was carried on. Every subject the boy's could think of was brought forth and discussed. Harlan, as usual was among the party and shot off his mouth with the rest. If anything about a hundred times more than any individual in the party, he has a natural gift of tongue. Knows how to use it and has always a reply ready no matter what the subject be.

At last when every other subject had been exhausted the weather was mentioned, and as we have been having excessive hot weather, which has been a great assistance to the flies and musquitoes in making it disagreeable for us. Harlan to wind up with expressed a hope that the weather would turn cold about 12 o'clock, and when he woke up in the morning he hoped there would be one inch of ice on every drop of water in this part of the country, and that every fly and musquito might be frozen. Such a thing under the circumstances seemed impossible, so we said good night and dispersed. I was soon asleep but how long I did not know.

Woke up feeling uncomfortable cold, wondered what had made such a change in the weather. Got under two blankets and was still cold, put on a third, felt more comfortable. Thought about Clints wish and wondered if it had anything to do with the change in the weather. Went to sleep again and slept until first call for Reveille was sounded by the Trumpeter. Went out to answer my name and found every person complaining about feeling cold. Harlan was around smiling all over his countenance, and saying "how is this weather for flies[?]" I told him I had always heard it said that the prayers of the unrighteous availeth naught. And as he was about as unrighteous as any person I knew, still his prayers to a certain extent had been answered. It did not freeze the water, but turned so cold it knocked the amination out of two or three hundred million flies, and as to the musquitous have not seen, felt or heard one since.

It has been, and is yet quite cold since the night of the 5th. Have had a little rain this last couple days. And it causes what flies there is left to seek shelter in our tents, but as soon as one is discovered making his entrance he is knocked down with out any ceremony and then kicked out in the Company street. We have hoisted the black flag, and so long as the weather remains cold no quarters will be shown the flies. They have caused us untold misery this summer, but their day is slowly passing away.

9 o'clock A.M., Monday, September 8, 1873

This minute one year from date my time of service in the Army of the U.S. expires. Four long years ago today I bound myself into slavery for five years. Four of the number have slowly passed away and the fifth and last will also pass by in due time. With the thought of this day one year hence brings a happy feeling beyond description. As each day slowly passes away it is counted as one less to serve the U.S. and I am nearer the loved ones at Home. Oh how my heart roes out to you this morning. We can now count my time by months and days, instead of years, months and days. May Our Father in Heaven watch over and protect us all. Keep us in health and permit us to be re-united once more is the fervent prayer of your own Eddie.

Wednesday, September 10, 1873

The Mail arrived a few minutes ago, but brought not a word from you loved ones. You no doubt can imagine the disappointment. This is the second time this Summer I have been disappointed in this way. Some persons wouldn't mind it, but to me it is the saddest disappointment I could meet with. The mail only arrives here once each week and I naturally watch its coming with great expectations. And if I only received a line from you "just to say you were all well," I would feel satisfied, but when I fail to get this (which I am glad to say is very seldom and far between), I am miserable. Now I must be content to wait until next Wednesday. I more than half expected to hear from Lizzie this mail and was disappointed somewhat in this. Well I have nothing else to write about this morning, and as there are no prospects of finding anything special to write about between this and tomorrow when the mail leaves I will close.

Summer Camp, Eighth Cavalry
On the Canadian River, New Mexico
SEPTEMBER 18, 1873

The mail arrived yesterday, and since its arrival I have been kept very busy "slinging ink" as Harlan calls it.

Received Father's ever welcome letter dated August 23rd. How is it you direct my letters now to Company D 8th Cavalry[?] There must be some mistake as this is the 2nd one in succession. I am still and will be for the balance of my enlistment carried on the Rolls of Company L. Perhaps you have taken one of my L's for a D. If that be the case please correct and for the future direct Co. L. However it don't make much difference how you direct my letters, so they come to Fort Union, as [I] am well known at Regimental Head Quarters.

Had my moustache shaved off last evening, and both look and feel awful funny about my upper up. Look like a young chap of fifteen. You can't imagine what a difference it makes in my appearance. Will let it grow out again this winter.

Expect the Scouting party to return saturday or sunday. No doubt they will have something of interest to report. Two of the Recruits received here few weeks ago Deserted the other night, each taking a good horse, set of horse equipments and their Arms. A detail was sent after them next morning but [I] don't suppose they will overtake them. Good commencement, we won't have a half dozen of them left by spring.

I can't see how it is my letters fail to reach you regularly, for I never allow a week to pass without writing to you. Something is surely wrong in the P.O. Dept.

The Pay Master is expected here about the time the scouting party returns and if [I] have an opportunity [I] will send you some money. Shan't want the Boots for Harlan and self until about the 1st of November. We will be in Union I suppose by that time.

When you receive this if Mr. Yingling has not made my boots I wish you would tell him to peg instead of sewing them, but sew Harlan's. However, it won't make any difference if he has them sewed now.[9]

---

9 At that time, the most common method for attaching the soles of boots and shoes to the uppers was with a double row of small hardwood pegs driven into holes around the perimeter. In dry western environments, however, experience proved that the pegs often shrank and worked loose. Stitching was also an adequate means for fastening soles, though rocky terrain and sandy soils quickly wore out the thread. See McChristian, *U.S. Army in the West*, 21, 74.

The weather is getting cooler here very fast, and I would not be surprised if the winter set in earlier than usual.

I am enjoying excellent health and feel splendid as each day passes by I feel better for [I] am one day nearer you loved ones.

You must excuse this hastily written and short letter, have some more Official Work to do in time to go off with this mail. And besides have no news to write you. Will try to do better next week.

Summer Camp, Eighth Cavalry
On the Canadian River, New Mexico
SEPTEMBER 23, 1873

All work for the day is over, and I feel like writing a few lines to you. This time of most every evening I find myself carried away (in imagination) back to Maryland and to my home. I am with you all. And we are all happy we talk about the past, the present and what we each intend doing in the future. How plain to me is every lineament of your features. If in these moments I am so extremely happy through imagination, I would like to know what my feelings will be when I am with you in person, heart and soul. Oh I know it will be happiness beyond expression.

Tomorrow another mail will arrive, and with it I shall expect to hear from you. If I am only sure you are well I am satisfied. The days and weeks of another month are rappidly passing away, but not too fast for either you or I.

Capt Young, with his Scouting party has not returned yet, although his rations were up today. It is the supposition here that he has gone to Union, and will return the latter part of this week. The Pay Master is expected here also this week.

Last night five or six citizens rode into Camp about 10 o'clock and reported that they had seen a party of Indians about twelve miles from here. First thing this morning ten men started off on a reconnaissance. They are to go as far as the Stone Ranch, 28 miles from here, remain there tonight and escort the mail here in the morning. As we are only a few men here now precaution has been taken in case of an attack. Orders were issued this evening in case of alarm we were all to take possession of a building which commands a view of the corral in which our horses are in. And where we could stand the Indians off for some time.

But I have no fears of being attacked so long as we remain here. And I can assure you I have no desire to be. I have seen all the Indian fighting I wish to for the balance of my enlistment. And when I return to civilization if at any time I should get blood thirsty I can attack the effigy of an Indian in front of some Tabacconist and it will be all the same. Will finish this tomorrow.

September 24, 1873

Have been sitting at the desk at hard work ever since the arrival of the mail at 10 o'clock this morning with the exception of an hour at dinner. Am feeling a little tired but before [I] leave [I] will write you a few lines. We are always very busy on Mail days and as this was one of them it was not an exception.

Was happy to receive Fathers letter of Sept 7, also received a paper. We have heard nothing more of the Indians. The party sent out to reconnoitre returned with the mail this morning without seeing any of them. Capt. Young, with his scouting party are scouting around Fort Stanton N.M. some two hundred miles from here and no telling when he will return. Suppose he must be after Indians or else he would have been here when his Rations were up.

Heard nothing about the Pay Master this mail, or when we are to leave here. If you have any payments to make soon you can ask the parties to wait a short time as I will have $100.00 to send you soon as [I] am paid. You can't imagine how proud I am to think of sending this amount. And I would not tell you of it only I thought perhaps you might need it now.

Lizzie, I suppose is with you now, and you are hearing lots of news from her. Would love to be home and hear her talk. Just wait though until I come if you want to hear some talking. Only eleven months and fourteen days yet and I have five years back talk to make good. And besides you know I am to have the pleasure of listening to what you all have gone through during the same period. Oh won't we have ellegant time in September '74.

I am going to stop writing now and finish tonight.

I have been to supper and now as it is dark [I] have lit a candle and see what I have yet to say. Not much I fear. Tomorrow I will commence on Quarterly papers. And will have a good steady job until the 30th.

Harlan has been disappointed in getting on General Service. I received a letter from a young soldier friend of mine now clerking at District Head Quarters in which he said the District Commander for some reason refused to approve of the transfer. And he said he would recommend me to take the vacant place if I wished him to. But as my time is getting so short it would not pay me to be transferred even if there would be no obstacle to prevent it. Supposing the transfer could be made, I would be put to considerable expense in procuring innumerable little necessities, and in the outcome I would find myself the looser by the arrangement. So [I] will write to my young friend, thank him for his Kindness and request him not to suggest my name.

By the way this young man can thank me for being on General Service himself. It occurred in this manner. He came to the Regiment a Recruit in '72, while I was in the Regimental Adjutants Office. I was introduced to him by an ex member of our Company who had been to the states and enlisted again and came back to the Regiment. This young man whose name is Frank Kingman, is quite a good looking boy. By the way a number of persons said he looked very much like me, and that the supposition was he was my brother. "Of course if he looked like me he must he good looking." At any rate I took a great liking to him and as he was a Clerk by occupation, I went to work to get him in the Adjutants Office, and succeeded in doing so. Got him in the Post Adjutants Office and when I left the Regimental Adjutants Office the Sergeant Major gave him my place. At the time I was rooming with the Chief Trumpeter of the Regiment and was fixed up elegant for a "buck soldier." I took him to my room gave him a complete suit of cloth[e]s and told him to make our room his Head quarters. You can rest assured he was thankful and is now anxious to return Kindness for Kindness.

Had I have been content to remain in the Regimental Office instead seeking Glory on the Plains, I would now be where he is. That was the only bad stop I ever took since I enlisted I think. Although in the long run I may come out a winner. Still I have no complaints to make. He writes exactly like I do, and to look in the Books each of us kept in the Adjutants Office you would suppose one person kept them. I intend keeping in the Captains good graces in hopes of getting the Clerkship in Washington. The Captain has always complimented me for accuracy and neatness in all my work for him, and I am satisfied he will help me when my time is out if it is in his power to do it.

Your letters (Descriptive) still afford me great pleasure and I feel that I know exactly where every person lives so far. Am somewhat surprised to find the greater part of those mentioned living in the same houses they did when I was home. Still I find a number of changes have been made. I have not heard from my several correspondents for some time. I don't know of a single person who can say I owe them a letter. Suppose though I will hear from them in due time.

Your letters are the greatest blessings I have, and I would certainly be a miserable creature if they were taken from me. And now my dear Sisters and Brothers let me hear from you as often as possible if only a line it adds one drop to my happiness. And I am never so happy as when reading one of your letters. It is no fault of my loved Mother, that you fail to write to me I know. I can see (or imagine I can) her telling you to write to me, and perhaps she often thinks you have written when you have not.

Clint just came to the tent and as it was tied up to avoid interruption [he] asked if the proprietor was in, [I] told him he was. He wanted to come in but I would not allow him, for if he got in and commenced talking there would be no telling when I would get this finished. Asked to be remembered to you all. And repeats his promise to visit us when we are all togeather.

I have just returned from a visit to the Captains tent who had sent for me to put an Endorsement on a letter for him. As I had to go to the Office to do it [I] will remain there until [I] finish my letter to you. Have put the endorsement on and now for the finish. Don't think shall be long about doing it. Am brought to this conclusion for three reasons, to wit: firstly am thinking [I] have written pretty near enough for one time; secondly, am quite tired as [I] have been writing hard all day; and thirdly [I] don't know what else to write about. I always like to write you long letters, [I] know those are the kind you like to receive. And also to repay you for the long ones you write me.

Don't suppose Jennie read my letter to you, or do I think she will ever answer it. Although there was nothing in it for her to be offended at, unless it was to read plain facts, or that I was not demonstrative enough, as Lizzie once told me not to be. Jennie and I corresponded for a long time. She always seemed very kind to me, and nothing gains my affections quicker than kindness. I liked her as a friend and correspondent but nothing more. All of a sudden her letters ceased. Supposing my letter to her had miscarried I wrote her a second, which shared the same fate. Concluded then I was dropped, and therefore retired heart whole, but not relishing the idea very much to be treated in that manner. Some time ago I was surprised to receive a letter from her. In it was many excuses for bad treatment on her part and hope that I would (as children would say) Kiss and make up. This I had no objection for doing, but could not let the opportunity pass without stating facts to her as they appeared. I had been wrongfully treated and wanted her to understand that I could not put up with a repetition of such treatment. Her letters were a pleasure, but rather than derive pleasure in that way where the other party did not derive an equal pleasure, I would rather dispense with the correspondence or service.

This is enough on the subject and as it is time to be in bed I will end this. Don't direct [to] Company D anymore, for I still belong to L.

Summer Camp, Eighth Cavalry
On the Canadian River, New Mexico
OCTOBER 1, 1873

Mail day and as usual [I] have been scratching away as hard as [I] could possible move my hand over the paper. Am not through yet, but have put away the Official for the more pleasant duty; that of answering your letter of the 16th of September. Will not promise you much of a letter for [I] am so tired writing [I] can hardly hold my pen. So you must be content with what I give you this time.

Will have to commence work earlier in the morning again, as [I] have a lot of Official business to send off by return mail. And [I] am also going to take a ride of fifty six miles tomorrow for exercise. An escort is sent out with the mail now, since the last Indian scare. And as I have been confined pretty close to the Office for some time, [I] have asked to go as one of the escort, and of course it was readily granted. The ride will do me good, and when I return [I] can go to work in the Office feeling like I have been at a Picnic or something of that Kind.

Don't suppose you would enjoy a horse back ride of a hundred miles would you Father[?] The Scouting party which left this Camp August 28th are still out. This mail brought news of their being at Camp

Supply, Indian Territory.[10] What they are doing there [I] don't know. Suppose they got down in that part of the Country and had to go in after Rations. They have been absent now thirty five days, and will before they return have [been] gone fifty, pretty long scout for the number of men. And [I] should not be surprised if they had some fighting to do. Will learn all in due time. The Indians reported as being in this vicinity have not put in an appearance, or is there much likelihood of their doing so.

Heard that the Pay Master would be here on the 7th inst. You can expect some money soon in case he comes. Will not send it though unless [I] can get a Money Order.

I am of the same opinion as you in regard to the Clerkship in Washington. I have not been carried away with the idea, but think under circumstances it would be a good thing <u>until</u> (as Wilkins Macauber [Micawber] in Dickens, David Copperfield, says) something turns up.[11] My own desire is to get something to do where I can be home with you loved ones, and where I can most assist in adding to your comfort and welfare. I have had enough of absence from home. And will endeavor not to be separated again.

I have no fears but shall get something to do where I can be with you. My term of service is beautifully growing less fast. Eleven months and one week from tonight. The days and weeks seem to pass rapidly away, but the months kind of hang heavy, but September '74 will roll around and I will be with you again before we know it. We are living in hopes of leaving here about the 20th of this month but have nothing Official for it.

The weather is getting quite cool now, and the nights in fact are cold, [I] sleep with four blankets over me, and am not too warm then. Quite a change from a few weeks back. The flies and mosquitoes are getting to be things that were, but are no more. Peace and happiness go

---

10 Captain John H. Page established Camp Supply, Indian Territory (Oklahoma) on November 18, 1868, as ordered by Lieutenant Colonel Alfred Sully, who commanded one of the expeditions sent against the Southern Cheyennes, Kiowas, and Comanches. Originally intended as a temporary supply base for Sheridan's winter campaign, it remained occupied and was redesignated as a fort in 1878. It remained active until 1895. See Frazer, *Forts of the West*, 124.

11 Wilkins Micawber was a salient character in the Charles Dickens novel *David Copperfield*. Micawber, once incarcerated in a debtor's prison, is eternally optimistic that his fortunes will always improve. Encouraged by that principle, and thus his reference to it here, Matthews believed that he would find meaningful employment after leaving the army.

with them I say, for we have suffered untold miseries here this summer, and principally from them, with odors of a Madam Skunk now and then added. Oh this is a pleasant place to dwell in the summer time. So sayeth Uncle Sams boys with an emphasis, to the word pleasant. I don't emphasise mine though, for I am good.

Clint was in the office a moment ago, and as usual asked to be remembered Kindly. I told him he could put his request in writing and you would be glad to hear from him. Said he would add a postscrip in the morning if you would not think him presumptuous. Told him he need have no fears for anything of that Kind.

Don't know what I am going to fill this out with. If [I] had an idea [I] would soon put it in paper, but [I] have not. And am feeling ever so tired. More so than [I] have been for a long time. Am well, and enjoying the best of health, [I] have not weighed for some time, but suppose [I] am at my regular standard 145 lbs.

Summer Camp, Eighth Cavalry
On the Canadian River, New Mexico
OCTOBER 8, 1873

Fathers long letter of September 19th arrived in the mail this morning, and with good news from home came the order for us to leave this place and return to Union on or before the 20th inst. You can imagine how happy we boys are to know that we will so soon leave a post so distasteful to us.

Our 2nd Lieut., one Sergeant, one Corporal and ten men will remain here this winter. How the boys who are so unfortunate as to have to remain will like it I can't say. Although if the whole Company was here there would be no trouble in finding volunteers to stay, for there are plenty of men who would rather remain here where there would be scarcely any duty to perform, and besides they would be under but very little discipline as our Lieutenant is very much of a boy and when he is away from other officers he never bothers himself about how the boys conduct themselves. But for my own part I would not remain here all winter for hardly any consideration. My principal reason for not staying would be the long interval between Mail days, for the Mail would only come and go on rare occasions, but there is no use speculating about the matter as I am not detaleable, And even if I was, [I] would have no fears of being left behind.[12]

Our Scouting party has not yet returned and there is no telling when they will, as we can't find out anything about them. They have been gone now forty two days, longer than we were absent from this place last year. Suppose they are wondering around the prairie somewhere between here and Fort Sill or Camp Supply, Indian Territory. I hope they are safe wherever they be.

Don't think Capt. Young displayed much judgment in marching sixty men in the heart of the worst Indian Country around here. He may return all right although he has been most too ventursome to suit my taste. I know he has been <u>blest</u> by his Command every day since the expiration of the original time to be absent. There is nothing that discourages men so much as keeping them out on a scout longer than the time set to be absent, for after they are out a few days they always commence to count the days until they are to return. And then if they should not get back on the specified day they naturally are sadly disappointed. I believe we would almost have mutanized [mutinied] last summer had General Gregg undertook to have kept us out longer than the forty days, for we were all sick of the trip before we had been out half the time. But why dwell on this subject when [I] am feeling so happy with the prospects of leaving this miserable place so soon[?]

I have this day put in four years and one month of my enlistment, and now at 7:30 P.M. have ten hours and a half less than eleven months to serve. Ain't it elegant to think my time is getting so beautifully short[?] Can almost imagine myself on my road home now so short seems to be my term of service. Let us all be of good cheer and make ourselves happy with the hopes of soon meeting. And oh what a meeting ours will be. As Sue said, "I guess there never was one like it." But why should it not be an unusual happy one. Five long years of separation certainly should entitle us to a happy reunion and I know ours will be one if there is such a thing as happy in Websters Unabridged.

I received quite a nice letter from Jennie. One of her old style, was very much pleased with it for [I] have always had a good opinion of her. In fact she has always shown more friendship and evinced a stronger desire to see me home safe again than any young lady correspondent I

---

12 Second Lieutenant Alfred H. Rogers commanded this detachment. See *ANJ*, October 25, 1873, 164.

have had excepting Ida and my dear Sisters. I have no doubt as soon as I return there will be lots of the young ladies who are so fond of new faces to flock around me and for a time make a regular hen out of me. Not that I by any means will be one in reality, but they will try to make me believe I am one. I have not forgotten their old tricks even if I have been isolated so long from their bewitching society. And when I come back I fear some of them will be disappointed in their expectations.

My dear Father your descriptions of the people of W[estminster] still afford me great pleasure, but I fear you write so much about them that you can't find room to write about yourself and the rest of the family. Everything you write me is read with the greatest of pleasure, but still nothing you can write gives me the pleasure that I derive in reading of yourself and the rest of my loved ones.

The Pay Master will not come down here now. And I don't suppose we will be paid before the 1st of November, but he may come to Union and pay us before another Muster which will be the last of this month. You can expect $100.00 just as soon as I am paid.

If Mr. Yingling has Harlan's and my Boots done I wish you would send them soon as you can and send the <u>Bill</u> with them, for it is not my intention to order anything from such a distance for either myself or Harlan without paying for it. And I don't want you to go the expense of sending them and only charging us for the boots. And I don't know if you charged us full price for them. Also let me know which pair is mine and which Harlans. Send them as you did the others and I guess they will come safe.

I guess this will be the last letter I will write you from this place. At least the last one this year. I may have to come down here again next year but I have one great consolation, I will not be here <u>this time</u> next year.

Shall expect to hear from Lizzie next mail, or as soon as we get to Union, and shall expect a long letter with a full account of her trip. The other night I was lying in bed thinking of you loved ones and of the time when I would be on the road home. Was trying to plan my route, which road I would travel on, thought about the Balto. [Baltimore] and Ohio and of stopping a day at Oakland. And then would think that won't do, because I came out over that road and besides stopping would keep me one day longer from seeing you. And as my heart and soul is bent on the speediest way of getting home I have decided it is better to take the fastest line let it be what road it may. Can you give me any ideas on the subject[?]

I finished the last of my Quarterly papers this evening, have worked steady and hard for the last couple of weeks. Have been scratching away day after day until the sight of pen and paper has almost become distasteful to me. Every return and letter has to be written twice, three and sometimes four times, so often in fact that one tires of the same thing. The returns are all duplicate and the letters have first to be written then briefed, giving the substance of the letter on the first fold and then copied in a letter book. I get so tired doing it at times that I leave the Office in disgust and almost wish I was doing duty in the Company, but I soon get over this kind of feeling and go back to my work in a different frame of mind.

There is nothing about soldiering nicer or cleaner than office work. And I will stick to it until my time is out.

I have written about all I can think of tonight, and guess I have written enough. And as this will be the last opportunity I will have of writing to you from this place, [I] will say good night and good bye and with it the hope it will be the last time I will have occasion to write from this the last place of Gods Creation.

Fort Union, New Mexico

OCTOBER 19, 1873

Arrived here on the evening of the 17th, and was never so happy to see this old place before. Every person was glad to see us. And I assure you we were equally as glad to see them. Have been ever so busy since our arrival fixing up and making ourselves comfortable. Am in my old room again and have it looking as cheerful as it is possible for me to make it.

Soon as [we] came in I had an offer of a Clerkship in the Regimental Adjutants Office (my old place) but declined accepting it, as [I] am very well pleased with my present place. I have made up my mind not to soldier anymore so long as [I] can keep in an Office. And I always find a desk waiting for me in any of them.

Col. Young and his scouting party have not returned yet. Heard that they expected to reach Bascom between the 15 and 20th of this month, they may be there now. Guess they will be surprised to find us gone when they come in.

I received Fathers letter on my arrival here in which he said Lizzie had written me a long letter four days before, but have not yet received it. The mail was sent to Bascom for us, and should have been back last night but has not yet got in. Suppose Lizzie's letter must have been in that mail. Am waiting ever so patiently for it to return for [I] want to hear all about Lizzie's trip and of her own dear self.

I have not time to write you much this evening as [I] have some work to do for the Captain, and the papers are all mixed up and have to be righted, but as I can write and mail a letter to you any day now, [I] will write to you at more length in a day or two.

Please send my boots soon as you can as [I] need them now very badly. The Pay Master has not yet put in an appearance and I hardly think he will come now until the first of next month.

You must not feel disappointed at receiving this short letter.

Fort Union, New Mexico
OCTOBER 26, 1873

Fathers long and welcome letter was gladly welcomed by me on the 23rd inst. And on the 24th inst. received the long looked for letter from Lizzie. And I must say it was elegant, if I did have to wait some time for it. She made up for it. Also received a very nice letter from Lec, with these and two home papers. I was made the happiest of Boys. They came in good time for I had been feeling quite sick, but am now well with the exception of a very sore mouth. Have taken no medicine for [I] never fancy going near a Military Hospital.

Have had a fearful lot of work to do in the office. Done all I could and the Captain done the balance. And now tomorrow [I] have to commence on Muster Rolls, which will furnish plenty to do until the 31st inst. Would not mind the writing but [I] am rather too nervous to do it neat. Tomorrow I will send you a Money Order (P.O.) for $100.00 directed to Father. Half of it is for my loved Father and the other half for my Dearest Mother. And out of this I will have to ask more than I like to. One of you will have to pay for Harlans boots and the other for mine. I wanted to and expected that I would have a $20.00 present for you each outside of paying for the boots, but the men who remained at Bascom owed me some money and was not here to get their pay.

Our Scouting party returned on the 21st inst. without having seen an Indian on the trip. Their horses are in a horrible condition and the men also looked very rough. They killed plenty of Buffalo and that is all they did. Don't think Col. Young will receive much credit for staying out over his intended time.

The Pay Master paid here on the 24th and will owe us two months more pay the last of this month, and is expected to pay about the 12th of next month.

You surely must have had an elegant visit from (excuse the below blot, the blotter slipped) your glowing discription of it, but there is nothing surprising about the welcome you received, for tell me where one of us ever goes that we do not meet with a hearty welcome. Even I have been welcomed in the U.S.A. but propose to sever my acquaintance in little more than ten months from date of this. My last year seems to pass away much faster than any of the former ones, but [it] cannot pass away too fast for either you or I.

You speak of my not mentioning Sues and Carries pictures. There surely is a great mistake some where, for I wrote you quite a long letter just after receiving it and the greater part of it was taken up about the picture, which by the way was splendid, with the exception of the style of wearing the hair, which I think is not pretty; although it may be fashionable. And besides her pretty face she must be a fine looking woman instead of the little Sister Sue I left in '69. It will not be so long now until I will be home to see in person.

You compliment my letters and writing more I fear than I deserve. And this one is written so poorly that [I] am most ashamed to send it. The room is awful warm and is making me feel sick and nervous.

I am afraid that I will not be able to send you much more money during the balance of my enlistment, for when I am discharged my transportation will only be to Cincinnati, and if [I] am discharged here it will take all of it to carry me to the Rail Road. Besides coming home I will have to provide myself with clothing out and out. There will not he a single article of wearing apparel but what I will have to buy. As Soldier cloth[e]s I guess are not very fashionable in the States, and besides I'll not have much of it when my time is out.[13] But in case I can send you any, you can rest assured it will be cheerfully done. And what is more, rather than you should suffer for anything during my absence I would send you the last dollar I had in the world, even if I had to return home with my shirt sticking out from the unmentionable part of my trousers. I know you would be none the less proud of me for that and that is all I care for.

Well Loved Ones I could write more this evening if [I] felt well enough to do it. So [I] will ask you to excuse everything.

Fort Union, New Mexico
OCTOBER 27, 1873

Enclosed find Money Orders for $100.00 a present from Eddie. I have not a moment to devote in writing this morning. But [I] will write in a day or two. Wrote to you last night.

Father,
    Divide equal with my loved Mother.
To John Matthews
    Westminster
        Carroll County, Maryland
From Wm. E. Matthews
    Fort Union
        New Mexico

Fort Union, New Mexico
OCTOBER 29, 1873

Lizzies ever welcome letter came to hand this morning and found me at the Desk where I have been for the last ten days. And even now Clint and I are sitting at the same Desk writing. I have put up my work for

---

13 Soldiers customarily sold their unwanted uniforms to other soldiers at the time of their discharge. The practice was advantageous to both parties as it raised extra cash for the dischargee and provided clothing at economical prices for former comrades, thereby saving them money on their clothing allowances. See Rickey, *Forty Miles*, 125–26.

tonight but Clint is not yet through, [I] have just helped him compare a lot of Q.M. papers and found them all correct. Just as soon as [I] get through with this Months work [I] will give you all the news to be found in and around this place.

The Book has not yet <u>arrived</u>, but [I] shall expect it in tomorrows mail. Almost forgot to acknowledge receipt of another of Fathers elegant Descriptive Letters, which wound up with Wm. (or commonly called) Bill Mitten.[14] Indeed I enjoy them exceedingly. And [I] have had no room for complaint of more arrival of letters from you since [I] returned from Bascom, and it is all I ask. If I can hear from you often I am always happy.

I made out the 1st Muster Roll for Capt. Hobart today for the coming Muster October 31st, 1873. Will try by hard work to finish two more tomorrow, but I tell you what it takes tall scratching to make out two Company Muster and Pay Rolls in one day.

The present [I] sent you on the 28th [I] hope will reach you in safety. Clint just told me to say to you in case some chap should take a notion to set up a Boot Store with our Boots, you might see us before you expect to, for we would be after him hot foot.

I have fully recovered from my slight indisposition and tonight Edward is himself again.

I am half owner in a little <u>Cat</u> now and it is really too funny to live long. Is continually crawling up my trousers leg, then upon my shoulder and down on the arm I am writing with [and] wants me to stop writing and play with it. Is now lying under my chin purring away every now and then looking up in my face as much as to say ain't you nearly done[?] I call it Tom, although [I] am ignorant as to what sex it belongs. You see instead of getting Old Bachelor-ish [I] am getting Old Maidish. Does this express my sentiments[?] Guess it does.

Well here I am stuck again. Guess [I] had better wind up as [I] have done a hard days work, and assure you not such scratching as this.

There are now four men in the room talking about their shares in

---

14 This man has not been positively identified. His name may have been omitted from the Registers of Enlistments, a not uncommon occurrence. The only likely candidate is William Madden, a member of Company M who enlisted in New York on February 7, 1872. However, he deserted on May 13, 1872, so it seems improbable that Matthews would have referred to him in this instance. See entry 142, p. 30, roll 39, ROE, RG 94, NA.

my Cat. Harlan says he ownes a tenth share and is going to cut it off. Told him his share was at the little end, the end the chap had hold of when the <u>bear</u> slipped in the hold. Enough of this nonsense for tonight.

Clint asks to be Kindly remembered.

Fort Union, New Mexico
"AFTER DINNER," NOVEMBER 4, 1873

While I am resting and having my after dinner smoke [I] might as well write you a few lines. Not that I have anything special or interesting to write you, but just by way of keeping my hand in.

We had quite a little bit of disagreeable news wafted to us on the wires last week and don't know but that it may prove still more disagreeable should the movement take place. We were building Castles for peace and quietness this winter, when dispatches were received from District Head Qrs. ordering L and M Companies to be in readiness for active and protracted field service. Boxes were packed and all the necessary arrangements made to move at a moments notice. Orders were then received to await further instructions. And we are doing the same thing now, "praying as only Soldiers know how" that the next Order will countermand the first and we be permitted to remain in our "little blue Bunks" this winter.

Seven months out of twelve is sufficient field service I think, but when it comes to twelve out of twelve it becomes monotonous. Winter campaigning is not the most pleasant thing I know of. But there is no use of crying before one is hurt (as I use to do), for even if the Company did move it is not certain that Clint and I would have to go with it.

I have still plenty of work to do. Last Saturday I made out two Company Muster and Pay Rolls, each one nearly the size of the "Balt[imore] Sun" and pretty near as much writing. Done this too from Guard Mount 9 o'clock to Retreat (Sundown). It was the largest bit of writing I ever done in one day. And when the Rolls were compared [I] only found two slight mistakes, one I wrote October instead of August, and the other I left out the letter "H" in a mans name. I have become quite a rappid writer now. And although I don't write so well [I] can get over a good deal of paper in a day, and do it with but few mistakes.

The Captain has a new set of Books (Company Record) for me to make out this winter. It will be a nice job and I will spend many a day very pleasantly in that way this winter.

I often think of the difference in me now and '71. Then I gave up my position for fear of not being capable of performing the duties. Now I do the same work for another party between times and find no difficulty in getting along. As Father says: Blanks are plenty and cost nothing, and when a Return don't suit me tear it up and try another. The advice has helped me along more than anything else. I have spoiled many a blank in my time, and still continue to spoil them and will until the day of my discharge.

Have only received one Boot yet. Guess the other will come in due time. Have you received the Money Order yet. (If you will take away one of those 's'es in <u>position</u> it will be spelled proper), but you need'nt mind for I have done it myself.

Now I have had my smoke and have soiled this sheet of paper, and must now go to work.

One of our Laundress'es just this moment sent me a plate of real good "plum pudding," and I got on the outside of it in less time than I have taken to tell you of it. If there is any[thing?] I like more than another it is plum pudding. "Well so long."

Fort Union, New Mexico
NOVEMBER 10, 1873

Father's long interesting and welcome letter mailed October 27th received on the 8th inst. Also my second Boot, and now so far as the robbery of the mails are concerned deponent careth not; provided Harlan's Boots or a letter from you is not aboard. Indeed I am thankful to you for sending them. And also to Mr. Yingling for making them. They are an exact and neat fit, and have proved satisfactory in every respect.

We are still under marching orders, but no telling when we will leave. I hope we are not to leave at all for the idea is not a pleasant one by any means.

B Company (Our regiment) returned to the post Saturday. They had been up in the Ute Indian Country (Colorado) looking after those Gentlemen's interest. We were glad to welcome them back. I got my horse and rode out four miles to meet them.

I have got another cold which has settled in my head, and the way I spoil handkerchiefs is a caution. On ordinary occasions I would sooner dispense with a shirt anytime than a handkerchief, but on these pleasant occasions I would sooner do without 2 Shirts than one h———f. "This word is too long to be repeated so often," you know what it means anyhow.

I don't know what [I] am going to fill this up with as there are no news floating around loose. This is meeting night for our "Soldier Lodge of Good Templers," perhaps when I return from it [I] will have some news to write you.

Tuesday Morning, November 11, 1873

Returned from the Meeting last night but without having learned of any news to write you, the meeting was as usual quiet and pleasant. Ten men members were added to our number and still the cause is progressing. My cold is much better this A.M. and the demand on handkerchief's decreasing.

Only 9 months and 26 days yet for Eddie. Will soon commence packing my traps. I have a lot of trash such as Indian trophies; petrified wood from the petrified forest which we passed through on our march from Arizona, a few little shells which I picked up on the Coast of Old Mexico, some different pieces of stone gathered at different parts of the Country in which I have traveled. Some from the great Montezuma Wells and Caves of Arizona. Some pieces of Wood from an Old Spanish Mission also in Arizona, some pieces of wood from the ruins of an old Church between here and Santa Fe, said to be as old as Montezuma himself.[15] But how old he was deponent knoweth not. I have also the "1st Chapter of Frontier Law," which will leave you to imagine what it is,

---

15 Located twenty-five miles southeast of Santa Fe, the site of Pecos Pueblo, today's Pecos National Monument, embraced the remains of a large multistory habitation and two Spanish mission churches, the foundation of one from the seventeenth century and the ruins of another dating to the eighteenth century. Eddie likely obtained his souvenir piece of wood from the latter. The place was a frequently visited landmark on the Santa Fe Trail. One of the best historical descriptions was recorded by Susan S. Magoffin, who accompanied her husband on a government mission to Santa Fe in 1846. See Drumm, *Down the Santa Fe Trail*, 99–102. Another, dating from the 1860s, is found in Ryus, *The Second William Penn*, 174–76. For a treatment of the site in the context of the trail, see Vestal, *The Old Santa Fe Trail*, 260–61.

besides these I have a lot of other trash which will have one virtue and one alone; that of filling up my "light Valise." This collection is intended for Arthurs Cabinet. And if he finds any pleasure in gathering that kind of curriosities I will be content.

Will have to close for want of a subject.

Fort Union, New Mexico
NOVEMBER 12, 1873

We received the good news this evening that L and M Companies would <u>not</u> have to put in a Winters Campaign as expected. The Order has been Countermanded and we poor Soldier boys are to be permitted to remain in good Quarters during this Winter at least. You can feel assured we feel happy this evening. I dreaded the move more on account of being so comfortable fixed up in my little room that [I] hated the idea of giving it up to live in a Common Tent. And as I have little else to write you, guess [I] can fill this up with giving you a description of the room and its occupants.

It is the same room I had last winter, to more fully describe the place just follow me in the front door (the only one in the room); the sides and out again and then you will see exactly how I am situated. Well here we go, just please step up about a foot from the pavement and you are in the room. Now turn to your right and you find yourself standing in front of a good size and pretty looking glass. Hanging a little below it is my watch case in the shape of a slipper, made of pasteboard silk and beads. A "Philopena" gift from a young lady. I intend bringing it (not the young lady) home with me so you can see how pretty it is. Below this is a small table with a blue blanket over it for a cover, and on it is our hair brushes, combs, cloth[e]s brushes etc. for cleaning our Arms.

Next on the programme is our side window, with double curtains made of some kind of calico. In this corner our washstand, soap and water is found with a bench for blacking our boots upon. And if you are thirsty by this time take a drink of "Adams Ale" (the only kind we keep) and move on. Between the washstand and fire place (four feet) hangs our first picture framed a 2 x 2 1/2 frame, and called "Harvest," it represents the farmer bringing in his grain from the fields, two steps further brings you in front of our fire place where at the present time you will find a cheerful fire burning.

Above this is the "Mantle piece" on which is to be found Clay and wooden pipes sufficient for half a dozen, and above this hangs a real pretty picture (steel engraving) called "Horses in a thunderstorm" and represents two beautiful horses terrified by thunder and lightning. It is admired by every person. Two steps more and you are at Eddies bed. On the floor in front of the bed is a piece of Carpet to stand on while dressing and undressing. And if you just take a peep under the bed you will see an elegant collection, consisting of the following Articles: 1 pr. Govt. Brass Screwed Boots, No. 7, (new) drawn for Scouting purposes, 1 pr. fine Boots No. 6 late importation from home, 1 pr Gaiters No. 5 1/2, slightly worn, (you see I have very convenient feet, can put them into anything in the shape of a Boot or Shoe between the Nos of 5 to 10) 1 nose bag, 1 larriat, 1 Hobbles (drawn also for the scout), 1 Canvas bag which I carry my cloth[e]s in when scouting, this is now filled with a lot of trash that [I] did not know what to do with.[16] And stowed it away for future use, and last but none the less useful is a large bottle of genuine "Bears Oil," which was rendered from the carcass of a <u>tame bear</u> that one of our boys killed at Bascom. I wish you had part of it, for it is elegant for the hair.

At the head of the bed is my box in which I keep my cloth[e]s, and I have quite a lot of them, above the bed at the head is a frame for photographs, at the top left corner is Lizzies picture, next Mothers, next Fathers, next a group composed of Johnnie, Arthur and Clellie, below these in the same order is Clara Wampler's, Joe Parke's, Mrs. Hurley and Sue's.[17] And below these are the pictures of John Reese, Andrew Thompson, Annie Lochead and Annie Reifeinder. The whole making a real pretty picture. On the side of the wall and over my bed is a picture called the "Evening of Love," representing a young lady in a pensive mood (guess her lover failed to make his appearance).

And now for the inventory of the bed: Pillow and Pillow Case, the pillow made of wool, not much wool and very hard, [I] guess when it was made wool must have been high; 1 Army Great Coat, folded to give

---

16 In 1872, the Quartermaster Department began contracting for boots and shoes with soles attached by machine-set brass screws, which made footwear more durable in the conditions encountered in the West. See McChristian, *U.S. Army in the West*, 74–75.
17 Joseph Parkes, 1796–1865, was a famous nineteenth-century English political reformer.

the pillow the requisite height, 1 pr. of Cavalry trousers, considerable worn (wore them all summer on the trip), five Army Blankets (to keep your son and brother from freezing this winter), 1 Bedsack single, the Bunk.[18] Bunk boards and Bed Bugs (not a bad bed is it to leave the bed bugs out[?]). I forgot to mention that the bed sack was filled with straw.

At the foot of the bed is another window looking out on the Parade Ground, with curtains same as the first, below it is another box with my belts and Arthurs curiosities in it. Next to this is my room mates bed who is a Sergeant and acting as Company Q.M. Sergeant, that rank having been done away with by the War Dept. His is quite a nice bed, much better than mine. He has only 4 years and two months to serve and can afford a good bed. He was discharged from the Company in '71 and came back to it and re-enlisted in '73, is quite a nice young man, married and has a little baby. His family is at his home in Indiana.

Above his bed on the side is a mate to the picture over mine, called the "Morning of Love" representing a pretty young girl who from her happy countenance one would naturally suppose she had just <u>seen</u> her lover. At the head of his bed is a picture called "Open your Mouth and shut your Eyes." You know what this represents, don't you[?] On the floor at the head of his bed is his box for clothing and above it a picture called the Rival Queens, "Queen Elizabeth and Mary, Queen of Scotts." Near this is a group of small pictures and frames, the latter made by Harlan and self, at the top is Fannie Shipley, following around in a circle are <u>Joe Parkes</u>, Ida's, Jennies, my room mates wife (a very pretty looking lady), two of my soldier friends pictures, another of my room mates wifes's pictures taken before she was married, and in the centre his little baby's picture. I tell you what they look pretty, (as the Dutchman say's; "Ain't it"). Next to these is a picture called "The Mischevious little Kittens," and represents three little Kittens playing with a Dog, very pretty, <u>but affecting to gaze upon</u>.

You are now nearing the door but before you reach it you will see our "Cloth[e]s rack" and by raising the curtain you will behold an elegant collection consisting of three or four Stable Frocks, two Caps for Stable wear,

---

18 A bed sack was the army equivalent of a mattress. It was made of either cotton drilling or duck and measured slightly less than seven feet long by approximately two and one-half feet wide by three and one-half inches deep. It was stuffed with hay or straw for padding. The bed sack was laid over four wood slats extending between the two iron bedsteads, or trestles, of the 1871 army bunk. See Greene, *U.S. Army Uniforms*, 12–15.

one little old Hat, for Scouting purposes, 1 Blouse with the elbows out, two Sabres, two Carbines, two Bridles, One Saddle Blanket and one canteen. Below this on the floor is one box for trash (but the trouble is we have too much of it, and the lid won't cover what is already in it), and by the side of the Box is 1 delapidated Camp Chair, which has been put aside for repairs. All of this comes under the heading of cloth[e]s.

Now turn around and look at our centre table with a collection of papers, books and other trash too numerous to mention. Around the table is two Q.M. Chairs and a Bench. And now face about and as you leave the door look in the watch case and you will see another picture of Joe Parkes.

You are very tired and so am I, so good night and happy dreams.

Fort Union, New Mexico
NOVEMBER 13, 1873

Good news and happiness seems to reign upon me fast, although I am separated by so many miles from Loved ones at home. Yesterday brought to us Soldier boys the good news that the Scout would not go out this winter, that of course was joyful news to us. I sat down at once and told you of it and to fill out my letter gave you a description of my room. And now [I] have just received your letter in which you acknowledge receipt of the Money Orders. Your kind words my dear Father, has filled my heart to overflowing, and I have not words to express my feelings. Suffice it to say that I am grateful to my Maker for giving me such loved and honored parents, sisters and brothers to work for. And it makes me the happiest of mortals to add to your comfort and happiness. My will and inclination are good, had I only the opportunity to assist you more, but situated as I am it is a hard matter to save money. My pay is small and what necessaries I buy costs so much that I often do without them. I don't want you to think that I deny myself that which keeps me in health and strength, for I know you would not have me do anything of the Kind.

Orders were received yesterday for the removal of the Regimental Head Quarters, Staff and Band to Santa Fe. General Gregg (Our Colonel) now Commands the District and through him I suppose the Order originated. Don't know when the move takes place. We shall miss them some, but the change will not effect the Companies stationed here.

No other news to tell you. Write soon and often. Only 9 months and 25 days to serve. And then as you say Eastward, Onward and homeward.

Fort Union, New Mexico
NOVEMBER 21, 1873

Father's Letter accompanied by one of Harlan's Boots just received. The letter read and now will answer at once, for [I] have neither received or written a letter to you for one week.

Have been pretty busy in the Office, and besides [I] am making out a Complete set of Books for Capt. Hobart, "Company Records." Have been working on the Company Descriptive Book to day.[19] And must say it looks very neat for me to do. Will finish the set about the last of this month.

Harlan is now out Scouting with a party of men under Command of Major Alexander, of our regiment. Expect them back sometime in the early part of next week. Clint has been relieved from Extra Duty in the Quarter Master Department as Clerk, and is now doing duty in the Company. [I] Expect he will be detailed in the Adjutants Office soon as he returns.

So you have a very poor opinion of my abilities as a "Sawish." Well since I come to think of it, I did use to love to saw wood. But it was always on some other boys wood pile, where I would have lots of Company. I can't say I am passionately fond of the exercise now, but would do a bit of it if Mother asked me to, but would rather she asked Johnnie, as he seems to take so kindly to it. And besides I am not strong like he is. And it always makes my side ache. If you have any eating of good things, or any light work like that to do, Eddie is your boy, for if there is any one thing more than another that I pride myself on doing, that thing is eating. Wish I had a Camp Kettle of Custard here now and a tin cup to eat it with. I bet you it would soon be of the good things that was.

---

19 Companies maintained a ledger-style book for recording each soldier's name, date and period of enlistment, physical description, former occupation, date of discharge, character rating, and, if applicable, the date of death, desertion, or transfer from the company. Also listed were the combat actions in which the soldier participated. See *Revised Regulations*, 20.

Last Monday night at our "Good Templars Meeting" I had the honor of being Elected Worthy Recording Secretary. It is an elegant Office but don't pay anything. I declined the honor, but the Lodge wouldn't listen to it. Last night [I] made up two back Quarterly Reports of the condition of the Lodge. It is just my luck to have a lot of back work to do every place I go. I never went in an Office to Clerk since [I] enlisted but had a lot of back work to do that some other Clerk had left undone.

We are going to have a little Ball at the Lodge Thanksgiving evening. Will tell you all about it soon as it is over.

Have had delightful weather here so far, not a single cold day yet or sign of snow. Hope it continues this way all winter.

Only 9 months and sixteen days yet. Ain't my time of service passing away fast[?] It won't be long before I am home with you (to saw wood).

It's pretty near time ain't it that Lizzie, Sue and the rest of them were writing to me[?] If you don't hurry up I will be home and then there will be no need of writing. There is nothing in the shape of news to write you. And I have no idea how I am to fill this out. (Guess I won't).

Fort Union, New Mexico
NOVEMBER 29, 1873

Our "Good Templars" Ball came off Wednesday night and we had a real nice time. Had our Hall decorated very nicely with Flags and pictures. At 8:30 nearly all the Officers and Ladies of the Post came in and opened the Ball for us. They danced one Quaddrill and one Waltz, thanked us for the pleasure and departed. Soon as they made their exit, dancing commenced in earnest and was kept up until 12.

Lunch in abundance consisting of Bread, Biscuits, butter, Ham, Tea, Coffee, Cake, Lemonade, Candy and Cigars to wind up with was then served. One hour was very pleasantly spent in that kind of pastime and then dancing resumed and kept up until 6 A.M. of the 27th.

Thirteen ladies (nearly all married) and about three times that many men composed the party. And I must say it was the most pleasant little party I have seen since leaving home. Soon as the dance was over I returned to my room and went to bed.

Slept until 11 o'clock A.M., got up and dressed for Thanksgiving dinner. Had an elegant dinner, best in the Garrison ([I] mean best of the Troops). Had four roast turkeys, (nice ones) none of your old Gobblers, two hams, fresh (some of our own pork), biscuits, butter, pickles (Cucumber and Beet), Coffee, bread and for desert pudding and pies in abundance. There was only about twenty of us for dinner, and we had enough left for our supper and breakfast that night and the next morning. You see we have not done bad this week.

About one hundred Recruits for the 15th Infantry arrived tuesday. And now we are expecting two hundred for our regiment next week. And indeed we need them bad enough. Our Company require 27, and we expect to have that many assigned.

You have not told me what Harlan's Boots cost. Wish you would let me know, he is so well pleased with them that he intends having another pair made some time this winter, provided it can be done. And I guess it can. Think [I] will take care of mine and wear them home 9 months from now.

Suppose you have read the Presidents proclamation pardoning all deserters from the U.S. Service who would surrender on or before January 1st, 1874.[20] They are flocking in from all parts of the country. Four men in our Company now, one of them a Sergeant and a married man besides, have surrendered as Deserters from different branches of the service. Received notification the other day of three others who deserted from the Company as having surrendered. Eleven all told have surrendered at this Post.

The weather still continues fine here, [I] hope it will continue so all winter.

And now Johnnie as to the collection of "Old Coin," I fear [I] will not be able to find many for you. Coins of any kind in this Territory is like Uncle Sams Greenbacks, very scarce, but if I can collect any for you [I] will do so with pleasure and bring them home with me, I have one very valuable piece of United States Coin in the shape of a one cent piece the only one I had to bless myself with when I enlisted in Cincinnati O. Sept 8th, 1869. Have preserved it and have also carried it with me from the time I left Cincinnati until the present time. Guess

---

20 GO No. 102, AGO, October 10, 1873, extended amnesty to all deserters who surrendered themselves at any military station on or before January 1, 1874. They would not be punished or penalized, except for loss of pay and allowances due at the time of desertion. They were restored to duty and required to faithfully serve out their remaining time.

that "one cent piece" has traveled about as many miles by water and land as any "one cent" in the country.

I have no news to write you. All quiet along the line. I am well, hearty, and have a nice place which [I] will keep until Sept, 74.

Fort Union, New Mexico
NOVEMBER 29, 1873

Father's long and very interesting letter was received this morning. And [I] will try to answer at once although [I] have nothing of much interest to write you, except the arrival of 224 Recruits for our Regiment today. Our Company will get about 21 which will make us 81 strong. And if they only remain we will do very well, but the great difficulty is they won't stick. I suppose the money panic in the States will be the means of filling the Army to over flowing. And rather than any unfortunate should be disappointed by finding the number required filled, I would surrender my place without a murmur. Any thing to keep peace in the family. Think by the time he had put in what is left of my time he would be satisfied; and content to live the life of a Civilian ever after.

Only 9 months and five days and then I will have faithfully fulfilled my obligations to the Government of the United States. It has been five long and disagreeable years too I assure you, but we will make this all up soon as we meet.

What am I going to do when I come home, do you ever think of that[?] But why do I ask such a question when I know you have many and many a time thought of it, but what I intended saying [is] have you ever arrived at any conclusion what I should do when [I] return[?] Or have you made up your minds to wait until I get there and take chances[?] We won't have very long to wait, and then the first situation I can find vacant which I can fill I'll take, let it be what it may, for I am not half so proud as [I] use to be. Guess this is because I am getting "Old" and as Father would [say] "Ugley."

The wind is blowing without at a fearful rate. Everything is covered with sand, and [I] think we will have some winter pretty soon. Have had elegant weather so far, but it is time now for cold snaps.

There is no use [in] me trying to fill out this sheet of paper, for I can't and don't know what I took such a large sheet for anyhow. You must not feel disappointed in receiving short letters, [I] would cheerfully write long ones if only [I] had subjects to write about. I have one great subject but am keeping it to tell you verbally when I come home, and that is my great Love for you all.

Fort Union, New Mexico
DECEMBER 10, 1873

Colonel, Laundresses and Staff of the Home Brigade:
Westminster, Md.

I have the honor and pleasure to acknowledge receipt of General Order No. 1, dated Head Qrs. Home Brigade, Westminster Md., Nov. 17th, 1873. Also <u>private</u> communication dated Nov. 30th. Both received yesterday. Please accept my heart felt thanks for the very handsome manner [in] which you complimented the Quartermaster for having performed his duties. I am very happy indeed to know that the Brigade is so well provided for in the line of clothing etc. And [I] have no doubt but the <u>men</u> [are] splendid appearance in their new Great Coats. Would love dearly to see them on Dress Parade and have the Colonel march them in Review. As you make no mention of the Laundresses having drawn any supplies on that requisition I presume they are already fully equipped for the coming Winters Campaign. This is the last winter of detached service for the Quartermaster. And I hope when [I] am present for duty with the Brigade, I will be better able to discharge the duties assigned me.

I had a good hearty laugh over the Colonels description of the Brigade. Especially of the prominent positions the Laundresses occupy.

There is certainly more freedom between the Commander and Subordinates than in any Military organization I ever saw or read of. But suppose this free intercourse is consistent with the best interest of the service.

There is little news of interest to write you. The Garrison is very dull, and [the] only thing going on is the drilling of Recruits lately arrived. But as I do not come under that head, it will not interest you or I to tell of it.

The Cubian Question is talked on considerable and all the boys [are] in favor of War, but this is more for a change of stations than any particular desire to set themselves up for a Target for the Spaniards to shoot at.[21] For my own part I am strongly in favor of War. And [I] think the difficulty will never be satisfactory to the American people until the outrage done the United States has been fully avenged. I would be perfectly willing to spend the balance of my enlistment in active service against Spain. And [I] think [by] about the time for my discharge, the War would be over. And Spain willing to make any reparation demanded by our Government. But I do not think the Spanish Government will comply with the demands already made, until they are forced to do so.

We have had but a slight fall of snow this winter. And it has disappeared, but ice about two inches in thickness has been formed on the pond. I was down skating this morning, first time have been on skates since the winter of 1868. Did not get a fall, but forgot nearly all [I] ever knew about skating. Will have to practice a little this winter, for [I] am very fond of the amusement. Only 8 months and a but now, time is passing nicely. And I will soon be home.[22]

Guess you will think this a very poor return for the two long and interesting letters just received from you, but I have nothing to write about and will have to close.

---

21 Matthews refers to the Cuban insurrection against its Spanish rulers that had started in 1868 and had continued more or less uninterrupted since that time. Although some American sentiment for armed intervention existed, particularly among naturalized citizens of Cuban heritage, President Ulysses S. Grant's administration resisted becoming directly involved for fear of igniting a war with Spain. The United States, with the Civil War fresh in its memory, had its own problems in the form of the Reconstruction of the South, economic depression, and the Indian situation in the West. Although war was averted in 1870 when Congress voted down a resolution recognizing the belligerent status of the Cuban rebels, relations with Spain again teetered dangerously in October 1873, when the Cuban-owned vessel *Virginias*, illegally flying the American flag while carrying revolutionaries and munitions, was captured by a Spanish warship on the high seas. Matthews and his comrades, like many other Americans, were incensed by the secret trial and execution of more than fifty *Virginias* passengers, several of whom were U.S. and British citizens. Diplomacy prevailed, however, when Spain responded to an ultimatum by paying reparations to the families of the executed Americans. See Bailey, *A Diplomatic History of the American People*, 379–81.
22 "Butt" probably derived from cigar butt and was soldier slang for the odd remaining portion of one's enlistment beyond a year or a period of months, i.e., the stub end. For example, "a year and a butt" meant a soldier had somewhat longer than one year remaining in his enlistment. In the context of Matthews's statement, he had eight months and about three weeks left to serve. See McConnell, *Five Years*, 120.

Fort Union, New Mexico
DECEMBER 16, 1873

I am not feeling very well this morning, have a bad Diarrhea. And [I] feel generally unwell, but [I] suppose [I] will be myself again in a day or two.

Last week a detail of men from M Company left here for Bascom to relieve the men of our Company now down there. When at Taylers Ranch second day out from here part of the Detachment got drunk and as a natural consequence a fight among them selves followed and in the melee one of the party, a young man named McCaffery was shot in the head and instantly killed.[23] A dispatch was sent back here stating the facts and a Board of Officers sent down to investigate the affair. They have returned and submitted their report to the effect that the killing was accidental. The body of the unfortunate young man was brought back and buried here saturday. It is too bad that a young man should be killed in that manner, but nearly all the deaths among Soldiers on the frontier occur in that manner. Very few die from sickness or at the hands of Indians.

I will have plenty of work now until about the 5th of January. And [I] will be kept pretty busy all that time. All the Rolls and Returns will be very heavy. These last Recruits have made plenty of work for me.

We have Drill here twice each day now, but as I have nothing to do with it, [I] am not interested. I attend no roll calls or stables now, and lye in bed as late [I] want to, whistle my own Reveille now.

Have been horseback riding most every day lately for exercise. The Captain told me to take my horse whenever I wanted to. Yesterday a Sergeant and I took our horses to go in the country after vegetables. Left the Post at 2:30 P.M. [and] rode out to the Ranch where we engaged the vegetables, distance from the Post 8 miles. Remained there an hour, then mounted up and rode to a little Town four miles away.[24] Got our

---

23 Private John McCaffery of Company M was killed "by accidental discharge of pistol" on December 12, 1873. A native of Philadelphia, where he had worked as a blacksmith's helper prior to entering the army, McCaffery had enlisted on September 5, 1872, at the age of twenty-one. See Eighth Cavalry Returns, December 1873; and entry 36, p. 198, roll 39, ROE, RG 94, NA.

supper and returned to Camp at 6:30 P.M. in time to attend Good Templars Meeting.

There is a great difference in the riding in the States and the way Uncle Sams Cavalry men ride out here. I remember when I was in the states that when a man rode a horse fifteen or twenty miles he thought his horse was gone up and that he had traveled an awful distance. But out here we think nothing of riding that distance in a couple of hours. Last summer when I came up here from Bascom I rode 72 miles first day and rested at Stone Ranch two hours besides. Next day [I] rode 53 miles and the next morning [I] came in to this Post by 11 o'clock distance rode 38 miles. And the following morning rode out about 10 miles for exercise for myself and horse. Guess when I come home [I] would make a good Deputy Sherriff or something else where there was a lot of riding to do.

Only 8 months and 14 days yet to serve. Am counting my time up to the 1st of September now, for [I] feel sure [I] will get my papers on the 1st, although my time is not out until the 8th. I should think a person ought to be allowed 8 days in five years.[25]

Had a splendid time last week skating. Was on the ice three days in succession. Beat all the Soldiers and Citizens around this post, and received several compliments for my agility on skates. Had not been on skates before since the winter of 68. But Eddie Matthews never forgets any kind of amusement, but if it was something beneficial my thick cranium would soon let it out and away it would go.

---

24 This village was known as La Junta until 1879, when it was renamed Watrous by the Atchison, Topeka & Santa Fe Railroad, to avoid confusion with another town on the line, La Junta, Colorado. The town's namesake, Samuel B. Watrous, was an influential merchant and rancher from Vermont who donated to the railroad a right-of-way across his land. La Junta was located at the confluence of the Mora and Sapella Rivers, making it an ideal location for growing vegetables to supply the fort. See Julyan, *Place Names*, 377. The two soldiers probably stopped for supper in Tiptonville, a tiny settlement on the Mora a short distance above La Junta. Its origins dated to about 1849, when William B. Tipton married Watrous's eldest daughter and established a residence at that location. Tiptonville supported its own post office from 1876 to 1908. Inhabited today by only a few people, Tiptonville is still a recognized place name in the local area. See ibid., 355.

25 Even after four years' service, Matthews gave the army too much credit for leniency. Regulations prohibited any soldier from being discharged prior to the expiration of his term of enlistment, nor could he be granted a leave of absence terminating with the date of his discharge. He was required to be present at his assigned station to personally receive his final statement and to settle his accounts. See *Revised Regulations*, 30.

Fort Union, New Mexico
DECEMBER 18, 1873

Have been for the past hour sitting in the Office enjoying my after supper smoke, and thinking of you loved ones. Happened to have Sue's letter (which [I] received few days ago) in my pocket so [I] took it out and read it. And [I] was at once put in the notion of writing home. Although it has only been a day since I performed that pleasant duty, but [I] know you will not complain if I write to you daily.

So you folks are all "distinguished" are you, and only found it out at this late day[?] No doubt but I too would have come under that head had my honored Father and Mother deferred their visit to America a year or two later, but as it now is [I] suppose I must be content with the knowledge that "I" am nothing but a poor American. I have the satisfaction of knowing my ancestors were "very distinguished." But why should I not also be considered distinguished if traveling entitles one to that distinction[?] Surely one who crosses the American Continent thence across the Gulf, up the Colorado River into the wilds of Arizona, visiting the Caves and Wells of the Old "Montazumas," traveling on the back of a wild Mustang through Lower California, Old and New Mexico, into Texas and finally back across the Continent over a different route to home and civilization. "Distinction of War," ask the good people of W[estminster] who seem very readily to accord one those high honors whether I am entitled to that claim or not, for I am anxious to know.

So the people of W. think that as I have lived such a roving life these five years that when I come home [I] will not be satisfied with the quiet life [I] will have to lead, that is just what I long for most, for [I] am sick and tired of wandering. And [I] have had so much roving these five years that the name will be sufficient for the future.

Only 8 months and 13 days, the time is passing away very well. Oh how happy I feel to think of soon being in the Arms of my loving and affectionate Mother, with my loved Father, sisters and brothers waiting in their turn to welcome the prodigal home. And if the mere thought of this reunion brings such happy feelings, what will they be when we meet[?]

Tomorrow I will commence to take an Inventory of all the Public property Capt. Hobart is responsible for. And [I] will be kept very busy with his papers until about the 5th of January.

I have made out a very nice Descriptive Book of the Company for him and was highly complimented for it by him. Sometime next month [I] will make out his Company clothing account book which will be a good job. Although a week ago I filled up a receipt book for Mrs. Hobart, 244 receipts [recipes] for making good things. I tell you what my mouth watered just thinking how nice some of them would taste when made. I took great pains in entering the receipts, and after [I] got them all entered up, [I] numbered them and underscored every word with red ink. All in all it looked very nice, [I] got "thank you" for it. And am expecting a dish of something nice soon as they make any thing of that kind, but if I should be disappointed in not getting any will always believe they only have the receipt book to show and look at, contenting themselves by thinking how nice and good they would be if they only had some.

The weather still continues elegant. Never saw nicer weather. Warm enough during the day to go in shirt sleeves.

Fort Union, New Mexico
DECEMBER 21, 1873

Sunday evening (after supper) and I [am?] seated in my "little room" with the best intentions in the world to write you something, deeming it the best and most pleasant occupation for whiling away an hour or two of an otherwise dull evening. But like a mariner cast adrift in the mighty Atlantic without either chart or compass to guide him to a haven of safety, so am I now situated in regard to a subject to write upon.

It is true I have two magnificent subjects: One and the first my gratitude to Him who has watched over and protected us through all these years. And second, but none the less for being so, my great love for you dear ones at home. These are elegant subjects, but I fear my ability to do them justice. I think I could better demonstrate my love in person were I only with you, than [I] could possible do on paper. And besides it would be so much nicer. But blessed be the name of the Lord, I will not be here this time next year.

The day's are passing away very rapidly. Each one bringing me nearer and nearer to home and happiness. Perhaps it is wrong to wish the time of our life to pass more rapidly as it is naturally short and sweet, but when situated as I now am, separated from home, friends and all that is dear to one, is it any wonder that I should pray for the time to more rapidly pass away[?] This is not living, but is a mere existence. (Kind of a half way). But what is the use of crying[?] Only eight months and nine day's, that won't be long passing.

I have all the work I can do in the Office for the next ten days and have little time for play (although the ice is splendid). Have vanquished all the Soldier boys at the post in the accomplishment of skating. No doubt you will say this is nothing new, as I could generally excell in play. And where I couldn't excell [I] could stand as much as any other boy.

The weather continues magnificent, not a cold day this winter. The nights are just cold enough for good sleeping.

Christmas will soon be here, but I know of nothing going on to enliven this place. But hope it may be a merry one to you "loved ones," and may you have a big dinner and think of your . . . Eddie.

Fort Union, New Mexico
DECEMBER 28, 1873

I am so tired writing that [I] can hardly hold the pen but as I have not written to you for nearly (if not quite one week) [I] must do so tonight. Have been sitting at my Desk writing all day long, and now at 8:30 P.M. am still at my post. Sunday or not Army work must go on. And as I am one of the necessary parts of the Machine [I] have to keep in motion, or else the machine couldn't _work_. You see I am an important part.

Had been working on a Muster Roll all day and finished it by supper, then sit down and wrote thirty invitations for a Social Party to be given by the members of our Order of Good Templars, New Years Eve. Guess you will say that was work that might be dispensed with. And so it might, but the trouble is we have not been effected yet by the Money Panic, and as we have a little Money in the Treasury [we] concluded it was [a] pious idea to Dance it off.

Harlan and [my]self were appointed as a Committee on Invitations, but H. has been sick all day and did not feel like writing tonight.

Christmas is over and New Years approaching. We had a very nice Dinner in the Company. In fact I believe all the Companies had something nice.

At night Major Alexander, Comd'g Officer, had a few fire works set off. No other excitement at the Post. And the day passed off quietly. Hope it was a Merry one with you.

We have received our New Uniform and are very well pleased with it. It consists of a Helmet with Cords, bands and plume with a large brass Eagle in front, the Cords, bands and plume are yellow (Cav'y Color). The dress coat is very nice, is trimmed with yellow (buff), pants same as issued before.[26]

Guess [I] will bring my Uniform home with me, to let you see the difference in the style in '61 and now. We all turned out this morning for Inspection in full rig for the first time and made quite a display. The style is taken from the Prussian Soldiers.

Tonight I have eight months and three days to serve. Time is passing quick, but none to quick.

From all accounts we will go to Texas in the Spring and by time we get settled down my time will be out. I can hardly wait until Sept. 74. Am getting more impatient every day.

I am too tired to write but will do better next week. Wishing you a happy New Year and very many of them.

Fort Union, New Mexico
DECEMBER 31, 1873

Father's ever welcome letter dated 21st inst. was received this morning. And I can assure you that I have felt good all day. All attributed to its reception. I have noticed many and many a time the effect your letters have over me. I may be angry with myself and imagine I am the same with every person in the world and one of your letters are handed me, my anger is gone like "Mark Twains Jack Ass Rabbit" with a flash and vanish. And I am at once at peace with all mankind. So you can

---

26 The dress uniform adopted by the army in July of 1872 was a radical departure from the one worn previously. As described by Matthews, the headgear consisted of a black felt helmet with brass trimmings and surmounted by a yellow horsehair plume. It also featured yellow worsted braided bands with draping cords fastened to the coat. The dress coat was a single-breasted Basque style reflecting strong European influence. It had a standing collar trimmed in yellow, with like-colored trimmings on the cuffs and tail. The basic style remained in use by the U.S. Army until 1902, and was one of the most distinctive uniforms in its history. See McChristian, *U.S. Army in the West*, 41, 52–53, 58–61.

imagine what influence your letters have over me. Without your letters I am miserable; with them the happiest boy in the world.

That surely was an elegant idea of mine when I suggested that you should commence at one end of town and describe the people and houses until you had taken in the whole place, for it has furnished a almost inexhaustable (excuse English) subject for you to write about, and has been of the greatest interest to me. Harlan always told me I hadn't an idea, but I knew I had all the time. Your idea's of something for me to do when I come home are mine exactly, with Rail Roading selling highest in the polls. But even this has it's objectionable faults. The main one is that I would be so seldom home. And I have been away so long now that I feel as though I want to remain by your side for the balance of my life. But we can wait eight months and a day. You see I am counting from the 1st of September, for I know Capt. Hobart will give me eight days if not more.

Capt. H[obart] has applied for a transfer into Infantry but I understand his transfer was disapproved, and for my part [I] am very glad of it, for [I] want him to remain in Command of the company as long as I am in it.[27]

The year we have been looking forward to for so long is almost at hand, only one day intervening. And then only eight months to serve, that time will pass away almost before we know it.

Enclosed find an invitation to our "Sociable." You won't come I know and will say perhaps that I am attending too many of them. But under present circumstances [I] don't think I can be blamed. It is very seldom that we have anything of the kind and in fact any other pleasure except that derived through the performance of our duty, and that I assure you is very little. But as there can be no possible harm in attending a dance where there is neither rowdyism or strong drink, I don't think you will find any objections to my attending.

Took a little horse back ride this afternoon (fifteen miles) to engage music for our dance.

---

27 Captain Hobart's application for transfer to the Third Infantry was approved on December 29. The Third was then posted at various forts in Kansas and Indian Territory, but early in 1874 was sent to the Department of the South. Hobart's motivation for leaving the Eighth Cavalry is not known, but may have stemmed from a desire for less strenuous service. The cavalry was constantly stationed in the West, and consequently life was often demanding for that branch. Hobart had served in the cavalry for thirteen years. See Heitman, *Historical Register*, vol. 1, 533; and Rodenbough, *Army of the United States*, 448.

I wrote a letter yesterday to the Commanding Officer of the Post requesting permission to give the Ball. And [I] received it back with an Endorsement that permission was granted provided the men attended in full dress Uniform, with waist belts and white gloves. And of course [we] have to comply, but I see no objections to this. As the Officers always attend our dances, and are always dressed in full uniform.

I have two Muster and Pay Rolls finished and they are big ones I tell you, about the size of the "Balto. [Baltimore] American" [newspaper].

I have been thinking of asking Ida White to go up home with me when I get to Baltimore. What do you think about it[?] Think it will be nice to have a few friends at our re-union, for I know it will be such a happy one that they will feel equally as good <u>almost</u> to see how happy we are.

Have nothing else to write about that will interest you. Good night and a happy happy New Year to you all.

CHAPTER EIGHT

"Every Day Is One Less for Me to Serve"

JANUARY—MARCH 1874

*B*y the beginning of 1874, disparate events were afoot in Kansas that would directly impact the remote Staked Plains that Eddie Matthews had traversed during Gregg's reconnaissance two years earlier. For several years following the Civil War, large herds of longhorn cattle had been driven from central Texas up the Chisholm Trail to end-of-track shipping points on the new Kansas Pacific Railroad, then being constructed across the state toward Denver. Abilene became the first Kansas town to attract the Texas cattle trade, followed a short time later by Ellsworth, as the rails extended westward, generally tracing the course of the Smoky Hill River. By the early seventies, a competing rail line, the Atchison, Topeka & Santa Fe, was building across central Kansas along the Arkansas River, reaching Dodge City in September of 1872. The fledgling town of Wichita, farther east on the ATSF, and conveniently near the Chisholm Trail, quickly established itself as a new shipping point for Texas cattle, vying with Ellsworth for supremacy in that business.

Dodge City, meanwhile, was too far off the existing cattle trails to provide an economical alternative shipping point to eastern markets. It was, however, advantageously located in the High Plains bison range. It was estimated that more than twenty-five million bison inhabited the region within a hundred-mile radius of Dodge. Beginning in 1871, concurrent with the development of markets for buffalo robes in England and New York, and for hides by leather tanneries in Pennsylvania and elsewhere, Dodge City catered to the commercial hunters swarming into the region to get rich from this new bonanza. The town boomed for the next three years as the railroad transported hunters to the plains, as well as supplies to merchants eager to outfit the scores of parties operating from that hub on the Arkansas. In 1873 alone, dealers shipped out over a quarter-million buffalo hides on the Atchison, Topeka & Santa Fe.

It was said that on any day, one could ride for fifty to seventy-five miles in any direction from the town and never be out of earshot of gunfire as hunters slaughtered thousands of the shaggy beasts, leaving most of the meat to rot. After the winter of 1872–1873, when it was estimated that as many as seventy-five thousand buffalo were killed, hide men were forced to range farther and farther from the Arkansas in search of enough animals to justify the hunt. By the spring of 1874, most of the southern herd, what was left of it, remained beyond "No Man's Land," as the Oklahoma Panhandle was then known, on the Staked Plains of Texas. The concern hide hunters initially had that they might be trespassing into hunting territory granted to the Indians by the Medicine Lodge Treaty of 1867 proved unfounded. The state of Texas had not agreed to such a concession, and therefore the Indians' hunting rights extended only east of the reservations situated in western Indian Territory. The Texas Panhandle, therefore, was wide open in a legal sense to anyone who wished to venture there. However, any interlopers daring to do so would find themselves in direct competition with the southern Plains tribes, who fully appreciated that the bison inhabited only that region and considered the Staked Plains as their exclusive domain. Nevertheless, white buffalo hunters, in their zeal to wring all the profits possible from a fast-dwindling market, invaded the northern Panhandle, threatening to exterminate the last of the Indians' natural commissary. The tribesmen relied upon the buffalo not only for sustenance, clothing, and tools, but for robes that could be traded to the New Mexicans for arms, ammunition, and other goods.

The Eighth Cavalry, meanwhile, pursued its mission to intercept the Comanchero traffic through eastern New Mexico Territory while serving as a buffer against Indian incursions from the Staked Plains. On the eastern side of the Staked Plains, troops in the Department of Texas concurrently defended the ranches and settlements south of the Red River against unremitting Indian raids by the Comanches and Kiowas. With the tribesmen still drawn to the remote northern Panhandle by the lure of game and trade with the Comancheros, and with that trade heavily reliant on the buffalo as well as livestock stolen from Texas ranchmen, the situation was fast approaching the kindling point.

Fort Union, New Mexico
SUNDAY NIGHT, JANUARY 4, 1874

Have been working in the Office from 8:30 A.M. until now, 8:30 P.M., Sunday though it is. Am tired to be sure but not too tired to keep me from writing a few lines to you loved ones. Have forgotten the date of my last letter, but don't think it has been quite one week.

After working hard all day I wrote two sheets of letter paper full in the shape of a letter to our Ex 1st Sergeant who is now desking in the War Department Washington, D.C. And in it asked what my prospects would be and the qualifications required for a Clerkship when I returned from the Wars.

Last Friday I done the biggest days writing I ever done in my life. Made out two Muster and Pay Rolls, the first one from 9 A. M. to 5 P.M. and the second from 5:30 P.M. until 9:15 P.M. If that was not a big days work no man ever done one of that kind. And the best of it was they were both without a mistake or erasure. And the best Rolls I have ever made out. To give you an idea (I mean that part of the family who have never been quartermasters) [of?] the amount of work on a Roll, we will take what plain writing paper it would take to cover the side of a room say 12 X 20 (we will take the 12 side) as that will be a little nearer facts. Now put this paper on a table, get your pen's black and red ink, etc. ready, take off your coat and collar, unbutton the shirt collar and then perspire a little at the prospects before you. The next motion is to calmly seat yourself in the chair, put a fresh piece of tobacco in your mouth, grasp the black ink pen in your right hand (if you are not left handed as most girls are) stick the red ink pen behind and resting on your right ear, the point to the front, inclining upwards. This is one time and two motions, and you are supposed to be ready to sling ink regardless of the price of the article.

The first part of the work is to put in the heading, viz: who's roll it is, Company, Captain, when and to what time paid. This goes clean across the top of the roll, say about eight feet of writing (more or less).

Next comes the Captains name and remarks, following his the Lieutenants, and then the Non Commissioned Privates according to rank. Then the Privates in alphabetical order, first the number, name, rank, enlisted when, where, who by, last paid, to what time, by what Paymaster. Amount of clothing money due Soldier or the U.S. as the case may be. Amount due for Tobacco, if the man is present write his full name, if absent draw a red ink line where his name would appear, then comes his remarks. (nearly all with some). For instance write this remark opposite say fifteen or twenty names viz: "Sentenced as promulgated in G.O. No.20, Hd. Qrs. district of N.M., to forfeit to the U.S. his Monthly pay for one Month." Or like this, viz: "Deserted at Fort Union, N.M. July 14th, 1873. Apprehended July 24th, 1873. Due U.S. for apprehension $30.00. Deserted from Confinement at Fort Lyons C[olorado] T[erritory] August 7, 1873, surrendered at Indianapolis, Ind. as a Deserter from Company L 8th Cavalry Nov. 10th, 1873, under the provisions of G. O. No. 102, War Dept. A.G.O. Oct. 10th, 1873. Due U.S. for Ordinance $126.27. Due U.S. for C.C. and G.E. $1.59, Due U.S. for Amt. paid Rice and Byers Depot Traders St. Louis, Mo $3.00."[1] Now this was all one remark and when you come to write this fifteen or twenty times it gets monotonous. Every word has to be written as you are not allowed to ditto a word on a Muster Roll. On these last rolls we had 3 Officers, 79 men, 1 Discharged, 1 Deserted, 6 Dropped, and 7 Attached, and four fifths of them with a long remark. It wouldn't be so hard if there was plenty of room to write, but the trouble is you are confined to a certain space and you have to write very fine to get it in. You have to make out four Copies.

Now this is a little Muster and Pay Roll of itself, and the one I will pay you on for the present week. I undertook to illustrate the thing to you and in doing so have spoilt a sheet of paper that might have been filled up with more interesting matter. But as it is now about 10 o'clock P.M. [I] will put this up until morning and then add a line. Good night and happy happy dreams.

---

[1] A person capturing a deserter was paid a reward of five dollars, plus reimbursement for reasonable expenses incurred in transporting the prisoner to the nearest military post or depot. See *Revised Regulations*, 515. "C.C. and G.E." stands for Clothing, Camp and Garrison Equipage. Some deserters, especially on the western frontier, took as much government property (arms, ammunition, a horse with equipment, clothing, etc.) with them as possible with the intention of trading or selling it to civilians to aid their escape. The cost of all this matériel was charged against the deserter if he were later captured. Most deserters were not apprehended. See Rickey, *Forty Miles*, 150–52.

Monday Morning 8:15

Have just had my breakfast. And before commencing the days work [I] will finish my letter to you.

Our little "Sociable" at Good Templars Hall New Years Eve was all any person could expect. We had a real delightful time. Danced from 8 to 12 P.M. [*sic*] and then got on the outside of a good substantial supper. At 1 A.M. resumed hostilities and kept it up until 5 A.M. I don't think there was one in the Hall that night but what enjoyed him or herself, and I guess they all felt like me, "tired but satisfied."

I was quite an important individual in the affair, was one of the Committee on Invitations, Music, and the only Floor Manager we had, besides served as Head Waiter at Supper, and in fact made myself generally useful.

News Year's day passed off quietly and was an exception to most holidays seen in the Army as no drunken Soldiers were seen meandering about the Garrison. I hope you had a happy time both Christmas and New Years. And that you may all live to enjoy many, many more.

I am marching over and into the affections of my last year very fast. Only seven months and twenty five days more.

We cut a dashing appearance in our new Uniforms and look quite flashy. I don't know but what I will bring my Helmet and Uniform Coat home with me. If you have never seen any of them, you will be surprised to how your Soldier boy looks.

The mail just came over, but no letter from you. Received "half sheet" Democrat.

Must stop pleasure for this time and attend to business. Got lots of it on hand.

Fort Union, New Mexico

JANUARY 9, 1874

Fathers letter with Lizzies picture was received two days ago, both were welcome I assure you. The pretty face of my loved sister of nearly five years back is plainly seen, but one part is not recognizable. And that is the present style of wearing the hair. I don't think it either becoming or pretty, but no doubt it is the style, and of course a young lady has to live up to it. Outside of this I think it very nice. And am very much obliged to you for it.

We have a Soldier Artist here now, who is taking pictures, but they are so poor that I would not have mine taken. Several of the men have had their pictures taken, but very poor ones they are. Perhaps after awhile he will be able to do better, and then I will send you one.

Well we have lost our Captain, and I am very sorry for it. We were all under the impression that his application for a transfer had been disapproved, but in this we were mistaken. Two days ago he received a Dispatch from District Head Quarters Ordering him to proceed at once to Fort Wallace Kansas and join his Company.

I had none of his Quarterly Returns made out at the time, but went to work with a will and worked until 12 M[id]night before last and had all of his Accounts closed by 11 o'clock last night. Fixed his papers all up nicely and delivered them to him at 11 o'clock last night. He thanked me for them and in bidding me good bye told me to write to him before my time was out giving him directions where a letter from him would reach me, and he would give me an elegant recommendation. And he would do more, [he] said he had some good friends at Washington and he would write to them to interest themselves in getting me a Clerkship in one of the Departments. Said he had no doubt at all but I could get a good situation. I thanked him and told him whether I applied for a Clerkship or not I would like to have a recommendation from him to take home with me, as I thought my parents would be glad to see me return with something to show that I had conducted myself properly during the five years of absence. Recommendations other than the character on a Discharge are seldom given in the Regular Army. And I may feel proud to have the promise of one.

Our new Captain is named Morris and is from the 3rd Infantry. Will be able to tell more about him when he joins the Company.[2]

---

[2] Captain Louis T. Morris began his army career in 1861 as a first lieutenant in the Nineteenth U.S. Infantry. He achieved the rank of captain by war's end, transferred to the Twenty-Eighth Infantry in 1866, and a year later was assigned to the Thirty-Seventh. Elements of that regiment had been stationed at Fort Union during the late 1860s and may have influenced Morris's decision. The army-wide reorganization of 1869 saw him transferred to the Eighth Cavalry. He would remain with the Eighth Cavalry until his promotion to major in the Third Cavalry in 1889. During the following decade, he would serve as lieutenant colonel of the First and the Fourth Cavalry, eventually retiring in 1898. See Heitman, *Historical Register*, vol. 1, 728. Officers of the same rank and standing in the army were permitted by mutual consent and approval of the War Department to exchange branches or corps, so long as the action was not to the detriment of any other officer in the respective receiving regiments. Lateral transfers were seldom approved and had to be properly justified. That both Hobart's and Morris's orders were cut on December 29, 1873, indicates this was such an exchange. See *Revised Regulations*, 12–13.

Was very sorry indeed to learn of Arthurs accident, but am glad it was no worse. Coal Oil is rather a dangerous article. I know this from past experience. I got in to the habit of lighting the stove fire with a little of the None Explosive kind myself, until one morning I put so much on the Kindlingwood that when the match was applied the top lid of the stove cushoned on the ceiling and your correspondent was knocked in among the flour barrels about six feet from the scene of disaster. And when he picked himself up and found no bones were broken he said he wouldn't make any fuss or say anything about it, but one thing he would never kindle another fire with coal oil. And if ever he kept his word he did this time. I would rather go without my breakfast anytime than kindle a fire with None Explosive.

I have not heard from my three young lady correspondents for some time viz: Ida, Jennie and Lec. Each of them owe me a letter, and time they were here ([I] mean the letters).

I am getting quite a collection of curiosities for Arthur such as they are. Their greatest virtue will be that they are far fetched.

Weather still splendid like spring, [I] have worked in the Office in my shirt sleeves nearly every day since first of the month.

I am afraid my eyesight is getting weak. I often have difficulty in running up columns on the different rolls, and when I read at night my eyes hurt and the sight gets dim. If I find they are getting any worse [I] will quit all night work and reading. Any person to look at my eyes would think they were strong enough but they are not.

Will look for Lizzies promised "Letter" for [I] have not had one from her for so long that [I] can't begin to remember. Would give anything to be with you tonight. Can picture and do what each of you are doing. Oh but won't it be nice for us all to sit around the fire next winter and tell of our doings during the past five years. I feel like I will want to sit by the side of my darling Mother all the time and hear her tell me what you all have said and done while I was away. And I know she will have lots to tell me of. I get to feeling so happy thinking of the good days in store for us that I don't know what to do with myself.

And now that we are getting a new Captain [I] suppose [I] will have to count my time from the 8th of September, for [I] don't suppose he would give me eight days. If Capt. Hobart had remained I would have got the eight days I know and perhaps more. But anyhow [I] can put in every day, and will be under no obligations to any of them.

Well I know of nothing more to write you tonight. Only seven months and 29 days "full time."

Fort Union, New Mexico
JANUARY 14, 1874

I have nothing much of interest to write you tonight, although [I] feel that [I] should write you something. Had not heard from you for more than a week, and yesterday morning at Mail time was in a feaver heat with great expectations. But when the 1st Sergeant returned from the Adjutants Office and seeing me look so wistful, and then to tell me there was nothing is beyond describing. Tears would have come had I not choked them down. I was sitting at the desk with a lot of papers before me, and commenced picking them up to put away for [I] could not think of work feeling as I did. The Sergeant saw that I was feeling pretty badly and thought he had gone far enough and to my great pleasure and surprise handed me a letter from Father and while I was tearing the envelope off [he] handed me another, this one from Ida. You can just imagine how good I felt then, for I can't begin to describe my feelings. And while in this blissful state the Sergeant handed me the third and only letter left for the Company (this one I recognized as from Sue). I just jumped up from the Desk and commenced dancing. If there ever was a happy boy for a little time, I was that identical individual, but shau [pshaw]; I can't begin to tell you any where near how good I felt, and am not going to try. Mind you I had arrived at this happy state by only looking at the envelopes. And now if you are very good at guessing, you can just guess how happy I was when [I] had finished reading the contents of the envelopes.

You are all well; that is the best of news to me. And then it will not be very long until we are all together again, and that is [the] best news. No, two. Then Sue is in Balto. [Baltimore] having a good time, and that is pretty good news, And then Ida, writes me a real nice letter, and tells me something that I must'nt tell you of in this, for she and Sue both told me not to, but I have a good, notion too any how. No, I won't, for you will find out soon enough. You needn't think Ida proposed to me, for she didn't. And besides I don't intend to marry any Girl that gets her hair up as high as she and Lizzie does. And another difficulty and objection is she wouldn't have me, but any how Ida is a real nice young lady and the older Ed Matthews gets the more he likes her, but don't tell any person that I said so.

My little Cat is on the Desk doing everything he can to make me stop writing, is now under my chin trying to catch the end of the pen. He has just now shifted positions and has made a bed out of Fathers letter which was lying open on the Desk.

I am very glad to know my letters come to hand regularily, for I try to write and do write as often as I can. Although it is very often I have nothing much to write about.

Our fine weather continues, and has put an end to our Skating. Many thanks to Mr. Warner for his compliment, but would have felt better if it had have been a compliment for some more useful accomplishment.

Have not yet got through with my work. Capt. Hobart's leaving threw me back considerable. It is getting late and as I want this to go off in tomorrow mornings mail [I] will close and take it to the Office.

Only seven months and twenty four days "full time" and then will mail myself for W[estminster].

Fort Union, New Mexico
JANUARY 18, 1874

Sunday morning 10:30 A.M. and I suppose you my loved ones, are either getting ready or on your way to divine Services while I your Son and brother am seated at my desk with intentions (the best in the world) to convey to you my thoughts and deeds.

I feel a sorrow this morning which cannot find words to express, and have never experienced a like feeling, except on one occasion when [I] received the sad, sad tidings that my loved and loving little Sister was no more. I suffered then what I pray never to be called on to suffer again.[3]

---

3 This is a reference to the death of Eddie's younger sister, Margaret. Since Eddie makes no mention of the event itself in any of the extant letters, she must have died sometime between April of 1871 and June of 1872, the period marking a gap in the Matthews correspondence. Margaret was listed among the Matthews family members in the census taken in June of 1870, but her name afterward disappears from public records. Moreover, Eddie did not address her directly in his letters after that time, making only this reference to the grief he had experienced upon receiving news of her death. Significantly, he mentions having "two Angel sisters" in his letter of June 20, 1874. The other was Frances, who was born in 1856 and died during the 1860s. See *1860 U.S. Federal Census*, last modified 2009, Ancestry.com; *1870 U.S. Federal Census*, last modified 2010, Ancestry.com.

And now [I] have just read the painful news of the accidental and sudden death of George Howard.[4] I can't describe my feelings, for George was a friend who I thought more of than [I] did of many of my old associates. It would not seem so hard had he died at home surrounded by kind and loving friends, but to die and be buried in a strange country separated by thousands of miles from home and friends. Perhaps without one kind friend to follow him to his last resting place, and when he was lowered in the silent grave to shed a tear over him. It is hard indeed to think of. For unfortunate George, how I would have loved to have been near you to perform the last sad rites over you. It would have been a painful duty I know, but surely a consolation at least to know that one kind friend was near to weep and mourn his loss.

None but those who have experienced a like situation can imagine my feelings when thinking of the possibility of meeting with any sudden accident which would result in my death. It is not the honor [horror?] of death alone which causes this indescribable feeling, but is the thought of dying and being buried in a strange land, away from home and loving friends.

It is strongly rumored that our Regiment will go to Texas in the spring. And in case it does I will surely visit the silent City of the dead in which lies the remains of my lost friend, I can write no more on this painful subject.

We are having miserable weather, not cold or rainy but a continued sand storm, for the last three days everything has been covered with sand. At times it would be impossible to see three feet ahead as the sand was flying so thick. But this is only Fort Union weather in reality.

Our new Captain has not put in an appearance yet. Expect him every day.

The days are passing slowly, and January more than half past. Every day is one less for me to serve, and never passes without being counted.

I don't know what to write about as [I] can find no news in Camp. I fear my letters for some time back must prove very uninteresting to you. There was a time when I could always find subjects to write a long letter to you, but lately I find the greatest difficulty in filling one sheet of

---

4 George R. Howard, an employee of the Houston & Texas Central Railway, was accidentally killed in Sherman, Texas, when he was crushed between two rail cars. See the *Democratic Advocate*, January 10, 1874.

note paper. This is not because I think less of you, for it is just the reverse if anything. I am thinking of you continually and of what we will all do next September.

P.S. What has become of my friend Jennie[?] She is neglecting me shamefully. "Tired again I suppose."

Fort Union, New Mexico
JANUARY 20, 1874

Your kind and welcome letter dated 11th inst. was received this morning. Also received one from Lec. You and my friends also, always write me such nice and interesting letters that I cannot help regretting mine are not better and more interesting. But this place affords so little news and that little is exhausted long since, that I find it a difficult matter to write you a letter unless I write exclusively of myself. And if [I] do that [I] fear you will think me egotistical.

I have received one letter from Sue, in which she speaks of enjoying herself very much, and from her description [I] imagine she is having elegant times.

Lizzie's promised letter has not yet put in an appearance although I have not despaired of receiving it yet. And now my darling Sister the more I gaze on your picture the better pleased I am with it and the more reconciled I become to the style of head dress. (Now this ought to bring you out I think).

Our Soldier Artist continues to improve in taking pictures, and I may have some taken after while, but I believe it would be better to wait seven months and 18 days and then see the original.

When I commence to mention your names I can hardly control myself, my heart gets full to over flowing and I can hardly wait until next September to see you. There is never a day allowed to pass without an hour spent in thoughts of you loved ones. And this thought of you brings such an ecstacy that I am happy for the balance of the day.

Our new Captain has not arrived yet. Is expected every day. We are very anxious to see him, and have our curiosity satisfied. From what I can learn of him he is a very good Officer, but is very military. That is just the kind of Officer's I like, and just the kind our Company needs to straighten the boys out.

A school of instructions for Signaling has been started here, with three men detailed from each Company in this regiment and the same number from the 15th Infantry.⁵

My darling Mother, I am begging again, and know I have but to ask you and I'll get what I want. Won't you please send me a couple [of] handkerchiefs. Those you sent me last Summer have bean pretty nearly washed away by my Laundress. And I could as well do without a shirt as a handkerchief.

It is getting late and I am tired [of] writing.

Fort Union, New Mexico
JANUARY 31, 1874

Tattoo Roll Call has this moment been sounded by the Trumpeter, and I am seated in my room with three letters before me to be answered before I retire to my virtuous couch (straw tick and six thin Government blankets).

First, foremost and most important is my dear Sister Lizzie's letter. First one [I] have received from her for so long that [I] can't remember dates. And if it were not contrary to an established rule of mine, [I] would confine myself exclusively to her in answering it, but I can't do this as it is generally a difficult matter here of late to find sufficient news to write about when [I] include you all in a letter.

I have been feeling quite unwell this last week, and felt worse today than [I] have for a long time. I got a half pound [of] tea from the Commissary this morning and had a strong cup for my dinner. Guess it must have been too strong for me, for [I] had hardly the tea and dinner down before it came up. And if there is anything in the world I despise its casting up <u>accounts</u>.

---

5 After the Civil War, the Signal Corps consisted of one man, Colonel Albert J. Myer, the chief signal officer of the army. Myer did his best to see that training in the various forms of signaling (most commonly with flags) was carried out at military stations throughout the country. Left to the discretion of post commanders, however, such training was sporadic and inconsistent, if done at all. Those commanders who appreciated the value of signaling sometimes designated one of their company officers as post signal officer to conduct training for assigned details of soldiers. Six months after Matthews wrote his letter, the Signal Corps was finally authorized a permanent cadre of officers and men. See McChristian, *Uniforms, Arms, and Equipment*, vol. 1, 264–65.

I had plenty of work in the office to do, but did not feel much in the humor for doing it. The Sergeant wanted me to go in my room and go to bed, but I would not do it. Sit at my desk all day and made out an estimate for a years supply of clothing, for the Company. Soon as [I] had figured out the amount of each article, [I] had to divide it up in different sizes, and when [I] had done this [I] had to make four copies of the estimate, in all quite a good days work for a well man. Will have plenty of work to do all next week in the Office, but lets drop work and take to more pleasant occupation.

Frank M. is surely very kind to carry my letters from the Office to you. And Eddie M. is also very dutiful to write those letters for Frank to carry, ain't he[?] And I am very glad my letters reach you regularly, for I never allow a week to pass without writing at least one letter to you. Would love ever so much to be home to attend your school exhibition, for [I] know I would enjoy it. Hope it will prove a success and when it has passed, write and tell me all about it.

No doubt your curiosity in regard to who Sue is going to bring home with her has been satisfied. She told me, but also closed my mouth, [I] wanted to tell you, but dare not. I asked Ida in my last letter to her to visit W[estminster] when I return, in fact asked her to go up with me. Do you approve of my action[?] Know you do without asking the question. Don't know what she will say to the arrangement.

I think your plan or contemplated visit to Oakland an elegant idea, and would love dearly to have you for my traveling companion from O. home, but am afraid I will not be able to reach home by the 15th of the month.[6] For as you know my time is not out until the 8th and I may not be able to leave here (provided [I] am discharged at this place) before the 10th, at least, for [I] will have to get my final statements cashed by the Paymaster before [I] can travel. I don't know whether I shall come home by way of the B[altimore] and O[hio] R.R. unless you are waiting for me at O. I came out over that Road when [I] "went west" but at any rate [I] will travel on the road which carries me to you loved ones the quickest. We will make our arrangements in regard to this matter at some later date.

I have a letter of Jennie's before me which [I] received the other day.

---

6 Oakland, Maryland is a small town located in western Maryland's Garrett County. It was in the vicinity of the Matthews's former home prior to the Civil War, so they undoubtedly had friends there.

It had been a long time since I heard from her, and had about made up my mind she had again tired of the correspondence. Be this as it may I should never have written the second letter to inquire why the former one had not been answered as I did some time ago, but I accept the excuse she makes, or at least she says my letter to her was received and also answered. And the way she found out her letter had not reached me was through some member of the family telling her I had not received an answer to my last letter to her.

You were surely very fortunate my dear Sister to receive so many Christmas presents. See how unequal the sweets of this life are distributed[?] One receives it all and the other nothing. For my part I had nothing to give. And imagine every person in this God forsaken Country was in a like predicament, for I received nothing. But I suppose those who give not, receive not. And I unfortunately am one of those fellows. Never mind, Xmas '75 will be different, for if [I] should not get anything then [I] would have the pleasure of looking at what some more fortunate one received. I was very sorry that [I] could not send you all something for a Christmas present but as it is you must accept the will for the deed.

Many thanks my dear Sister for your corrections of bad Grammar. Must try to do better, and in fact do try, but it seems without success. You must put up with some mistakes for as you know my schooling did not amount to much (all my own fault however). And what little I do know has been learnt from you at home and some of my associates. I do not offer this my dear Sister to exonerate myself of any Grammatical errors, and will promise to do the best I can in the future.

I was very glad to meet an old friend of mine the other day, one who use to be my <u>bunky</u> when we were recruits. I remember writing to you from Angel Island, California, and speaking of him. I use to read my letters to him and he always seemed interested. And almost the first word he said to me on shaking hands was (how is your Sister, the one who use to write you those nice letters) and on being told you were all well and especially my big sister he seemed to feel greatly relieved. He is one of a detachment from G Co. sent here to learn signaling. He was down to see me tonight and on leaving told me I should remember him to you. And in reply to this please make some mention of him, for I know he will greatly appreciate a kind word from you. His name is

"Pendergrass" (no doubt you will say it is not very aristocratic) but what's in a name[?][7]

Our new Captain has assumed Command of the Company, and I can't say I like him, although [I] have no reason to dislike him. He has treated me well enough so far. I think he is inclined to be a little more Military than Capt. Hobart was, but this is no fault. Will know more about him after while.

Well I am tired and fear [I] will have to wait until tomorrow before answering the other letters. Excuse and correct mistakes. And write often to me.

Only Seven months and seven days from tomorrow morning.

Fort Union, New Mexico
FEBRUARY 4, 1874

Have this moment received a letter from Father and Ida, both mailed from home January 27th and both at hand same time. Have finished reading them, feel happy and will reply at once.

I imagine our winter has just set in this morning. When [I] came out of my room [I] found about six inches of snow on the ground and more still falling. Suppose it is now about eight inches deep and still coming. If only [I] had a sleigh and a pretty Girl [I] might have some elegant fun, but unfortunately have neither.

I saw a letter yesterday from my friend Bradbury who is in the War Dept. as Clerk, and he says there is strong talk of reducing the Clerical force in the Dept.[8] And if they commence to reduce now, my prospects

---

7 On January 17, 1874, Private William Pendergast of Company G was detailed on detached service to Fort Union to attend "signal school." He remained there until April 22, when he returned to duty with his unit. See Eighth Cavalry Returns, January and April 1874. The ROE does not list Pendergast.

8 Sanford Bradbury was a veteran soldier who served through the Civil War, first with the Twenty-Seventh New York Volunteer Infantry (1861–1863) and afterward with the First New York Cavalry, from which he was mustered out as a first sergeant in July of 1865. His record indicates that he was a second lieutenant in the regulars for a few months in 1866, but the circumstances are not clear. However, Bradbury enlisted again on November 1, 1866, at Washington, D.C., and was assigned to Company L, Eighth Cavalry, in which he rose to the rank of first sergeant. Bradbury was cited for "conspicuous gallantry in action" in a fight with Apaches at Hell Canyon, Arizona on July 3, 1869, and was awarded the Medal of Honor. On July 11, 1872, nine months after he was discharged from his first enlistment, Bradbury enlisted again at the age of thirty-two and was assigned as a General Service clerk in the Adjutant General's Office. After serving in that capacity for two years, he secured an early discharge through the secretary of war to take a civilian position as a clerk in the same office.

I fear will be but poor. Poor or not will make but little difference to me, for to tell you the truth I am getting tired of Office work.

Have not been feeling as well as usual for the past week or two and attribute it all to confinement. Another thing is the weakening of my eye sight. At times when I have been working on Clothing Rolls, Quarterly Returns or anything of that kind, the paper would disappear from my sight altogether. And very often I have to take a Ruler and put it along a column of figures before I can run them up. And to look at my eyes you would imagine they were as strong as any persons. Taking every thing into consideration I am of the opinion that out door work would be better for my health, but there is time enough to decide on what can, and will be best to go at when [I] return to W[estminster].

Ida has declined my proposition to visit W. in company with me. Say's she thinks it best not to come with me, although it would give her pleasure to do so. Say's she wants you home folks to have me awhile all alone. And then soon as the first act is over, she will put in her appearance. I am perfectly satisfied with the arrangements although it would be very pleasant to have her with us.

You will soon be through with your descriptive letters. I am looking forward with great interest for your next letter. As I suppose it will carry you home. And I want you to give me a full description of house, store and of yourselves, for you are perfectly acquainted with this family, and can describe them minutely. I will be very sorry when your letters are finished on this subject for they have been both interesting and pleasant.

Seven Months and three days from Guard Mount (9 o'clock this morning). I think of you loved ones and of the day we shall meet again, from morning until night. And before closing my eyes to sleep [I] ask our Heavenly Father to watch over and protect you all. How eagerly I glance through your letters until I find that you are "all well." And then I go back to the beginning of the letter and read it carefully through, then carry it around in my pocket four or five days reading it over most every day. Then they are put away in my box where they remain until

---

See entry 1267, p. 107, roll 31, ROE, RG 94, NA; and entry 605, p. 92, roll 38, ibid. Contained within the Register of Post Quartermaster Sergeants is a section giving the service records of General Service soldiers. See ROE, Ancestry.com; and *Decorations*, 10.

they number twenty five or thirty, [I] take them out and read over carefully and then consign them to the flames. This is not done without a feeling of pain, but I cannot very well preserve them, but I have many times regretted that I ever destroyed one of your letters. Had I preserved them all until my time was out it would have been like destroying myself to have destroyed them all together.

Well my darling ones, it will not be so very long until we can dispense with pen, ink and paper for conveying our thought and wishes.

A sleigh without bells has this moment passed my window, in which were three or four Officers. This is the first one [I] have seen this winter.

Am feeling much better today. Weighed myself yesterday 138 1/2, not very heavy weight.

Fort Union, New Mexico
FEBRUARY 8, 1874

Sunday Morning 10 1/2 o'clock, and your correspondent has from this very moment just one hour and a half less than seven months to serve Uncle Sam. It is not that I have any great amount of news to write you that I am seated at my desk this beautiful Sabbath morning, but more in accordance with an established rule and custom, and also because it is a pleasure for me to do so. I rather expected to hear from you this morning, but was not very much disappointed when [I] found there was nothing for me.

Quite a strange and fortunate accident happened about one mile from here last week. Doctor Moffatt, Post Surgeon, left the Post during the day to attend a patient living in the country a few miles from the Post. On his return in the evening and when within a mile of the Post his horse slipped on the ice and fell, falling upon the Doctor's leg and breaking it below the Knee. The Dr. was unable to get up and try to catch his horse although the horse remained near him. And there the Dr. and horse remained until about 10 o'clock the next morning. The night was bitter cold and the ground covered with six inches of snow. How the Doctor lived through that night suffering with a broken leg is a wonder to every person. Next morning a Mexican happened to come along and seeing the Doctor hurried in to the Garrison and reported the circumstance. An ambulance was sent out at once and brought the Dr. in.[9]

He is doing well now, and in giving his account of the accident states that the horse (which by the way is a race horse, and also very spirited) remained close to him all night. That he (the Dr.) tried to crawl up to the horse for the purpose of tying his handkerchief to his tail and then to try and drive he horse away from him in hopes he would return to the post and assistance be sent out. This failed, and the Doctor next commenced making snow balls and threw them at his horse to make him leave, but the animal was too faithful and would only run around him, and could not be induced to leave his Master alone. I commenced this narrative by stating that it was a strange and "fortunate" accident. The fortunate part of it is that the Doctor lived through such a bitter cold night suffering as he surely must.

I don't suppose the Doctor would dispose of that horse now for any amount of money. I know I would not if I had been in the Doctor's place. It is true that the horse was partly the cause of the accident, and after it happened failed to render his master any assistance, but what I claim for the horse is that he was as true and faithful as it was possible for a dumb creature to be, and although his faithfulness might have been the death of his master he is nevertheless entitled to all praise.

Dinner is ready, and I am also ready for it. I am quite well again, and truly hope this may find you all well also.

Fort Union, New Mexico
FEBRUARY 15, 1874

"Sunday afternoon." Have received no letter from home since the early part of the week. The greater part of which was Arthurs letter in telegraph. I will answer it in the same style soon as have finished this. I see by his "alphabet" I made some mistakes in my letter to him.

---

9 Dr. Peter Moffatt, a native Canadian, migrated to California, where he secured an appointment as an army surgeon on October 9, 1867. He died in service on June 15, 1882. See Heitman, *Historical Register*, vol. 1, 718. Dr. Moffatt suffered fractures of both the tibia and fibula as a result of this accident. Fortunately, Fort Union's large hospital also supported an acting assistant surgeon (contracted civilian), Dr. C. M. Clark, who treated Moffatt by applying a plaster splint to his leg. See MH, Fort Union, NM, February 1874, RG 94, NA.

An Order from Post Head Quarters just came in to detail two Non Commissioned Officers and ten privates from our Company to go to Fort Bascom, and relieve the party now stationed there. I expect we will all have to go to Bascom again this Summer, but in case we do I will have the blessed consolation of knowing it will be my last Summer at Bascom or in fact any place else in the Army.

Six months and twenty six days yet. I have been scratching my head for the last ten minutes trying to scratch an idea out but it is no go.

Will surely hear from you tomorrow morning and will write again in answer.

Excuse short letter and write to me often.

Fort Union, New Mexico
FEBRUARY 16, 1874

Oh, what a happy morning this is for me. I feel so light hearted and joyful that [I] can scarcely sit still long enough to put my feelings on paper for your mutual benefit.

I had about an hours work to do this morning in making out Ration and Tobacco Returns for the party which leaves our Company for Fort Bascom tomorrow morning. And all the time was doing this work was figeting about in my chair all impatience for the mail to come over, finally it came; and out of the four letters for Battery L, three were for Eddie Matthews.[10] No doubt you have all seen the picture of the man who had inhaled "Laughing Gass." Well I can just inform you his laughing countenance was not a circumstance to mine.[11]

Out of these three letters one was directed by Lizzie, one by Father and the third by Capt. Byers. Home letters always take precedence, and so Lizzies letter was opened first and in it [I] found quite a nice letter from herself, one from Miss Mary Shellman. Which by the way was very nice and shall be answered by return mail, and a nice little letter from my little Brother Arthur, with a complimentary ticket to your school exhibition for

---

10 Matthews was being facetious in referring to his company as a battery. He well knew that that term was reserved for the artillery branch, particularly light, or mounted, batteries.
11 The discovery of nitrous oxide dated to the eighteenth century, but it came into widespread use as a local anesthetic, mainly in the field of dentistry, only around the time of the Civil War. It was commonly known as "laughing gas" for the euphoric effect it had on those to whom it was administered.

myself and Cat. Accept my sincere thanks for your kind consideration: "Love me; Love my Cat." Owing to the inclemency of the weather Tom and I were unable to venture out. Nevertheless our united thanks are tendered you for the "Complimentaries," but I am digressing.

Lizzie's letter was carefully read and in its perusal I experienced a pleasant feeling hard indeed to describe. Oh my kind and loving Sister, you are a noble Girl. And the sacrifice of your own happiness for a period, in order to promote that of our ever kind, loving and devoted parents, will never be a cause of regret to you. And when the day comes in which you are made a happy bride, your happiness will only be the greater for having for a time sacrificed your own in order to promote others. And I love you more (if such a thing be possible) this morning my darling Sister, for making me your confident in this affair, than I ever did before. I hope the day may never come when you will feel a regret for having confided in your Brother.

My darling Sister I fear you are inclined to flatter me in your praise of my writing. You write a far better hand than I do, and still you speak of being ashamed of your writing in comparison with mine, and if I could only write as well as you <u>do</u> and <u>can</u>, I should never make any excuses. I have corresponded with a number of young Ladies, and out of the number only one, "Lec," could write any way near as good as you do Lec is a beautiful writer, every letter is as plain as print.

If it is not too much trouble I would like very much to have a couple [of] Calico shirts. I have been wearing the two sent me while at Summer Camp ever since their arrival. And they are still very good, but my Laundress is not the best hand in the world to do up shirts. If you can make these low in the neck (I mean in front) I wish you would do so. And also please send me Collars to match. I had a couple of Calico shirts at Summer Camp last Summer and found them very comfortable during the excessive hot weather. I wear a 14 1/2 inch Collar.

We had a little snow storm last night and a little rain this morning, but both have almost disappeared now. The soil in this Country is so sandy that snow or rain is soon absorbed.

I wrote you a short letter yesterday. Had then six months and twenty six days to serve the U.S., but this morning [I] have not quite that long.

Will stop writing for today. Once more accept the heartfelt thanks of your boy, and brother for the pleasure given him this morning.

I will answer Miss Mary's letter this evening.

Fort Union, New Mexico
FEBRUARY 22, 1874

"Sunday night 10 o'clock," and your disappointed Son and Brother is seated at his table in his little room for the purpose of writing you a few lines.

Guess you think my life is made up with pleasures and disappointments and that I change as the case may be.

Have not heard from you since last Monday. Answered at once in the most cheerful style, and here I am tonight pouting because [I] have had no letters from you for six days. But some how I felt so sure of hearing from you this morning that when the 1st Sergeant returned from the Adjutants Office and said the mail would not be in until 4 o'clock this evening, I would not believe him. Got up and went down to the post Office and asked the Telegraph operator who told me the same thing. Was restless all day, and at four o'clock was at the Adjutants Office, where [I] found one letter for me from Lec, but nothing from home.

I almost forgot to tell you the handkerchiefs arrived safely two days ago. They are very nice indeed. Please accept my sincere thanks for them. They will last me the balance of my time in Uncle Sams Service.

We have had a very severe snow storm this last two days. And I am afraid [we] will have more of it. In case we do, you can attribute the non-receipt of letters from me to this, as it is likely to delay the mails. Guess we will pay up for the fine winter [we] have had all along before [we] get through yet.

Only Six Months and thirteen days to serve the U.S.

We have to commence on the Company Muster and Pay Rolls on the 24th inst. Will have seven days steady work, four on the M. and P. Rolls and three on other Company work.

Will have three more sets of Rolls to make out for the Company after these. Am commencing to build up hopes of getting the eight odd days of my time now. Believe the Captain will give it to me, [I] like him better than [I] did at first. He has no suggestions to give me about the Company papers. Lets me make them out alone, and signs anything I place before him. Guess he would sign a blank sheet of blotting paper if I placed it before him and said it was all O.K.

I have just cause to feel proud of my Office work so far as accuracy is concerned for in all the work [I] have done in different Offices [I] have only had <u>one</u> paper returned for correction. And that was a "Statement of Charges," and in it I had short charged a few Articles of Ordinance [ordnance].[12] Even this was no mistake of mine for at that time a new price List of Ordinance had just been issued, which we had not then received. And I charged the Articles at the old price. I am vain enough to believe that there is not another Clerk in the whole service who has done the same amount of work I have that can show as clean papers in this connection. And this is the most particular part of the work.

The books and papers in our Office are full of corrections made by Harlan and other Clerks before him, but not a single one is to be found since I have had charge of them. This speaks pretty well don't you think so[?] And unless I forget it when my time is out, [I] will have papers from my Company Commander to substantiate what I have said in this, just to show you, if for nothing else.

You may think this most too much self praise, but I don't think I should hesitate in writing you what is actually the fact.

I am going to stop writing now and go to bed, to dream of expected letters from you Loved Ones, on the morrow, and if I should fail to hear from you, you can expect to be burdened with another of these letters.

Fort Union, New Mexico
MONDAY EVENING, FEBRUARY 23, 1874

I have made up my mind to burden you with a letter daily until [I] hear from you. Last night this punishment commenced, and as todays Mail only brought me a paper, you find me once more with the weapon of punishment in my hand prepaired to inflict the full penalty of the Law.

Was again disappointed this morning by not hearing from you, and to make matters worse [I] had only a cup of tea and slice of bread for my

---

12 A statement of charges was drawn up prior to a soldier's court-martial. In it were listed the charges and specific allegations, as well as a list of any government property he had stolen or destroyed in committing the alleged acts.

breakfast, as the meat had all been issued out. Could have put up with this very well had it been the first time it happened, but only the morning before it was the same thing. I happened to hear the Acting Q. M. Sergeant give the Cook orders to get fifty five pounds of Beef for the days rations. And Knowing that fifty nine men eat at the Company Tables, it was not surprising that some of the men should go without meat. My American English blood was up at once and I told the 1st Sergeant that I wanted to make a report to the Captain in regard to the messing of the Company. And that I wanted him to go with me to see that I only stated facts. The Sergeant said it was not necessary for him to go with me, but for me to [go] and make my report.

So off I started, and when in the Captains presence [I] stated that I had the 1st Sergeants permission to make a report to him in regard to the messing of the Company, and asked if he would listen to it. He answered certainly. I told him in these exact words, that yesterday morning I had but little meat for my breakfast, not enough for any man, and that this morning [I] had none at all, that fifty nine men messed in the Company, and that only fifty five pounds of Meat was drawn for them, which would be 1/4 lb. less than twenty pounds short rations, that when the meat was brought to the Company Kitchen the Non Commissioned Officers in charge had the choice part of it cut off and wasted in bulk and put on the Non Com's table. That the bread for the Non Comd. Officers was cut up in slices and put on their table, and when they had eaten it they could call for more and get it, while for the rest of the men it was cut up in rations put on their table in front of them and in case they wanted more, it would only be want, for they could not get it. Told him I knew I was not an unusual big eater, but had frequently gone away from the table hungrey, and that I knew when I went away hungrey there were many more in a like predicament.

The Captain told me he would attend to this matter at once, and came over to the Orderly Room with me, made the Acting Q.M. Sergeant get his beef book and after examining it and asking a few questions told the Sergeant hereafter he wanted him to have bread cut up in slices for the men and that they should have Corn bread three times each week in addition to all the wheat bread they could eat, that he (the Sergeant) should go [to] the butcher shop each morning, get every pound of meat the men were entitled to, see it weighed and then see that the men got it after it came to the Kitchen.[13]

This is the first time during my service that I made a report of the kind. And would not have made this one, only the living was getting too bad. And as my time was getting short [I] did not want to die of starvation at this stage of the game. The men of the Company have been praising me all day for making such a change in their living. And say had any other man in the Company made the same report [he] very likely he would have been put in the "Guard House" and no change made after all. My room mate the identical Q.M. Sergeant has taken it all in very good grace, although I was the cause of him getting stired up a little by the Captain. I know exactly the duties of a Q.M. Sergeant, and also how a Company can live if their rations are properly managed. And I will not quietly submit to the bread which rightfully belongs to me being taken out of my mouth.

We are to have a "lecture" at our "Good Templars Hall" tomorrow evening. The Lecture[r] being the Assistant Surgeon of the Post.

Can't I prevail on my dear Father, to give me his ideas of Temperance in writing in the form of an address, so that I can study it up, add my own ideas to it and deliver the whole thing ("original"), as Father is such an elegant hand at anything of this kind and I know he can do it with but little trouble, while I find any such thing very difficult and almost impossible unless I borrow (mind you only borrow), other peoples ideas. Don't mean to say [I] would borrow the whole subject and then spout it out as though such things were as easy for me to do as rolling off a log. Will expect something from you in reply my dear Father on the subject.

Lots of snow on the ground, and more falling.

Will commence the Company Muster and Pay Roll's tomorrow or the day after.

Another day less to stay away from home than [I] had yesterday.

---

13 Eddie's complaint about short rations was valid. The daily army ration called for each man to receive one and one-quarter pounds of salt or fresh beef, or twelve ounces of bacon. Accordingly, the company should have drawn seventy-three and three-quarters pounds of beef for fifty-nine men, rather than fifty-five pounds. Each man was also apportioned twenty-two ounces of soft bread or flour, or twenty ounces of corn meal. Most companies drew the flour ration in bulk, knowing that a surplus would result. The excess flour could either be baked into additional loaves for the company, as in this instance when the captain insisted that the men be given all the bread they wanted, or the flour could be sold or bartered to local civilians. See *Revised Regulations*, 244.

"Six Months and twelve days. It is quite late and besides I have nothing else to write about.

Fort Union, New Mexico
FEBRUARY 24, 1874

Have this moment finished a letter to Ida, which was in answer to one received from her this morning, and although it is quite late my head shall not press my pillow (made of wool) or my eyes close in slumber until I have informed you that no letter has been received from you today. And once more your big Son and Brother has drank from the cup of disappointment. Something must be wrong. And I know it cannot be through delays of the Mails for Ida's letter came through in seven day's.

What ever the trouble may be it shall not keep me from writing to you daily until an answer is received. Wrote to you Sunday night, last night and am at it again.

The Monotony of Garrison life was disturbed a little by the Lecture delivered by Dr. Clark, Acting Post Surgeon, this evening. Subject "A trip to the Moon." The Hall was crowded, and every person anticipated a Comic Lecture, for the subject would naturally impress one as being if not Comic (rather flighty).[14]

Finally the Lecturer arose with a pile of Manuscript before him which looked like he intended business, but alas for great expectations, for a sillier discourse I never listened too. Neither sense or nonsense could be heard. Nothing but the foolish ideas of an idiot who's small brain was destroyed altogether from the influence of liquor. After listening to this lunatic for an hour we returned to our homes feeling something like I suppose a dog would that had been caught in the act of sheep stealing. We were badly sold. In case the Dr. should deliver another lecture I will assure him plenty of [seating?] as the attendance would be very slim.

There is about 10 inches of snow on the ground, and prospects for still more, I thought we were having most too fine a winter for this country, and knew there must be some mistake.

---

14 Dr. C. M. Clark was ranked as an acting assistant surgeon, i.e., a civilian physician contracted by the army to provide medical services to the troops. Acting assistant surgeons were first authorized during the Civil War to accommodate the larger wartime forces. They were paid $125.00 per month and granted certain allowances. See *Revised Regulations*, 518.

Will commence on my Rolls tomorrow, and a hard job [I] will have I know. Guess though [I] will get through with it.

I don't know how I am going to fill this sheet of paper. Unless I tell you [I] have only six months, ten days and about nine hours (it may be a few seconds more) to serve the U.S.

Now if I don't get a letter from you tomorrow, you can expect to hear from me in genuine earnest tomorrow night.

Fort Union, New Mexico
FEBRUARY 25, 1874

Another disappointment, what in the world is the reason I do not hear from you[?] Are any of you sick, and you want to keep me ignorant of it[?] Or what can possible be the matter[?]

This morning got my Pay Rolls out and undertook to commence them, but was so anxious and felt sure [I] would receive a letter from you soon as the mail came over that [I] could not think of anything else, so [I] told the Sergeant there was no use in me trying to write until the mail came over. Finally it came and when [I] found there was nothing for me [I] could have sit down and cried. I did not know what to think. After spending half hour over my trouble commenced work on the rolls and at Retreat this evening had one nearly finished, but how in the world I done it [I] am not able to say for [I] am positive [I] never wrote a line without thinking of you. Could not drive you out of my mind. Expect [I] will find a lot of mistakes when [I] compare my roll. It will be very strange if [I] do not.

You need not expect anything cheerful from me until I get a letter from you. Would not write this if it was not to make my word good. When [I] said I would write to you every day until [I] got a letter from you, [I] had no idea [I] would be obliged to write this often. And now if such a thing be possible that I do not hear from you tomorrow you will hear from me in earnest for this suspense is terrible. Still one day less to remain away from you.

Hoping my next letter will contain something more pleasant and that my expectations will be gratified on the morrow.

Fort Union, New Mexico
FEBRUARY 26, 1874

Will I ever hear from you again[?] Or do you think because I have only six months and nine days to serve that it is not worth while writing for that short time[?] I have never felt as much disappointed since [I] have been away from home and can't for the life of me imagine why I do not hear from you. Sunday morning I felt pretty sure [I] would get a letter but as none came [I] consoled myself with the thought that [I] would get one Monday but Monday's mail failed to bring me a letter, [I] was truly disappointed. Would almost have bet my existence that [I] would hear from you Tuesday, but as I feel that your letters are too sacred to gamble on did not bet, if [I] had [I] would have lost. There is no use talking, I felt miserable. Wednesdays mail brought me nothing, and I felt miserable. And as I drew a blank in Thursdays (todays mail) I felt and still feel wretched. Have been sitting at my desk working hard all day and trying to drive you and my disappointment out of my mind but every line seemed to have a thousand thoughts of you. If I only knew that you were all well I would feel easier, but this uncertainty is terrible. I have suffered more this week than [I] have during the balance of my life all put together.

Little did I imagine when [I] said Sunday night that [I] would write to you every day until [I] did hear. And will keep my promise if only [to?] say "No letter yet."

The weather still continues cold, and plenty of snow on the ground. Capt. Morris told me today that he did not think we would leave the Territory this year. And would only make short Scouts from this post during the summer, but I guess he knows little more about what we will do than I do.

I see that the Bill for the reduction of the Army has passed the House, and will no doubt become an Act. In that case I believe our Regiment will be consolidated with the 7th Cavalry and I might get out before the expiration of my term.[15]

---

15 The acts of June 16 and 23, 1874, further reduced the size of the army from thirty thousand enlisted men to twenty-five thousand, plus the officer corps in proportion. It was truly the army's "dark age." Recruits were not only hard to come by, but were of generally low quality. Matthews was wrong in his supposition that regiments would be consolidated as they had been in 1869. Rather, the strength of companies was reduced by attrition. See Heitman, *Historical Register*, vol. 2, 611–13; and Ganoe, *History of the Army*, 334.

Fort Union, New Mexico
FRIDAY NIGHT, FEBRUARY 27, 1874

"No Letter yet." Can't say that [I] am disappointed, for [I] am use to that feeling, and suppose [I] might get hardened after while so that [I] would not care whether I had a friend in the world or not. God forbid that I should ever feel this way. Imagined when [I] sit down to comply with my promise made Sunday night, that [I] would just say have not heard from you yet, but could not end with saying that hardly, if my life depended on it. Tonight I love you all with my whole heart and nothing can change that love. It seems almost as though this love has grown more intense by the many disappointments I have experienced this week.

My one thought has been of you and you alone. No matter what I tried you were foremost in my mind.

Write to me for God's sake and set my mind easy. If I knew you were all well [I] would be satisfied.

Fort Union, New Mexico
FEBRUARY 28, 1874

Have just returned from "Degree Meeting" at Good Templars Hall. Have taken a dose of salts; and am now going to write a few lines to you.

I have not yet heard from you as the mail from the East will not be in until 4 A.M. tomorrow. The roads are reported as being in very bad condition. The stage for the last few days being drawn by six mules, whereas when the roads are good only four are required. But with all the bad weather and bad roads we have had a daily mail until today, so I cannot attribute your long silence to delays of the mails.

Received two letters from Balto. [Baltimore] during the week both coming through in seven days.

This will make the eighth letter, or attempts at letters since [I] have heard from you.

I have only six months and eight days more to serve. Guess I might as well say six months, for [I] do not think there will be any doubt but that the Captain will give me eight days.

It seems to be the general opinion here that we will not go to a summer Camp, this year, but will go on short scouts from this Post. I wish it would turn out to be this, as in this way my six months would soon pass away. And now you can rest assured that in the future I shall never go so far away or remain long enough absent to require a letter. Will be sure In this case not to be disappointed.

Have only two of my Muster Rolls done. Have ninety three names on the Roll and out of this number seventy three have long remarks attached to them. Some filling four lines. I never saw such heavy rolls since [I] have been in the Army.

If I do not hear from you tomorrow morning I don't know what I shall do, something desperate I fear.

Fort Union, New Mexico
MARCH 2, 1874

No letter from you yet. And last night I was compelled to break my word about writing to you every night until I did hear from you.

The mail this moment from the East for the Company has come in and as usual am sadly disappointed. And I feel now that I do not care whether I ever get another letter while [I] am in the Army, for if this should be the case I could not feel worse than I do now. My heart is too full to write more. A Love to you all which can never grow less, no matter what may occur. And a Kiss to you, is all I can say.

Fort Union, New Mexico
MARCH 2, 1874

I have only this moment returned to my "room" from "Good Templars" Meeting. Imagine [I] have been benefitted by the meeting. As [I] am feeling far different than did this morning. If in my letter to you Loved Ones this morning I said anything displeasing to you, or which has wounded your feelings, <u>forgive me for it</u>. For I was so sadly disappointed and have been for the last week that I scarcely know what I have done. I know tonight that you have not neglected writing to me, and that your letters must have been lost or delayed.

I was thinking when [I] dated this that the 6th inst. would be Mother and Lizzies birthdays and dated this the 8th.

I know how old Lizzie will be, but not my darling Mothers age. It will not be so very long until my twenty fourth birthday. Better look out Lizzie, I am only two years behind you.

I have completed my Muster Rolls. The Captain asked me yesterday if I could have them done by today. Only had two done then, but told him [I] could do it. Worked from 1 o'clock yesterday until 11 o'clock last night and had at that time made one roll and entered all the names on another (my fourth). This morning [I] finished it, and compaired them, and the only mistakes found was "one cent" not charged on three of the rolls. Pretty close shaving for correctness wasn't it[?]

It is getting quite late and I know of nothing of Interest to write you. I will surely hear from you in the morning, but in case I should not, no word of reproach shall be uttered, for I feel satisfied that everything will be explained when I do get a letter.

Forgive me I pray for anything I have said.

Fort Union, New Mexico
TUESDAY EVENING, MARCH 3, 1874

"Peace on Earth; Good Will to all mankind." I have heard from you; know you are all well and am as gloriously happy tonight as it is possible for one to be who had not heard from the kindest of Father's, Lovingest of Mother's and most devoted Sister's and Brother's for sixteen days. Two long and most welcome letters from you received this morning. One was dated February 15th and the other the 22nd, but both Post marked February 23rd. So your letter of the 15th must have either been detained at home or else neglected in the Post Office. If I knew the latter was the case would write Mr. Postmaster a letter "from homes" and one he would not appreciate very much. Hereafter I will not be so sanguine of hearing from you at regular intervals—will always expect letters from you, but will not allow myself to be so sadly disappointed in case none come for a week.

You will know exactly how I felt and I know [you] will sympathize with me, and will also say I have acted foolish by allowing myself to be carried away in this manner. But all I now ask is that you write and say I am forgiven for all that I have said displeasing to you, in my letters during the past week, and that you will write to me often in the future.

I like long letters to be sure, but rather than wait so long [I] would have you write, if you could only say you are all well.

I hardly know what to think of the doings of the <u>good people</u> of Westminster. They have surely changed for the worse since I left home, or else they are only now being found out—and shown up in their true light.

In the case of Mr. Woods, [I] imagine the subject most too delicate to express myself. Man is (as Father says) weak—and women are weaker, and both together are <u>weakest</u>. I am sorry indeed to hear of so much of this frailty.

So my heavy weight does not frighten you it seems, [I] imagine [I] will have to keep a very civil tongue when [I] come home for fear [I] might rile that big brother blood of mine, and in the game that would probable ensue, your Quartermaster (and light weight) would come out second best.

My occupation is not calculated to very largely develope my muscles, while this big brother of mine is getting himself in elegant trim to insure of my walking in the way of the righteous on my return.

Now I have never said anything to you Johnnie to get you hostile. And if I ever done anything to you in days long since past (when I was not afraid of you), I am willing to be forgiven.

How are Arthur and Clellie on the mus[c]le, perhaps you think I am afraid of them too, but I am not, unless they each weigh over 138 lbs. And as for this "one hundred and seventy two pounds," all I have got to say is when I come home—if he says saw wood; "I'll saw." And if while I am resting after sawing wood, he should say dig potatoes, I'll dig. In fact I will be willing to make myself generally useful and scarce if necessary, but if I catch any sick or lame people shooting off their mouth, I'll make it rather uncomfortable for them.

I imagine you try to impress upon my memory that a "certain family" are <u>consumptive</u>, this may be only imagination of mine, but if it is not, and you have reasons for doing so, I can easily set you at rest, "as [I] have no serious intentions in that quarter," and in fact but little in any other. Guess my matrimonial ideas were nipped in the bud, in the early part of my summer. And my inclinations in that direction since have not been very great.

If I were you folks I would scald the first butcher that stuck his head in the house and hollowed "Veal," for you have sufficient proof that Veal is not good for you. But if you were compelled to eat as much tuff beef as we soldiers boys, beef that has crossed the plains so often that they have grown old in the service, and too old to draw a "prairie schooner" any longer, you would relish a bit of veal, or in fact anything else that would assist your digestive organs. Salts for instance.

Compaired my "Muster Rolls" this evening at the Commanding Officers Office, and had a very flattering compliment paid me. General Alexander (Commanding Officer) told me in the presence of my Company Commander, that my rolls were <u>handsome</u> and could not possible be neater. Very good of him I think.

Fort Union, New Mexico
MARCH 10, 1874

I have not written to you for a week, or have I received any letters from you during that time. Intended writing to you the 8th inst. (Mothers and Lizzies birthday), but had so much work to do, that [I] was too tired to write a letter. In fact here of late [I] have been doing work for three Officers, and have been obliged to work pretty hard.

Have now started into my last six months in the Army. And into my last six months of absence from you loved ones. Feel elegant tonight with the exception of being a little tired after a days hard writing. There is little, if any news to write you. The snow has disappeared and we are having some fine weather.

Weighed myself the other day and pulled the beam down at 143 1/2, quite an improvement. The prospects for a change of stations during my service are I think rather meager. And I suppose I will be discharged at this post. It seems to be settled that the troops here will make short scouts during the summer from this post, instead of going to a Summer Camp. This will suit me very well. For [I] am fixed up real comfortable, and can put in five months and twenty seven days very easily with the thought of soon meeting you loved ones. Oh happy days, how patiently [I] am waiting for your dawn. To be with you all, and know your thoughts, wishes and desires is to be happy.

Will expect a letter from you in tomorrows mail. And will write again soon.

Fort Union, New Mexico
SUNDAY NIGHT, MARCH 13, 1874

Wanted to write to you several times during the week, but put it off from day to day in hopes of hearing of something interesting to write about. Have heard of nothing, and cannot delay writing longer. We are having regular March weather here now. So windy at times that it is almost impossible to keep on one's feet. In fact it blows a perfect hurricane all the time. Every now and then you are struck on the back of the head with a stone about the size of your fist. One naturally looks around to see who threw the brick and finds that Mr. Wind done it.

I have a miserable cold in my head. Have blown my nose so much that it is now so sore [I] can hardly touch it.

We Good Templars are going to have a cold water dance at our Hall on the 17th of Ireland.[16] Guess it will be my last dance in the Army. Time is passing happily away. Only 5 months and twenty three days.

I think it is pretty certain we will remain here during the summer. Only going out on a few days scout at a time. And I hardly think I will have to leave at all until I leave for home. So your boy will not be exposed to much danger during the last five months of his time.

You folks seem to weigh pretty heavy, but you are not tall enough. Was this moment measured and stand 5 feet 9 inches, with boots on. And weigh 143 1/2 lbs.

Have received no letter from you for a week, but suppose [I] will get one tomorrow. Will write again as soon as [I] hear from you. Excuse shortness for can think of nothing to write to you this time.

Fort Union, New Mexico
MARCH 21, 1874

Father's, Sue's, and Arthur's and Clellie's letters were welcomed by me yesterday.

---

16 Considering the large number of regulars who were either Irish-born immigrants, or were only a generation removed, it is not surprising that the rank and file of the army traditionally celebrated St. Patrick's Day with much drinking and merriment. On this occasion, however, the Good Templars at Fort Union were hosting a "cold water" dance, meaning only nonalcoholic refreshments would be served.

Father's ridecule is pretty severe in regard to my uneasiness in not hearing from you, but [I] suppose he is right, and I am wrong. And now if you will let the subject rest, I will never refer to it again, but before I do this I must say a word to Sue, who has also been an accomplis with Father in shaming me. She opens on me by calling me a "silly goos[e]" and all such things as that. Now you just wait Miss Sue, until I come home and I'll attend to your case. You needn't think because you aspire to the position of a school marm, and that by a word or look you make the most ferocious inclin [?] in Lizzie's school succomb to your will, that you can do the same by me. I am not afraid of you, even if I am of Father and Johnnie. "You don't weigh enough."

My friend Bradbury, in the War Department, sent me the Speed on the Army Appropriation Bill made by Senator Albright, which strongly disapproved the reduction of the Army. But it seems the bill has passed. I am of the opinion that the reduction will be made by consolidation, the number of regiments will be reduced, but the same number of men will be kept. The strength of the Regular Army is not more than 25,000 total. And if a country like the United States cannot afford to keep a standing Army of that number, I think it had better sell out, and close up business. For my part I wish Congress would abolish the Army altogether, and disband it at once.

Only five months and eighteen days. And then for some of those spring chickens of Mothers. I will have a good appetite for spring chickens after eating salt pork and tough beef for five years.

Received a home paper today, it always comes regular.

Have heard nothing about going Scouting yet, and am in hopes of remaining here the balance of my time.

I have nothing in the shape of news to write you. You must excuse poor letters here of late (or rather for some time back) and take the will for the deed.

I suppose Jennie has put an end to our correspondence, as [I] have not heard from her for a long time. Imagine the fellow the Captain spoke of has supplanted me in the affections of the fair Jennie. Well such is life.

Fort Union, New Mexico

MARCH 24, 1874

Fathers good, and affectionate letter dated 15th inst. this moment received and read. Will try to answer it at once. Have a very bad cold and do not feel much like letter writing.

We are having the most changable weather I ever saw in this country. One day it rains, next it snows and next day is fine. Every person has colds, but as long as there is nothing worse, need not complain. To know that you are all well and doing well is happiness for me.

As each day of service and absence from home draws to a close I become more anxious in regard to the health and welfare of you loved ones. And when your letters reach me if you can only say "we are all well," I am happy.

It is true I love long letters from you, but know how hard it is at times to write them. We have not heard a word about going scouting, and may not leave this post during the summer.

General Alexander, Post Commander, received a telegram yesterday from St. Louis, that his Mother was dying and for him to come on at once. The Stage going East had only left the post about ten minutes before he received the telegram. An Ambulance was ordered out at once and in a few moments the General was off in pursuit of the Stage. And overtook it about ten miles from here.

I attended a little party at the Post Hospital last Saturday, given by the Steward and Lady. Had a very pleasant time, danced a little and had an elegant supper.

I will have to commence a set of Quarterly papers for my Captain in a few days, will only have one more set after these to make out. Sometimes I can hardly realize that my term of service will soon be ended, although it seems an age since I left home. Since I joined the Company, [I] have seen three different detachments of men discharged from it, by reason of expiration of terms of service. And to bid those men good bye, knowing they would soon be surrounded by their friends, while I was compelled to remain in this Country was the hardest of all for me to bear, but now comes my turn. And most every day some person will say, "how long now Ed[?]" When I say, "five months and a <u>but</u>," the answer is invariable, "Oh, how I wish my time was out as soon." I tell them to have patience, as I had the same time once to serve as they have now. I remember when Father, congratulated me for having only 57 months to serve. And [I] often laugh over it.

Only five months and six days, intended to correct short time hereafter, for [I] feel sure the Captain will give me the eight days.

Mother be very careful with the young chickens, for I am counting the days until the time when you and I can sit over our Cup of tea, and while leasurely picking a chicken bone talk of the past, present and make plans for the future. Oh no, that won't be a happy day for us (as the dutchman says) "don't it[?]"

Give us your ideas on temperance when ever you feel so inclined. No particular hurry.

Mary Shellman told me in her letter that Geo. Winters had asked to be remembered to me and said that he would meet me some place when I returned. Told her, it was not necessary for him to go to any trouble to meet me, as I was not particularly anxious to see him.

Somehow it is impossible for me to write you a readable letter any more. And besides not having a subject to write you, the writing is miserable.

Excuse everything and answer soon.

Fort Union, New Mexico
MONDAY NIGHT 10:30, MARCH 30, 1874

Intended writing to you yesterday but as [I] received no letter from you in the mail [I] concluded to wait until this morning, feeling sure [I] would hear from you. The mail came, but no letter from home for Ed. (Don't imagine I am disappointed, for am not.) I will hear from you in due time [I] feel sure. Could not delay any longer, although like always to have a letter to answer.

Returned to my room about an hour ago from "Good Templars" Meeting, since then have been chatting with one of the members who dropped in. Our Order is in a flourishing condition and increasing in number every meeting night. Initiated three new members tonight and received propositions for membership of two others.

A womans praying hand would, I think add greatly to the cause here, (provided they were <u>white</u>), as we have so few white ladies out here to see and talk to one. Is a pleasure few would deny themselves, when an opportunity afforded the happiness.

New Mexico would be the place for a "Female Suffragish" to hold forth. She would never be denied a building to Lecture in, and would always have a sympathizing audience, who would admire her for being a woman, if they did not advocate the cause.

The frontier is the best place in the world for Old Maids or <u>fat</u> women to migrate. They can always get a husband, and will always be admired by the rough frontiersman and boys belonging to Uncle Sams outfit, whether they are pretty or not. This beats all the places in the world for fat women. I have attended several Dances this winter, and the array of heavy weights of the female persuasion was astonishing. One might as well try to encircle a sugar hogshead with his arm, as to try to put his arm around one of their waists. I enjoy round dancing very much, and am never happier than when [I] have my arm around the <u>slender</u> waist of some pretty girl whirling around in a "Dutch Waltz," but out here where female loveliness consists of a "two ton weight" [I] am like the old gentleman at a fashionable Ball in the states, "content to sit with my arm around one of their waists," while others make themselves dizzy waltzing. If I had only stuck to this all through [I] would be happy tonight, for my arm is still sore from the strain on it at our last Ball, trying to hold up on her No. 14-teens, "two thousand weight of female loveliness." But this is enough of this or you will think this a heavy letter.

Have commenced making out my Quarterly Papers. And will only have one more set to make out after these. Five months and ten hours "short time."

No orders yet about a summer scout, and we may remain in Camp here all summer, but [I] am afraid this will be too good to be true. In case though the Companies only went on short scouts during the summer from this post, I will not have to go out. Assure you [I] am not anxious to go, for [I] have done all the scouting [I] have any desire to do.

We are having fine weather again, and hope our winter is over. I have a cold now, which is not as welcome as something good to eat would be, "spring chickens for instance."

I must try and answer Arthur's and Clellie's letters soon, but my delay in answering them at present need not keep them from writing again. Their letters, like all others from home, are like a ray of sunshine, and always gladdens the heart of your son and brother. Am never happier than when reading your letters. It is time to go to bed, so [I] will wish you good night and happy dreams.

Fort Union, New Mexico
MARCH 31, 1874

I finished one letter to you at about 11 o'clock last night, took it to the Post Office first thing this morning, and returned to my room with Fathers letter of March 23rd. So you see if I had waited until this morning [I] would have had a letter to answer.

If you have not heard from me regularily it is no fault of mine, for I have written you at regular intervals, still do so and will continue to do so as long as [I] am separated from you. The letter you speak of as being sent same time as Capt. B's, did not arrive with his, but came to hand a couple of days afterwards and was answered as all letters from you are. You worry me, to imagine that a letter from Capt. B, or any other friend could be of such interest to me as to make me think less of yours, so little in fact as to fail to speak of it. No indeed, my loved ones, no matter how good and interesting others letters may be, a line from you is always more welcome and treasured in the heart more. And if I should fail to express my happiness at hearing from you, it is no reason I do not feel it. Capt B. letter was elegant and the best letter of the Kind I ever read. And still it was not so good as to carry me away altogether and make me forget a letter from you.

You say all are home to Breakfast and supper. Not all, as there is one who left in '69 who did not carry his dinner with him. And as he has drawn no rations from the home Commissary during the five years, upon his return next September the A[ssistant] C[ommissary] G[eneral] can expect a ration return for all back rations. Will make out a special ration return for myself, and instead of the usual headings such as Bacon, hard bread etc., will insert others more suitable to my taste, such as "spring Chicken," fresh oysters, hot rolls, fresh butter, 1 wash tub full of Custard, plum pudding, brandy sauce, (a little weak so that it will not hurt a Good Templar) and then have a <u>table cloth</u> on the table and a clean Knife and fork to eat with. I imagine this would be a good deal of happiness.

The new preacher does not seem to be as popular as the Rev. Mr. Richassm, perhaps when you are better acquainted with him you will admire him more. I know I will enjoy a sermon when [I] return, for [I] have not attended divine service since August 1869, except on three funeral occasions when [I] heard the Episcopal burial service read and nothing more. The last church I attended was an Episcopal, in Cincinnati. Guess you will think I am pretty bad. Will try to make up for lost time when [I] return.

I will be very happy indeed to have a pair of shoes made by such a skillful workman as my honored Father must be from all accounts. And although my feet are not so handsome as you would make me believe, they are nevertheless very highly valued, and would not be disposed of, for [I] hardly think I could buy another pair that would answer the purpose so well.

I am very sorry to hear that Lizzie is suffering with Neuralgia, for [I] remember how she use to suffer when I was home. Father with the Earache, Mother with the headache, Lizzie with the Neuralgia, Eddie with the toothache, Sue with geathering in her ears, and Clellie with sore toe, what have we ever done that the Good Lord should inflict us with such punishment. I don't mean to say we are afflicted in this way now, for I have not the toothache, and Clellie has not a sore toe (that I know of), but I remember when we were thus afflicted, I have not had the toothache since the fall of 70, when we were stationed at Cimerron, N.M. Suffered four days and then had a tooth drawn by a drunken Doctor, who gave the balance of my teeth such a scare by the way he handled one of their number, that they have never had courage to ache since.

I am not impatient for the "temperance production." No particular hurry, will answer when ever you feel so inclined.

Can think of nothing interesting to write you, and imagine you will have some trouble to read what [I] have already written.

CHAPTER NINE

"When Eddie Comes Marching Home"

APRIL–AUGUST 1874

In the spring of 1874, a group of enterprising Dodge City merchants, aware that the buffalo hunting grounds were shifting southward as the number of animals steadily declined in Kansas, seized upon a bold plan to establish a trading post on the Canadian River, thereby staking an early claim both on the hide business and supplying the hunters. The place they chose was well known as Adobe Walls, site of the eroded remains of a trading post built some thirty-five years earlier by the well-known firm of Bent, St. Vrain and Company. The place had also been the scene of an 1864 engagement between Indians and a force of New Mexico Volunteers from Fort Bascom under the command of Colonel Kit Carson. Within a short time after the Dodge City traders arrived, the new Adobe Walls complex, consisting of two stores, a saloon, and a blacksmith shop, was well stocked and open for business.

The Indians, cognizant of the threat posed to their culture and very existence by the decimation of the buffalo, were incensed by this blatant invasion of what they considered to be their exclusive hunting domain. Incited to general war by an influential new medicine man, Comanche, Kiowa, and even some

Cheyenne war parties struck the whites—hunters, teamsters, surveying parties, and soldiers alike—wherever they encountered them over the region south of the Arkansas River. Particularly repugnant to the Indians were the buffalo hunters and their trading post at Adobe Walls, situated just 150 miles downstream from Fort Bascom, which would again be Eddie Matthews's summer home away from home.

Fort Union, New Mexico

SUNDAY NIGHT, APRIL 5, 1874

I have now returned to my room after spending an hour very pleasantly at one of our Laundresses quarters, and will before [I] retire answer Lizzies, and Clellies letters which [I] received yesterday. Was ever so glad to hear from you, and know that you were all well, but not all well, for a person suffering with neuralgia is far from well.

I will not complain of any neglect on your part my dear Sister, for writing to me so seldom, for I know your time is so much taken up and when you do have a spare moment to yourself you do not feel like letter writing but rest assured your letters are appreciated and read with pleasure. Blessed be the name of the good Lord, the time is nearing when we can dispense with letter writing. Won't it be nice when we can all sit together around the family board and have a general talk.

The letter of Fathers you speak of was received and answered so it must be my letter that is missing instead of his. You folks will never get me <u>mixed</u> up again and get the laugh on me for not hearing from you at regular dates, for [I] am never going to allow myself to be disappointed. If I hear from you [I] will be happy, and if [I] do not [I] will make myself happy with the prospects of hearing from you some time.

Wish I could have been home at Johnnies party. Remember the one we had at East End. And a real nice one it was. We will have another one next September, won't we? Guess my big Sister will look awful stylish in her new silk dress. Won't you be too proud to associate with an ex-soldier when I come home?

No news yet about our summers scout. General Alexander who has been East is expected here during the coming week, and then perhaps we will find out whether there is to be a scout or not. The weather is fearful windy, and every thing covered with sand. Can almost shovel it out of our room.

Received a letter from Jennie the other day, first one for a long time.

Enclosed find a note from a friend of mine who is Post Commisary Sergt. and to who I gave the Capt. letter to read.

I have finished making out my Quarterly papers, compaired them without finding a single mistake.

I can't think of a single thing to write you and am most ashamed to send this. Will write to the boys sometime during the week, and if [I] can scare up an idea will write to you.

Fort Union, New Mexico
APRIL 6, 1874

I have this moment returned from Good Templar Meeting and before I get under my Government Blankets, will write you "just a few lines."

Fathers "Roll of Company" for the week ending March 29th received this morning has been examined, found correct and placed on file. We have new forms now for rendering this Return, but as yours is a Home organization and a Kind of independent Company, this Office will not be particular in the examination of your Returns, expecially as they are so good. I think my honored Father is as fluent in his language as some other people I know, for in this letter he says he has nothing particular to write about and then produces an elegant letter. If I could only do as well in return [I] would not offer any excuses.

I never saw this place as quiet as it is at present. Nothing going on to give one an idea to write about.

Some of the boys seem to think our regiment will be consolidated with the 7th Cavalry in the reduction of the Army. Should this take place it would hardly be in my time, or would it help my case any.

My time is passing away finely. And will be home with you almost before you know it. Imagine [I] can almost taste those new potatoes and spring chickens already. Just wait until I come home, and we will then decide on leaving W[estminster] to better our conditions. I am in hopes that when we are all together, we can devise some plans to get along well.

Fort Union, New Mexico

APRIL 11, 1874

It is now 9 o'clock P.M. and I have just returned to my room from Deg[r]ee Meeting at Good Templars Hall.

The Shirts and Collars arrived this morning. How can I thank you sufficient for your Kindness to me? Rest assured loved ones I shall never forget it, and the day is not far distant until I will be with you all and prove by deeds my love and devotion for you all. The shirts and collars are very nice, and will last me until [I] come home. They will be splendid for the summers scout in case we have to go on one, but [I] have heard nothing in regard to one yet.

Received a nice little letter from Ida this morning. And [I] will answer tomorrow, Sundays are generally devoted to letter writing.

It will soon be my birthday (April 26th) "24 Years of Age." And what an <u>enviable</u> prediciment I'm found in. I ought to feel proud of it but I don't. Will commence life anew next September, and will try to make a better start than [I] did nearly 24 years ago. I am satisfied that you loved ones pointed out the right way for me to travel when I first started out, but you see I strayed from the right, took the wrong and have now wound up in New Mexico. "But courage old boy," we will soon take a new stock, and I think with our present experience we will do better next time.

"Four Months and nineteen days" and then homeward bound. That time will soon pass away. My friends use to tell me that the last year of my Enlistment would seem as long as any two former ones, but I have found it just the reverse. The days, weeks and months of my last year have passed seemingly faster than any of the others. As each day passes by I feel happier and life becomes more dear, for I feel that there is something for me to live for. When I had four years and more to serve I had no thought of danger and was afraid of nothing, felt as though it would be but little loss to either you, Uncle Sam or myself whether I was Killed or not, but I have got bravely over all such nonsense as that, and have no inclination to put Uncle Sam to the trouble and expense of erecting a "Head board" to mark the resting place of this individual.

I have not written to my little brothers yet, but will very soon. Have been very busy in the Office all week, and have still some work on hand.

We have just received the new "Tactics" for the use of all branches of the service.[1] Don't think they will interest me much, and it is not necessary any person should go to the trouble of teaching me, or putting me to the trouble and inconvenience of being taught for the time I have yet to serve.

It is time for me to close this, take my bath and go to bed. Perhaps, I will hear from you tomorrow, and if [I] do [I] will write again at once.

Fort Union, New Mexico
APRIL 13, 1874

Fathers and Clellie's letters dated April 5th this moment received and read.

Out doors it is blowing a perfect hurricane, and sand flying so thick that one cannot see two yards ahead. Everything in the Office was covered with sand, [I] dare not open my desk, so [I] have adjourned to my room to commence with you loved ones for an hour or two. You folks ought to be caught in one of these little wind storms to appreciate them. If there is a religious wash woman in this Territory your correspondent knoweth not, but religious or not; when they shuffle off their mortal souls, wring out the last Government shirt, fold their wash tubs and say "adeos" (good bye) to things earthly they should be permitted to enter that land above where Wash tubs and sick things are below par, for surely they have had enough punishment here below. It is enough to make one weep to have a line strung over with nice white linen, and without a moments warning have one of these gentle zephers come up.

Father commences his letter by saying he has nothing to write about. Read that portion to the 1st Sergeant, and then showed him the length of the letter. The Sergt. wanted to know how long the letter would have been had he had something to write about. You always manage to write me

---

[1] Lieutenant Colonel Emory Upton, an innovative tactician, rejected the concept of closed-rank battle lines in vogue during the Civil War. In 1863 and 1864, he began experimenting with light-column formations to demonstrate the soundness of his theories. He later authored a manual of infantry tactics, which was adopted by the army in 1867. Although Upton proposed that his tactics also form the basis of an assimilated system for artillery and cavalry, the War Department failed to act immediately upon the recommendation. The cavalry continued to use an earlier system developed by Colonel Philip St. George Cooke prior to the war. Only in 1874, with the strong support of Commanding General William T. Sherman, did the army adopt Upton's assimilated tactics for all branches of the service. See Jamieson, *Crossing the Deadly Ground*, 6–10.

long and interesting letters, and they generally come regular. And to this is attributed the greatest pleasure and happiness [I] have had the nearly five years [I] have been away from home. With your letters I am happy beyond expression, without them am as miserable as it is possible to become so you see what an effect they have over me.

The time is drawing to a forcus [focus?] when letters to and from us will be of the things that were, "four months and seventeen days" the days seem to pass more rappid than ever, and I hardly feel the time slipping away; but still it cannot pass too quick for either you or I. To Know that you are all well and doing well is the most comforting news you can write me, and when a letter is received from you, the first thing looked for are the words: "We are all well." Can then go back to the first and read your letters with pleasure.

You are having cold weather, but we are having the most changeable weather I ever saw. First snow, then rain, then a few hours of sunshine, and the whole wound up with a sand storm.

I am glad to hear the chickens still flourish and are progressing finely, take good care of them my darling Mother, until I come home and then I'll help you (to eat them).

I think you have done remarkable well, my dear Father, in the shoe business. And you are deserving of all praise. And still I cannot help feeling a regret that at this time of your life you are obliged to do such work. And when I read of you working at this business I most deeply feel my inability to render you such assistance as would keep you from such work, but unfortunately I cannot give you that aid at present, but am living in hopes that when [I] get home will get in some situation where [I] can help you more. I will have but little (if any) money left when [I] reach home and buy what clothing [I] will necessarily require. And will expect to go to work at once.

I have spent more money perhaps than I should have since [I] have been in the Army, but everything you buy in this country you have to pay three prices for. The Government provides its men with plain and substantial food and clothing, but one tires of the former and in five years will spend considerable money for little extras which help his health and living wonderfully, and which added to his government rations one can live very well.

The great trouble with the clothing is it will not fit you, and for one to dress in Government issue without having it altered is to make yourself a rediculous looking object, and to feel generally uncomfortable. And to have your clothing altered costs considerable. In fact it costs more to have them made over than the original price of the article. A blouse costs $4.55 and the tailor charges $5.00 to make it over and line it. A pair of trowsers unmade costs $3.99. Made as the Government issues them $4.59, and the Tailor charges you $4.50 for altering. These are shameful prices we all know and still cannot help ourselves. If we did not have them altered for our own comfort, the officers would make you have them so for appearance sake.[2]

Then comes your Laundry bill $1.25 each month, and unless you shave yourself, your barber bill is another $1.00 per Mo. If you shave yourself, you cannot also cut your own hair and this takes a 50¢ scrip each time. One cannot wash his hands and face with Gov't. Soap, and this takes a few more dimes.

Nearly every soldier wears paper collars in Camp 40¢ a box, if you wear two a week, 4 2/7 and 4 3/7 in a month, and 10 collars in a box. Multiply, divide and subtract this problem and the remainder will increase a little the list of expendiatives. Then comes combs, hair and tooth brushes, a little hair oil occasionally (for bacon grease won't answer) and unless you have some kind of oil your hair becomes stiff dry and hard, and you will soon find yourself bald headed. (How would your correspondent look in this predicament?)

The Gov't. does not provide you with towels and one cannot always use his shirt tail, another expenditure. Nearly every soldier wears fine boots on stated occasions such as Inspections, Musters, Sundays and many other times. (This subject wears them all the time when in Garrison.) This article of itself in this country costs a months soldiering, but thanks to you loved ones, and the Shoemaker at home mine does not cost so much, and are of a better quality. These boots will not look well all the time without they are blackened, and blacking out here costs stamps 25¢ per box, and than you cannot blacken them without a brush,

---

2 Improperly fitting clothing was a problem that plagued the army for more than a decade after the Civil War. Unscrupulous wartime contractors often made garments smaller than the marked sizes in order to use less cloth, thereby increasing their profits. These discrepancies usually were not discovered until a soldier actually drew the clothing and put it on. In the case of postwar regulars, the discovery was not made until years later. Soldiers learned that their only alternative was to requisition uniforms of larger sizes, then have the company tailors remake them to fit the individual. Over time, this resulted in a surplus of small sizes, which few men could wear, and a corresponding dearth of large garments. See McChristian, *U.S. Army in the West*, 8–9, 38–39.

(a horse brush Gov't. issue won't do this work) another 75¢ added to necessary expenses, (1) cloth[e]s brush 75¢ then you need several little brushes for cleaning your arms and equipments. The Govt. won't issue them and the Arms are obliged to be clean or else be punished. So the boys generally clean them.

White shirts is another virtue to the majority of the boys, but as for myself, my sincere thanks are due you for this comfort. Although we are so far from civilization and have no pretty Girls, (God bless them), to rumple our slick fronts we still like to look clean and feel comfortable. Paper, envelopes, stamps, pens, ink and paper [sic] are an expense to some, and if I had to buy mine it would amount to more than the "paper collar" expenditure I can assure you, but I have been so situated nearly all the time that [I] had all of these articles furnished me by Uncle Sam, except now and then I buy a $1.00 [worth of?] stamps. I keep a Postage book for the Company Commander and many a 3¢ is entered that was not for Official matters.

Another little necessary and indespensible article is tobacco, most every soldier uses it. It is one of the greatest comforts we enjoy, these we nearly all smoke and have to buy pipes. Cigars are too expensive and Uncle Sam has failed to supply us with pipes, so you see this is an expense that could not possible be avoided. (Mother says it can I know.) Many and many are hour have I spent performing Guard duty, perhaps in an Indian Country without a soul near me except the sleeping forms of my comrades unless some prouling Injin was watching near by to raise some fellows hair, and at these times a piece of the nasty weed was more highly prised and afforded more company than a friend would be, for when on Guard duty you are not supposed to enter into a conversation with any person, but if you have a bit of the weed you can chew away to your hearts content and be happy. How often I have held silent communion on these occasions with you loved ones. No thought of danger would enter my head and the tour of Guard would slip away without me knowing it, besides using tobacco because I like it. I have every reason to believe it has preserved what few teeth I have left. This alone would be sufficient benefit to continue its use. I often think I will quit chewing when [I] leave the Army, for with all the comfort I imagine I enjoy from its use, I am well aware of it being a very nasty habit. There are many other little necessaries to be purchased with our little $13.00 per month, and when it is all added up it leaves a balance of $000,000.

The little store does not seem to amount to so very much, and still I guess it adds considerable in the aggregate to the support of the family. It was surely a relief to read a letter from W[estminster] free from an account of some vile deed of scandal. Having read of so many acts of the vilest character occuring almost daily, one would naturally imagine W. to be a second Sodom. It is to be hoped we have heard the last of these bad deeds, and that the inhabitants better nature will show itself to drive away the remembrance of so much bad.

Johnnie seems to be progressing finely and is beating me in everything. If he wears a 6 1/2 Boot he beats for big feet, for I can wear very comfortable a 5 1/2. He don't outweigh me yet, ain't better looking, and had better stay away from my Girl. I never could sing and never could learn, it was a good deal like sawing wood, "had no taste for the accomplishment."

How is Arthur progressing with the Telegraphing, doing well I hope. Clellie says he has a collection of shells, stones and a little counterfeit money. Very fine collection I must admit, but wait my little brother until I come home, when I promise to bring some little trophies that will increase your collection some. I will have neither counterfeit or good money to give you, but lots of shells, stones etc. They will be a curiosity for being far fetched, if for nothing more.

Left you a moment to go to my dinner, dined sumptuously from roast beef, ration about the size of a small sized mouse. And that little piece of meat contained about as much toughness as anything of its size I ever saw, not excepting rubber. I hardly think there is a dog in the Garrison; (and there are about five hundred) that could make an impression on that bit of meat. Am sure he could not eat it and live. Then I had soup, soup that would make an invalid die to look at, and a well man sick to indulge in. This soup was composed of three nearly equal parts, namely cabbage, rice and sand, if there were any perceptible difference in the equalization of the ingredients it was in favor of sand. Of course I enjoyed the soup, for desert we had dry bread, so you can imagine how good I feel at the present moment. It is [a] singular thing that here in one of the best stock raising countries in the world we get the poorest meat. One would imagine from the toughness of the meat served up to us that we were consuming some of the old pioneer cattle that crossed the plains in 49. And I guess some of it did.

Now for supper I will have bread and Coffee, with no milk in it, and very little sugar. So you can imagine how amiable I am when [I] retire tonight. If I don't make those chickens wish they had never come out of their shells when I come home, it will be because I can't run fast enough to catch them.

Many thanks my honored Father, for the very valuable information found in your letter. That Sunday April 5th was Easter and the next day, "Monday" was Easter Monday. We <u>wouldn't</u> have known it if you had not told us. The next subject in your letter we will pass over without comment as it is rather a s———subject unless carefully handled, have reference to the removal of a necessary outbuilding.

The shirts and collars came safe and have been acknowledged in a former letter. Have one of them on now. Guess that is what makes me write so much. Again accept my sincere thanks for them. Shall not want anymore clothing while [I] am away from home, and will have some left when my time is out.

The "temperance subject" will await your pleasure. No particular hurry, the reason I asked you for it, was we do a little talking and speechifying at nearly all our meetings. And as I know your ideas are so good on most any subject [I] thought you could give me a few. I hold the second highest Office in our Lodge, "Worthy Vice Templar." Was Secretary the quarter before. The Lodge is in a flourishing condition and new members [are] joining every meeting night. We meet again tonight and will have four or five to initiate. What has become of your Debating Society? Never see anything in the home paper about it. Have you disorganized?

I read yesterday in a Santa Fe paper that the Troops in the Territory would likely start on the Summer Campaign in a couple of weeks, but nothing of an Official nature in regard to it has been received at this Post. One Cavalry Company will have to remain here during the summer unless another Infantry Company is sent here. The Infantry Co. now here are all on Extra Duty in the Qr. Ms. Department. The Civilian Employees all being discharged. Anyhow if we should go in the field, I will only have about four months to remain and I could almost stand on my head in a corner that long.

Wrote to Ida last night, and now am indebted to no person for a letter, except my little brothers. And somehow [I] don't know what to write that would interest them. Will try to think of something.

And now my loved ones, it is time for me to stop. Had no idea of writing so much when [I] commenced. It will take you some time to decypher it I know.

Always remember me to those who inquire after me, and when they ask you when Ed is coming home, tell them next September, for I am not going to re-enlist.

Harlan this moment came in the room and says a woman out in Ohio had five children at a birth. Says that woman wants to break her husband up. Sends his Kind regards to you all.

Fort Union, New Mexico
APRIL 21, 1874

Fathers third edition of the Pay Roll Letters was welcomed by me yesterday evening. And a good letter it was. The mails had been delayed a couple days by bad roads. I never saw anything to equal the weather we are having. Snow, rain, hail and sunshine in regular order.

Last friday a Lieutenant with one Ambulance wagon and five men left here in the morning for the Rail Road.[3] A fearful snow storm was blowing at the time. Sometime during the day one of the Escort returned to this Post and said his party were lost on the prairie. Two of our Company were ordered to saddle up and try to find the Lieutenant and party and have them return. The two started out but returned in an hour saying it was impossible for them to travel as they could not make their horses face the storm. Next morning another party was sent out to look for the missing, and found the Lt. and Ambulance at a ranch six miles from here and the wagon with the rest of the men at another ranch eighteen miles distant. All were safe and well.

You can imagine from this what kind of storms we have out here. If you remember I got snowed in the Raton Mountains with a party of

---

3 The Atchison, Topeka & Santa Fe Railroad, building westward across Kansas and southeastern Colorado Territory, had by this time reached the vicinity of Big Timbers, a patch of woods that served as a favorite Indian camping ground on the Arkansas River near present-day Lamar, Colorado. Progress was slow, however, and the company's immediate goal of reaching Pueblo was not achieved until 1877. Only then did the ATSF pursue its secondary goal to connect Pueblo with Albuquerque, New Mexico Territory, via Raton Pass. Thus, Fort Union did not gain convenient access to rail transportation until early summer of 1879, and then only at Watrous, some eight miles from the post. See Waters, *Steel Rails to Santa Fe*, 54–56. The significance of Big Timbers is discussed in Inman, *The Old Santa Fe Trail*, 233–34.

men in 1871. The snow was so deep then that before we reached the Ranch we were trying to get to at times horse and rider would disappear in some gulch, and a queer time we would have to get the unfortunate one out. The Lt. in charge and his horse disappeared so suddenly one time and went down in the snow so awkwardly that we all burst out laughing, and laughed for five minutes while the Lt. and horse were floundering around in the snow, with the Lt. on top one time and the horse next. Finally we went to his rescue and put him on higher ground, but it frightened him out of riding anymore that day. And for the next hour or two a mysterious looking object could be seen plowing through the snow dragging a Government horse after him. I shall never forget that trip, or the Lieut. and his horse.

Last night when I went to bed the thunder was spealing forth terrible sounds. Lightning flashing and rain failing fast. This morning when [I] came out of my room [I] found the ground covered with <u>snow</u>. Never saw anything like it in my life, I had quite a sore throat last week, got a Gargle from the Hospital and am about well once more.

Received an elegant letter from Mary Shellman yesterday, in which were some little "Forget Me Not's." Oh, but they did smell sweet. Mary in describing the rising generation of young folks of W[estminster] told me that those who were wearing pinafores when I left, now consider them selves young ladies, and that when I come home [I] need not be surprised if [I] am pointed out as "Old Mr. Matthews." Says she is considered quite <u>Ancient</u>. I just want to catch some of those snipes calling me Old, and if I don't make some of them think they have been jumped by a Comanche Indian it will be a wonder. I cannot help commending Mothers idea of Poultry raising. Expect she will become a "Granger" soon. May every success in the world attend you my noble Mother in your undertaking is the wish of your boy. And if I am permitted to feast on a turkey of your own raising it will only be relished the more for being so.

I attended a Party on the 18th inst. given by the Post Commissary Sergeant, and had a real nice time. Initiated four men members in our Lodge last night. (Three citizens and one Soldier.) We have seven Citizen members now and about seventy soldiers. The Soldiers fill all the Offices at present except one.

I will be 24 next Sunday and will then have four months and four days to serve. Time is passing finely. Nothing about Scouting yet.

Fort Union, New Mexico
APRIL 26, 1874

"Twenty four years old today" and celebrated it by playing a match game of Base Ball, which by the score you will see was not a bad game for Soldiers to play. Our side won and of course that makes the game better. We have received our marching orders, and leave this post for Fort Bascom May 5th, 74. The three Cavalry Companies at this post will go.[4] I will only have four months to serve, and don't suppose [I] will have to leave Bascom. You can rest assured I'll run no chances of getting an arrow stuck into me at this late day.

I will have lots of work to do in the Office from now until the day we start. Am so tired this evening that [I] can hardly write. You must never miss a week in writing to me when [I] leave here, as we only have a Mail once each week at B[ascom]. It will be an awful disappointment to have one come without bringing me a letter from you.

The "Democrat" always comes regular, and is I assure you read from beginning to end, and is always interesting to me.

I am sure I do not know what [I] am going to fill this up with, as can think of nothing that will be interesting to you. Expect [I] will hear from you tomorrow and will answer at once. Am real tired and will go to bed soon as [I] close this. Excuse such a short note.

Fort Union, New Mexico
APRIL 28, 1874

Fathers always welcome letter (4th edition of Pay Rolls) came to hand this morning and was read with pleasure. Before I go any farther I want to ask you a question. "What is the definition of the word <u>Missah</u>." I saw it some time ago on a book mark, and have searched through Websters Unabridged without finding the word. Have asked every soldier in the Garrison who I thought knew anything, but none of them could give information. Few days ago I asked the Chaplain, he could not tell me at

---

4 Companies C, L, and M left Fort Union on May 5, 1874, on a six-day, 148-mile march to old Fort Bascom to occupy the "Summer Camp" on the Canadian River, whereupon they began patrolling the region to the south and east. See Eighth Cavalry Returns, May 1874.

the time, but said he would hunt the word up and let me know.⁵ Saw him this morning and inquired if he had found the meaning of the word, said he had not. And then asked me if the word was not "Pisgah." It is my opinion the old Chaplain knew as little about the word Pisgah as he did "Missah." I think it is a Biblical word, if it is a word. Don't fail to answer.

Some time ago the Chaplain took it into his head to get up a Vocal and Instrumental Concert and called upon all—who could sing or play any kind of instument to meet at the Chapel the following tuesday evening. I with several others attended, not however to sing or play, but to look on. Several of the boys brought instruments such as Violins, Banjos, Guitars and Brass Horns. A Mrs. Dr. Welden presided at the Organ. This lady sings and plays elegant and is a very sweet looking lady. Several Hymns and Comic songs were sung accompanied by the different instruments. The evening was spent very pleasantly, and since that time we have had music and singing once each week. Had one this evening and the Chapel was crowded. More than it ever is when the Chaplain preaches. The Chaplain seems to enjoy it more than any person. And the more noise the better he is pleased.

The Companies are all getting ready to leave here on the 5th of next month. Extra Duty men are all relieved and sent to their Companies for duty. I will remain in the Company Office the balance of my enlistment, and will have but little to do. Don't suppose I will leave Bascom in case the Company should go out for a fifteen or thirty day scout. You can feel assured that I'll not run into any unnecessary danger this summer.

In regard to the injunction "Men should always pray" I obey it so far as to offer each night a petition to the God above to protect and keep you loved ones under his care, and that I may be permitted to return to you in good health. My prayer is not long, but is as fer[v]ently uttered as any your New Minister sends up.

I can't imagine how Father finds so much to write about each week, his letters are always long and interesting. I wrote you a short note the other day. "Sunday."

Same old cry, "have nothing to write about." Am well and have but four months and two days to serve. Guess this is about the best news I could write you.

---

5 Chaplain David W. Eakins served at Fort Union from July of 1870 until his death on March 5, 1876. See Oliva, *Fort Union and the Frontier Army*, 683; and Heitman, *Historical Register*, vol. 1, 393.

Excuse writing and mistakes as it is getting late and I have written this in a hurry.

Fort Union, New Mexico
MAY 4, 1874

I have but a few moments in which to write to you. Every person is working, some packing boxes, others loading them in wagons and the balance are at the Qr. Mrs. Store now unloading. I have just finished packing my field desk, and getting everything ready for the march. We leave here tomorrow morning. The Troops for a six months scout, your boy for less than four.

Have not heard from you since last monday, but am in hopes of receiving one in the morning before we start.

I have left what clothing here I will need to travel to the states in, and also my few trophies which [I] intend to bring home. Will wear my Soldier clothing until [I] reach St. Louis, or some point east of that City, and will then equip myself with something decent to appear before you loved ones. The time is drawing very near now for me to start in the homeward march. I have never felt better since [I] have been in the Army than [I] do at present. And you can rest assured I will take good care of myself this summer.

I will write to you every opportunity and you must not allow a week to pass without writing to me. I must now say Good bye, until I reach B[ascom] when [I] will write again. You must excuse this short and hastily written note, for I have yet considerable work to do this evening.

Fort Bascom, New Mexico
MAY 11, 1874

Well here I am, and here I expect to remain until Sept. 1st, 1874. We arrived at this place right side up side at 12 N today.

Since then [I] have been busy fixing up my tent. Have a wall tent for my Office and to sleep in. And am as nicely and comfortably fixed as it is possible for a buck soldier to be in Camp. Have my desk up, and papers arranged and am now open for business.

We left Union the morning of the 5th and marched to Los Vegas distance 28 miles. Wind blew a perfect gale all day, which made the riding very disagreeable. Every person was covered with dust and few of the Command washed that evening before turning in for the night. The great trouble in traveling in this country is the Alkali dirt and water. In marching you get considerable of the fumes on you, and the less of the latter you use the better you feel.

Wednesday morning we broke camp at 7 o'clock, and marched to Taylors Ranch distant from Los Vegas 15 miles. Got in Camp early and had a good rest.

Thursday May 7th, left camp at 7 A.M. and marched to Whitmores Ranch (15 miles). Friday May 8th, left camp at 7 o'clock (our usual hour). I was not feeling very well and thought it would be better for me to ride on one of the wagons. Gave my horse to one of the men and mounted a wagon. Had to ride on the top of the load and there I rode all day. You can imagine how I felt that night when [I] got into camp after riding 24 miles, perched on a loaded Army wagon and up in the air about 16 feet. The road was not very smooth and to fall off was either death or six months sickness. The former I could not think of and the latter would keep me in this country longer than Uncle Sam has rationed me to, and longer than I wish to remain, so you can rest assured I kept a good hold on the wagon cover, and was happy when [I] arrived at the Concha[s River] (our Camp for the night) to be alive and bones unbroken. That days ride cured me of any future inclination I might have to ride on an Army wagon. And for the balance of my service in ranks of Uncle Sams fighting Cavalry whenever I have any marching to do, [I] will do it on the back of my little pony.

That morning I had completed four years and eight months of my apprentiseship to the U.S. Saturday morning broke camp at the usual hour and marched to McClary's Ranch 28 miles. Wind blew hard all day and it was after dark when [we] finished our suppers, [I] felt pretty tired and slept pretty sound that night. Sunday morning May 10th left Camp at 7 o'clock and rode to Johnsons Ranch, (26 miles) and Monday morning rode into this place (12 miles), total number of miles traveled 148.

Went to the river after supper and took a bath, water pretty cold. Changed clothes, had my hair cut, and face shaved and now [I] feel pretty well. Guess the next time I travel that road it will be with my discharge in my pocket and on my way home. Guess the scouting done this summer will be by Companies, each taking their turns. Don't think I will have to go on any. And shall not get angry if I do not.

The mail from Union will be down tomorrow or the next day, guess I will hear from you by it and will finish this then. Good night and pleasant dreams to you all.

Tuesday morning. Wagons now leaving for Union and not a moment to spare. Will write by next mail.

Fort Bascom, New Mexico
MAY 13, 1874

This has been a happy day for me. Mail arrived at 10 A.M. and brought me two letters from home, and one paper. Father's mailed April 27th and Sue's, May 2nd, both long interesting and welcome.

Have been writing a lot of official letters today, and have now nothing more to do of that nature until the arrival of the next mail. Major Alexander, Commanding Officer, left for Union early this morning and the mail will not leave here until he returns, which will be next Sunday or Monday, so I need be in no particular hurry to close this. I sent you a letter yesterday morning by some wagons which started back to Union. And [I] will not allow an opportunity to pass without writing, if it is only to say I am well.

I never was so comfortable fixed at this place as [I] am at present, and will have an easy time during the few remaining months of my stay on Uncle Sams frontier. I have plenty of reading matter with me, and a couple of my friends at Union have promised to keep me supplied with papers. And as I will have but little to do in the Office [I] will devote the balance of the time to reading and writing.

Miss Martin, Major Alexander's wife's Sister, presented me with a book just before we left Union, entitled "Helena's Household." It is a tale of Rome in the first century. She also gave me a Testament, both very good books to read. The latter especially.

The men here have been quite busy since our arrival cleaning up the Camp and making themselves comfortable, [I] suppose by the time all are nicely fixed they will be ordered out for a month or two. Don't think I will have to go out on any of the expeditions, and [I] am sure [I] have no inclination to go.

In regard to the question of money, it was written for several reasons. First, I like to tell you of all my doings, second, I would love to assist you if in my power to do so, and third the subject was a change and helped to fill up my letter. I thank you all sincerely for your praise of the help I have been able to afford you, and I only regret that [I] am not now situated so as to continue to assist you, but you know as well as I can explain how I am situated. It would not be possible for me to get transportation farther than the point where I enlisted and that is not sufficient to carry me to Cincinnati, but I will have enough saved to carry me home respectable.

Sue says she wants to see me return looking as nice as when I left. I will try not to disappoint you my dear Sister. And in regard to whiskers etc. you need have no fears as I only possess a small dark colored "mustache" and unless you consider that an improvement in my appearance [I] can soon dispose of it. I want to do everything and anything that will please you all, and nothing that you do not approve of. Will also consume what tobacco [I] expect to during the balance of my time in the Army, for [I] intend to quit chewing if possible to do so before [I] come home. And I have no doubt [I] shall be successful in my efforts, but know it will be hard to give up. Capt. B[yers] wrote me of a struggle he was undergoing in the effort to give up smoking. And although I have not been consumer of the weed as long as he, I can feel that it will require no little resolution and will be sacrificing and old friend and comforter to dispense with its use. Nevertheless the effort and sacrifice shall be attempted, and I guess accomplished.

Sue say's never mind the teeth, I can buy better ones. Perhaps I can, but this also will cost both pain and inconvenience for a time. Although what few teeth I have left are not very good, I hate to think of parting with them. And [I] don't think I shall so long as they answer the purpose nature intended them. Maybe Sue only wants Company when she has her [own?] drawn, as the old saying says "misery loves company." You may get new teeth if you want them my dear Sister, but Ed intends to stick to his.

It is now after Taps, and as there is no hurry to close this [I] will add more if [I] can find an idea. So Good night and happy dreams to you all, for I am going to turn in and seek morpheus.

Thursday night May 14th, 1874. A citizen leaves here in the morning for Union, so [I] will try and send this by him. And write again when the mail leaves. Everything is quiet here and weather very warm. Only three months and sixteen days to serve, this will soon pass.

Sue asks what has become of Clint, he is here, is Clerking for the Adjutant, is doing very well, has about as easy times as I, and is just as lazy. His enlistment expires May 30th, 75, and says I can expect him for dinner on the 4th of July following. He always asks to be remembered to you all.

I might as well end this and take it to the man who is going to Union in the morning, or I may not get to see him. Excuse all mistakes etc.

Fort Bascom, New Mexico
MAY 18, 1874

General Alexander returned from Union tonight, bringing the mail with him. In it was Fathers letter dated May 3rd and mailed May 5th (the day we left Fort Union for this place). Also received the Democrat dated May 9th but your letter and the paper were blessings untold. You are all well, that is the greatest blessing of all. And if the good Lord will only keep you so the blessing will be still greater.

I unfortunately am not exactly blessed it seems tonight, have quite a sore eye. First intimation I had of any thing being wrong with my left optic was while lying down reading this afternoon. Felt rather an unusual sensation in that organ and upon looking in a glass found it very much inflamed and matterated. Have applied a wet handkerchief to it since then, but it still continues sore. I have either caught cold in it, or have been reading and writing too much. Especially at night. I know I do wrong to spend so much time in this pleasure, for I am well aware my eyes are not strong enough to stand it.

Besides reading an writing, there is still another great an injurious evil to one afflicted with weak eye sight. It is the fine sand which is so plentiful all over this Territory. The wind which blows in all seasons and almost continually out here, keeps this sand in motion nearly all the time. You might go to bed one night with a large sand bank at your front door, and wake up the next morning to find the whole pile moved around to the opposite side of the house. And then again before the day had passed find the same pile of sand placed back again to the first point. It has ever been this since my arrival in the country, and I suppose will remain so, until the good Lord sees fit to order it otherwise, and this I am very much afraid will never come to pass, as the inhabitants of the Territory are not a God fearing people, and in no way deserving of a change for the better. In fact it is my opinion that any white man in the Territory who was free to leave it and would not ought to be smothered in one of these sand banks. And a board placed at his head with this epitaph: "I remained in this God forsaken country when I was free to leave it."

Since our arrival here the men have been kept busy cleaning up around Camp, and now everything is as clean as could possible be. I suppose the greater part of the summer will be spent in teaching the new Tactics just published and sent out, but I shall not be called upon to receive any of its benefits. The old Tactics will answer me for the balance of my enlistment, and as I don't think I shall re-enlist, it would only be so much instruction in the art of Killing thrown away. It is my opinion but little scouting will be indulged in during the summer.

The weather is very warm, almost sufficating at times. At night though it is generally cool, so that one can sleep comfortable.

Only three months and twelve days to serve. The time continues to grow less fast. Will soon be home with you. And although not absent as long, by a good many years as Mr. Norris'es Brother, or ever numbered for as dead. I know our meeting will be more the less joyfull, I cannot imagine how a brother could separate himself from a brother and remain silent for so many years. Can one do this and feel the love which should naturally exist between brothers? Surely I could not live in this way.

I expect now the mail will leave in the morning and that hereafter we will have a weekly mail. I have written twice since [I] arrived here to you besides this. One I sent by a wagon train which returned to Union and the second by a citizen who left a couple days later. It is now about 10:30 P.M. and my eye is not feeling very pleasant, and this writing by candle light is not calculated to help it any, besides [I] have nothing interesting to write you.

Fort Bascom, New Mexico

MAY 20, 1874

A wagon leaves here tomorrow morning for Union and I cannot resist the temptation of writing you although I have but two items to write of, viz: I am well and the weather is extremely hot. So warm in fact that your boy is actually melting away. This is not caused from over exertion, for I have at present hardly enough work to do, to give me an appetite for my ration of pork and beans. My eye is almost well, and will try to keep it an its twin in better condition hereafter.

The dutch members of our Company have got together tonight and are making the Camp fairly ring with their songs of "My Faderland." Some of them sing splendidly. Their favorite song is the "Watch on the Rhine." Their singing has one virtue at least, if no more, it helps greatly in whiling away the monotonous hours of Camp life. Generally spend an hour or two of an evening with bat and ball. The match game we played at Union on the 26th of last month, Harlan and I sent to the "New York Clipper" and just received a copy of the paper with the score of the game. Although there was a number of games reported played by professionals, ours was the best game of all. The dutch singers have just congregated around my Tent, and are giving me a benefit. They are singing something very pretty now. "I know what they say, but not what they mean."

No talk yet of any scout yet, and no person spoiling for one.

Can't prolong this any longer so [I] will have to close. Expect the mail back next Tuesday, will have something then to write about.

Fort Bascom, New Mexico
MAY 24, 1874

This is Sunday night, and while your son and brother is slowly melting away he will write you a few lines for mutual pleasure before vanishing entirely. It is so hot here now that one almost suffocates. This afternoon after dinner I took off all my clothes, except shirt, drawers and stockings and took out an arm full of old letters (in fact all I had), and while lying on my bed perused them carefully through. And assure you I found plenty of pleasure in their perusal. I never tire of reading and re-reading your letters and those from my friends. I noticed one thing this evening, although I have several regular correspondents, Father writes me as many letters as all the rest put together. And as length his, leaving out a couple from Capt. Byers, would double all the rest. Many, many my honored Father, for the happiness your letters convey to your absent son. I hardly know what I should do were it not for you. But then I know Mother reminds you often that a letter should be written to the absent one. Only continue as you have done for the past for "just three months more" and then there will be no occasion for letter writing so far as we are concerned.

Some ten or twelve wagons containing Commissary Stores arrived this evening from Union. The Mail was also expected, but has not put in an appearance yet. Wish it would come, for [I] just feel like reading a letter from you.

A wagon leaves here for Union tomorrow and I guess [I] will not wait to hear from you but send this up. There is plenty of work here for the boy to do. And as I have but little else to write [I] might as well fill this up with the routine of duty.

First thing in the morning is Reveille, at sunrise, when the men fall in line and answer "here" when their names are called by the 1st Sergeant, they are then marched to the picket line, where they exercise themselves for an hour on their horses. This gives them an appetite for their breakfast. This call is sounded on the trumpet at 5:30. And consists generally of fried bacon, bread and coffee. Sick Call comes next 6 A.M. when the sick, lame and lazy repair to the Hospital Tent and receive their pills and quinine, scarcely any other medicine is used in the Army. If you have a sore back, three pills are prescribed for you, if a bad cold, three pills, and for anything more a dose or two of quinine is considered just the thing. Following the sick comes Fatigue Call, and this takes all the men not detailed on other duty, the way work is done here.

Guard Mount is sounded at 7:30 when the 1st Sergeants march on their guard details, these are inspected by the Adjutant and are then marched to the Guard House where they relieve the old Guard. Drill Call comes next, but as all the men are on fatigue this does not hurt any person. Next is Water Call 9 o'clock, but as the horses are sent out to herd soon as breakfast Call is over, no person is hurt again. Next is Re-call from fatigue 10:30, this is the call what makes the boys laugh. They hunt the shade then and speculate on what there will be for dinner, whether it will be bean or rice soup, the rice generally turns up. Dinner Call 12 N. rush to the Kitchen, grab a tin plate, cup, knife, fork and spoon, get your fried bacon, rice soup, and piece of bread. Devour it and be thankful it is no worse.

2 o'clock Fatigue Call is sounded when the boys commence hostilities again. Some with brooms, policing the Camp, others with axes and

wagons after brush to put up shades over the Officers tents. Drill Call is passed over again. Recall from fatigue, water and stable call is sounded at 5:15, when the boys spend another hour at stables. Supper (Coffee and bread) comes after stable call. As there is but little of this, it is not necessary for a trumpet call. Retreat at Sunset when the men answer to their names and the details are made for the next day. Tattoo at 8:30 P.M. and Taps at 9 when the lights in the Camp are supposed to be out and men go to bed. It is very near that time now, but as I am a Kind of independent organization [I] can burn a candle as late as [I] want to.

Sunday mornings at 7:30 the men turn out mounted for inspection and have the balance of the day or until stable call to rest themselves for the morn. I have now given you the general duties of the men.

Will now tell you the duties of the boy (myself). Generally raise up in bed about 7 o'clock A.M. and <u>whistle</u> my own reveille, get up, call my name to see if I am all there, say here, if I find the command all present. Make my toilet, also my bed, the latter by spreading the top blankets smoothly over the rest, as it is no use making up my bed until [I] get ready to turn in, for the loafers in the tent during the day sit on it and rumple it up. Go to my breakfast, which is kept warm for me by the Cooks. Come back to my tent, light my pipe and start out for a mornings walk, and look for bugs.

Have a very nice collection of these little animals, which any lover of curiosities would be glad to have. Perhaps they are smaller animals than Barnum would care to have in his mammoth Wippodrouse, they consist so far of Tarantulas, Centipedes and Scorpinons of the poinsonous insects, horned toads, lizards, swifts, beetles, butterflies, grass hoppers, spiders and many other specimens of different bugs which I have not learned the name of. These will be a splendid addition to my other curiosities. Have them preserved in alcohol.

When [I] return from my walk [I] either read or write until dinner. After dinner [I] take a smoke and if [I] feel like it, a sleep. Go to supper when it is ready, and then put in the balance of the time from dark until [I] get sleepy the best way I can. Get sleepy sometime during the night, whistle Taps and get under the blankets. So you see I have no stables, roll calls or fatigue to do. Sunday morning instead of turning out under arms and mounted for Inspection, all I have to do is to spread my books out on my desk for Inspection and remain in my tent until the Capt. has signed them (if there are any for his signature), put them up and roam at will.

My soldiering for the last year has been very easy, but sometimes, such as at the end of each month, Quarter, half year and year I have but few spare hours to hunt bugs or anything else, except <u>papers</u> for five and sometimes ten days, but then I can stand to work a few days now and then.

I like our new Capt. very well, he is one of the independent kind not too proud to listen to a suggestion from a subordinate. In facts he allows me to make out all the papers which ever way I think is right, and he has never had occasion to complain, as but one paper has ever been returned to him for correction since I have been in the Office, and that one was returned from Regimental Headquarters for correction of an imaginary mistake where none existed. And was sent back to the Regimental Adjutant with the brief endorsement "That the return was correct, no error appeared in it." And I guess the Adjutant found out it was correct, for he never sent it back again.

When ever a letter is to be written or an Endorsement to be put on, the Capt. tells me to do it, but does not give me a copy. I use my own judgement and he is always satisfied.

I had a fearful dream the other night, thought I had been discharged from the service, through [for] some cause [I] had reenlisted within three days, and had made every preparation to desert the same night as [I] reenlisted. Thought some of my friends had made up a purse for me to travel on. I must have been in terrible agony, woke up suddenly and when [I] found that it was only a dream and that I was still serving my first enlistment, with little more than three months to serve, the exclamation of "thank God" rolled out so suddenly that I was almost startled at my own voice. I was too happy to sleep any more that night, and spent the remaining hours until morning thinking of what might have been had my dream been a reality instead of imagination. You can rest assured my loved ones, that every time I re-enlist in the Army of Uncle Sam, it will be in my sleep. It is now getting late, and no mail from Union, so [I] will proceed to close, and will send this to Union by the wagon tomorrow. It is trying to rain a little and I hope may succeed, for we need rain very badly, if for nothing more than to cool the atmosphere. You must excuse mistakes for I cannot take time to read this over.

"Only 3 Months and 6 days." How are the chickens?

Fort Bascom, New Mexico
MAY 25, 1874

Could not possible feel better under present circumstances than [I] do tonight. The mail arrived an hour ago, and brought me Fathers long, welcome and always interesting letter dated May 10th, and my little brother Arthur's interesting missive dated [missing], also a home paper which is always read with pleasure. I have read my letters, the Local News, and Marriages and Deaths in the paper, and will answer your letter tonight as will have some official writing to do tomorrow.

Many thanks my dear Father, for the deffinition of the word "Missah." Perhaps had I perused the Bible more, [I] would not have had occasion to ask the question. And [I] am sure our Reverend Chaplain should have been conversant enough with the teachings of the same book to have given me the information instead of sending me a little puny Dictionary for me to look for the word. The deffinition given by you corresponds with my idea of the word, as expressed to several of my friends. I am highly pleased to learn of Johnnies advancement in trade, but am not a bit surprised, for [I] always knew he was a mechanical genius, and if [he] had an opportunity would make an elegant workman. And besides this he is such a good boy, and deserving of all the praise you all bestow upon him. This makes me feel very proud of my brother, I can assure you.

Arthurs letter was very good indeed. And I am delighted to know he has progressed so finely in his trade or profession. You are little, my dear brother, but from all accounts "you are all there." You'll get along I know, stick to your business, learn all you can, for a good Operator can always get a situation, and the pay is good and also sure.

Where is my "second self," (the better part of myself I mean) what is he doing, and what trade or profession is he thinking of following, or is he too young to decide on his calling yet? I rather imagine he is destined to fill some pulpit and help to reclaim the fallen. If such should prove his calling, may he meet with every success. And prove a good worker in our Masters Vineyard, is the best wish and earnest hope of his absent brother. I never knew him to be anything but a good little boy, and manly in all his doings and sayings. And sincerely hope the past five years has added to his advancement in manliness, as it has in years. But your big brother will soon be home to see, hear and decide for himself. And as two of my correspondents have called me their "critic," you had better look out as I may judge as a critic, instead [of] as your big brother.

And still there are some left to speak of. Sue's prospects for a school seems fair, in fact almost sure, but as she was disappointed before, one cannot feel certain, until the object sought is gained. I might say until she finds herself in her schoolroom, with 25 or 30 little urchins around her, and with a teachers certificate to prove that she is the identical individual who is authorized by the School Commissioners of Carroll County in the State of Maryland to knock the dust out of those 30 little jackets whenever they required dusting. I sincerely hope there is not another disappointment in store; not only for her, but for all of us, of the Matthews family.

Next on the list comes the "school marm with the specks," the school marm without a doubt, and a successful one beyond my greatest expectations. I always knew my English Sister could sling ink, talk as much and as fast, knew as much, (and a good deal more) and was as competent to impart what she knew as any Girl I know, but with all this I had no idea she would prove so successful in her undertaking. But I also know her success has cost considerable labor and study.[6] I am proud to call you Sister, and although I am so far your inferior in intellect, I will promise you that no act of mine in the future shall cause you to regret that I am your brother Eddie.

And now comes my loved and loving Mother. God bless her, and make her years many and pleasant on earth. I see she has taken a new departure since I left home, "a connoisseur of poultry," may your judgement and treatment of your flock keep them well and fat, until the arrival of your boy, who I believe has a kind of weakness for roast turkey and chicken. You will not have to wish long and it is my opinion you will be surprised to see me get on the outside of fowl.

And now last, biggest, (more properly speaking largest) but none the less loved and honored by his son Eddie [remainder of letter missing]

---

[6] He refers to Elizabeth (Lizzie), who was born in England in March of 1848, just a few months prior to the Matthewses' migration to the United States.

Fort Bascom, New Mexico
JUNE 1, 1874

Received Fathers ever welcome letter dated May 17th this morning. And will now give you any news to be found down here.

Capt. Morris (our new Captain) with all the company except 16 men (myself among the 16) left here on the 28th of May for a ten days Scout. They will go to Old Fort Sumner, 85 miles from here, remain two days and then return.[7]

We have had a regular deluge here, raining very hard three days and now the Canadian River is running all over the country. The men had built shades (made of cotton wood brush) over mine and the 1st Sergeants tents, and had planted poles all along the other tents, intending fixing shades over all. When they were ordered on the scout, work was suspended until their return, but now the shades are of the comforts that were.

Two nights ago while the rain was falling in torrents, one of the men ran to my tent where I was, and told me to get outside quick as possible if I wanted to return home alive as the shade was falling. I was not long in getting out and had hardly got from under the falling poles and brush, when down come the whole business crushing in my tent so that it looked like an old hat with the crown kicked in. The boys all gathered around and assisted in pulling the brush away, when all was cleared, got new tent poles, (as the others were broken) put my tent up and have now concluded that it is not necessary to have any shade. Had I remained in the tent when the brush fell, [I] guess I would not have been hurt very badly, but would have been badly frightened.

Yesterday afternoon while I was sitting in front of my tent, picked up a broom straw, (nothing very remarkable in this, imagine hearing you say) and in trying to bite into it, broke one of my <u>front teeth</u>, (upper one) one that Dr. Chas. Billingslea filled for me in 67. You ought to have seen this individual dance around, lamenting his misfortune about that time for although my teeth are ever so poor, I would not have had this

---

7 Captain Morris formed a command of fifty enlisted men by drawing soldiers from both Companies C and L for this patrol. Combining men from various units was a common practice during the era, when the desired complement was not available from a single unit, considering those who were sick, in confinement, detached, and on extra or daily duty, such as Matthews. See Eighth Cavalry Returns, May 1874.

one broken for anything. I am sure it has not enhanced my beauty any, and as I possess but little [I] am very careful to keep (or rather try to keep), what little I have. What must I do, stop in Baltimore and have my teeth fixed or come home toothless? If my mustache was only a little heavier and I laughed less it might do very well as it is. But I am continually laughing whenever [I] see or hear anything to laugh at, and like my big sister, have to open my mouth very wide and let it all roll out. And of course this makes a display of my poor teeth. Give me your advice and I will act accordingly.[8]

Three months from this morning I expect to have my discharge in my pocket and be on my way to Union. And then as soon as [I] can get my papers cashed start for home.[9] And expect to arrive at that blessed place about the time <u>those potatoes</u> are <u>out</u> of the <u>ground</u>.

Mr. Johnny needn't think he is going to stick me in a potato field the moment I get home, this is a good deal like a saying the boys have when a scout is talked of. They say: "they have not lost any Indians and don't want to find any." I haven't planted any potatoes and have no particular desire to dig any, but am willing to sit on the fence and watch him dig them. Will send $10. to Union with the Mail Carrier, and let him get a Post Office Money Order for it and send in this, to pay for my boots. If this is not sufficient, you must tell me, and I will send more, for I want a nice dress boot.

I sympathize with you my darling Mother, and hope long ere this your teeth have ceased to ache. I have suffered enough with the same complaint and know what it is. There is little if anything more for me to tell you, and this is rather a poor letter and very badly written. I am well and doing well and hope this may find you one and all the same. I will write every opportunity.

---

8 Dental care was still something of a luxury in the late nineteenth century, particularly in the West. Because the army had no dentists, garrisons relied upon itinerant practitioners who appeared irregularly, if at all, at frontier posts. Most of the time, however, army personnel were at the mercy of the post surgeons, who possessed little if any dental training, or even the enlisted hospital stewards, who performed extractions in the most primitive fashion. See Ashburn, *History of the Medical Department*, 108–9; and Rickey, *Forty Miles*, 133.

9 The "papers" to which Matthews refers were his discharge certificate and his final pay statement. On the latter were recorded his identity and personal information, the date on which he was last paid, deductions for outstanding debts, the balance of his clothing account, the amount of his retained pay, the amount of travel allowance to the place of his enlistment, and the total amount due. The catch was that the statement could be cashed only by an army paymaster, and finding one could be problematic on the frontier. See *Revised Regulations*, 371.

Money Order in favor of
> John Matthews
>> Westminster
>>> Carroll County
>>>> Maryland.

From
> William E. Matthews
>> Fort Union
>>> New Mexico

Summer Camp, Fort Bascom
JUNE 14, 1874

Mail day, two letters and one paper from home, and one letter from Ida. Have had my <u>tea</u> (bread and bad coffee), and now while the flies, gnats and musquetoes are singing their praises to his Satanic Majesty, only stopping every second to torture and try to get me mad, but I am not mad and would not harm one of these innocent insects which were created for some wise purpose (to torment both good and bad), unless I couldn't catch them. Last year we were only persecuted by musquetoes and flies, but this summer buffalo gnats have been added, and they are if any thing worse than the others.

As for warm weather, we can see yours, and go you ten degrees better. Never experienced hotter weather except while at Fort Yuma. And that place is said to be just a little hotter than the place wicked people are supposed to go when they shuffle off this mortal civil [coil?] here below (or here above) as the case may be. I once heard a story about this Fort Yuma, but as it is as well known as the departed Horrace Greeleys ride to California you may have heard of it before. Anyhow [I] will tell you all about it. Two of Uncle Sams boys died and were buried at the post one summer. A few nights after their buriel some of their late comrades were surprised to see these chaps come in the squad room and upon being interrogated said they had been to hell, and found it so cold in comparison to Yuma, that they had come back after their <u>blankets</u>. Now I do not ask you to believe this, for I <u>hardly</u> believe it myself.

There seems to be some doubts as to whether it is hair, or no hair, on Johnnies upper lip, and from the impartial description given by Father, I must take the side of hair, and although it may be like a Base ball nine, five on one side and four on the other, still the hair is there. I remember one Sunday away back in 66, I was down at the Engine house in Company with some other boys, some of the party had an old razor and shaving brush, and as my virgin face had never had a razor drawn over it, although something resembling hair could be perceived. I was persuaded to indulge in a shave. After [I] had been properly scraped, I viewed myself in a piece of looking glass, and imagined some great transformation had taken place in my appearance. Worked myself up to such a state that [I] was afraid to go home for fear you folks would ridecule me. (as you have my big [little] brother). Kept away from home all day, and when darkness enveloped the town an urchin about my size might have been seen making his way home. Arriving at that place he entered the house with throbing heart and when he found himself in the presence of the family he almost gave way, but as the moments passed and no remarks were made by any of the family, he commenced to feel more comfortable. And it was not discovered until I had been regularily shaved for more than a year.

In regard to my future employment I hardly know what to say. A Clerkship in one of the Departments of W[ashington] would be a very good situation I am well aware. And if I once secured a place there [I] am satisfied [I] could keep it. Capt. Hobart, our late Captain, told me to write to him before my time was out and give him my address. He will do anything in his power for me I know. If I had my choice of some good out door situation to a Clerkship of any kind, [I] would take the former. Know it would be better for my health, especially for my eyes. I think it will be just as well to wait until I come home. I will find some employment. I am very grateful to you my dear Father, I assure you, for your promised aid.

Only two months and sixteen days short time. It hardly seems possible that my time is so near out, although [I] have been away from home an age. Nothing new to tell you of. All quiet along the line. Have no idea of doing any more scouting for Uncle Sam. And [I] am sure [I] have done my share. Went fishing yesterday, caught a dozen very nice Cat fish, but came very near being eat by musquetoes.

Summer Camp, Fort Bascom
JUNE 20, 1874

The regular mail arrived this evening and I was the happy receipient of a regular letter from you. Fathers long and interesting letter dated June 7th was received. It is now 9:30 P.M. and as it is a great deal more comfortable writing at night than in the day [I] will answer your letter.

There is nothing to fear in regard to my health, for I am strong and healthy, and have a constitution that would almost require an earthquake to undermine. During the past five years I have been at times exposed to most every danger, privation and hardship man is called upon to endure, from being nearly ship wrecked, to nearly starved and famished, while at other times have suffered both extremes heat and cold, and am tonight as strong (if not stronger) physically than [I] have ever been. But why have I branched off on my own troubles in this way? It was not my intention I assure you when [I] commenced this. All I can say or do my Loved Ones is to advise you all to be careful, very careful of your health.

The [time?] is drawing very near when I hope we will be united, and I pray none of you will be sick at that time. Oh what a joyful day that would be could we all clasp hands, you I and those two Angel sisters, but they are far happier than we can expect to be. God bless both them and us, and help us so to live, and that when we are called we will all [be] worthy and deserving of entering that home in heaven where we shall meet those loved ones never more to separate.[10]

The days seem to pass away very fast now, and I'll soon be home. Let us endeavor to be happy and not give ourselves any unnecessary trouble, for it generally comes soon enough, without being borrowed.

There are no Camp news to write you. No Indians around and no more talk of a Scout. The weather continues excessively hot, but as I have had no work to do that amounted to anything [I] have spent my time in the shade, under a mosquito bar, either reading or sleeping, but now busy days for me are approaching.

The last of this month is general setting up of all the books and papers for the fiscal year, for the Quarterly Returns of Q.M. Stores. C[lothing], C[amp] and G[arrison] E[quipage] and Ordnance Stores I have twenty days grace, but always endeavor to get them off within

---

10 By "two Angel sisters," Eddie refers to his deceased sisters, Frances and Margaret.

three days after the quarter, for the Muster and Pay Rolls [I] have three days and for the Quarterly and monthly returns required at Regimental Head Quarters, [I] have two days grace. These latter consist of Company Fund Account, Return of Horses, Return of Company, Descriptive list of Deserters, Return of Regimental Recruiting Party. Report of Scouts, Report of Ammunition, Return of Books and Blanks. Statement that an inventory of all public property pertaining to the Company has been taken and then the letters of transmittal. All have to be made in duplicate, except the M. and P. Rolls and they are made quadruplicate. You can imagine that considerable paper and ink will be consumed. To say nothing of the drops of sweat this working in such hot weather will come out, but I will make these papers out with a lighter heart and in a more cheerful manner than any previous ones, for these will be my last quarterly returns. And when [I] have made out the M. and P. Rolls for July and August [I] will write a notice and post [it] up in front of the Company Office. Clerk wanted, as the late incumbent has abdicated for a position in the Home Brigade.

I have seen the bug you describe. One of our boys received a letter from home [a] few days ago, and in it a sample of these animals but as there are plenty to be found out here, it was not much of a curiosity, although it came from the States for our bugs are now State bugs also. Guess a couple of these bugs would be no addition to Arthurs Cabinet. So [I] will not embalm any of them in Alcohol.

Have finished my sheet. Will stop for tonight. If [I] hear of any thing interesting before the mail leaves [I] will add a postscript.

Summer Camp, Fort Bascom

JUNE 26, 1874

Fathers always welcome and interesting letter of June 14th was received a couple hours ago. Will answer at once, although [I] cannot promise you a letter. The heat is terrible, and the least exertion one indulges in, the better he will feel. It is ten degrees hotter here this Summer than either 72 or 73.

I have not done anything with the papers yet, but intend making a start tomorrow. Will have to work early in the morning and late at night, for [I] could not possible work during the middle part of the day.

I received orders this morning to turn in everything in my possession, belonging to the U.S. Done so and have now neither Arms, Ammunition, or equipments of any Kind. So now in case the Company should go on a Scout, I would not have to go. Not a single word of a Scout and I hardly think any will be made until the latter part of the Season, and then I will be scouting towards the rising Sun.

I am altogether undecided as to what route shall travel when [I] return. My inclinations at present are to take the Balto. [Baltimore] and Ohio. Father advises me to take a good look at the country, as it will very possible be for the last time. I have seen all that [I] wish to, and shall have no regrets when my back is turned towards the Mississippi River. As for answering questions innumerable as to country etc., and do without exaggeration and in few words. I have no intention of writing a history of my travels when [I] return or of ever drawing descriptions of oceans, adventures etc. I am certain this five years [of] "roughing it" has furnished me with a subject or subjects sufficient to spend many an evening relating. And it will not be necessary for me to prevaricate. Besides I am [a] son of the George Washington family.

And if I could only step in at home tonight, none of you would "Sir" me, but would recognize me without any trouble. Think I must return home without letting you know the day, but I fear if I should do this I could not control myself long enough to see whether you would know me or not. Guess about the time [I] came in sight of the house, [I] would drop bag and baggage and make a rush for the door, and when [I] arrived in your presence [I] should be so over come that [I] could not tell you that I was the returned prodigal. You shall know when I am coming and almost to the hour, for I have no desire to surprise you.

Am glad the money order arrived safe, and hope the boots will reach me as safely. Tell Mr. Yingling please to make them exactly the same height across the instep as the last pair, for they fit me exactly. I can just feel myself melting away, and guess [I] will have to stop.

If any of you should see Mary Shellman ask her if she received an answer to her last letter, as I wrote to her some time ago, and that has been the last of it. Jennie, I imagine has discarded me entirely for [I] have not heard from her for an age. Ida (the dear Girl), has been more prompt in writing to me than any of my friends. And I guess if the truth must he told, I think more of her than of any of the others. Lec's letters are also very regular, but with the others it is rather uncertain. And when I answer one of their letters [I] would not bet on hearing from them again. They seem to take spells, a kind of inspiration and the letters some of them write is a carbin [carbon], but as Capt. B. says: "there is always a Calm after the storm in the affairs of life," and just so it is with my correspondants.

Matthews was unaware that on June 27, the day after he wrote the above letter, a small party of hide men and traders at Adobe Walls would be in a fight for their lives against more than two hundred Cheyenne and Comanche warriors, who attacked the place early that morning. At the conclusion of the famous all-day battle, a couple of dozen tribesmen lay dead, as well as three of the defenders. The assault on the post caused the traders to abandon it a month later, as the Indians continued to attack hunters whenever they found them that summer.

Summer Camp, Fort Bascom
JUNE 30, 1874

It is 9 o'clock P.M. I have this minute finished making out the Company Muster and Pay Rolls for May and June. Have been working in the mornings and nights while the weather was the coolest.

A general change has been made here since my last letter was written. A dispatch from Dept. Hd. Qrs. was received here last Saturday night for Gen'l. Alexander to break up the Summer Camp at once, and for him with two of the Companies to proceed to Fort Union N.M., leaving one Company here until the Q.M. and Commissary Stores were removed to Fort Union. And then for the Company Commander left here to use his own judgement as to where he would Scout or Camp. Capt Morris, our Capt., is off on a fourteen days leave of Absence. The next morning an order was published detailing our Co. to remain here, rationed to include August 31st. B and M Companies left here early this morning, and Battery L is quietly sleeping in their little Tents.[11] The 5th Cavalry in Arizona and the 6th Cavalry in Kansas are ordered to change Stations. And I think B and M Companies of our regiment will march to some point in Colorado, and Scout the country until the arrival of the 5th Cavalry.

---

11 Mahnken, AAAG, to Alexander, June 26, 1874, in LS, District of NM, RG 393, copy in v. 29, Arrott Collection, NMHU.

I am very sorry our company was left here, for had we went to Colorado my time would expire shortly after our arrival, and I would be near the Rail Road. In that case my transportation would almost if not quite carry me home, while to be discharged here would take nearly all the transportation to carry me to the Rail Road, but it can't be helped.

And now I intend asking the Captain to give me my discharge on the 15th of August, twenty three days before my time expires. He may possible allow me this time, as Commanding Officers have authority to give an Enlisted man 30 days furlough. He could give me this time, but I could not get my final Statement Cashed by the Paymaster until the day my term of service expired. But this would make very little difference as I have money enough to take me to Fort Leavenworth, Kansas or St. Louis. And I could have my papers Cashed there.

It is rumored here that our Capt. has gone off to get married and no doubt when he returns he will be feeling pretty good and may have compassion on a poor fellow, who might want to do likewise (but he don't). He is to marry Miss Reese, Chaplain Agguilla Rees[e]'s daughter of Fort Wallace Kansas.[12] This Reese is from Maryland, and I suppose is related to our Reese's at home. Anyhow if he is married when he returns, [I] will tell him I am acquainted with his wifes relations, and that may have some effect.

I have now just two and a half hours to enjoy the blessedness of a chewess and smokers life, for at the hour of 12 M. tonight, I break my pipe, then [throw?] away my tabacco and burn what matches I have left. And if I have strength and resolution enough, quit the use of an article which has afforded me many an hours comfort, although at the same time I knew it was an injury to self to continue its use. It seems hard to throw away a friend which I have stuck to so long. And were it not for my darling Mother and Sisters I would not do it. Although it were an injury to use it. But I know they will love me more for the sacrifice and I want to do any and every thing that will please them. Chewing and

---

12 Aquilla Asbury Reese, a native Marylander, served as the chaplain at Fort McHenry from 1862 to 1867. Immediately thereafter, he was appointed post chaplain in the regular army and served in that capacity for ten years. He died in 1878, shortly after his retirement. Captain Morris, his soon-to-be son-in-law, had previously served in the Third Infantry, posted in western Kansas at that time. He undoubtedly met Ms. Reese when they both resided at Fort Wallace, prior to Morris's transfer to the Eighth Cavalry in December of 1873. See Heitman, *Historical Register*, vol. 1, 728, 821; and Rodenbough, *Army of the United States*, 448.

smoking tabacco does not look so nasty I know in the eyes of my Father and brothers as it does to Mother and Sisters, for were this the case I guess Father would have quit its use long ago.

I am making the most of the time left me, and don't know but [I] shall keep awake until the last minute in order to enjoy the pleasure so soon to be of the things that were. I know it will require resolution to accomplish this end but I believe I will have the requisite amount.

The mosquitoes are getting so bad that [I] will stop writing for tonight. Will not close this until after the mail arrives from Union, which will be a couple of days.

July 1st. 5 o'clock P.M. The mail arrived unexpectedly this evening and brought me Fathers, Lizzies and Johnnies letters of June 21, a paper and two lines from Jennie asking if I had forgotten to write. As I wrote some time ago in answer to her letter I shall not write again. Our correspondence has been the most disconnected affair I ever heard tell of. And as I will soon be home [I] can settle all difficulties.

I was very happy indeed to read a line from the pen of my Sister Lizzie, and also from Our Machinest.

You folks needn't think I am toothless entirely and require a whole set. I had the piece drawn by the Hospital, [I] mean the piece left by the broken tooth. It makes quite a hole in my [illegible—smiles?]. My mind is about made up to have a tooth put in either in Cincinnati or Baltimore. It will only delay me an hour or two, but you need not say anything about me having a <u>bought</u> tooth.

Last night at near 12 M. I took my pipe and had my last smoke at least for many a day. If I have put my hand in my pocket once today for my Tabacco, [I] have done it fifty times. Whenever [I] would catch my hand in the act, [I] would pull it back with the exclamation: "No tabacco there old boy." After breakfast this morning gave my pipe tabacco and matches away. And [I] have felt forlorn all day, but feel confident [I] shall win.

Our Captain has not returned yet. Expect him here this week. I will not ask him about the furlough until next month.

I hope when this reaches you my darling Mother will be quite well again, and that she will try to keep out of the hot Sun. I am exposed to enough of Old Sol's rays for both of us.

I have one official writing to do tonight and have but little time yet to do it in, as the mail closes at Tat-too.

Write often for the time is drawing very near when there will be no occasion to write to each other. Have wanted something bad all day, you know what it is.

Fort Bascom, New Mexico
JULY 10, 1874

I have not heard from or written to you for more than a week. And [I] have but a few minutes now to devote to that pleasant duty. We have not had a mail from Union since July 1st. Can't imagine what is keeping it. Capt. McCleave of our Regiment leaves here at 2 o'clock A.M. (now 9 P.M.) for Union, so [I] will send this with some Official Matter that [I] have written and have yet to write.[13]

A ranch man living some 40 miles from here came in Camp yesterday afternoon and reported that Indians had attacked his ranch and had run off five head of horses. Capt. Morris with 10 men and Lieut. Rogers with 7 men of our Company saddled up at once and started out with 3 days rations. Lieut. Rogers and party returned this afternoon without having seen any of the Modocs.[14] Expect the Captain and his party in the morning. I don't suppose there is an Indian within a hundred miles of this place. And that this report has only been started to keep our Company down here all Summer. The Citizens here are afraid we will be ordered to Union like the other two Companies, unless they can get up an Indian scare to keep us here.[15]

---

13 Captain William McCleave had a long and colorful army career. Enlisting in the First Dragoons in 1850, he held positions ranging from private to first sergeant in Company K during the following ten years. Early in the Civil War, Brigadier General James H. Carleton, formerly a major in the same regiment, was selected to command a column of California Volunteers marching to the Rio Grande to secure New Mexico Territory for the Union. In recognition of McCleave's experience, Carlton had him appointed as a captain in the First California Cavalry. During the march eastward, McCleave was captured by Confederates and thus achieved the dubious distinction of becoming the first prisoner of war in that campaign. He was later exchanged, promoted to major in 1863, and subsequently brevetted as a lieutenant colonel for bravery in action against Apaches. After his wartime service, McCleave was selected to fill a lieutenancy in the Eighth Cavalry. He was promoted to captain in 1869, and retired from the army ten years later. See Heitman, *Historical Register*, vol. 1, 655. For further details concerning McCleave and his capture, see Masich, *Civil War in Arizona*, 16–17, 31–33, 186–88, 190–91.

14 Matthews's reference to "Modocs" is facetious, for he well knew that they were an Indian tribe in the Pacific Northwest.

15 Such ploys by civilians to keep troops in their vicinity were commonplace on the frontier. Then, as now, a military presence was a boon to the local economy. The populace profited by selling hay, grain, beef cattle, wood, vegetables, and other commodities to the troops. Likewise, saloons, gambling houses, and brothels were eager recipients of the currency paid to soldiers. See Rickey, *Forty Miles*, 128–29, 168.

We had a terrible hurricane here last nights came very near blowing all our tents down. I had gone to bed before the storm came up, but as it was so furious, [I] got up and dressed and then sit down on my bed to think and await events, when [I] got through thinking found it was Sun up, and that I had just slept about 7 hours with my cloth[e]s on. No damage was done by the storm.

I have finished nearly all the Company work [I] will have to do for Uncle Sam. Have a couple of Official Letters to write tonight, and then [I] will have little or nothing to do while [I] am in the Service.

I have three days less than two months to serve even though [I] have to serve full time, but feel almost sure [I] can get the eight days in September if no more. In this case, [I] would only have one month and twenty days. I tell you what the time is getting short, but not too short.

You can hardly imagine how nicely I have succeeded in the dispensing with the use of Tabacco. Have not used the weed in any manner since 12 o'clock of the night of June 30th. Have no idea I shall ever use it again. I can assure it required considerable resolution to keep from it. A more than 16 year habit broken of in a moment. Love will accomplish most anything won't it?[16]

Now I have not time to write a moment longer. We will surely have a mail in a day or two when I will hear from you.

Hope this will find you all as well, and feeling as well as I do tonight. Excuse mistakes and write often.

Fort Bascom, New Mexico

JULY 12, 1874

No mail from the East yet. But [I] expect one tomorrow. A new mail route from Las Vegas to Fort Stanton has been opened and one mail each week will pass here. And I suppose the Mail from Union will be taken off.

The two Scouting parties that went in pursuit of the Indians, returned, one party the next day without having seen any signs, and the other party under Command of Captain Morris last night. This party

---

16 If we are to believe this, Matthews began using tobacco in some form at age eight. This may have been one of the sources of strife with his parents.

found their trail and followed it a short distance until they came up with some Mexican Sheep herders who informed the Captain that the Indians had passed there on the night of the 8th inst. and that they were about 52 miles ahead of him. The men only had three days rations leaving here, and it would have been foolishness to follow them any farther. I have no idea that they will visit this place during the summer, and suppose this was only a few on a thieving expedition. I am suffering terrible with the heat tonight, have finished all the Company papers, and will have comparitively nothing to do for the remaining "<u>month</u> and a <u>but</u>."

Have almost become reconciled to do without tabacco, but still miss it very much, shall never use it again.

When my boots are finished I wish you would please direct them to Frank C. Ingraham, Commissary Sergeant U.S.A., Fort Union, N.M. and he can send them from there to me by some other conveyance.[17] I am afraid if you were to send them to me and they had to pass through so many of these territory P[ost] M[asters], I would not get them.

Our dutch are making the Camp ring with their dutch songs.

Will write to you again tomorrow or the next day.

Fort Bascom, New Mexico
JULY 14, 1874

The citizen mail from Las Vegas arrived this P.M. It was some time before any person could be induced to open it and distribute the letters. The trouble arose in this manner. 1st this is a new Mail route just started, 2nd No Post Master has been appointed yet, and 3rd there was no key

---

17 Frank C. Ingraham first enlisted in the army at age twenty on November 11, 1866, at San Francisco, California. Assigned to Company M, he was one of the original members of the Eighth Cavalry. He was born in Cleveland, Ohio, and had worked as a clerk before joining the army. Immediately following his discharge in 1871, he again enlisted and served in the Eighth until he was appointed to the position of commissary sergeant in June of 1873. Ingraham left the army after his discharge in 1876, and found employment as a clerk for nearly two years in Washington, D.C., then elected to return to the army on April 4, 1878. He was assigned to the Fourth Infantry, first to Company E and later to the field staff as regimental quartermaster sergeant, a position he held until his discharge in 1883. Ingraham immediately reenlisted in the Fourth at the age of thirty-one. On January 8, 1885, he was promoted to the rank of post quartermaster sergeant. Tragically, he committed suicide by slashing his own throat on October 25, 1885, at Fort Hays, Kansas. See entry 799, p. 97, roll 31, ROE, RG 94, NA; entry 280, p. 151, roll 39, ibid.; entry 58, p. 134, roll 42, ibid.; entry 72, p. 164, roll 42, ibid.; and Register of Post Quartermaster Sergeants, RG 94, NA.

here that would open the lock. A regular Council of war was held between the Citizens here and our Officers. Every person wanted the mail bag opened but none cared to open it, did not like the idea of tampering with the U.S. Mail, had the bag been submitted to the buck Soldiers for their action, it would have been kicked open in a minute. However the Council decided that our Captain as Commanding Officer was the proper person to open the Mail and he done so. And when the strap had been cut and letters thrown out, lo and behold it was discovered that only five or six letters and a couple of papers was there. And two of these for your humble Servant. There must surely be something wrong for this is the first mail for two weeks and only half a dozen letters. Why, I ought to have had that many my self. And still I don't see how it can be when Father's letter was mailed July 2nd and one from Lec. June 30th.

I don't know what I am going to fill this sheet up with, for there is nothing here to write about, except the excessive hot weather and that subject has been exhausted long since.

The Indians I understand have threatened to come here and run off our horses. I would just like to see them try this experiment for we have two 12 lb. Guns here and plenty of grape and canister and if some of their dusty hides would not get perforated, it would be a caution.[18] But these Kiowa and Comanche Indians have no "stinking regard" (as the Soldiers say) for 12 lb Guns. This we learned one night on the Plains in 72, when they ran off our beef cattle. B and M Companies of our regiment that left here on the 30th of June are now at Cimerron N.M. in persuit of Indians that murdered a couple of Ranchmen near there [a] few days ago.

Only one month and 16 days. I tell you what, it is getting short. I asked the Captain the other day if he had any discharges (blanks) down here with him, said he had, and asked if I wanted any. Told him not just yet, but would want a couple for his Saddler and myself next month.

---

18 "Grape and canister" was a trite expression used by writers of the era who had little or no technical knowledge of artillery. Grape shot was used only in large-bore cannon, particularly seacoast and naval guns, to destroy ships' rigging and kill personnel. A "stand" consisted of nine iron balls, in three tiers, sandwiched between two iron plates secured by a central bolt and two iron rings. The diameter of the balls varied according to the caliber of the gun. Canister, on the other hand, was employed in field pieces ranging in size from twelve to forty-two pounders. It was an anti-personnel round consisting of a tin cylinder containing a quantity of iron balls (lead musket balls for mountain howitzers). Canister had the effect of a shotgun and was devastating against an enemy in the open at ranges of up to a couple hundred yards. See *Ordnance Manual*, 36, 271, 284.

I am glad the potatoes are doing so finely and that the prospects are good for a large crop. Also hope they may be out of the ground and safely housed by the time I reach home.

My appetite for tabacco has about disappeared and I have but few thoughts of it anymore. Have surprised myself greatly.

I am getting tired and sleepy, and as [I] can think of nothing interesting to write you will stop.

Fort Bascom, New Mexico
JULY 17, 1874

It is now 11:30 P.M. and time your boy was in his "little bed," but he is so gloriously happy, that such a thing as sleep would be an impossibility. Have never felt so happy since my absence from home, except the day [I] returned from the 40 days Scout in 72, when I received about thirteen letters and an arm full of papers.

Tonight about 10 o'clock Capt. McCleave, 8th Cavalry, A.A.Q.M. [Acting Assistant Quartermaster] returned from Fort Union. I was sitting in front of my tent talking to one of the Company at the time the Ambulance drove in. And being always anxious and eager to hear the news and find out if any mail was aboard, [I] rushed over to the driver and was handed an arm full of mail for the Company. Took it to the tent and for my portion, (Guess I got a little more than an equal share), five (5) letters, one (1) postal Card and three (3) papers. Letters were from Father, Ida, Capt. Byers, a young friend on General Service at Santa Fe and from the Veterinary Surgeon of the Regiment. The Postal Card was from our Ex 1st Sergeant, now Clerking in the War Department and a particular friend of mine. Two of the papers were from home the other from my friend the Vet. Surgeon. And now if this is not a glorious feeling to be in Ed Matthews never experienced anything of that description. It would make one of our innumerable Donkeys (Boroe's) laugh to see my smiling countenance. It resembles the picture of "Pluck" in the "Danberry News." Well we won't say anything about this, but proceed to business.

Your 4th of July was considerable more exciting and eventful than ours. Here there was nothing unusual except the firing of the National Salute of 38 guns, and that the boys had bacon and plum pudding for dinner. There seemed to be an abundance of the latter and as we had eaten nothing but beans and bacon for a month, the boys (your correspondant included) just gorged themselves and the result all were seen walking around an hour or so after to assist digestion. No cases resulted fatal and all hands were willing to attack a piece of supper, but there was none to attack.

There must have been fine fun at the "Fair Ground" on the 4th from your description, for I have not taken time to look [at] my papers, although there will be no opportunity to send this off for several days, [I] could not resist the temptation of writing tonight. The last time I was at the Fair Grounds was on the 3rd of July '69 when I won the Velocipede race and $25. and came near dying from exhaustion and the heat of the Sun. Had it not have been for Dr. Shipley (poor fellow) and his little flask of "Old Rye" [I] guess [I] would have fainted.

Am glad the Money Order is all right and now if the boots only come as safe all will be well, but [I] guess they will.

The question of time, distance, and roads, I shall travel over next Sept. is not easily answered. In the first place I cannot tell whether I will be able to leave Fort Union before the 10th of Sept. or whether I will be in Leavenworth Kansas at that date. I have heard that there has been an order published to the effect "that no Soldier would be allowed to leave the District in which he was serving without having a furlough from the Dept. Commander in which the District was located."

Saturday Morning. When [I] had finished the first sheet last night, or rather this morning, for it was about 1 o'clock, [I] concluded to cease hostilities, and look at the locals in the home papers. Was quickly disrobed, for [I] only had on trousers, shirt and slippers and lying down on my bed perused the papers until about 3 A.M. when [I] extingushed the "dip" and was soon unconcious of things earthly.

Awoke about 7 o'clock washed, dressed and went to breakfast, more from habit than anything else, for [I] knew [I] should find nothing palatable. Bacon, dry bread and a cup of badly made coffee is not calculated to tempt to any great extent ones appetite. Many and many a time when I <u>was addicted</u> to the use of <u>tobacco</u>, I have gone away from my meals without having satisfied[?] my mouth by anything placed on the table, and having a good smoke, cheated my stomach in the belief that something had been taken inwardly. This is a strange country and stranger people when one will try to cheat himself, but with all this fastidious taste of mine I can eat anything when I am hungry from a buffalo chip down to a ten-penny nail.

I was never passionately fond of vegetables as you well know, but circumstances over which we have no control, sometimes work wonderful changes in one's customs etc. And so it has proved in regard to my tastes for Vegetables. When I say we have had bean soup for dinner, and baked beans for supper every day for the past month and that I have eaten heartily of them at every meal, and that I like them, [I] only tell the truth. Still when one has beans for about a thousand meals in succession the thing becomes monotonous and considerable on the order of sameness. And I have no doubt but that I would fight if any person said beans to me when I leave this bean bellied Army. (Excuse the expression).

Another Indian Report was brought in yesterday morning. A Mexican herder rode frantically into the Camp and reported that the Indians were twelve miles from this place and were killing cattle that belonged to a Mr. Stapp, a ranchman living close by our Camp. Our horses were run in from the herd and twenty men including our Capt. and Lieut. saddled up and started out hot foot with one days rations. They have not returned yet. I came near going out with the party and only remained in Camp on account of the excessive hot weather. Have no idea our men will get to see the Indians and even if they should come in sight of them, would not get a shot.

Our dinner bell, (big piece of steel and bar of iron) has rung, so [I] will stop until [I] have conformed with a regular habit of mine: "that of going to dinner when ever [I] had an opportunity," but before I leave you I will bet my interest in the Civil Rights Bill against a counterfeit Nicle [nickel], that there is "bean soup" for dinner. "Any body take that bet?" Well here I have returned to my desk and writing after half an hours absence and am in the most Angelic feeling imaginable. Lost my bet on the bean soup. And would be willing to have lost the whole Black race besides. We had no beans for dinner. When the remnant of Co. L now in Camp gazed on that dinner, and found roast beef instead of bean soup, they could not suppose the exclamation of Nasby, when the Crusaders had destroyed all the liquor at the "X roads." And a new supply had been received at "Old Bascoms," viz: "We are saved." Some of our boys must have been out foraging and to save themselves from being bit by some persons Cow, had to kill it, but the least intimation of anything of this kind the better. A frontier Soldier seldom asks you "where you got it or how," but instead, "Are there anymore of the same kind where that come from?"

But to return to our Warriors now in pursuit of "Mr. Lo," I have no doubt but that they are now riding around over the sand, searching for the trail of the wiley Comanche, while the sun is more than burning them.[19] Am glad now I had sense enough to remain in Camp.

In regard to time, route etc. of my return, [I] will resume the subject where [I] left off last night. I have never seen the Order spoken of, but would have seen it had one been published. It is just this, I cannot get my "Final Statements" cashed until the day my Enlistment expires. Perhaps I could sell them to some person at a discount of 8 or 10 percent, but this I would not do under any circumstances for I could not very well afford to pay $20 or $25 in order to get away two or three days sooner. At present I shall count on leaving Union about the 10th of Sept.

As to transportation to the Rail Road, [it] will altogether depend on circumstances. The distance from Union to Las Animas C[olorado] T[erritory] is 218 miles. This is the remains of the Kansas Pacific so far, this distance will have to be traveled by Stage or foot transportation, if by Stage the fare will be about $45 and if I should be fortunate to meet with some Government wagons or Ambulance's going through, the transportation would be nothing.[20] And the only difference would be that I would be four or five days later in reaching home. My transportation to Cincinnati amounts to about $65. At Las Animas, I would take the K[ansas] P[acific] to Kansas City, and from there to St. Louis would take the North Missouri, from St. Louis [I] will go to Cincinnati where [I] will discard Soldier blue, and Equip myself with something suitable in the line of Clothing, and will perhaps at the same time have my lost "Ivory" replaced.

The quicker I can get out of Cincinnati the better [I] will be pleased for [I] have no particular love for the place. Will go from C. to Bell Air on the B[altimore] and O[hio] R[ail] R[oad] ([I]think it is at this point the Rail Road from C. crosses the River). And will then take the Old Balto. and O. to Balto. From B. will take the Western Maryland, as far as

---

19 "Mr. Lo" was a common soldier nickname for Indians. It derived from a poem by Alexander Pope.
20 Matthews was misinformed on this point. The railroad that had reached Las Animas, Colorado Territory, was the Atchison, Topeka & Santa Fe, not the Kansas Pacific, which lay farther north (paralleling modern Highway 40) on the route to Denver. The possibility that he might hitch a ride on government wagons refers to the supply trains that were still plying that portion of the Santa Fe Trail from end of track to Fort Union.

Westminster. Arriving at the Depot [I] will disembark, take the middle of the pike and take a "foot march" until [I] reach the Corner of Main and [word missing] Street, make a right turn and rush into the arms of my darling Mother. This is my route as well as [I] know at present.

As to time [I] can only suppose and guess. Supposing I cannot get away from Union before the 10th of Sept., this will come on "Thursday," if [I] travel by Stage (which [I] will suppose) [I] will arrive at Las Animas Saturday Morning Sept. 12th. It will be guess work through out. I have no "time table" or schedule, so [I] will average the rate of travel at 20 miles per hour from Las Animas to St. Louis and at 25 miles per hour from the latter City to the end of my destination. Say I leave Las Animas the evening of the 12th, [I] will arrive at Kansas City late in the evening of the 13th. If [I] should connect as we would wish, and will suppose [I] would arrive in St. Louis the morning of the 14th. Leaving same day [I] would arrive in Cincinnati on the 15th. Here I could transact any business I wanted to and leave on the 16th (evening) and would arrive in Balto. the morning of the 18th. Do any little shopping and visiting [I] wanted to, and leave on the 4:00 o'clock train, and arrive home Friday evening at 5:37 P.M. just in time to have a hug, kiss, cry, laugh and shake hands all around before we eat something. I am an exception to the general rule in putting [off?] a thing of this kind. I don't suppose there is another soldier in the U.S.A., but would have put the eating part first.

And now comes the cost which [I] calculate will amount to $1.00 just about $35. more than the Government transportation will amount to. There is no telling yet to a certainty where I will be at the end of my enlistment, but the prospects of being at this delectable Camp are almost sure.

Our Warriors returned to Camp an hour ago. They saw the greatest quantity of Indian signs, but nary a Modoc. One Mexican had been killed before the party arrived. That is the only casualty so far as reported. Suppose we will now have Indians on the half shell, for the balance of the Summer.

I have just learned that B and M Companies are full of business. B had went from Union to Cimerron, N.M. shortly after they arrived at the former place, but had returned to Union again, and again been sent out on the road. Also heard that the Indians had Killed some 20 persons around Trinadad C[olorado] T[erritory] and the day Cimerron N.M. and that a Citizen volunteer Company was being orgainized. This is only a rumor so far, perhaps I will find out something more authentic before [I] close this.

My friend in Washington sends me a "postal card" to know why I do not write. About three weeks ago I received a "Card" from him, but did not consider it an answer to my letter, but as I did not hear from him again [I] concluded to write, so [I] sit down and filled up two sheets of this kind of paper for him. The letter is still in my desk awaiting the next mail. Told him in it that he wrote too good a letter to put me off with a "postal card" and that I couldn't stand it.

My Vet. Surgeon friend has resigned his position and intends locating in Denver City.[21] He thinks there is no person in the world like Ed. M. He has manufactured a "Horse Powder" which may become as popular as the great Stonebaker or Foutz (or Pfoutz) I don't know which, wish I was certain of the matter, would make a fortune out of it for us both.

Tuesday 21st. The Citizen Mail from Las Vegas arrived this afternoon, but one letter for our Company and that not for me, but can assure you [I] was not disappointed for [I] did not expect much. And [I] am feeling good still from the effects of the last dose.

Am still firm in my resolution to quit the use of Tabacco. The inclination has not left yet, but is not so very strong.

The Comanche and Kiawas have been stealing some stock in this neighborhood and have Killed several Mexican Cattle herders. Our boys went out twelve miles today and brought in the body of one of the Killed. It is a good thing for the Country when Indians Kill the Mexicans, for when they do this they shut off their supplies and also information. Rest assured that I shall not expose myself to any unnecessary danger.[22]

Fort Bascom, New Mexico
JULY 28, 1874

The U.S. Mail arrived [a] few moments ago, and brought me Fathers letter dated 12th inst. And the nicest fitting boot I ever put on my foot.

---

21 The Eighth Cavalry had two veterinary surgeons at this time, both attached to District Headquarters in Santa Fe. The second-class, or junior, veterinarian was Absolum W. Blackburn, who had been on detached service at Fort Union since December of 1873. See Eighth Cavalry Returns, June 1874.

22 The raids alluded to apparently occurred on Ute Creek, north of Fort Bascom. Gregg was properly critical of the ranchmen for not taking the necessary precautions after being warned by Captain Morris. Gregg to AAG, Department of MO, July 24, 1874, in LR, District of NM, RG393, copy in Arrott Collection, v. 29, 102.

The "Modocs" have not been seen for some time around here, but last night some Mexican horse thieves run off a dozen horses from a herder within a half mile of Camp. The report was brought to Camp about 11 P.M. last evening, and a party of men sent out. They have not returned yet, so [I] cannot say tell what success they met with.

My term of service is drawing to a fine end and I have every reason to believe that it all lays with Harlan, whether I get away from here on or about the 20th of next month, or not until after the 1st of September. Harlan left here yesterday for Union where he will have some papers to make out for the late Quartermaster of this Camp. It will take him about a week to do this work. And if he wants to, he can get back here by the 10th and not latter than the 15th of August. He is the only man in the Company that can take my place, and unless he gets back I will have to remain here to make out the August Returns, Muster Rolls etc. But he promised me by all that was holy, that he would return as soon as he possible could in order to give me a chance to get off before my time was out. I have not said anything to the Captain about giving me any time as I thought it was most too soon to speak. Our Company Saddler's Enlistment expires August 9th, and the Capt. let him go to Union with the Wagons yesterday. That was the same as giving him 14 days. Would have given him his discharge but when [I] come to look for them, [I] found they had been left at Union, so [I] will have to send up by this mail for some. It will not make any difference in this case as the man intends to reenlist in the Company.

I intend to go to either Fort Leavenworth Kansas, or St. Louis Mo. to have my Final Statements Cashed. In regard to the transportation it is paid only to the place of Enlistment and at the following rate, viz: for every 20 miles, you are allowed a days pay, and a days rations. Computed at 30¢. This would make 83 1/3 c. per day. The distance from here to Cincinnati is 1534 miles, making my transportation $64.20. The Gov't. pays its discharged men as though they were to <u>foot</u> the distance, and does not provide for staging and Railroading. My transportation will not begin to carry me to Cincinnati, let alone 624 miles farther, if I have to travel to the Rail Road by Stage, but I'll get home all right and get home respectable.

Sue said in one of her letters some time ago that she did not want me to wear Soldier Cloth[e]s home. And wanted me to look as nice as [I] did when [I] left home. It is true one ought to make and save a little money in five years, and I have made enough and saved enough to give me a complete and respectable outfit, and have a few dollars besides. (Not very many though, not enough to start a National Bank). All I ask is that my health will continue as good in the years to come, as it has in the past. I will find some way to make a respectable living and help you loved ones along.

I guess you had better not write to me after August 20th, and also stop the paper at that time for I expect to get away from Union sometime near the last of August, provided Harlan gets back to make out the Companies papers. I will continue to write to you every opportunity. I am feeling splendid and am as happy as a King at my prospects of so soon meeting you all.

You must give Mr. Yingling my sincere thanks as well as the price of the boots, for they are a splendid pair of boots, and fit as nicely as a Kit Glove. It is not necessary for me to wear them to break them in so as they will fit and feel comfortable on my feet, for they are that now. Many thanks to you also my dear Father, for the trouble I give you, and also to the person or persons that put the stockings in the boots.

Enclosed is another Order for a pair of Boots with size etc. You can give the enclosed to Mr. Yingling and if he will make them I will pay him the money soon as [I] return, as that will omit all risk of sending the money.

Every man in the Company has been to my tent to see my boots, and all have spoken highly of quality etc. If Mr. Y. consents to make the boots for this friend of mine, I guess you had better have them done up and addressed as follows: Sergeant Richard Williams, Co. L 8th Cav'y., Fort Union, N.M.[23]

---

23 Richard Williams began his military career in 1866, when he enlisted in the Eighteenth Infantry at the age of twenty-one at Camp Douglas, Utah. Previously a miner, the six-foot Williams was a native of New York City. As a result of the army reorganization of 1869, he was reassigned to Company G, Fourth Infantry, from which he was discharged at the end of his term on August 18, 1869. He reenlisted in the Ninth Infantry in November of 1870 at Omaha Barracks. Ten months later, however, he deserted and shortly thereafter enlisted again, but under an assumed name in Company L, Eighth Cavalry. He subsequently surrendered himself during the amnesty of 1873, and was permitted to make good the lost time and to serve out the remainder of his unexpired term using his real name. He was discharged as a sergeant with an excellent rating at Fort Brown, Texas, in 1878. After working as a cook for a few months, Williams reenlisted in Company M, Eighth Cavalry and served another five years. He was again discharged as a sergeant with an excellent rating. He then tried civilian life for nearly four years, but returned to the army in May of 1887, to serve three more enlistments. Williams was finally discharged for disability at the age of forty-nine at Fort Sill, Indian Territory, in the spring of 1898. See entry 1517, p. 265, roll 32, ROE, RG 94, NA; entry 1299, p. 305, roll 37, ibid.; entry 319, p. 116, roll 43, ibid.; entry 198, p. 281, roll 45, ibid.; entry 214, p. 314, roll 46, ibid.; and entry 440, p. 299, roll 48, ibid.

I know of nothing more to write tonight and as it is getting late will close. "Only One Month and three days, I guess." Tell all that ask that I will be home about the 15th or 18th.

Fort Bascom, New Mexico
AUGUST 4, 1874

Mail day and happy one for me as usual. Fathers welcome letter dated July 19th came to hand, also an elegant letter from Capt. B. and two home papers. Since the arrival of the mail [I] have been very busy working [on] an Official matter but have finished all in that line and must now answer yours, and Capt. B's.

I am more than happy tonight for [I] have asked for, and been promised a "25 days Furlough." Soon as [I] had finished the Captains work this evening [I] concluded it was a good time to speak and done so. I asked for 25 days on my time so as [I] could go to Union, and wait for some opportunity to travel to the Rail Road, instead of going by the stage so as to save $40.00 or $50.00. Then to go as far as Fort Leavenworth Kansas and get my Final Statements Cashed.

Told the Captain that I thought I was entitled to that time, as I had served my enlistment about as faithful as the majority of Soldiers. He told me that he knew that very well and would do what he could for me. Said soon as the wagons returned from Fort Union, which will be some time about the 10th, he intended sending them right back and that I could go with them. Oh, but I tell you I have been hopping around pretty lively since then.

Now I expect to be in Fort Leavenworth by the 1st of September and think [I] can get my papers cashed on that day, and in this case would be home about the 4th of September, just one month from tonight. Anyhow I will be able to tell you in a later letter almost the hour [I] will be with you. You see it will be impossible for me to get my papers Cashed before the 1st of Sept. by the Paymaster at Ft. Leavenworth. As a letter will have to be written from the Co. to him stating that I would present my Final Statements to him to be Cashed. And they are not in the habit of cashing them until your time is out. Will write you more definitely by the next mail.

I can't account how it is that you have not heard from me for so long, as [I] have never missed a week in writing to you, but I suppose it has been through some delay in the mail, and that all my letters have reached you ere this. And anyhow the time is drawing near when we will have no occasion to write.

There is nothing much for me to write you. Everything is quiet here now, but I think our Company will have to remain here until the 15th of October. However it will make no difference to me how long they remain here after I get away, except that I will be a little sorry to leave a few of my friends in such a miserable place as this.

You need have no fears that I shall expose myself to any danger at this stage of the game, time is too short for that and besides there is too much happiness in store for me when I return to do anything foolish now.

Why don't you folks say something about my not using Tabacco? Have been kind of disappointed for [I] expected to see something like this: "My noble boy, to make such a sacrifice etc, etc.," but you have not said a word. I am doing splendid and have not used the article since the 30th of June. Sometimes [I] am almost sorry that [I] gave up smoking, as we are living so badly now and if I smoked I could cheat my stomache sometimes in the belief that I had eaten something when I had not. There is nothing like a good smoke after eating. "Father will agree with me in this I know."

I acknowledged receipt of boots and general satisfaction they had given in last weeks letter. You needn't think Father that your foot is smaller than mine, yours is very small I know, is in fact a good deal smaller than mine if the difference in our weights is taken into consideration, for I only weighed 141 today, but we are not going to allow anything for this.

I am glad and happy to hear that so many are anxious to see me return home, and will be happier if some of them will give me something to do that will give me an honest living.

Fort Bascom, New Mexico
AUGUST 11, 1874

Father's ever welcome letter dated July 26th was received about an hour ago. It was very interesting indeed and I consider [it] as one of the best letters I ever read, although in the commencement of it you expressed doubts as to your ability to fill the sheet of paper.

For your <u>praise</u>, I sincerely thank you and trust through no act of mine in the future you will be disappointed in me. My services in the Army will soon be dispensed with, owing to my having no desire to renew my engagement. And as you say I will not have the U.S. to pay me for my services. And may not find in Civil life as sure and regular pay for my services. Well we will wait and see. When I return [I] will not have much more than will equip me in a new outfit, but I will have good health and strong constitution to resort to. This added to a determination to succeed in anything I undertake will meet with its reward, I am sure. Well we will wait and see.

I have lots of news to tell you, but as [I] will be home so soon [I] am going to write short letters hereafter. Made out a discharge and set of final Statements this morning for our Co. Saddler, and unless I get away from here pretty quick [I] will have to make out a set of reenlistment papers for him, as he intends to re-enlist in [the] Company.[24] I am now next on the programme for a discharge and have 27 days full time. Do not expect to serve it down here, but have not yet learned when the Captain is going to let me off. Even if I was a free man tonight [I] do not know how [I] would get up to Union. The transportation is the trouble, but we will trust to luck, and when my discharge is given to me I will find some way of getting home. You must excuse short letters for the balance of my time. I will write to you again in a few days when [I] expect to have something more definite to tell you, as regards my home movement.

Fort Bascom, New Mexico
4 O'CLOCK A.M., AUGUST 13, 1874

I am happier this morning than [I] have been for five long years. And why, you ask, because in half [an] hour your Son and brother will be on the road home.

Yesterday Capt. Morris said to me: "have you your Books and papers all posted up?" Told him I had and that there was no back work

---

24 Michael Shanahan was born in Limerick, Ireland, and later immigrated to the United States. Having worked previously as a stone mason, Shanahan enlisted in the army on August 9, 1869, at New York City. As Matthews predicted, the saddler immediately reenlisted in the company and served a second five-year term, taking his discharge at Fort Brown, Texas. Although Private Shanahan enlisted a third time on August 19, 1879, he died less than three months later from the effects of a broken skull. See entry 675, p. 115, roll 37, ROE, RG 94, NA; entry 220, p. 259, roll 40, ibid.; and entry 369, p. 199, roll 43, ibid.

of any description to do. Asked if I had given any person in the Company instructions how to render the necessary returns, etc. etc. Said I had. He then told me to settle up my own account, make out my discharge and Final Statements and be ready to go to Union with him this morning. Oh no I didn't feel happy about this time. Was so happy that [I] was nervous and could hardly make out my papers. Will leave here in [a] few moments in an Ambulance for U[nion]. Will be three days going up. I have to stop now as everything is ready. Will mail this at Las Vegas as [we] pass through and will write more definitely soon as [I] reach Union.

Excuse everything for [I] have only had a moment to write. And besides just imagine how good I feel.

Fort Union, New Mexico
AUGUST 17, 1874

Well here I am and on my way <u>home</u>. Oh what a blessed name. Left Bascom the morning of the 13th in an Ambulance, and in Company with our Captain. Arrived at Las Vegas the evening of the 15th. Mailed a letter to you, and received Father's of August 2nd. Was delighted to hear from you. Left Vegas the evening of the 16th and arrived here that night. Was kindly received by Sergt. Williams (of our Co.) and Lady, taken in and cared for.

While at breakfast this morning the Adjutants Clerk came in and gave me Father's excellent letter mailed on the 10th Inst. The Clerk said he had heard I was in the Post, and knew I would be glad to hear from home. They all know Father's writing, and also how anxious I always am to hear from home. Here I found Major Price, with three Companies of our regiment. They will leave here on the 19th inst. join our Co. at Bascom and make a big and general Scout against the Indians. In fact all the Cavalry and part of the Infantry on the frontier are now scouting or will start in a few days. The Indians seem to have made a general outbreak all over the country. I would not be surprised if the boys found plenty of work to do before the Summer is over. It was getting pretty lively for us at Bascom, but of this [I] will tell you soon as [I] return.

"2 hours later." Captain sent for me at this stage of the game, so [I] had to stop and go to him, found him and was handed a copy of a report in regard to number of men, amount of transportation etc. in the

Company ready for field service, and was told to copy it and bring it to him at once so that he could hand it to Major Price. I have done it and am now in my room lying down with a small box for a desk and pencil to write with, as [I] have nothing better and cannot get in either the Adjutants Office or B Co.'s Office to finish this. But why go into such lengthy detail when [I] know you will not complain so long as you can decypher what I write you. Guess though you will not be able to do any thing more than that with this. I will have a good deal of writing yet to do for our Capt. during the next two or three days. And soon as [I] have finished I will ask him again for my Furlough. Have no doubt but [I] will get it, and be able to reach Fort Leavenworth by the 1st of next month. There are a good many of the men here now doing duty, that came out from the states same time as I did, who are waiting here for their discharges. And if I have to remain here until the last day of my time [I] will not [mind?] much, for now that [I] am away from Bascom [I] feel ever so much better, and besides [I] am out of all danger.

Will write to you every opportunity or whenever [I] have any thing to write to you. The time is very short now and we will soon enjoy the happiness of our meeting which you so beautifully illustrated or described in your last letter.

I am truly grateful and happy to know that I have so many good friends in Westminster, and shall always endeavor to conduct myself in such a manner that they will continue to think well of me.

Col. McKellip was very kind to say what he did of me, and if he can aid me in getting some good situation when [I] return will be more thankful, but as to a Commission in the Army [I] would not want it even if such a thing were possible, for [I] am tired of the army and everything connected with it.

You must pardon such a scrawl, as my facilities just now for writing are not very good, and besides I cut my first finger on my right hand today and it is rather sore tonight.

Will write again in a day or two.

Fort Union, New Mexico

AUGUST 19, 1874

I am now fixed to remain here until the last day of my service in the Army of Uncle Sam. Our Captain left here this evening for Bascom, but before he left he done everything in his power to get me a Furlough so that I could go through Fort Leavenworth by the lst of September, but late Orders and U.S. Regulations will not allow furloughs in cases like mine. And I must be content to submit to the rules and regulations governing the land forces of this glorious Union. But what is the difference? I have served faithfully my enlistment, less the few remaining days, and I can now serve them and be under no obligation to any person in the U.S. Service. Suppose I am as well off here as in Leavenworth until my time is out, and am sure [I] will be at less expense. The stage fare from here to the Rail Road is $43., which I will have to pay unless [I] have an opportunity to travel by some cheaper conveyance.

Major Price, with his Command of three Companies of the 8th leave here for Bascom tomorrow. They will be joined by our Company at B[ascom] and together go on a Scout for perhaps two months. From present indications I have no doubt but that they will find Indians before the Summer is over, as they seem to be plentiful down in that country.[25]

Am happy to say that this individual will have no more of that kind of amusement, if [I] can call it by that name. I have nothing particular to write about this evening, and expect you will have to be content with short letters for the balance of the time [I] am away.

You can write to me now as late as August 28th, as I do not expect to get away from here one day before my time is out.

Adjutant's Office
Fort Union, New Mexico
AUGUST 24, 1874

Have the best news to tell you now that [I] ever had for the last five years. <u>I leave here tomorrow morning for the Rail Road with a detachment of our regiment. And will not be at one cents expense to go there</u>. I am in better spirits this evening than [I] have been for many a day. Only heard of this party going away [a] few hours ago. Thought there was nothing to loose if nothing gained by asking to go. Started in a hurry for the Commanding Officer of the Post and stated my case. The present C.O. is

---

25 This operation involved four companies of the Eighth Cavalry: C, H, K, and L, totaling almost three hundred men. See Morrison to Price, August 8, 1874, LS, District of NM, RG 393, copy in Arrott Collection, v. 29, 128.

1st Lieut. [Edmund Luff] of my Company, and soon as [I] had explained every thing to him, he said, "Certainly Matthews, if it is any accommodation to you and will save a dollar for you, you can go." Told me to see Capt. McCleave, (of our regt.) who will go in charge of the Outfit and ask his permission to go along. Done so, and was told to get ready. This was in the Quartermasters Office. Capt. McCleave turned to Capt. Smith, Depot Q.M. and said, "This young man wants to go with the transportation tomorrow. I have known him a long time and know him to be a very worthy Soldier, and that I had been a Sergeant and Company Clerk ever since he knew me." Very good of the Capt. wasn't it?[26]

I will be at Fort Lyons, terminus now of the Atchison, Kansas [sic] and Santa Fe Rail Road, about the 1st of September. And may not receive my discharge until the 8th. Will write to you soon as [I] reach the Rail Road. Have left word here for any Mail coming for me to be sent back home. So if any of your own letters should come back just keep them for me and I will read them soon as [I] return. I don't want you to destroy them just because I am coming home.

I hope none of you are sick and will all be well when Eddie comes marching home about the 12th or 14th of next month.

You must excuse everything in this not according to regulations for am so happy that [I] guess am kind of Lo[o]ney.

Much to his satisfaction, Eddie missed participating in what would be known later as the Red River War, the largest field operation involving his company during the entire era. During the spring and early summer of 1874, Cheyenne, Comanche, and Kiowa bands retaliated against the Indian Bureau's withholding of rations and the concurrent mass slaughter of the southern buffalo herd by commercial hunters. General William T. Sherman, commanding the army, received permission in July to launch a campaign against those tribes, now roaming the Staked Plains and raiding on the northern Texas frontier.

---

26 Captain Gilbert C. Smith had served as quartermaster of Fort Union Depot since July 5, 1873. He was another of the men hailing from the eastern United States who migrated to California prior to the Civil War and wound up serving with that state's volunteer forces. Smith was initially first sergeant of Company D, Fifth California Infantry, but was soon thereafter promoted to the rank of second lieutenant, a rank he held until 1864. He served as a captain and assistant quartermaster of volunteers for the next two years. In 1866, Smith received an appointment as a second lieutenant in the Ninth U.S. Infantry, and remained with that unit until 1868, when he transferred to the Quartermaster Department. Smith eventually rose to the position of deputy quartermaster general of the army in 1895, and died in 1899. See Heitman, *Historical Register*, vol. 1, 898.

The army's proven strategy called for several columns of troops to converge on Indian haunts, in this instance the Texas Panhandle. The army's spearhead, composed of eight companies of the Sixth Cavalry and four of the Fifth Infantry, along with a section of artillery, under the overall command of Colonel Nelson A. Miles, struck south from Fort Dodge, Kansas. A second column, acting as "beaters" to help corral the elusive tribesmen, moved east from Fort Union down the Canadian River. This battalion of three companies of the Eighth Cavalry, commanded by Major William R. Price, passed through old Fort Bascom on August 23, where it was reinforced by Eddie's Company L, though he was then at Fort Union about to embark on his homeward journey.

Completing the encirclement of the region, two additional columns penetrated the Staked Plains from the vicinity of Fort Concho, Texas, and another advanced west from Fort Sill, Indian Territory. During the late summer and fall, troops and warriors clashed in several engagements, three of them involving Eddie's old company. By the end of the year, most of the Indians had either been defeated or had realized the futility of further resistance and returned to their agencies. Only a few remained out until early the following year, when they too finally capitulated.[27] *The near extermination of the bison, coupled with the displacement of the native inhabitants, left the boundless grasslands of the Panhandle open to swift occupation by Texas cattlemen operating on a grand scale.*

Meanwhile, ex-private Eddie Matthews went "marching home" to Maryland following his discharge. He was clearly embarrassed to be seen in uniform because regular soldiers were widely thought of as shiftless and too lazy to work. Unlike the experience of veterans returning from the Civil War, there was no band to greet him at the train station, no parade in his hometown, no fanfare of any kind beyond that extended by a family grateful to have him back alive. Like other ex-regulars of the western Indian campaigns, Matthews quickly melded back into the local populace, his service to his country barely noticed and soon forgotten.[28]

---

27 See Utley, *Frontier Regulars*, 212–33. Company L, Eighth Cavalry, saw action in the vicinity of Sweetwater Creek, Texas, on September 12; near Gageby Creek, Indian Territory, on October 13; and near Muster Creek, Texas, on November 28. The company suffered no casualties, though it reportedly inflicted some among the Indians. See *Chronological List of Actions*, 58–59; and Heitman, *Historical Register*, vol. 2, 440–41.

28 The local newspaper noted only that "Edward Matthews, son of John Matthews, Esq. of this city, returned home Thursday last from the West, where he has been serving in the United States Regular Army for the past five years" (*Democratic Advocate*, September 12, 1874).

EPILOGUE

"If I was only out of this miserable mob and home they would never catch me in it again," Eddie Matthews once swore. For a man who found army life so distasteful and had so eagerly anticipated the day of his discharge, he would seem the most unlikely of candidates to ever again don army blue. Yet, as implausible as it may seem, Eddie did just that.

At the age of twenty-seven, after being out of the service for more than three years, he again sought out a recruiting office, this time in nearby Baltimore, where he signed up for another five-year hitch on January 18, 1878.[1] His motives for reenlisting are unknown, but he obviously considered soldier life preferable to whatever he had encountered as a civilian. Stranger still, when the recruiter asked his previous occupation, he responded, "soldier," providing no clue as to what he may have done after returning to Westminster. He may have been employed by a railroad, an option he had once considered, or he may

---

[1] See entry 4, p. 1, roll 42, ROE, RG 94. That he enlisted at Baltimore suggests that Eddie found employment and remained in Westminster during the intervening three years. Had he gone directly to Sellersville, Pennsylvania, following his first enlistment, he undoubtedly would have reenlisted at Philadelphia.

have found work in the budding regional cigar industry, or he may have done something entirely different. Whatever it was, the recruiting officer chose not to question him too closely. Any honorably discharged veteran presenting himself for reenlistment was indeed a prize catch.[2]

During the interim since Matthews had passed through the old cavalry depot at Carlisle Barracks, Pennsylvania, the army had closed that facility and established a new one at Jefferson Barracks near St. Louis, Missouri, to be in closer proximity to operations on the western frontier. Eddie soon accompanied a draft of recruits to the depot, where he spent only a short time because, as a veteran, he needed no introduction to army drill, comportment, and discipline. Despite his criticism of his former comrades, he nevertheless must have found them tolerable, as evidenced by his request to return to his former company of the Eighth Cavalry. That its Captain, Louis T. Morris, his old company commander, was willing to accept him back in the unit spoke well of Eddie's conduct and performance during his previous enlistment.

During Eddie's time as a civilian, the Eighth Cavalry had been transferred from New Mexico Territory to the Department of Texas, where it took its turn occupying a line of forts and picket camps along the lower Rio Grande from Brownsville northwestward to Fort Clark. Smuggling, cattle rustling, and banditry by Mexican revolutionists and common outlaws were rampant along the international border, a situation with which the army had contended for years. At the time Matthews returned, Company L was stationed at Camp Santa Maria, 236 miles from its home post at Fort Brown. Even though he was added to the company rolls effective February 16, he probably was assigned to temporary duty at the post until his troop returned from its up-stream patrolling at the end of the month.[3]

With the exception of an overnight pursuit of some Mexicans early in April, the company settled into the usual humdrum of garrison life at Fort Brown for the next several months, a routine Matthews found all too familiar. As an old soldier, and an experienced company clerk, he must have maneuvered his way into that job soon after his arrival. If Eddie Matthews had learned anything during his previous five years' service, it was how to avoid the tedium of troop duty. As a clerk, he worked regular hours in the relative comfort of the orderly room, answered to no one except the first

---

[2] The recruiting officer was none other than First Lieutenant Emmet Crawford, Third Cavalry, who was instrumental in coaxing the famed Geronimo into surrendering. His untimely death at the hands of Mexican troops during the 1886 campaign attracted national attention.
[3] See Eighth Cavalry Returns, February 1878.

sergeant and his company commander, and was exempt from guard duty, fatigue, and drill.

Eddie readily readjusted to army life until the summer of 1879, when he committed an act that should have been contrary to his better judgment. On June 11, he abused his position as company clerk by preparing a fraudulent statement over the mark of Private William Snider, an illiterate member of his troop. The document authorized George Willman, a Brownsville grocer, to submit a claim of five dollars against Snider's pay. Eddie further incriminated himself by forging Captain Morris's signature as approving the action. From what we have learned about Eddie Matthews's character, it seems unlikely that he would have perpetrated a scam for his own gain. The wording of the order suggests that Willman had advanced credit to Snider, who may not have repaid the debt. If that supposition is correct, Willman may have prevailed upon Matthews, as company clerk, to produce the forged document to recover the money, rather than taking his grievance directly to Captain Morris for redress.

Regardless of Eddie's motives, the army came down hard. When the fraud was discovered on the following payday, July 1, he was promptly arrested and incarcerated in the Fort Brown guard house to await trial. A general court-martial in August found Eddie guilty on two counts of forgery, ordered him to be dishonorably discharged, and sentenced him to imprisonment for eighteen months at hard labor. Recognizing his previous good conduct, however, the members of the court unanimously urged the reviewing officer, Department Commander Edward O. C. Ord, to show Eddie clemency. Nearing the end of a forty-five-year army career, General Ord concurred and accordingly mitigated the sentence to twelve months.[4]

Matthews was incarcerated at Fort Brown until after his formal discharge from the army on September 13. Some two months later, he was transferred to Fort Leavenworth Military Prison in Kansas, where he was registered as an inmate on November 29, 1879, to serve the remainder of his sentence. We cannot be certain just how he spent his time there, but he likely worked either in the prison boot and shoe factory, or in the woodworking shop that produced barracks chairs for the army. In any event, it is interesting to note that when a census taker interviewed him in 1880, Eddie again gave his occupation as "soldier," rather than prison inmate, thus providing an insight to his self-perception despite his current circumstances.[5]

---

4 See *GCMO* No. 61, Department of Texas, September 2, 1879, RG 393, NA.

5 See entry 461, p. 380, v. 1, Registers of Prisoners, Military Prison Records Division, RG 94, NA; and *1880 U.S. Federal Census*, Ancestry.com, 2010.

It was common knowledge among the prisoners that requests for early release were sometimes granted to men convicted of less serious crimes, and who had records of good behavior. Matthews considered it worth a try. Early in March of 1880, he submitted his application for remission of two months of his sentence to Captain Asa P. Blunt, the prison commander. Blunt, rating Matthews a model prisoner, favorably endorsed the request and forwarded it to the judge advocate general for consideration. Army lawyers, apparently of the opinion that Matthews had been shown leniency enough by having his original sentence reduced, denied the request.[6]

Thus, Eddie had to resign himself to serving out his time until he was released on July 1. But at that point the trail goes cold. Just where he went and what he did in the decade immediately following his prison term have not been discovered. Chagrined by a dishonorable discharge and a prison record, he may have avoided returning to Westminster. He was well known there, and friends undoubtedly would have asked prying questions as to where he had been and why he had come home early. If he did return to Maryland, it seems likely that he would have fabricated a story about receiving an early discharge for one reason or another, a not uncommon occurrence.

Sometime after leaving the military for good, at least by 1892, Matthews found employment in the cigar manufacturing industry in Sellersville, Pennsylvania, a small rural town midway between Philadelphia and Allentown.[7] Although we cannot be sure, his reasons for migrating there may have stemmed from prior experience in that line of work in his hometown, which also supported at least two commercial cigar factories by the mid-1870s.[8]

Settled originally by German immigrants, Sellersville existed for many decades on a sluggish agrarian economy that supported relatively few local merchants and tradesmen. The mid-nineteenth century witnessed a gradual change as cigars gained in popularity over pipes as the smokers' preference. The climate and soils of southeastern Pennsylvania were conducive to the growing of tobacco, and by the 1840s, farmers in Bucks County discovered its practical and economic benefits as a cash crop.

---

6 See March 6, 1880, v. 1, Registers of LR, 1875–89, in Records of the Military Prison Division, RG 94, NA.
7 A 1932 obituary for William E. Matthews states that he had resided in Sellersville, Pennsylvania, for forty years. See *Doylestown Intelligencer* clipping files, 1850–1900, Bucks County Historical Society.
8 By 1874, John L. Reifsnider, a prominent and diversified Westminster businessman, was operating a wholesale cigar factory. Four years later, the newspaper editor noted, "Our cigar makers are doing a thriving business. Mr. Charles V. Wantz has fifty men employed" (*Democratic Advocate*, February 2, 1878). Matthews may have been employed by one of these firms between his enlistments.

Farmers and their families in the vicinity of Sellersville occupied the dreary winter months by making crude cigars from unsold tobacco. The cigars, usually long, slender, and of irregular shape, were then marketed through local taverns, as well as grocery and general mercantile stores. As business increased, groups began assembling at some designated neighbor's house to work as teams, thereby developing divisions of labor to promote efficiency and output.[9]

Word spread about Bucks County, and by the outbreak of the Civil War, scores of villages in the area, including Sellersville, Perkasie, and Quakertown in the North Penn Valley, were firmly established as "cigar towns." The industry grew rapidly during the 1870s and 1880s as manufacturers in Philadelphia, New York, and elsewhere began extending branch factories into this burgeoning cigar-producing district. While small privately owned shops having only a few employees continued to operate alongside the larger factories, cigar manufacturers increasingly used molds and other devices to speed production and increase the uniformity of the smokes. The North Pennsylvania Railroad, along which these towns were located, enabled the parent firms to deliver raw tobacco and the local shops to ship out the finished product, which was then sold to jobbers and wholesale grocers for distribution in saloons, barber shops, and grocery stores throughout the region.[10]

By the time Eddie Matthews arrived in town, Sellersville was well established in the popular five-cent cigar industry. A step up from the cheaper two-for-a-nickel stogie, the five-cent cigar had become an institution among the American working class. The town boasted a population of more than five hundred people and three or four commercial cigar factories, in addition to the traditional independent makers, which by that time supplied cigars to the large companies by subcontract. Each of the outside firms employed twenty-five to seventy people, both men and women, and thus almost everyone in the area was dependent on the domestic cigar industry in one way or another.

Despite his education and considerable experience as a clerk, Eddie hired on as a cigar maker at a factory, perhaps Otto Eisenlohr and Son, one of the principal companies operating in the area. The job was tedious and anything but glamorous.[11] Cigars were hand rolled by experienced men and women who were paid by the piece, with the wage averaging $5.00–$5.50 per thousand. At that, some companies paid half the worker's earnings in cash, the

---

9 See Baum, *Two Hundred Years*, 102.
10 See Cooper, *Once a Cigar Maker*, 13–15.
11 See Grim, *Bucks County Directory*, 202; and Cooper, *Once a Cigar Maker*, 199–200.

other half in cigars (which he peddled as best he could), or even in vegetables from company-owned gardens.

True to the pledge he made to himself during his army days, Eddie did not rush into marriage. In fact, he remained single until 1899, when at the age of forty-nine he married Annie J. Freed, a thirty-seven-year-old milliner and daughter of James and Sarah Freed of Sellersville. It was a first marriage for both. Their wedding date, April 26, would always be easy for Eddie to remember—it was also his birthday. Little more than nine months after they wed, Annie gave birth to William E. Matthews Jr., who, like his father, would be known as Edward. He would be their only child.[12]

Eddie Matthews spent the next three decades laboring in the factory at Sellersville, making cigars and packing them in cedar boxes until he was eighty-one years old. Annie, meanwhile, operated her own dry goods business for many years, and later owned a variety store. For the rest of his life, Eddie was a solid citizen of the community, being active in both the Reformed Church and the local Masonic lodge. Shortly after Annie's death in 1931, he went to live with his son in Jersey City, New Jersey. The old ex-cavalryman survived his wife only a short time, however, dying of a heart attack on May 24, 1932. His body was returned to Sellersville for burial.[13]

It seems unlikely that Eddie Matthews ever shared with anyone, perhaps not even Annie, the story of his second enlistment and subsequent time in prison. Certainly, his brothers and sisters were aware that he had served twice in the army, but his second term seems to have been overlooked, for reasons we now know. Nevertheless, time assuaged the sting of that unpleasant memory, and in later years, Eddie became something of a local celebrity as "an Indian fighter . . . in New Mexico and Arizona."[14] With so many Civil War veterans residing in every community in those days, it is easy to visualize a middle-aged Eddie swapping stories of his experiences on the western frontier and contrasting his life in the regulars with that of the volunteers. Ever a

---

12 Annie J. Freed Matthews, a native of Pennsylvania, was born in September of 1861. See *1900 U.S. Federal Census*, Ancestry.com, 2004; Marriage License Number 10, William Edward Matthews and Annie J. Freed, April 24, 1899, Bucks County, Pennsylvania, microfilm collections, Bucks County Historical Society; and records of St. Michael's Lutheran Church, Sellersville Church and Cemetery Corporation records, Bucks County Historical Society.
13 See Death Certificate, William Edward Matthews, Bureau of Vital Statistics, State Department of Health, New Jersey.
14 *Sellersville Herald*, September 19, 1907. It is interesting to note that when the census taker interviewed Eddie in 1930, with Annie present, he denied being a military veteran. See *1930 U.S. Federal Census*, Ancestry.com, 2002.

gregarious personality, he eagerly shared with those who showed an interest his treasured collection of Indian artifacts and souvenirs acquired during his army days in the Southwest.

Looking back over his long life, Eddie undoubtedly considered his service as a frontier cavalryman to have been the highlight. With the passage of time, he came to appreciate that he had "seen the elephant" and experienced what relatively few others of his generation had—being in a long column of horse soldiers snaking its way across the barren plains, being at long-since-abandoned western garrisons during their heyday, banging away at Indian enemies with a "Sharps Improved," and parading mounted in full dress uniform, arms and brasses glistening. Truly, his memories of that bygone era were to be cherished. That Eddie Matthews's family preserved the letters he penned as a young soldier is indeed fortunate. He could not have imagined that those threads, so vital in binding him to his distant family, would one day form a rich, vibrant personal legacy of life in the frontier army. Knowing Eddie as we now do, we can assume he would have found that immensely gratifying.

ABBREVIATIONS USED IN THIS VOLUME

AAG	Assistant Adjutant General
AAAG	Acting Assistant Adjutant General
AGO	Adjutant General's Office
ANJ	Army and Navy Journal
ARSW	Annual Report of the Secretary of War
CO	Commanding Officer
G&SO	General and Special Orders
GCMO	General Court-Martial Orders
GO	General Orders
HQ	Headquarters
LR	Letters Received
LR&O	Letters, Reports, and Orders
LS	Letters Sent
MH	Medical History
NA	National Archives
NM	New Mexico
NMHU	New Mexico Highlands University
PR	Post Returns
RG	Record Group
ROE	Registers of Enlistments in the U.S. Army
SO	Special Orders

BIBLIOGRAPHY

Unpublished Material

Chaplain's Records. Fort Union Collection, Donnelly Library Special Collections, New Mexico Highlands University, Las Vegas, NM.

District of New Mexico Letters, Reports, and Orders. Typescript copies of selected documents from RG 393, National Archives. Arrott Collection, Donnelly Library Special Collections, New Mexico Highlands University, Las Vegas, NM.

Eighth U.S. Cavalry, 1869–1874. Returns from Regular Army Cavalry Regiments, 1833–1916. Record Group 94, National Archives and Records Administration, Washington, D.C.

Enlistment Papers. Record Group 94, National Archives and Records Administration, Washington, D.C.

General and Special Orders Issued, 1871–1875. Eighth Cavalry, Regimental Records, 1866–1918. Record Group 391: Records of U.S. Regular Army Mobile Units, Cavalry, National Archives and Records Administration, Washington, D.C.

General Court-Martial Orders. Department of Texas, Headquarters Records, 1870–1913. Record Group 393: Records of U.S. Army Continental Commands, 1821–1920, National Archives and Records Administration, Washington, D.C.

General Orders. Department of the Missouri, Headquarters Records, 1861–1898. Record Group 393: Records of U.S. Army Continental Commands, 1821–1920, National Archives and Records Administration, Washington, D.C.

Historical Map Files. Arizona Historical Society, Tucson.

Historical Map Files. Donnelly Library Special Collections, New Mexico Highlands University, Las Vegas, NM.

Letters Received, 1872. Department of the Missouri, Headquarters Records, 1861–1898. Record Group 393: Records of U.S. Army Continental Commands, 1821–1920, National Archives and Records Administration, Washington, D.C.

List of Medical Officers and Physicians. Record Group 94, National Archives and Records Administration, Washington, D.C.

Marriage Licenses, Bucks County. Bucks County Historical Society, Doylestown, PA.

Medical History, Fort Union. Copied from RG 94, National Archives. Center for Southwest Research, Zimmerman Library, University of New Mexico, Albuquerque.

Medical History, Fort Union, New Mexico, 1868–1891. Record Group 94, National Archives and Records Administration, Washington, D.C.

Photo Archives. New Mexico History Library, Santa Fe.

Printed Orders and Circulars, 1873. Department of the Missouri, Headquarters Records, 1861–1898. Record Group 393: Records of U.S. Army Continental Commands, 1821–1920, National Archives and Records Administration, Washington, D.C.

Records of the Adjutant General's Office. Record Group 94, National Archives and Records Administration, Washington, D.C.

Register of Post Quartermaster Sergeants, U.S. Army. Record Group 94, National Archives and Records Administration, Washington, D.C.

Registers of Enlistments in the U.S. Army, 1798–1914. Record Group 94, National Archives and Records Administration, Washington, D.C.

Registers of Letters Received, 1875–1889. Records of the Military Prison Record Division, 1865–1889. Record Group 94, National Archives and Records Administration, Washington, D.C.

Registers of Letters Received, 1880. Department of the Missouri, Headquarters Records, 1861–1898. Record Group 393: Records of U.S. Army Continental Commands, 1821–1920, National Archives and Records Administration, Washington, D.C.

Registers of Prisoners. Records of the Military Prison Record Division, 1865–1889. Record Group 94, National Archives and Records Administration, Washington, D.C.

Returns from Regular Army Cavalry Regiments, 1833–1916. Microforms collections, University of Arizona, Main Library, Tucson.

Returns from United States Military Posts, 1800–1916. Microforms collections, University of Arizona, Main Library, Tucson.

Sellersville Church and Cemetery Corporate Records. Bucks County Historical Society, Doylestown, PA.

Vital Records, June 1878–Present. Bureau of Vital Statistics, State Registrar's Office, New Jersey Department of Health, Trenton.

William E. Matthews Letters. Typescript. Fort Union National Monument library, Watrous, NM.

Books, Articles, and Theses

Adjutant General's Office. *Chronological List of Actions, &c. with Indians from January 15,*

1837 to January 1891. 1891. Reprinted with introduction by Dale E. Floyd. Fort Collins, CO: Old Army Press, 1979.

Alexander, David V. *Arizona Frontier Military Place Names, 1846–1912.* Las Cruces, NM: Yucca Tree Press, 1998.

Annual Report of the Commissioner of Indian Affairs. Government Printing Office: Washington, D.C., 1870.

Annual Reports of the Secretary of War. Government Printing Office: Washington, D.C., 1868–1874.

Ashburn, P. M. *A History of the Medical Department of the United States Army.* Boston: Houghton Mifflin, 1929.

Bailey, Thomas A. *A Diplomatic History of the American People.* New York: Meredith, 1964.

Baker, T. Lindsay and Billy R. Harrison. *Adobe Walls: The History and Archeology of the 1874 Trading Post.* College Station: Texas A&M University Press, 1986.

Barns, Will C. *Arizona Place Names.* Revised and enlarged by Byrd H. Granger. Tucson: University of Arizona Press, 1960.

Battle, J. H., ed. *History of Bucks County, Pennsylvania.* Philadelphia: A. Warner, 1887.

Baum, Walter E. *Two Hundred Years.* Sellersville, PA: Sellersville Herald, 1938.

Billings, John Davis. *Hardtack and Coffee: The Unwritten Story of Army Life.* Chicago: Lakeside Press, 1960.

Billings, John S. *Circular No. 8: Report on the Hygiene of the United States Army with Descriptions of Military Posts.* 1875. Reprint, New York: Sol Lewis, 1974.

Bourke, John Gregory. *On the Border With Crook.* 1891. Reprint, Lincoln: University of Nebraska Press, 1971.

Boyd, Mrs. Orsemus Bronson [Frances]. *Cavalry Life in Tent and Field.* 1894. Reprinted with an introduction by Darlis A. Miller. Lincoln: University of Nebraska Press, 1982.

Brown, William L., III. *The Army Called It Home: Military Interiors of the 19th Century.* Gettysburg, PA: Thomas, 1992.

Carter, Robert G. *On the Border With Mackenzie; or, Winning West Texas from the Comanches.* 1935. Reprinted with a foreword by Charles M. Robinson III. Austin: Texas State Historical Association, 2007.

Cooper, Patricia A. *Once a Cigar Maker: Men, Women, and Work Culture in American Cigar Factories, 1900–1910.* Urbana: University of Illinois Press, 1992.

Decorations of the United States Army 1862–1926. Washington, D.C.: Adjutant General's Office, 1927.

Dobak, William A., and Thomas D. Phillips. *The Black Regulars 1866–1898.* Norman: University of Oklahoma Press, 2001.

Drago, Harry Sinclair. *Great American Cattle Trails: The Story of the Old Cow Paths of the East and the Longhorn Highways of the Plains.* New York: Dodd, Mead, 1965.

Emmett, Chris. *Fort Union and the Winning of the Southwest.* Norman: University of Oklahoma Press, 1965.

Farrington, Dusan P. *Arming & Equipping the United States Cavalry, 1865–1902.* Lincoln, RI: Andrew Mowbray, 2004.

Foner, Jack D. *The United States Soldier Between Two Wars: Army Life and Reforms, 1865–1898.* New York: Humanities Press, 1970.

Frazer, Robert W. *Forts of the West: Military Forts and Presidios and Posts Commonly Called Forts West of the Mississippi River to 1898.* Norman: University of Oklahoma Press, 1977.

Ganoe, William Addleman. *The History of the United States Army.* 1942. Reprint, Ashton, MD: Lundberg, 1964.

Goetzmann, William H. *Army Exploration in the American West, 1803–1863.* New Haven, CT: Yale University Press, 1959.

Grim, Webster. *Bucks County Directory, 1894.* Doylestown, PA: James D. Scott, 1894.

———. *Bucks County Directory, 1898.* Doylestown, PA: James D. Scott, 1898.

———. *Bucks County Directory, 1905 and 1906.* Doylestown, PA: James D. Scott, 1906.

Haley, James L. *The Buffalo War: The History of the Red River Indian Uprising of 1874.* New York: Doubleday, 1976.

Harlan, Anna Louise. "The Fort Smith-Santa Fe Trail." Master's thesis, University of Southern California, 1933.

Hart, Herbert M. *Old Forts of the Southwest.* New York: Bonanza Books, 1964.

Heitman, Francis B. *Historical Register and Dictionary of the United States Army: From Its Organization, September 29, 1789, to March 2, 1903.* 1903. 2 vols. Reprint, Urbana: University of Illinois Press, 1965.

Heth, Henry. *A System of Target Practice: For the Use of Troops When Armed With the Musket, Rifle-Musket, Rifle, or Carbine.* Washington, D.C.: Government Printing Office, 1862.

Hinton, Richard J. *The Hand-Book to Arizona: Its Resources, History, Towns, Mines, Ruins and Scenery.* 1878. Reprint, Tucson: Arizona Silhouettes, 1954.

Hodge, Hiram C. *Arizona As It Was, 1877.* 1877. Reprint, Chicago: Rio Grande Press, 1965.

Hotaling, Edward. *They're Off! Horse Racing at Saratoga.* Syracuse, NY: Syracuse University Press, 1995.

Hunt, Roger D., and Jack R. Brown. *Brevet Brigadier Generals in Blue.* Gaithersburg, MD: Olde Soldier Books, 1990.

Inman, Henry. *The Old Santa Fe Trail: The Story of a Great Highway.* Topeka, KS: Crane, 1899.

Jamieson, Perry D. *Crossing the Deadly Ground: United States Army Tactics, 1865–1899.* Tuscaloosa: University of Alabama Press, 1994.

Julyan, Robert. *The Place Names of New Mexico.* Albuquerque: University of New Mexico Press, 1998.

Kautz, August V. *Customs of Service for Non-Commissioned Officers and Soldiers as Described from Law and Regulations and Practised in the Army of the United States.* Philadelphia: J. B. Lippincott, 1864.

Kenner, Charles L. *The Comanchero Frontier: A History of New Mexican-Plains Indian Relations.* Norman: University of Oklahoma Press, 1994.

King, Charles. *Campaigning With Crook, and Stories of Army Life.* New York: Harper & Brothers, 1890.

Knight, Oliver. *Life and Manners in the Frontier Army.* Norman: University of Oklahoma Press, 1978.

Koster, John. "The Forty-Day Scout: A Trooper's Firsthand Account of an Adventure with the Indian-Fighting Army in the American Southwest." *American Heritage.* 31.4 (1980): 98–107.

Leckie, William H. *The Buffalo Soldiers: A Narrative of the Negro Cavalry in the West.* Norman: University of Oklahoma Press, 1967.

———. *The Military Conquest of the Southern Plains.* Norman: University of Oklahoma Press, 1963.

Lindmier, Thomas. *The Great Blue Army Wagon: The History of Wheeled Transportation in the Frontier Army.* Lexington, KY: Carriage Museum of America, 2009.

Lord, Francis A. *Civil War Collectors Encyclopedia: Arms, Uniforms, and Equipment of the Union and Confederacy.* Harrisburg, PA: Stackpole, 1965.

Magoffin, Susan Shelby. *Down the Santa Fe Trail and Into Mexico: The Diary of Susan Shelby Magoffin, 1846–1847.* Edited by Stella M. Drumm. New Haven, CT: Yale University Press, 1926.

Masich, Andrew E. *The Civil War in Arizona: The Story of the California Volunteers, 1861–1865.* Norman: University of Oklahoma Press, 2006.

McAulay, John D. *Carbines of the U.S. Cavalry, 1861–1905.* Lincoln, RI: Andrew Mowbray, 1996.

McChristian, Douglas C. *An Army of Marksmen: The Development of United States Army Marksmanship in the 19th Century.* Fort Collins, CO: Old Army Press, 1981.

———. *Uniforms, Arms, and Equipment: The U.S. Army on the Western Frontier, 1880–1892.* 2 vols. Norman: University of Oklahoma Press, 2007.

———. *The U.S. Army in the West, 1870–1880: Uniforms, Weapons, and Equipment.* Norman: University of Oklahoma Press, 1995.

McConnell, H. H. *Five Years a Cavalryman, or Sketches of Regular Army Life on the Texas Frontier, 1866–1871.* 1888. Reprint, Freeport, NY: Books for Libraries Press, 1970.

McDermott, John D. *A Guide to the Indian Wars of the West.* Lincoln: University of Nebraska Press, 1998.

McPherson, James. *Battle Cry of Freedom: The Civil War Era.* New York: Oxford University Press, 2003.

The Medal of Honor of the United States Army. Washington, D.C.: Government Printing Office, 1948.

Murray, Keith A. *The Modocs and Their War.* Norman: University of Oklahoma Press, 1969.

National Park Foundation. *The Complete Guide to America's National Parks.* New York: Viking, 1986.

Oliva, Leo E. *Fort Union and the Frontier Army in the Southwest: A Historic Resource Study, Fort Union National Monument.* Professional Papers No. 41, Southwest Cultural Resources Center. Santa Fe, NM: National Park Service, 1993.

Quartermaster General of the Army. *U.S. Army Uniforms and Equipment, 1889: Specifications for Clothing, Camp and Garrison Equipage, and Clothing and Equipage Materials.* Foreword by Jerome A. Greene. Lincoln: University of Nebraska Press, 1986.

Revised United States Army Regulations of 1861. Washington, D.C.: Government Printing Office, 1863.

Rickey, Don, Jr. *Forty Miles A Day on Beans and Hay: The Enlisted Soldier Fighting the Indian Wars.* Norman: University of Oklahoma Press, 1963.

Riddle, Kenyon. *Records and Maps of the Old Santa Fe Trail.* West Palm Beach, FL: John K. Riddle, 1963.

Rodenbough, Theophilus F. *From Everglade to Canyon With the Second United States Cavalry: An Authentic Account of Service in Florida, Mexico, Virginia, and the Indian Country, 1836–1875.* 1875. Reprint, Norman: University of Oklahoma Press, 2000.

Rodenbough, Theophilus F., and William L. Haskin, eds. *The Army of the United States: Historical Sketches of Staff and Line With Portraits of Generals-in-Chief.* 1896. Reprinted with a foreword by Joseph P. Peters. New York: Argonaut Press, 1966.

Ryus, William H. *The Second William Penn: A True Account of Incidents That Happened along the Old Santa Fe Trail in the Sixties.* Kansas City, MO: Frank T. Riley, 1913.

Shakespeare, William. *The First Quarto of Hamlet.* Edited by Kathleen O. Irace. Cambridge, UK: Cambridge University Press, 1998.

Steele, Volney. *Bleed, Blister, and Purge: A History of Medicine on the American Frontier.* Missoula, MT: Mountain Press, 2005.

Steffen, Randy. *The Horse Soldier, 1776–1943. The United States Cavalryman: His Uniform, Accoutrements, and Equipments.* Vol. 2, *The Frontier, the Mexican War, the Civil War, the Indian Wars, 1851–1880.* Norman: University of Oklahoma Press, 1978.

———. *United States Military Saddles, 1812–1943.* Norman: University of Oklahoma Press, 1973.

Tate, Michael L. *The Frontier Army in the Settlement of the West.* Norman: University of Oklahoma Press, 1999.

Taylor, Morris F. *First Mail West: Stagecoach Lines on the Santa Fe Trail.* Albuquerque: University of New Mexico Press, 1971.

Thian, Raphael P. *Notes Illustrating the Military Geography of the Unites States, 1813–1880.* 1881. Reprint, Austin: University of Texas Press, 1979.

United States Army Military Division of the Missouri. *Outline Descriptions of the Posts in The Military Division of the Missouri Commanded by Lieutenant General P. H. Sheridan. Accompanied by Tabular Lists of Indian Superintendencies, Agencies and Reservations, and a Summary of Certain Indian Treaties.* Chicago: Headquarters Military Division of the Missouri, 1876.

United States Army Ordnance Department. *The Ordnance Manual for the Use of the Officers of the United States Army.* Philadelphia: J.B. Lippincott, 1861.

Upton, Emory. *A New System of Infantry Tactics, Double and Single Rank: Adapted to American Topography and Improved Fire-Arms.* New York: D. Appleton, 1867.

Upton, Richard. *Fort Custer on the Big Horn, 1877–1898: Its History and Personalities as Told and Pictured by its Contemporaries.* Glendale, CA: Arthur H. Clark, 1973.

Urwin, Gregory J. W. *The United States Cavalry: An Illustrated History, 1776–1944.* Norman: University of Oklahoma Press, 2003.

Utley, Robert M. *Fort Union National Monument, New Mexico.* Washington, D.C.: National Park Service, 1962.

———. *Frontier Regulars: The United States Army and the Indian, 1866–1891.* New York: Macmillan, 1973.

———. *Frontiersmen in Blue: The United States Army and the Indian, 1848–1865.* New York: Macmillan, 1967.

Vestal, Stanley. *The Old Santa Fe Trail.* Boston: Houghton Mifflin, 1939.

Walker, Henry Pickering, and Don Bufkin. *Historical Atlas of Arizona*. Norman: University of Oklahoma Press, 1986.
Waters, Lawrence L. *Steel Trails to Santa Fe*. Lawrence: University of Kansas Press, 1950.
Wheeler, Keith. *The Railroaders*. The Old West series. New York: Time Life Books, 1973.
Williams, Jerry L. *New Mexico in Maps*. Albuquerque: University of New Mexico Press, 1986.
Wilmer, L. Allison, J. H. Jarrett, and George W. F. Vernon. *History and Roster of Maryland Volunteers, War of 1861–1865*. 2 vols. Baltimore: Guggenheimer, Weil, 1898.

Periodicals

Army and Navy Journal
Doylestown (PA) *Intelligencer*
(Westminster, MD) *Democratic Advocate*
(Prescott) *Weekly Arizona Miner*
(Santa Fe) *Daily New Mexican*
Sellersville (PA) *Herald*

Electronic Resources

Ancestry.com
American Civil War Regiments.
England 1841 Census.
England and Wales, Free BMD Marriage Index, 1837–1915.
New York Passenger Lists, 1820–1957.
U.S. Civil War Soldier Records and Profiles.
U.S. Federal Census Collection, 1850–1930.
U.S. IRS Tax Assessment Lists, 1862–1918.

Map Resources

"Map of the Territory of Arizona," General Land Office, 1869, Arizona Historical Society Library, Tucson.
"Map of the Territory of Arizona," C. Roeser, General Land Office, 1879, Arizona Historical Society Library, Tucson.
"Map of the Military Department of New Mexico," Capt. Allen Anderson, Fifth U. S. Infantry, 1864. Reprint, Western National Parks Association: Tucson, Arizona, n.d.

INDEX

Adobe Walls, Tex., 337
Albuquerque, N. Mex. Terr.: described, 81–82
Alcatraz Island, Calif., 45, 45n8
Alexander, Andrew J., 36, 36n2, 47, 284, 295, 329, 332, 338, 353, 355, 370
Angel Island, Calif., 18–21, 311
Apache Indians: Jicarilla, 103; Mescalero, 232n; shooting incident with, 140–41, 142; Tonto, 20–21
Arapaho Indians, 75–76
Arkansas River, 298, 338
arms: cleaning of, 344; Colt revolver, 60, 60n19; how stored, 133, 140; illicit trade in, 213–14; Indian, 213; personal, 88; Remington revolver, 60n19; saber, 133; Sharps carbine, 86, 86n10, 103, 141, 399; Spencer carbine, 46n, 86
Army, U.S.: composition of, xii, xvi; reorganization of, xi–xii, 1, 87–88, 87n12, 93, 93n, 215, 215n, 324, 331; role in combatting Comanchero trade, 74–76

artillery, 94, 94n, 157, 157n, 376
Atchison, Topeka & Santa Fe Railroad, xvi, 298–99, 347n, 380n20

Baker, Edward D., 43–44, 44n6, 46–47
Baltimore & Ohio Railroad, xiii, 310, 369, 380
Bank, First National of Santa Fe: shipment of currency for, 122–23, 123n51
Bankhead, Henry C., 158, 158n15, 180
Barnum, P. T., 153, 153n10, 359
baseball, 3, 8, 100, 100n, 142, 349, 357
bathing, 120–21, 140, 352
Baumgartner, William N., xv, xvn, 2–3, 7, 19
Beam Ranch, 47
Bent, St. Vrain and Co., 337
Big Tree (Kiowa), 227, 248–49, 249n
Blackburn, Absolum W., 382, 382n21
Black Kettle (Southern Cheyenne), 75
Blanco Canyon, 167–69, 168n, 179
Blunt, Asa P., 396
Bowers Ranch, 61–62

409

Boyd, Orsemus B., 154, 176, 176n31
Bradbury, Sanford, 312n8, 331
Bublitz, Ora (granddaughter), xvii, xviii
Bucks County, Maryland, 396–98
Buntline, Ned. *See* Judson, Edward Z. C.

Camp Date Creek, Ariz. Terr., 33, 33n, 55
Camp Rawlins, Ariz. Terr., 59
Camp Supply, Indian Terr. (Okla.), 265–66, 268n10
Camp Toll Gate (Camp Hualpai), Ariz. Terr., 36, 36n1, 51, 57, 64, 66
Camp Verde, Ariz. Terr., 60–61, 60n21, 63
Canadian River, 72, 75, 148, 337; danger crossing, 243–44; flooding of, 363
Carleton, James H., 74
Carlisle Barracks, Pa., 395. *See also* Cavalry School
Carrick, Robert, 81, 81n
cattle drives, 298–99
Cavalry School (Carlisle Barracks), 2, 3n4; recruit experience at, 4–5, 7–8
chaplain, 130n, 350
Chino Valley, 59
Chisholm Trail, 298
cigar industry, 396–98
Cimarron, N. Mex. Terr., 135; attack on ranch near, 376, 381; disturbance at, 110–15, 142; Indian agency at, 90, 90n, 110–13, 110n, 111n33, 141; shooting incident at, 113–15
Clark, C. M., 315n, 322, 322n
Clendenin, David R., 135, 135n, 137–38, 144–45
clothing, civilian worn by soldiers, 343–44
Cobb, Edmund M., 113n, 116n, 140, 220; gift to, 118
Coe, Samuel, 107–8, 108n
Cofran, Sarah F., 130–31, 130n
Colorado River, dangers in crossing, 243
Comanche Indians, 72n, 73–76, 144, 184, 212, 227, 299–300, 337; raid Fort Sumner, 253; soldiers' opinion of, 142, 376
Comanchero trade: discussions of, 73–76, 144–45, 183–84, 299–300; interdiction of, 144–45, 183–84, 246, 249, 252; Matthews's views on, 213–14
company fund, 234
Conchas River, 352
Coon, C. E., 123n51
court-martial, 88–89; of Matthews, 395

Crook George, 198, 231
Cuban insurrection, 289, 289n21

Davis, A. P., 202, 204n11
Davis, John, 128n1
Department of Texas, 148, 299
Department of the Missouri, 148
depredations, Indian, 63, 92, 94, 253, 263, 373–75, 379, 381–82
desertion, 13, 16, 23–24, 45, 66, 69, 88, 92–93, 128n1, 138–40, 143–44, 262; amnesty for, 286, 286n
Devin, Thomas C., 68, 68n
District of New Mexico, 74, 132, 132n, 145, 148, 265
Dodge City, Kans., 298–99, 337
drunkenness, 39–40, 94, 118, 130, 136, 146–47, 290
Dutchman's Ranch, incident with Indians at, 140–41

Eakins, David W., 130n, 350n
Eighth U.S. Cavalry, xviii, 2, 7, 12–15, 20–21, 25, 28, 94, 339; band, 92, 103, 103n; desertions from, 13; expedition to Staked Plains, 148–49, 183–84; headquartered at Santa Fe, 283; interdicts Comanchero trade, 76, 245–46, 249, 299–300; pursues thieves, 95, 106; quells disturbance at Cimarron, N. Mex. Terr., 111–15; recruits for, 252, 286–87; in Red River War, 392; route of march to New Mexico, 70–71, 70n; scouting after Indians, 232, 232n, 245, 254, 267–68, 274, 277–78, 280, 284, 329, 330, 334, 338, 352–53, 363; transfers to New Mexico, 42, 54–55, 60, 67, 72–73, 78–81
Eisenlohr, Otto and Son, 397
Elizabethtown, N. Mex. Terr., 116
Emery Gap. *See* Emeryville
Emeryville, N. Mex. Terr., 106, 106n
entertainment, 56, 97–98, 103, 204, 285, 289, 290–91, 294, 296–97, 302, 330, 332, 348, 350, 357
Epizootic catarrh, 194, 194n, 196, 199–200
Expedition to Staked Plains (1872), 157–84; attacks on, 162–64, 167; distance marched, 182; preparation for, 156–57; rations on, 158–59, 159n18, 160

INDEX 411

field service, preparation for, 138, 351
Fisher, Thomas M., 15
fishing, 90, 366
Fitzgerald, Michael J., 16
Foley, Timothy, 128n1
food, army, 9–10, 12, 14, 54, 62, 77–78, 87, 98, 124, 129, 201–2, 259, 329, 345–46, 358–59, 378–79; in field, 176; misappropriation of by noncoms, 319–21; prices of in Arizona, 40; special, 102, 278, 285–86, 377–78
Foos, John, 202, 204n11
Ford, William, 114, 114n, 116
Fort Bascom, N. Mex. Terr., 72, 72n, 79, 94, 144–45, 178, 181, 242, 388–89; detachment remains at, 269, 290, 316; distance by road from Fort Union, 224, 291; expeditions from, 75, 117, 337, 390, 390n; horse thieves active near, 383; and Red River War, 392; skirmish near, 202–4; summer camp at, 148–49, 316, 325, 329, 349, 349n, 350–51, 370; threat of attack on, 246; use of ramadas at, 149n5; war parties active near, 263, 373–75, 379, 381–82
Fort Craig, N. Mex. Terr., 72
Fort Dodge, Kans., 392
Fort Garland, Colo. Terr., 72
Fort Leavenworth, Kans., 383, 385, 389; military prison at, 395–96
Fort Lyon, Colo. Terr.: expedition from, 75; special escort from, 123n51
Fort Mojave, Ariz. Terr., 27, 27n26, 28
Fort Selden, N. Mex. Terr., 72
Fort Sill, Indian Terr. (Okla.), 392
Fort Smith Road, 74, 76, 144–45, 158, 158n16
Fort Stanton, N. Mex. Terr., 264; mail route from, 374
Fort Sumner, N. Mex. Terr., 74, 96, 144; raid on, 253; scout to, 363, 363n
Fort Union, N. Mex. Terr.: adobe construction at, 131; arsenal at, 73, 133, 133n8; barracks at described, 133; as base of operations, 75–76, 148–49, 392; cemetery at, 86; chapel at, 86; garrison at, 131; ice houses at, 121; laundress quarters at, 133; location and role of 72–75; military prison at, 233–34, 237, 234n27; military reservation at, 109n; wedding at, 130–31
Fort Union Quartermaster Depot, 73, 89; employees discharged from, 346

Fort Wallace, Kans., 303, 371
Fort Whipple, Ariz. Terr., 21, 21n, 26; fire at 65
Fort Wingate, N. Mex. Terr., 79, 96, 118, 131
Fort Yuma, Calif., 19, 20n, 24, 27; joke concerning, 365
Foster, Charles W., 43–44, 44n6, 57
Fourth U.S. Cavalry, 148, 149n4, 154, 199
Franco-Prussian War, 98, 98n18
Freed, Annie J. See Matthews, Annie J.
Fulkerson, Michael D., 119n

Gageby, James H., 123n51
Gageby Creek, skirmish at, 392n27
Galisteo, N. Mex. Terr., 82n
Gartten, Patrick, 128n1
General Service, 252–53, 253n, 265
Getty, George W., 74, 124, 124n, 132n
Good Templars, Independent Order of, 199, 199n, 204, 279, 285, 291, 294, 302, 321, 325–26, 330, 333, 340, 348; Matthews elected secretary for, 285; office held in, 346
Granger, Gordon, 145, 148
"greaser": defined, 99n20, 214
Gregg, John I., 76, 91–92, 96, 99, 102–3, 104n, 105, 112, 127, 133, 226, 382n22; combats illicit trade, 76, 144–45, 147–49, 148, 204, 220; commands district, 132, 132n, 283; demotes Matthews, 146; leads expedition on Staked Plains, 150, 158, 168, 176, 179, 183, 270; Matthews opinion of, 159; relinquishes command of district, 145
Gregory, S. S., 123n51
guard duty, 10, 54, 77, 82–84, 86, 88, 96, 100, 175, 247; care of prisoners, 136; in field, 166–67, 180, 197, 247; inspection for 8, 11, 83, 125, 129
guard mounting: described, 83–84, 358

Hannan, John, 175–76, 175n
Harlan, Clinton C., 146, 196–97, 196n3, 205, 208, 237, 240, 249, 251, 257, 260, 265–66, 269, 276–77, 284, 319, 347, 355, 383
Harry Bassett (race horse), 166, 166n
Harvey, Daniel G., 251n5
Hawkins, John L., 101n, 127, 127
Hennissee, Argalus G., 138–39, 138n15, 165
Hobart, Charles, 43n, 99, 102, 110, 146, 150, 232, 240, 243, 245, 266, 276, 296, 296n, 304, 312, 366

Hodges, William, 243, 243n
holidays: Christmas, 124, 126, 294–95, 311; Independence Day, 93–94, 245, 377–78; New Year's, 294, 302; St. Patrick's Day, 330, 330n; Thanksgiving, 119, 285–86; Washington's birthday, 55
horse racing, 55–56, 128
horses, 30, 121; breeds discussed, 102–3; colors of, 120; remounts, 136
Howard, George R., 307, 307n
Hubbell's Ranch, 74
Hunter, Pendleton, 19–20
hunting, 47–49, 160–61, 170, 172–74, 177–79, 181, 222; commercial hide, 299, 338
Hurley, John M., 120, 120n42, 136, 142

ice, harvesting of, 121
Ingraham, Frank C., 375, 375n
inspections, 5; guard mount, 8, 11, 359; Sunday, 53–54, 121, 121n46, 220, 359

Jewett, Horace, 132
Jicarilla Apache-Ute Agency, 125. *See also* Cimarron, N. Mex. Terr.
Johnson, S. A., 123n51
Johnson's Ranch, 352
Judson, Edward Z. C ("Ned Buntline"), 106–7, 107n

Kansas Pacific Railroad, 132, 136n11, 298, 380, 380n20
Kauffman, Albert B., 52, 130n; wedding of, 130–31
Kiowa Indians, 72n, 73–76, 212, 227, 299–300, 337–38; attack Gregg's expedition, 162–64, 164n21, 184; skirmish with near Fort Bascom, 202–4; soldiers' opinion of, 376
Kit Carson, Colo. Terr., 132, 136, 136n11

La Junta, N. Mex. Terr. *See* Watrous, N. Mex. Terr.
Las Animas, Colo. Terr., 380–81, 380n20
Las Vegas, N. Mex. Terr., 82, 99, 126, 154–55, 224, 227, 352, 388; described, 92; district court at, 75; mail route from, 374–76
laundresses, 101–2, 101n, 121n45, 124, 257, 278, 341; lack of at Fort Bascom, 224; prices charged by, 133, 343
Lee's Ranch, 49

Loma Parda, N. Mex. Terr., 82, 82n, 93, 99, 109–10; raid on, 184, 184n
Luff, Edmund, 113n, 123n, 220, 225, 391

Mackenzie, Ranald S., 148
Mahnken, John H., 90, 90n, 128, 132
Matthews, Annie J. (Freed), 398, 398n12
Matthews, Arthur W. (brother), xiv
Matthews, Elizabeth ("Lizzie") (sister), xiii; announces marriage, 201–2, 230; as teacher, 362
Matthews, Frances (sister), xiv, 18
Matthews, George B. McClellan ("Clellee") (brother), xiv
Matthews, John (father), xii–xiv; as tax collector, 230
Matthews, John J. ("Johnnie") (brother), xiv, 25, 230
Matthews, Judith Newton (mother), xii–xiii
Matthews, Margaret ("Maggie") (sister), xiv; death of, 306, 306n
Matthews, Susan M. ("Susie") (sister), xiv, 230
Matthews, William Edward ("Eddie"); adopts cat, 276, 306, 317; as clerk, xv, 31, 31n, 37, 43, 45–46, 147, 150, 152, 240, 250–52, 254, 256, 267, 272–73, 276–78, 284, 292–93, 297, 300–301, 303, 310, 316, 318–19, 326–27, 329, 339, 350, 359–60, 367–68, 383; collects insects, 359; combat, experience in, 163–64, 167; as cook, 40, 42–43, 64, 77, 84, 87, 110; on cost of living, 343–44; court-martialed, 395; deals in watches, 239; demoted for being drunk, 146, 254; dental problems of, 354, 363–64, 372; describes daily routine, 235–36, 358–59; describes quarters, 208, 229, 280–83, 351; on desertion, 217, 223, 252; discharge of, 274–75, 303, 332, 369, 390–91; domestic problems of, xiv, xivn5, 4, 6, 9, 25, 42, 340; as duty sergeant, 228–30, 232, 234, 240, 243; education of, 311; employment, post-service, 155, 268, 291, 300, 303, 312–13, 366; enlists, xii, xv, 2, 393, 393n; as escort for money, 122–23; health of, 22–23, 42, 77, 87, 100, 119, 135–37, 156, 194, 221, 241, 250, 279, 304, 309, 311, 313, 330, 336, 348, 352, 355, 367; Hispanics, opinions of, 99–100, 109, 214,

333; hometown acquaintances, opinions of, 89–90, 328; imprisoned, 395–96; on Indian policy, 227; Indians, opinions of, 60, 99, 142, 160–61, 222, 227; as "laundress," 257–59; on liquor, 14, 27, 37, 39, 43, 52, 66–67, 117, 143, 210–11; literary pursuits of, 134, 209, 236–37, 353; on marriage, 206–7; on militia for fighting Indians, 231–33; nickname, 223; officers, opinions of, 12, 24, 40, 68, 89, 118, 165, 269–70, 308, 312, 322, 360; opinion of Quakers, 227; as orderly, 96, 122, 127, 129, 132; physical description, 2n, 152, 330; political views of, 98, 132, 289; promotion of, 125, 139n, 145, 193; promotion, views on, 37–38, 45, 85, 117, 123; as quartermaster sergeant, 193, 197, 197n5, 205, 215–16, 219, 222, 225; reduction to private, 250–51, 251n5; regular army, opinion of, 248, 331; on religion, 76–77, 86, 152–53, 335–36, 350; rescues comrade, 137–38; romantic interests of, 44, 97, 271, 297, 305–6, 310, 313, 328, 369–70; sister's marriage, views on, 155, 206–7; souvenirs collected by, 279–80, 286, 304, 345; on suffrage, 132, 333; on tactics, 213, 340–41, 356; as teamster, 153–54; on temperance, 321, 336; tobacco use by, 32, 160, 259, 292, 344, 371–72, 374, 378, 382, 386; transportation, means of to return home, 380, 383; travels to Ohio, xiv–xv; the West, impressions of, 13, 25, 70, 89, 110, 117, 135, 161, 172, 230, 234–36, 307, 330, 341, 348, 352, 355–56; women on the frontier, opinion of, 333–34
Maxwell, Lucian, 253. *See also* Maxwell Grant
Maxwell Grant, 104n, 112, 112n36
McCaffrey, John, 290
McClary's Ranch, 352
McCleave, William, 148, 172, 199, 373, 373n13, 377, 391; commended, 164n21
McGonnigle, Andrew J., 128, 128n2, 256
McGrath, Michael, 128n1
McKellip, William A., 98, 101
Mescalero Apache Indians, 72
Middleton, Passmore, 57
Mitchell, John J., 77, 77n, 93

Mitten, William, 276
Modoc Indians, 198, 198n, 231–33, 248, 254–55, 373n14
Moffatt, Peter, 314–15, 315n
Montezuma Castle, 63–64, 63n
Morris, Louis T., 303, 303n, 308, 312, 324, 363, 370–71, 373, 387, 395; Matthews's opinion of, 360
Muster Creek, action at, 392n27

Navajo Indians, 79, 96, 118, 131
Ninth U.S. Cavalry, 221, 221n

Ocate, N. Mex. Terr., 142
Omaha Barracks, Neb., 14–15
O'Neal, Charles (Charles O'Neil), 164n21
Ord, Edward O. C., 395
"Oregon Jake." *See* Smith, Jacob

Parkes, Joe, 281–83
pay, 8, 17–18, 18n, 31, 33, 60, 62, 84–85, 88, 118, 140, 140n, 154, 223, 227, 229, 283, 342; as clerk, 250; of duty sergeant, 228, 228n; final statement of, 385; of quartermaster sergeant, 223
Pecos Pueblo, 279n
Pecos River, 75
Pendergast, William, 312, 312n7
Perkins, Bejamin R., 36, 36n1
permanent party (recruit depot), 6, 6n, 7
Pope, John, 122, 122n, 144
Prescott, Ariz., 28, 33, 53, 59, 69–70
Price, William R., 388–90
prisoners, escape of, 127–28, 136, 136n, 237
Pueblo Indians: involvement in Comanchero trade, 73–76, 144
Pullman, John W., 256

quarters, soldiers': described, 53, 280–83
Quitaque, Tex., 183

Randlett, James F., 165, 165n24
Red River, 299. *See also* Canadian River
Red River station, 105–6, 105n
Red River War, 184
Reece, Aquilla Asbury, 371, 371n
Reece, Mary, 371
Reifsnider, John L., 396n8
Rio Grande, crossing of, 80–81

Robbers' Cave. *See* Stone Ranch (Colo. Terr.)
Rogers, Alfred H., 246, 256, 373
Rollins, Gilbert, 153, 153n11
Rowalt, John F., 173–74, 182, 207–8; skirmish with Kiowas, 202–4, 204n11, 243; medal awarded to, 173n

Sandia Pueblo, 82n
Santa Fe, N. Mex. Terr., 73, 82n, 145, 158; described, 124; shipment of currency to, 123–24
Santa Fe Trail, xvi, 73, 108n, 125, 380n20
Satanta (Kiowa), 227, 248–49, 249n
Sayer's Ranch, 243
Sellersville, Pa., 396–98
Seventh U.S. Cavalry, 75; 82, 339
Shanahan, Michael, 387, 387n
Sheridan, Philip H., xiii, 75
Sherman, William T., 74
Shorb, (Joshua?), xiv–xv, xvn, 2–3, 19
Sixth U.S. Cavalry, 370, 392
signaling, training in, 309, 311
Signal Service (Corps), 244, 309n
skirmishes: with Kiowas, 162–64, 167, 202–4; with Tonto Apache, 61–62, 63
Smith, Gilbert C., 391, 391n
Smith, Jacob ("Oregon Jake"): death of, 59–60, 59n18
Smith, Samuel P., 15–16, 19–20
Smoky Hill River, 298
Snider, William, 395
soldiers: of African-American decent, 7, 11; character of, 24; deaths of, 111, 118, 153, 175–76, 210–11, 243, 290; foraging by, 379–80; German-born, 357, 375; as officers' servants, 42–43, 43n
Soldier Spring, skirmish at, 75
Southern Cheyenne Indians, 75, 184, 214–15, 338
Staked Plains (Llano Estacado), 73–76, 170, 299–300, 392
Stapp Ranch, attack on, 379, 381
Stone Ranch (Colo. Terr.), 107–8, 108n, 112
Stone Ranch (N. Mex. Terr.), 221–22, 291
summer camp on Canadian River, 148; description of, 150
Sweetwater Creek, action at, 392n27

tailor, company, 91, 259, 343
target practice, 46
Taylor, John, 210–11, 211n
Taylor's Ranch, 290, 352
Third Regiment, Potomac Home Brigade, Maryland Volunteers, xiii, 16
Third U.S. Cavalry, 68, 70, 74–76, 82, 108n, 111
Tompkins, James S., 1
traders, New Mexican. *See* Comancheros
Trinidad, Colo. Terr., 138–40; Indian attack reported near, 381

uniforms, 9, 9n, 64n, 274–75, 281–83, 302, 351; altering and prices of, 342–43, 343n; new pattern issued, 295, 295n, 297
Union Pacific Railroad, 16, 77, 206
Upton, Emory, 341n
Ute-Apache Indian Reservation, 226. *See also* Cimarron, N. Mex. Terr.
Ute Creek, attack on ranch near, 382, 382n22
Ute Indians, 90, 90n, 102–3, 142, 239, 243, 278

Valois, Gus (Gustavus Haenel), 32, 32n, 221

wagons, army, 137, 137n, 352
Wallace, George W., 60, 60n21, 61
Wantz, Charles V., 396n8
Watrous, N. Mex. Terr., 290–91, 291n24
Weier, Sigmund, 118n
Westminster, Md.: Matthews family relocates at, xiv
Wheaton, Frank, 51, 51n, 53, 57–58
Wheeler, Mortimer M., 90, 90n, 99–101
White River, 168n
Whittemore's Ranch, 145, 352
William, Richard A., 174, 174n
Williams, Richard, 384, 384n, 388
Williamson Valley, 36, 47, 53, 59
Willman, George, 395
Wilson, William P. (Indian agent), 90, 90n, 102, 104n

Young, Samuel Baldwin Marks, 2, 66, 128, 130–32, 222, 222n, 240, 243, 246–47, 256, 263, 264, 270, 272, 274

www.ingramcontent.com/pod-product-compliance
Lightning Source LLC
Chambersburg PA
CBHW030104010526
44116CB00005B/85